PARLIAMENT AND LIT
MEDIEVAL EI

Parliament and Literature in Late Medieval England investigates the relationship between the development of parliament and the practice of English poetry in the later fourteenth and early fifteenth centuries. During this period, the bureaucratic political culture of parliamentarians, clerks, and scribes overlapped with the artistic practice of major poets like Chaucer, Gower, and Langland, all of whom had strong ties to parliament. Matthew Giancarlo investigates these poets together in the specific context of parliamentary events and controversies, as well as in the broader environment of changing constitutional ideas. Two chapters provide new analyses of the parliamentary ideologies that developed from the thirteenth century onward, and four chapters investigate the parliamentary aspects of each poet, as well as the later Lancastrian imitators of Langland. This study demonstrates the importance of the changing parliamentary environs of late medieval England and their centrality to the early growth of English narrative and lyric forms.

MATTHEW GIANCARLO is Assistant Professor of English at the University of Kentucky.

CAMBRIDGE STUDIES IN MEDIEVAL LITERATURE

General editor
Alastair Minnis, *Ohio State University*

Editorial board
Zygmunt G. Barański, *University of Cambridge*
Christopher C. Baswell, *University of California, Los Angeles*
John Burrow, *University of Bristol*
Mary Carruthers, *New York University*
Rita Copeland, *University of Pennsylvania*
Simon Gaunt, *King's College, London*
Steven Kruger, *City University of New York*
Nigel Palmer, *University of Oxford*
Winthrop Wetherbee, *Cornell University*
Jocelyn Wogan-Browne, *University of York*

This series of critical books seeks to cover the whole area of literature written in the major medieval languages – the main European vernaculars, and medieval Latin and Greek – during the period c. 1100–1500. Its chief aim is to publish and stimulate fresh scholarship and criticism on medieval literature, special emphasis being placed on understanding major works of poetry, prose, and drama in relation to the contemporary culture and learning which fostered them.

A complete list of titles in the series can be found at the end of the volume.

PARLIAMENT AND LITERATURE IN LATE MEDIEVAL ENGLAND

MATTHEW GIANCARLO

CAMBRIDGE
UNIVERSITY PRESS

CAMBRIDGE UNIVERSITY PRESS
Cambridge, New York, Melbourne, Madrid, Cape Town, Singapore,
São Paulo, Delhi, Dubai, Tokyo, Mexico City

Cambridge University Press
The Edinburgh Building, Cambridge CB2 8RU, UK

Published in the United States of America by Cambridge University Press, New York

www.cambridge.org
Information on this title: www.cambridge.org/9780521147729

© Matthew Giancarlo 2007

First published 2007
First paperback printing 2010

A catalogue record for this publication is available from the British Library

ISBN 978-0-521-87539-4 Hardback
ISBN 978-0-521-14772-9 Paperback

For Krista,
sine qua non

Contents

Illustrations

Preface

The basic argument of this study is simple and can be simply stated. The last quarter of the fourteenth century and the first decades of the fifteenth – from about 1376 to 1414 – was a period of fundamental importance for the development of both the English parliament and English literature. These developments are related, and this study investigates that relationship. Each in their own way, the growth of parliament and the development of poetry have motivated intense study. The intersection of the two, despite their especially close contact during the later English middle ages, has largely been ignored.[1] What I undertake here is to treat them together, and to do so proceeding from the premise that, as it has been put recently, "textual practices do not exist within a social vacuum. [They] are produced by, and themselves sustain, particular social and political formations."[2] I pursue this operative principle in its softer and less deterministic (but no less substantive) form. That is, my point will not be to argue that parliament "made" the literature of the period or that the literature made parliament. Either proposition would be unreasonable, and in any event their relatedness is not one of direct historical causality. Nor will parliaments in literature (artistic renderings of the political body and practice of parliament) be the sole focus of inquiry, although they are key to this study. Rather, these two hallmark institutions of British culture, parliament and literature, are connected as important elements in a mutually informing and mutually dependent set of discursive and textual practices. They came into contact in a time and setting when *parlement*, as "discussion" and "deliberation," was becoming critical for both literary and political life. The same men whose identities and institutional activities were integral to parliament were also audience to the remarkable changes and new styles of poetry practiced by Langland,

---

[1] Notable exceptions include Pieper, "Das *Parlament* in der me. Literatur"; Strohm, "The Textual Environment of Chaucer's 'Lak of Stedfastnesse'"; Steiner, "Commonalty and Literary Form."

[2] Simpson, "The Other Book of Troy: Guido delle Colonne's *Historia destructionis Troiae* in Fourteenth and Fifteenth-Century England," 401.

Chaucer, and Gower. These artists, in turn, had extensive parliamentary connections. But as close as these social spheres were, it is in the broader and overlapping concerns of both political and artistic practice – anxieties about voice, representation, and the vision of a cohesive community in a fractured world – that we find this era's more fundamental connection of poetry to parliament. In a way that had not been seen before and would not be repeated after, imaginative literature and parliamentary politics were mutually expressive of the same cultural moment. That moment, which was characterized by a particular desire for (and the particular dangers of) speaking "with one voice," is the wider context in which this historiographical narrative is set, and for which it provides a unique perspective.

My hope is that this study will find interest among both literary and historical scholars, as its subjects and texts are equally important to both. Recent exemplary studies have blurred the lines between these disciplines, and it is from these that I take my cue. My focus is primarily on imaginative or "high" literature, also in the hope, as Janet Coleman puts it, of reaching "a happy medium between reading the imaginative literature as mere sources of social history . . . [and] according to standards of literary judgment."[3] At the same time, the long tradition of research on English constitutional and parliamentary history provides constant guidance, as well as a rigorous model for approaching parliament's influence on the literary writing of the age of Chaucer. Bringing these two fields into dialogue would be, it seems to me, sufficient justification for an inquiry of this sort. The impetus for that dialogue is made stronger by the apparent need for literary scholars to have a useful digest of historical work on parliament, not just for the decades that are the main focus but for the longer period from about the thirteenth to the early fifteenth centuries. This, therefore, provides the most general aspect of the tripartite subject matter of this book: an investigation of the specific historical and literary influences of the English parliament during the later fourteenth and early fifteenth centuries, especially during the reign of Richard II, which "saw the medieval parliament as much involved in political action as at any time in its history"[4]; a related inquiry into the issues of representation and voice, and the literary-political practices motivated by them; and some consideration of the historiographical significance of it all, from a later perspective which includes us as participants in this long political and cultural tradition.

[3] Coleman, *English Literature in History 1350–1400*, 46.
[4] Taylor, *English Historical Literature in the Fourteenth Century*, 209.

Acknowledgments

Research for this study was begun in 2001 during a Morse Fellowship sponsored by Yale University. It was completed and the book drafted in 2004–5 while I was the Walter Hines Page Fellow at the National Humanities Center, Research Triangle Park, North Carolina. Publication has also been supported by a grant from the MacMillan Center for International and Area Studies at Yale University. It is my pleasure to gratefully acknowledge this institutional support, without which this book could not have been written.

I would like to thank a host of colleagues who in various ways have assisted my study, thinking, and writing. At the National Humanities Center, I benefitted from the tireless assistance of the library staff: Eliza Robertson, Jean Houston, and Betsy Dain. A draft of Chapter Four was read by the 2004–5 NHC literature symposium under the astute direction of Geoffrey Harpham. My thanks are due also to Joe Luzzi, Karin Schutjer, and Mary Favret, who were particularly generous members of that collegial group. The complete first draft of the book was read, commented on, and much improved by Annabel Patterson, for which I am deeply grateful. Other colleagues at Yale and elsewhere have been helpful with comments, corrections, and friendly advice: Roberta Frank, Traugott Lawler, Jose Cheibub, Mark Ormrod, Gwilym Dodd, Emily Steiner, Nelson Minnich, Lynda Coon, David Frederick, Fiona Somerset, Andrew Galloway, Steven Justice, Clementine Oliver, Robert Meyer-Lee, James Simpson, Lee Patterson, Alastair Minnis, and the anonymous readers for Cambridge University Press. I owe particular and heartfelt thanks to Maura Nolan, whose counsel and feedback were simply indispensable for the development and completion of this project. I am also grateful to Linda Bree for her patient editorial guidance, to Jordan Zweck for meticulously checking the manuscript, and to Diane Brenner for indexing.

Chapters Three and Five have been previously published in different versions, in *Viator* 36 and *The Yearbook of Langland Studies* 17 respectively. I am grateful to these annuals for the permission to republish here.

My deepest debt is to my wife, Krista, and to my entire family, for their love and support. Thank you.

Abbreviations and textual note

Brinton, *Sermons*	*The Sermons of Thomas Brinton, Bishop of Rochester*
Butt	Ronald Butt, *A History of Parliament: The Middle Ages*
DNB	*Dictionary of National Biography*
Guisborough	*The Chronicle of Walter of Guisborough*
MED	*Middle English Dictionary*
Modus	*Modus Tenendi Parliamentum*
OED	*Oxford English Dictionary*
Powell and Wallis	J. Enoch Powell and Keith Wallis, *The House of Lords in the Middle Ages*
PROME	*The Parliament Rolls of Medieval England*
RP	*Rotuli Parliamentorum*

* * *

Since this study was begun, new editions of key texts have become available and electronic media continue to improve our scholarly resources. While many citations have been updated from previously published material, I have retained the older standard references to the eighteenth-century edition of the *Rotuli Parliamentorum* (*RP*) instead of adopting what will certainly become the new standard, the *Parliament Rolls of Medieval England* (*PROME*). Because most of my research was conducted before the publication of *PROME* in 2005, and because the older *RP* provides some petitionary texts that have been omitted from the newer edition, I have maintained the original citations. Where possible, these have been cross-checked with the new *PROME* CD-ROM edition.

Introduction:
parliament and literature

Where, in any account of reality, narrativity is present, we can be sure that morality or a moralizing impulse is present too.
    – Hayden White, "Narrativity in the Representation of Reality"[1]

Literature is our Parliament, too.
    – Thomas Carlyle, "The Hero as Man of Letters"[2]

* * *

Almost from its indefinite inception, "parliament" has been the object not only of historical inquiry but of historiographical rewriting. Parliament has been a vehicle for, and an object of, the desire for origins, from about as far back as the documentary trail will take us. Not long after King John was forced to negotiate the great charters with his barons on the field of Runnymede in 1215, this political and military conference was retroactively re-dubbed a *parlement*, a "colloquy" or "parley."[3] This Franco-Latin term was relatively new to the English side of the Channel and competed with (and ultimately replaced) the then-current Latin terms *colloquium* and *consilium*. The word *parliamentum* was apparently first used in this context in 1236.[4] At this time and after, until the early fourteenth century, a "parliament" was still an occasion and not an institution, as Maitland famously noted; the meaning of the word *parlement* as simply gathering or colloquy was available well into the later middle ages. The word could be used by Gower or Chaucer in contexts where clearly it means nothing more than

---

[1] White, "Narrativity in the Representation of Reality," in *The Content of the Form*, 24.
[2] Carlyle, "The Hero as Man of Letters. Johnson, Rousseau, Burns," Lecture V of *On Heroes, Hero-Worship, and the Heroic in History*, 164.
[3] See Butt, 87; Treharne, "The Nature of Parliament in the Reign of Henry III," 214–5. The reference, in a royal writ by Henry III dated 14 April 1244, refers to the "'parleamentum de Runemed' quod fuit inter J. regem, patrem nostrum, et barones suos Anglie."
[4] Butt, 79–80. See *MED*, s.v. "parlement(e)", *OED*, s.v. "parliament." Both provide very late citations (14th c.) as earliest attestations in English. For analyses see Pieper, "Das *Parlament* in der me. Literatur," 188–93; Treharne, "The Nature of Parliament in the Reign of Henry III," 209–15; Brown, *The Governance of Late Medieval England*, 156–7; Richardson, "The Origins of Parliament," 137–149.

that.[5] Nonetheless the specific meaning of *parlement* as the deliberative and consultative assembly of the king's court grows with the development and growth of parliament's power, and its significance is manifest by the later fourteenth century. The first parliamentary manual, the *Modus Tenendi Parliamentum*, has been dated anywhere from the 1320s to the 1370s. Whenever its origin, this guidebook for the the procedures of holding a parliament – very clearly understood as a regular institution of government, not just an occasional meeting of magnates – indulges the historiographical urge by positing its own account of the origins and justifications of parliaments. It tersely mythologizes parliament's historical beginnings and regularizes its capacities as a judicial and deliberative body.[6] For the *Modus*, parliament was a familiar and special court of the king usually (but not always) centered at Westminster. It was one that, Russian-doll-like, was itself a court of courts, the king's assembly wherein, as the law-manual *Fleta* describes it in the late thirteenth century, "the king holds his court in his council, in his parliaments" (*habet enim Rex curiam suam in consilio suo in parliamentis suis.*)[7] Parliament did not replace baronial councils or the feudal *magnum concilium*, nor sittings of the King's Bench, nor the operations of the king's judicial and legal ministers, nor the traditions of consultation and consent in political and fiscal matters. Rather it accreted aspects of all of these to itself so that by the 1400s the English parliament had been, for the better part of a century, a uniquely multifaceted and increasingly important part of government, "absolutely distinct from any other assembly."[8]

The personnel of parliament developed as it adopted new functional roles. Early parliaments were characterized by irregular summonses for the nobility and infrequent attendance by the commons. By the time of

---

[5] One of the first literary texts brought to mind when thinking of parliaments, the poem *The Parlement of the Thre Ages*, uses the word with only that meaning. Hence it is not treated here.

[6] The *Modus* begins by asserting the origins of parliament in the practice of William the Conqueror as passed to Edward son of Ethelred: see *Modus*, 67 and 103. The *Modus* is discussed further in Chapter Two.

[7] Butt, 83; Musson, *Medieval Law in Context*, 186.

[8] Brown, *The Governance of Late Medieval England*, 169. The medieval English parliament has been treated extensively in a number of excellent studies in the last fifty years. Major reference works are Butt, Powell and Wallis, and the historical and analytical apparatus of *PROME*. Also central are the essays collected in Davies and Denton, *The English Parliament in the Middle Ages*; Fryde and Miller, *Historical Studies of the English Parliament*; Sayles, *The King's Parliament of England* and *The Functions of the Medieval Parliament of England*; Edwards, *The Second Century of the English Parliament*; Brown, *The Governance of Late Medieval England*; Musson, *Medieval Law in Context*; Musson and Ormrod, *The Evolution of English Justice*; Harding, *Medieval Law and the Foundations of the State*. These studies and others build on the foundational work of Maitland, Stubbs, Cam, Tout, Clarke, Baldwin, and Chrimes. An early monograph of enduring value is Pollard, *The Evolution of Parliament*. A short and excellent overview of the fourteenth century parliament (especially its documentary history) is given by Richardson and Sayles, "Introduction," in *Rotuli Parliamentorum Anglie Hactenus Inediti*.

Edward II, a largely regular noble peerage had developed, and after 1325 no parliament was summoned without representatives from the shires and boroughs. Altogether, the personnel of parliament constituted a relatively small group of a few hundred men. Two representatives were sent from each of the thirty-six shires and from each of one hundred or so boroughs and cities, constituting the Commons. Among the Lords, the number of barons, abbots, priors, and other upper nobility receiving summonses totalled about seventy. The clerical element of early parliaments was variable and contested as the English Church struggled to remove itself from liability for attendance and, thus, from the taxes raised in parliaments. After the 1340s no representatives from the lower regular clergy were required to attend, and clerical summonses were restricted to upper prelates (archbishops, bishops, abbots) who held their positions as baronial dependents of the king. Clerical convocations shadowed parliaments and were frequently held at the same times, often making parallel grants of taxation. An ecclesial presence was linked to parliament both through the attendance of the church's highest officials and through the mutually informing assembly-structures they represented. For example, in 1395 when the Twelve Conclusions of the Lollards were pinned to the doors of both Westminster Hall and St. Paul's Cathedral, it was through the dual presence of these secular and sacred convocations that the Wycliffites sought to advertise their protest. Nominally clerical issues (heresy, clerical endowment, relations with Rome, discipline of the church) sometimes came to dominate the secular assembly. But one striking feature of the development of parliament during the fourteenth century is its steady laicization, as the upper prelates attended by virtue of their status as landholders of the king.

Conversely, as the representatives of the Church largely exited parliament during the fourteenth century, the "commons" as Commons grew in presence, giving the English assembly some of its most distinctive features. The regular summons of town burgesses finds many counterparts in continental practice, but the representation of the shires – the historical, local communities of the vill and the hundred – was relatively unique. That uniqueness has played a crucial part in the mythologization of the English parliament, as the "Commons" came to both represent and misrepresent the *communes*, the commons or community at large (*communitas, universitas, communitas regni*) of the realm.[9] Knights of the shires, present sporadically in early parliaments, acted as conduits for information and for requests for

---

[9] For the sake of clarity, throughout this study I make a provisional distinction between the institutional Commons (capital C) when referring specifically to parliamentary personnel, and the commons (small c) when referring to the *communitas regni*, the "commons of the realm."

redress of grievances. As their role at parliament normalized, these knights, who could be noble or non-noble, came to assume an important role in the political and legislative aspects of the assembly, as well as in its imagining by writers and poets. In the Commons, members of the lesser nobility mixed with city burgesses and fellow- but non-noble representatives of regional communities, *les Communes*, forming a mixture of discrete estates in one assemblage that contrasted with both the estate of the barons and upper nobles (*les Grauntz*) and the upper prelates (*les Prelatz*) among the Lords, and with the estate of the king (*le Roi*).

The greatest single power of the Commons was control of taxation. From the mid-1340s onward, it was not just custom but recognized statute that no taxes could be levied by the king, or for the king by the authority of the Lords, without the assent of the Commons in parliament. This was in fact the primary reason for calling parliaments, to induce (or extract) grants of taxation in support of military ventures. In return the king promised justice in the form of reaffirmed charters, re-enforced or modified statues, the hearing and trying of petitions, and the introduction and acceptance of new laws. As wars played on (alternately or concurrently French, Scottish, Welsh, Spanish, or Flemish campaigns from 1307 onward), the representatives in parliament found themselves in the somewhat paradoxical situation of gaining more power through their increasing fiscal liability for military ventures largely not of their own choosing. As kings needed money, so the power of parliament grew, as did the power of the Commons in parliament. At the same time the individual members of the Commons, both burgess and shire-knights, were often the dependents of the lords of the upper assembly, or directly of the king. And the king and Lords, in turn, could themselves be liable to the wealthier segments of the Commons, thus creating a complicated web of class and estate associations, regional loyalties and prejudices, dependencies and alliances. These networks, while certainly not limited to parliament, were nonetheless an important part of it. As has been recently acknowledged by both social and political historians, it is too simplifying to say that the Commons were entirely dependent or entirely independent of the men nominally above them. Political affiliation and action was, as we might reasonably expect, a complicated matter. Parliamentarians had to negotiate an increasingly complex system of social and political connections.[10]

---

[10] See especially McFarlane, "Parliament and 'Bastard Feudalism'"; Clark, "Magnates and their Affinities in the Parliaments of 1386–1421"; Ormrod, *Political Life in Medieval England*, 54–6; and Edwards, *The Commons in Medieval English Parliaments*, who notes that "'dependency' in later medieval England was an almost infinitely variable phenomenon" (14).

This social complexity in the composite estates of parliament (an issue dealt with at greater length in Chapter One) is further deepened by the complexity of the bureaucratic and political functioning of the assembly itself. What began as a judicial assembly focused primarily on matters of law and equity – the "capping" of the English judicial system with a highest court of royal appeal – evolved during the late thirteenth and fourteenth centuries into a court of politics and policy. However, it is essential to remember that these functions were never strictly separated.[11] What was sought in parliament was political justice *through* the law, by way of the courts, of which parliament was the highest. Its judicial function was a durable and consistently important part of its identity.[12] Up through and beyond the middle ages (and still to the present day in Britain), parliament was the highest court of legal appeal. It had original jurisdiction in matters of treason and impeachment, as well as in issues of specific relevance to the royal household. Petitions for private justice continued to be submitted to parliament all through the medieval period. As the system of royal courts matured and took over much of the necessary lower-level judicial functioning, parliament developed as a court of taxation and legislation. At long but remarkably regular intervals, parliament attempted to impose control over royal policy by the imposition of permanent or advisory councils. The process of impeachment developed in parliament, and the most divisive political struggles from 1327 to 1414 – two royal depositions, executions, banishments, legal and political standoffs, state trials – all occurred either in or around parliament as a combined legal and political tribunal. Social and commercial legislation, what Musson calls "the regulation of everyday life," also increasingly emanated from parliament.[13] They attempted to control (usually unsuccessfully) such things as wage and price levels, staples and commercial boundaries, sumptuary laws, ecclesial and town liberties, monopolies and guilds. Even picayune matters such as the disposal of offal and the price of pepper make their way to the parliamentary rolls, recorded alongside the most extreme political crises of the period.[14]

---

[11] See Musson, *Medieval Law in Context*, 184–216; Harding, *Medieval Law and the Foundations of the State*, 170–86 (the phrase "capping" of the judicial system by parliament comes from Harding, 147); Musson and Ormrod, *The Evolution of English Justice*, 25–8; and Lyon, *A Constitutional and Legal History of Medieval England*, 408–30.

[12] For analysis, see recently Harding, *Medieval Law*, 181, and Musson, *Medieval Law in Context*, 189. The ideological appeal of justice in parliament remained strong throughout the fourteenth and early fifteenth centuries. See also Tout, "English Parliament and Public Opinion."

[13] Musson, *Medieval Law in Context*, 207–9. [14] *RP* 3.87; 3.662.

With the development of its representative element, parliament was gradually endowed with the *plena potestas* of its members to speak for, and to, the communities of England. In this regard the Commons came to represent the *communitas* or commons of the realm even as they were, individually, drawn from the relatively restricted classes of the shire gentry and burgesses. During the fourteenth century, parliament assumed both a legal and a political form of representative speaking authority and was recognized to have this voice as more than a baronial gathering. As chief justice William Thorpe remarked around 1365 regarding the publication of a legal statute, "though proclamation has not been made . . . everyone is held to know a statute from the time it was made in parliament, for as soon as parliament has decided anything, the law holds that everyone has knowledge of it, for parliament represents the body of all the realm."[15] Thorpe's assessment of parliament's representative and legislative power is in some ways unique, and it elides a long developmental history. But it is not misleading, either in the overall authority it grants or the bodily metaphor used to justify it. As Anthony Musson describes it, the assembly "embodied for medieval people a triune nature: an occasion or venue for discussion of royal business (and at times popular concerns), a wing of royal government . . . and a collection of particular people and particular groups of people providing through their pool of knowledge and experience an element of national consciousness."[16]

Additionally, it is necessary to recognize the importance of parliaments and parliamentarism not only for England during this period but also for Europe as a whole. Almost all of the specific elements of the English parliament have analogues in other deliberative assemblies of the era. English practice was influenced by both ecclesial and continental (especially French) practice.[17] Equally if not more important than the secular developments of the European assemblies was the Conciliar Movement that began at about the start of the Great Schism (1376), lasting until the end of the Schism following the Council of Constance (1414–18) and, in its waning years, the collapse of conciliar efforts at the Council of Basle in 1439. As ubiquitous as it was, secular parliamentarism developed no body of theory to match

---

[15] Cited in Chrimes, *English Constitutional Ideas in the Fifteenth Century*, 76, from the legal Yearbook for 39 Edward III.

[16] Musson, *Medieval Law in Context*, 185.

[17] See extensively Marongiu, *Medieval Parliaments*; Lord, "The Parliaments of the Middle Ages and the Early Modern Period."

the extent and vigor of church conciliar theory.[18] By the later fourteenth
century, this was a Europe-wide intellectual movement that drew on earlier
philosophy in developing a conception of church authority based on the
tradition of authoritative councils in direct competition to papal supremacy.
In the writings of Marsilius of Padua in particular (c. 1275–1343), the Church
as the "body of the faithful," the *universitas fidelium*, finds its most accurate representation in a General Council set in opposition to the papacy.
Decrees of a council (representing the *pars valentior* or *major et sanior pars*
of the Christian community) would have greater authority than any papal
decree, and even the power to depose the Pope.[19] Parallels to contemporary and later fourteenth-century parliaments as putative representatives of
the community, the *universitas*, were both natural and inevitable. Occasionally they provoked conscious comparisons between church and secular
practice.[20] In England, assemblies of provincial convocations also provided
an immediate parallel. The principle of delegate representation – a concept so basic to our political tradition that it is surprising to think it ever
needed an origin – was in fact borrowed from church practice. In 1215–17,
in the same years King John was haggling with his barons, Innocent III
convoked the Fourth Lateran Council, the greatest representative gathering ever assembled to date.[21] Parliaments and convocations looked to each
other, and competed for legitimacy, in shared forms and procedures. Later
the next century, when Edward III wrote to the Pope and declared that
his requests carried the weight not only of his royal person but also of the
English nobility and community assembled in parliament, this was not a
gesture of royal weakness but of recognizable power.[22] The kingdom, like
the church, claimed the authority of its *universitas* through deliberative and
representative assembly. In both secular and clerical spheres, in all parts of
Europe, and for the period both preceding and immediately following the
decades that are the focus here, parliamentarism and conciliarism were not
isolated practices but important and widely spread cultural developments,

---

[18] On the intersections of conciliar theory and secular political practice see the relevant chapters of *The Cambridge History of Medieval Political Thought, c. 350–c.1450*; Quillet, "Community, Counsel and Representation"; Black, "The Conciliar Movement." See also Oakley, *The Conciliarist Tradition*; Tierney, *Religion, Law, and the Growth of Constitutional Thought, 1150–1650*, and "The Idea of Representation in the Medieval Councils of the West"; Black, *Council and Commune*, 194–209, and *Political Thought in Europe*, 162–85.
[19] Quillet, "Community, Counsel and Representation," 561.
[20] Black, *Council and Commune*, 194–8, *Political Thought in Europe*, 166–9.
[21] Tierney, "The Idea of Representation," 27–8.
[22] Richardson, "The Commons and Medieval Politics," 36–7.

as well as sources of theoretical and practical controversy. They permeated political, intellectual, and religious life. As Pronay and Taylor have noted, in this regard England was squarely in the midst of Europe-wide developments.[23]

In this context the decades from the 1370s to the early 1400s can be situated as both completely congruent with earlier and later developments, and, as A. L. Brown has summarized, as pivotally important for England in particular:

> [T]he significance of the period [from 1377 to 1422] in the long-term history of parliament seems clear. Parliament's development had already gone far by the beginning of the 1370s, and in the following half-century it continued along the same lines. But the pace quickened. Procedure hardened markedly, classic parliamentary rights began to be recognised, the importance of the commons increased significantly, interest in election and elections grew, and again and again parliament was the great national assembly and high court where major issues were aired and decided, sometimes in scenes of high drama.[24]

Similarly, Ronald Butt has concluded (with an architectural, as opposed to organicist, metaphor) that by the time of Richard's deposition in 1399, "the essential groundwork of medieval parliamentary power had been laid, and on it during the sixteenth and seventeenth centuries would be built the basic structure of the modern Parliament."[25] These characterizations of the liminality of the later fourteenth century help to remind us of two things. First, while parliament's institutional identity and practice was solidifying, it had not yet solidified completely into bureaucratic and governmental forms familiar to later ages. All eras are transitional, and we cannot expect that the parliamentarians of the time had any definite sense of their own pivotalness in the growth of the institution. At this time parliament was still a "clearing house and talking shop" with much less formal rigidity than it would later have.[26] On the other hand, this was a period when the post-plague *communitas regni* lurched from one crisis to another: the waning of Edward III and court crisis of 1376–7; the minority of Richard II; the Uprising of 1381; the magnate upheavals of 1386–8; the king's conflict with London in 1392; Richard's revenge and "tyranny" of 1397–8; the deposition of 1399; the uprisings of 1401–6; the omnipresent war with France and the specters of heresy and social unrest. Historians do not engage entirely in back-projection when they note that parliamentarians sensed – like their

---

[23] *Parliamentary Texts of the Later Middle Ages*, 3–5.
[24] Brown, "Parliament, c. 1377–1422," 139.   [25] Butt, 451.
[26] Harriss, "The Formation of Parliament, 1272–1377," 35.

poet counterparts – new developments taking hold. Crisis forced change, which suggested opportunity. Without descending into Whiggist teleologism or inevitabilism, we can responsibly acknowledge these developments as creative and still plastic ur-formations.

Secondly, it is equally important to stress that what we find is not representative democracy, or democracy in its assumed, post-enlightenment forms and liberalist definitions, but a species of democratic activity that violates most of what we associate with that word. We find only tightly restricted "representation" in the usual sense; no universal suffrage or even gestures towards universal suffrage; no conception of inalienable personal rights or civil liberties, or minority protections; no respect for the discreteness of offices and institutions, checks between spheres of governmental power, or principled separations between Church and state or between economy and society. And if we were to use "democracy" to describe these developments in England and Europe, frequently it would devolve to its original meaning, namely "mob rule," the community representing itself to itself, accurately or inaccurately, as speaking "with one voice" in the voice of communal will or the outcry of gang violence. As will be discussed in the next two chapters, parliament frequently stood at these junctures as well: between royalty and rabble, narrow interests and wider community, court of justice and lynch mob.

All of these observations militate for a more socially nuanced understanding of the environment of parliament.[27] From a specifically literary point of view, the question thus is not, why would artists be influenced by all of this?, but rather, how could they *not* be influenced, given the ubiquity and intensity of these parliamentary matters in both intellectual and political life? With a few exceptions, the connections between parliament and literature in this period have been only lightly touched upon even where one might expect otherwise. The potential problem appears to be one of conceptualizing the points of contact between art and institutions in a usefully illuminating way. There is a flatly historical approach available, and it is helpful to list some of the demonstrable connections between these artists and parliament. Chaucer was a parliamentarian in 1386 as an MP for Kent, and he had regular contact with others who served

---

[27] Compare Maddicott, "Parliament and the Constituencies, 1272–1377," 78: "We ought to view parliament, then, not only as a political assembly and a court but as an occasion for the complex interplay of private hopes and fears – for the seeking of royal favour, the promotion and supression of petitions, the maintenance of friends and the thwarting of enemies. These things are revealed to us only fragmentarily . . . yet they are suggestive of many currents of personal conflict and ambition which ran beneath the political surface of parliamentary life."

as MPs (Henry Bailiff, the probable model for the host of the *Canterbury Tales*, was MP for Southwark). As Justice of the Peace and Controller of the wool customs he held offices in the sphere of parliamentary concern and control, especially as Controller, since the wool tax was a major source of parliamentary revenue. Chaucer's son Thomas was repeatedly elected as speaker of the Commons during the reigns of Henry IV and Henry V. His paternal-poetical ancestry may have helped to give him the aura of a uniquely representative voice of the community. John Gower's history is murkier, but we know that he had a troublesome legal case brought before parliament in 1366. As Chapter Three explains, his name appears repeatedly in the parliamentary records for that year. In this and other matters, Gower also had business dealings with parliamentarians. At his death in 1408 his will was witnessed by Sir Arnold Savage, one of the speakers of the Commons. Gower's *Cronica Tripertita*, a late Latin addendum to the *Vox Clamantis*, is a biased account of the downfall of Richard II that is structured with reference to parliaments, and it displays a working familiarity with the circulated records of parliament. For Langland, our lack of any reliable extra-poetical biography does not allow these kinds of close connections to be known. But we do know that manuscripts of *Piers Plowman* were in the possession of parliamentary households, one of them (as discussed in Chapter Five) a contemporary of Langland's, and another owned by a late speaker of the Commons, Sir Thomas Charleton (d. 1465).[28] The poem makes veiled allusions to parliamentary events, and similiarities between elements of the *Visio* and the Good Parliament of 1376 have long been recognized. Perhaps the best evidence of a connection between Langland and parliament comes from his later imitators, the anonymous poets of the "Piers Plowman tradition" who composed *Mum and the Sothsegger, The Crowned King*, and *Richard the Redeless*. All of these are in a Langlandian idiom with extensive references to parliament. Helen Barr has suggested that the author or authors may have been parliamentary clerks.[29] If so, it gives some indirect evidence as to who was reading Langland as contemporary literature: not just the knights and burgesses of parliament but also the clerks who worked for them.

Indeed, as much recent scholarship has demonstrated, to be a poet in this period was, by and large, to be a clerk and to have clerkly–clerical training. All of these poets moved in the clerical and bureaucratic circles that were a distinctive feature of the London-Westminster environment. Chancery and

---

[28] Noted by Edwards, "The Early Reception of Chaucer and Langland," 4, and McFarlane, *Nobility of Later Medieval England*, 237–8. Charleton's inventory also included a copy of the *Canterbury Tales*.
[29] "Introduction," *The Piers Plowman Tradition*, ed. Barr, p. 17.

Paternoster Row were as central to parliamentary developments as they were to literary ones.[30] Recent research has confirmed what we could reasonably expect, namely that some of the clerks and scribes who made their livelihood in the production and copying of legal and governmental documents also worked on literary texts. This in turn should be contextualized by the explosive growth of documentary practices in later medieval culture.[31] From the late thirteenth century onward, the "bill revolution" of the court system extended and deepened the reach of specifically clerkly elements of textual production.[32] As the greatest court of the land and the apex of the judiciary system, parliament was both a source and subject of this trend. It was the highest court of petition and, as I discuss in Chapters Two and Four, this petitionary aspect of parliament had a profound effect on literature. The thousands of medieval parliamentary petitions extant to this day in the National Archives, the vast majority of them still uncatalogued until very recently, testify not only to the social importance of legal petitioning but also to the ways this typically scribal business could be present in everyday life. They informed literary practice even as literate practices, like parliament itself, were developing in new ways.

In addition to this straightforward historical contextualization, a second means of presenting the links between parliament and literature is even more obvious and, in commensurate ways, limiting. That is, we can note the simple presence of parliaments *in* literature and the literary representations of parliaments that proliferate in this period. Each of the works analyzed in this study contains a parliament or extensive references to parliaments. One of the notable aspects of later fourteenth-century literature is the cross-cutting interest in representing parliament *per se* in ways both connected to, and different from, what had come before. As Chris Given-Wilson has noted, a newly-stressed attention to parliaments is one of the most salient characteristics of later fourteenth-century history-writing.[33] In Chapter One, I outline this shift in the representations of parliament from a baronial to a communal model. Understood narrowly as the governmental institution or more widely as the practice of talk, colloquy, and debate, "parliament" has a correlatively strong presence as an element entered into

[30] Harriss, "The Formation of Parliament," 32.
[31] See Clanchy, *From Memory to Written Record*; Green, *A Crisis of Truth*; Steiner, *Documentary Culture and the Making of Medieval English Literature*; Kerby-Fulton and Justice, "Langlandian Reading Circles." On scribal practice, see recently Horobin and Mooney, "A *Piers Plowman* Manuscript," especially 94–102.
[32] The phrase comes from Harding, *Medieval Law and the Foundations of the State*, 160–70; see also his "Plaints and Bills in the History of English Law, Mainly in the Period 1250–1350."
[33] Given-Wilson, *Chronicles*, 177–9.

imaginative narratives. It has obvious affinities to other recognizable tropes and literary forms that it frequently draws from and re-combines: debate poetry, estates satire, romance, courtly lyric, and drama. But for analytic purposes, "the literary representation of parliament" itself quickly becomes too limiting as a rubric for understanding the dynamics of these works, as if, for example, Chaucer's *Parliament of Fowls* could be reduced to a simple allegory of an institution, or Langland's use of the "Parliament of the Rats and Mice" fable were no more than displaced contemporary commentary. They *are* that, but more as well.

One way of incorporating this representational aspect into something potentially more insightful is to think of parliament itself as a special forum and form for court literature, related to but different from the kinds of literature that circulated around the *camera regis* and the courtly affinities of noble households. Parliament was a "house" – first so-called in 1376 – but not a household. The public sentiment attending to it was unique. Parliaments were viewed as courts with all of the attendant problems of one, but also as special assemblies for the publication of popular opinion and reputation, or of what interested parties tried to pass off as such. An early and familiar vignette provides an amusing hint of the social sensibility available through parliament. It comes from one chronicle account of the Earl of Warenne's response to Edward I's *Quo warranto* inquiries:

Soon thereafter the king disturbed some of the landed magnates by way of his justices, wishing to know by what warrant (i.e., with writs of *Quo warranto*) they held their lands; and if they did not have a good warrant, he immediately seised their lands. And, among the others, the earl of Warenne was called before the judges of the king and interrogated by what warrant he held his land. He produced in their midst an old and rusty sword and he said, "Behold, my lords, behold my warrant. For my ancestors, coming with William the Bastard, conquered his lands by the sword and defended those same lands by the sword against whomever wished to occupy them. For the king did not conquer and subject the land by himself, but our ancestors were with him as fellows and helpers." And the rest of the magnates held with him and his response, and they left, raucous and unplaced. When the king heard this, he feared for himself and he quieted down from his initial error. Shortly thereafter the Welsh rose up, and the king had great need of his magnates. When the king was holding a certain parliament (*quoddam parliamentum*) and the sons of the magnates stood before him in the evening, he said to them, "What do you say among yourselves when we are in council with your fathers?" And one responded, "You won't be offended if I speak the truth?" And the king said, "No." "Certainly, my lord king, we say:

> *Le roy cuuayte nos deneres,*
> *e la rayne nos beau maners,*
> *e le Quo voranco,*
> *sale mak wus al at do.*"[34]

The little French-English jingle at the end can be translated, "The king covets our money, / and the queen, our beautiful manors. / And the *Quo warranto* / will do us all in." The story of Warenne is familiar as a classic exemplum of the clash between legal–documentary forms and folk–traditional assertions of right.[35] Around 1285 Edward I had instituted newly invigorated and invasive *Quo warranto* inquiries into the landholdings of the nobility. The response given to his justices was less than enthusiastic. Warenne's reply – which gains eager assent from fellow magnates – is bold but consonant with the forceful self-assertion of Edward's barons, even in the king's parliament. More subtle but equally interesting is the scene that follows in the unspecified later *parliamentum*, when the king attempts to get a better sense of his magnates' mood by questioning their sons. If we imagine the exchange as a living tableau – the king consulting his barons while engaged in another political struggle with them, the attendance of the peers' families at the high court of parliament, and the social exchange going on both within and outside the assembly meetings – we can better understand parliament as a social and literary event as well as a political one. Parliaments were big events, gatherings of the nobility and community representatives in the most public regular assembly in the kingdom. They

---

[34] Guisborough, 216: "Cito post inquietauit rex quosdam ex magnatibus terre per iusticiarios suos scire volens quo Waranto tenerent terras et si non haberent bonum varentum saysiuit statim terras illorum; vocatusque est inter ceteros Comes de Warenna coram justiciarios regis et interrogatus quo Warento teneret produxit in medium gladium antiquum et eruginatum et ait 'Ecce domini mei ecce Warentum meum. Antecessores enim mei cum Willelmo bastardo uenientes conquesti sunt terras suas gladio et easdem gladio defendam a quocunque eas occupare volente. Non enim rex per se terram deuicit et subiecit sed progenitores nostri fuerunt cum eo participes et coadiutores.' Adheseruntque sibi et sue responsioni ceteri magnates, et tumultuantes et inpacati recesserunt. Rex autem cum audiret talia timuit sibi et ab incepto errore conquieuit. Et cito post insurrexerunt Walenses et magnatibus suis rex multum indiguit. Cum teneret rex quoddam parliamentum et filii magnatorum starent coram eo in vesperis dixit eis, 'Quid loquimini inter vos quando nos sumus in consilio cum patribus vestris?' Et respondit vnus, 'Non offendamini si veritatem dicam?' Et rex 'Non.' 'Certe, domini mi rex, nos dicimus sic:

> Le roy cuuayte nos deneres,
> e la rayne nos beau maners,
> e le Quo voranco,
> sale mak wus al at do.'"

[35] See the analysis of Clanchy, *From Memory to Written Record*, 35–43; also Musson, *Medieval Law in Context*, 23. The poem is noted by Wilson, *Lost Literature of Medieval England*, 195–6.

were also gossipy and showy affairs, a crossroads for political rumor and conflict as well as an important arena for public display, discussion, and, presumably, for poetical and artistic efforts a bit more polished than the quatrain recorded here. As we shall see in Chapter One, the early baronial focus of parliamentary writing shifts but never completely dies. The image of parliament as a forum for this sort of popular communication actually expands. This small scene also touches on elements of enduring thematic concern in poetry: the question of truth-telling versus remaining mum; the desire for, and danger of, a single voice speaking the opinion of a community (as one son stands forth to be a representative speaker); the combination of humor and seriousness. But most importantly, what also emerges over time is the sense of parliament as a *notional forum*, a place or site for the representation of conflict and colloquy and a fitting form for the tensions and debates of the day – the things that *sale mak wus al at do* – in both sage and satirical tones.

   In this regard, what parliament provided – and, I will argue, what made it appealing to poets – was a way to approach the issue of representation itself, since parliaments in literature are *representations of representation*, in both aesthetic and electoral senses. They are portraits of portraits of the community. In parliamentary poetry, what we repeatedly encounter is not just historical topicality or allegorism. Rather, the intersection of social form and literary practice facilitates new conceptual horizons, making possible modes of narrative that, while not strictly new, could be received and represented in new ways. Correlatively, a "literary" and social understanding of parliament helps to flesh out its historical and institutional growth in a time when history and literature were not easily separable, especially in chronicles and romances. Parliaments in literature allowed authors to exploit topical resonances and institutional forms, as did other formal models of composition directly borrowed for literary use (especially petitions and bills, as discussed in Chapters Four and Five). At the same time, the second-order or meta-poetical possibilities of parliament enabled writers to muse on the act of writing itself in a manner directly relevant to an interest in the *bonum commune* and the developing public sphere. As we shall see, the poetry of *parlement* was also poetry about its own expressive capacity. What is meant by a parliamentary form or style of poetry is therefore an experimentally capacious approach to artistic work that is set in specific political contexts as well as the broader setting of parliamentary changes, in England and beyond, that fundamentally enabled these poets to write as they did. This is not to claim that all literature responded to this context. The works of the *Pearl*-poet, for example, have little or nothing to do with the aesthetics of parliamentarism. But for authors, clerks, and audiences in and around Westminster, parliament was an immediately important part of community affairs as a self-conscious construction of the "body politic." Simply put, parliament and poetry worried about the same things. Poets borrowed from parliament many of the terms and forms needed to express those issues, and more.

What we find at this intersection is thus a locus of public discourses artistically representing the conflict over what it meant for a voice to *be* "common" or public in the first place. In an article of fundamental importance not just for this book but for a whole generation of critics, Anne Middleton identified Ricardian "public poetry" as "best understood not as poetry 'about' contemporary events and abuses . . . rather it is poetry defined by a constant relation of speaker to audience within an ideally conceived worldly community, a relation which has become the poetic subject"; it is a form of expression in which "poetry was to be a 'common voice' to serve the 'common good.'"[36] The anxieties so evident in the labors of Gower, Chaucer, and Langland were centered on the dual demands of representation, the anxiety about "the poem's adequacy to his [ie. the poet's] world, not only as a representation of it, but, even more important, as an address to it."[37] What Middleton identifies as characteristic of Langland's obsessive rewriting of *Piers Plowman* is, I would contend, equally true of Gower and Chaucer (and of the lesser later poets treated in Chapter Six). The salient issue is representation, the question of who can "stand" or speak, who can represent, in the artistic and social communities, and for that matter what *can* count as a community, a *universitas*, or as the community of communities, as parliament was often called. As the voice of "*the* commons," the lower assembly of parliament arrogated to itself a name that was coterminous with the larger realm it sought to speak for, even when – as during the Uprising of 1381 – the very identification of the "true commons" was violently at stake. Who *can* speak in the name of the commons? Correlatively, the challenge to the poets was one of both representing-to and speaking-for the community, addressing it but also standing *for* it as a medium for self-knowledge and deliberate action.

Again, not surprisingly, these durable cruces of representational adequacy can be traced back to this period. They find their earliest mature

---

[36] Middleton, "The Idea of Public Poetry in the Reign of Richard II," 95; more recently see also Watts, "The Pressure of the Public on Later Medieval Politics."
[37] Middleton, "The Idea of Public Poetry," 98.

formulations in the philosophy and law of the day.[38] From a narrow and strictly legal sense of representation in classical and early medieval usage, the later middle ages developed, through the mediation of canon law, an understanding of representation as necessary for the conception of aesthetic and social totalities. For Ockham, Marsiglio, and others, "*repraesentare* is essentially part of the process of knowledge."[39] In this view, something can be understood or comprehended correctly only when it is represented correctly in aesthetic, spiritual, or political terms. It is in the concept of representation where these categories closely meet. In an inchoate but easily recognizable fashion, the desire to identify the king as symbolically representative of the community, at the same time that parliament was held to be a descriptive representation of the *universitas*, creates a remarkable but little remarked tension. The unity of the sovereign is opposed to the fragmentation of a communal body that is reconciled in the figure of a corporate social totality, the king in his court of parliament, a political representation that is curiously re-doubled, fragmented, self-antagonistic, and yet unified.

Of course this was a long-term tension that did not arise whole cloth out of only parliamentary developments. There is no need to assume that earlier periods were gripped by a naïve monarchialism or by the simple fascination with the subject of the king as coterminous with the subject of the community. The ethic of the *universitas* and *communitas* was at least as long and strong as that of monarchy. As an early poetical polemicist under Henry III asserted,

> Premio preferimus uniuersitatem;
> Legem quoque dicimus regis dignitatem
> Regere, nam credimus esse legem lucem,
> Sine qua concludimus deuiare ducem . . .
> Dicitur uulgariter: ut rex uult, lex uadit;
> Veritas uult aliter, nam lex stat, rex cadit.[40]

[We give first place to the community (*universitatem*): we say also that the law rules over the king's dignity; for we believe that the law is the light, without which we conclude that he who rules will wander from the right path . . . It is said commonly, 'As the king wills, so goes the law.' But the truth is otherwise, for the law stands, but the king falls.]

[38] See especially Cam, "Mediaeval Representation in Theory and Practice," and "The Theory and Practice of Representation in Medieval England."

[39] Quillet, "Community, Counsel and Representation," 562. See also de Lagarde, "L'idée de représentation dans les oeuvres de Guillaume d'Ockham."

[40] *The Song of Lewes*, ed. Kingsford, 847–50, 871–2; On the ubiquity of *universitas* as a framing concept of medieval thought, see especially Michaud-Quantin, *Universitas*.

It was entirely conceivable that the *universitas* could and should come first, and that the community stood across from its king as subject and petitioner but also as the source of authority. The poet of this long and eloquent Henrician lament thus assumes a similar position of speaking for the community – the undefined "we" of his subject-position – as the advocate of law and community voice, even as that community tries to incorporate *and* distance the image of a unifying and virtuous sovereign as its organic avatar. This tension is absolutely central to the form and content of much of later medieval poetry.

Whether a representative could be independent of the thing represented – whether the parliamentarian could exercise independence from his constituency (a particular worry that surfaces in *Mum and the Sothsegger*, for example); whether, or how, a king was answerable to his subjects as their symbolic head (a worry of *Piers Plowman*); whether a poet could stand in an independent relation to the *communitas* as both a critic and a member (as in Gower's incessant self-representations, but also of Chaucer's more subtle ones): these are points that strike not only at the heart of the public poetry of the time, but at the perennial issues of political and parliamentary representation. As noted by Hannah Pitkin in her classic study of political representation,

A writer's position in this range of views is correlated with his conception of political life in the broadest sense: his ideas on the nature of political issues, the relative capacities of rulers and ruled, the nature of man and society – in short, what we might call his metapolitics. . . . In the broadest terms, the position a writer adopts within the limits set by the concept of representation will depend on . . . his broad conception of human nature, human society, and political life.[41]

The "range of views" concerns the power of the representative, bound or free, mandated or independent from the body or constituency putatively represented. Without doing too much violence to Pitkin's formula – and without ascending into airy generalities – it is my argument here that the public poetry of the late Ricardian and early Lancastrian era is dealing with these same questions by way of the institutionally-grounded and timely formations of parliament, in the "endless ambivalences" of mediatory poetry.[42] The metapolitics of later medieval poetical writers thus bears a close relationship to our own era through these issues of representation and consent, and through the forms and historiography of parliamentary writing and politics. For these authors, metapolitics and metapoetry were correlative

---

[41] Pitkin, *The Concept of Representation*, 146, 167.
[42] Middleton, "The Idea of Public Poetry," 103.

practices, as both poetry and parliament dealt with the conditions of discourse and complaint, public expression and individual voice.

To conclude by returning to my epigraphs, Carlyle's assertion that "literature is our parliament, too" is thus a thesis this study will cautiously uphold in its dual potential interpretations. Literature was a form of public discussion, of *parlement*, at the same time that parliament was a form and forum for creative "literary" expression. While neither was causally dependent on the other, they both stand to be illuminated by each other's light. At the same time, the potential dangers of this metapolitical turn can be manifest (if not conscious) in the inevitable tug towards a triumphalist narrative such a project invites. In an article from many years ago, the historian Helen Maud Cam found a reasonably good straw man in Arthur Hallam, the pre-eminent Victorian historian, as an example of this tendency. Writing of the constitutional history of medieval England, Hallam began,

No unbiased observer who derives pleasure from the welfare of his species can fail to consider the long and uninterruptedly increasing prosperity of England as the most beautiful phenomenon in the history of mankind. In no other region have the benefits that political institutions can confer been diffused over so extended a population; nor have any people so well reconciled the discordant elements of wealth, order and liberty.[43]

This unabashed whiggery was no more acceptable to Cam in 1948 than it is today. It was in reaction to assertions like this that Stubbs composed his magisterial *Constitutional History of England* in 1878 – and in reaction to Stubbs, that Maitland composed his; and in reaction to Maitland, that we have McIlwain, Pollard, Chrimes, Lyons, Cam and Clarke, Richardson and Sayles, Musson and Ormrod, and so on, to the present day, in a remarkable catena of historical scholarship. Truthfully and unpejoratively, in each case – Hallam's formulation is only more obvious and less embarrassed – the desire to arrive at that "beautiful phenomenon," and to comprehend it more usefully, is always the driving force for historical narrative. So the presence of a moralizing impulse (to use Hayden White's phrase) is both as unavoidable as it is frankly necessary in any such inquiry. What this study attempts to provide is a new but definite form of narrative continuity in dealing with the early parliamentary tradition. When combined with an assessment of the literary tradition, the other massive *grand récit* of British culture, the temptations to moralizing whiggery are strong.

One always tentative solution, as Maura Nolan has argued, is the suspension of metaphoric elements that are not then allowed explicitly to be

---

[43] Hallam [1818] in Cam, "Stubbs Seventy Years After," in *Law-Finders and Law-Makers*, 189.

arranged in metonymical sequence, forestalling a comfortable narrative of historical continuity even as the assumption of *some* continuity (why else study this history and literature?) remains, perhaps morally, in the background.[44] The question is, again, of representation, historical and therefore imaginary, where now the "embrace of the fragmentary" – in one sense a necessity itself, given the fragmentary state of medieval parliamentary records – becomes an explicit historiographical principle. Fragments are juxtaposed to suggest a form of completeness or an interaction between them, but the final assertion of totality is foregone. Such a principle of analytical practice is also potentially a political one. Recent theorization about "aesthetic representation" in parliamentary contexts calls for the recognition of fragmentation, and of the inevitable distance between representation and represented, not as a fault to be overcome but as the actual source of legitimate political power, since all power, like knowledge, arises from the act of representation.[45]

This essentially aestheticist (post)modern perspective is notable for its contrast to a medieval one. Repeatedly in medieval texts, what is desired is the identity of a single voice and a unity of public representation that would close the gap or fissure between the authoritative image of society – sovereign, assembly, council, convocation, or the figure of the poet himself – and its tenor, the *communitas*. The contrast, however, becomes less severe, and in fact might elide into similiarity, if we recognize that in this period, the artistic renderings of parliament – and the art influenced *by* parliament – not only leave this representational space open, but also explore it, problematize it, and take trouble over it in unique ways. The desire for a narrative of this trouble thus suffers the embarrassment of plot less as the tidy construction of an historiographical good story (the "growth of parliament" and the "growth of literature"), but as the account of contingent forces, variously arrayed in art and politics, that have made our world much of what it is today, for better or worse.

* * *

The ensuing chapters are arranged in chronological sequence and paired by thematic interest. Following this Introduction are two historical chapters

---

[44] Nolan, "Metaphoric History: Narrative and New Science in the Work of F. W. Maitland," 559, 562, 568.

[45] On "Aesthetic representation" as a political concept – the necessary gap between represented and representative being both the space and source of political power – see the work of F. R. Ankersmit, especially: "On the Origin, Nature, and Future of Representative Democracy," in *Political Representation*; the other essays gathered in that volume and in *Historical Representation*; and his *Aesthetic Politics*. For a critique of Ankersmit's arguments about aesthetic representationalism and the philosophy of *juste milieu* politics, see Zammito, "Ankersmit and Historical Representation."

analyzing a set of important topics: the literary development of the representational element of parliament away from baronialism, and the related model of Arthurianism; the idealized, quasi-spiritual notion of parliament as the *vox Dei*; the centrality of complaint and the development of a communal voice of complaint in the documentary practice of petition; and the conceptual dynamics of representing a single voice that is, by definition, the voice of a multitude.

After these chapters and building from them, the literary analyses begin in Chapter Three with the author who is perhaps the least "representative" and most socially critical of the commons, John Gower. My analysis centers on an understudied work of Gower's canon, the *Mirour de l'Omme*. Gower's poetry reflects the baronial model of idealized royal counsel, but it also reveals a unique perspective on the tensions of representation and on the question of who can speak for the community. His poetry is, counterintuitively enough, heavily invested in a parliamentary model of representation by being the most critical of it from a public poet's point of view. Chapter Four approaches Chaucer similarly. Chaucer also presents parliaments in a traditionalist and courtly manner and from a critical perspective. But his own interest is both deeper and, in the end, more artistically generous and insightful. My analysis naturally centers on the *Parliament of Fowls*. I also contend that the General Prologue of the *Canterbury Tales* should be understood as an expression of aesthetic parliamentarism, which is a more native English focus in contrast to recent assertions of Chaucer's Italianate political influences. Chaucer's idiosyncratic treatment of erotic and marital matters also necessitates a better understanding of the social collocation of marriages and parliaments, which is a point of contact for all three authors.

Gower and Chaucer thus form a relatively natural pairing. In Chapters Five and Six, Langland and his minor successors also stand together. They are distinguished by a different approach to parliament and by a more practical conception of what a communal voice could include and the political work it might achieve. The portraits of society presented at the beginning and end of *Piers Plowman* are dependent on a parliamentary model in both direct and abstract forms. The poem's attempt to arrive at a functioning totality in parliamentary form – a workable image of deliberative social exchange in the "House of Unity" – is but one of many models that crumble, in the end. Similarly, the poets of the Piers Plowman tradition, treated in Chapter Six, appear to have sought a political solution for contemporary crises in the meliorative role of parliament. Theirs is a much more bureaucratized vision of the assembly, expressed in Langlandian verse, as a safety valve or salve for the community. However humble, these post-revolutionary poems indicate an attempt to think through the trauma of 1399, and beyond, in parliamentary and poetical terms.

The suggestive assemblage of incomplete poems treated in the last chapter is inadvertently symbolic of the way the incomplete project of parliament was slowed, if not halted, by Henry V's victory at Agincourt in 1415. With success in war and popularity at home – success an English king had not experienced since the 1340s – the Crown's dependence on parliament lessened, and the frequency of parliaments dropped significantly. Following its ascendence in the early part of the fifteenth century, parliament went into a period of relative decline in terms of its political power even as it maintained its identity (sometimes vigorously) as the voice of the community. For the most part, parliament drops out of literature as both a topical element and a structuring form. The book thus ends with a short consideration of this turn of events. But the powerful aesthetic forms of a parliamentary idea of the *communitas*, which lay behind the unique and deliberative communities of poetry, had already been created. They were left, as it were, as compelling fragments of social self-imagining for later recuperation.

For the exposition of this thesis, I have incorporated into each chapter a fragmentary historical episode: Gower's parliamentary law-case of 1365–6; Chaucer's involvement in the Wonderful Parliament of 1386 and the developments of 1388, and also, with regard to parliament and marriage, the case of Elizabeth de Burgh from 1322 and 1327; Langland's prescient reflection of the events of the Good Parliament of 1376 and some of the chronicle stories related to it; and for the parliamentary poems of Chapter Six, a reading of some remarkable petitions submitted by the Commons and by a commoner in the two parliaments of 1414. Each of these parliamentary episodes provides insight into how parliament was viewed and why people looked to it for communal or personal redress, and how the ideologies of parliament could be manipulated, sometimes quite artfully, for different ends. As partial as such observations must necessarily be, they provide points of intersection between the aesthetic and electoral representations that were bound up with parliament and literature.

CHAPTER I

Parliament and voice in the thirteenth and early fourteenth centuries

My Lord Coke tells us Parliament *is derived from 'parler le ment' (to speak one's mind). He might as honestly have taught us that* firmament *is 'firma mentis' (a farm for the mind), or 'fundament' the bottom of the mind.*

— Thomas Rymer, "On Parliaments"[1]

* * *

Writing about a century after the eminent legist and parliamentarian Sir Edward Coke (1552–1634), the poet, historian, and critic Thomas Rymer (1641–1713) had good grounds to poke fun at his predecessor's poor etymologizing. However naïve his claim about its origins, Coke's fanciful calque-derivation of the word "parliament" is nonetheless revealing in its combination of two elements: the desire to get at parliament's origins by way of words, and the correlative wish to align those origins with a form of speaking that is at once individual (to speak *one's* mind) and institutional, and hence authoritative. In the seventeenth century, when competing histories of the origins of the "ancient constitution" were themselves part of a national struggle between the authority of the crown and parliament, the political need to derive and define the power to *parler le ment* led, as in Coke, to some creative historiography of parliament.[2] As I will demonstrate here, that creativity and fictionality itself has some history behind it, as the roots and early development of parliament were bound up with shifting representations and narratives. This history of the creative conception of parliament provides a necessary background for understanding how, and why, its discourses and forms became central to the practice of later fourteenth-century poets – and, indeed, beyond, desultorily to the age of Milton. It also serves as an interesting story in itself, as several speculative observations can be made about the parameters of parliamentary

[1] Quoted from *Brewer's Dictionary of Phrase and Fable*, 685.
[2] See Pocock, *The Ancient Constitution and the Feudal Law*.

consciousness, for this early period, from the intersection of literature and institutional development.

Much of the historiographical narrative presented in the next two chapters is familiar from later medieval English constitutional history. Looking at it through the lens of literary and cultural history, and with a view to contextualizing some of the literary developments of the period, leads to a different set of emphases. The focal points of analysis, in this chapter and the next, are five: 1) the representation of parliament as a gathering of estates or classes, and the flexibility of those notions prior to the fifteenth century; 2) the early, almost exclusively aristocratic model of parliament in the thirteenth and early fourteenth centuries – what I call romance baronialism – and the expansion and development away from an exclusively baronial focus during this period; 3) the concomitant representation of parliament as a divinely inspired gathering that derives from clerical assembly; 4) parliament's importance as a court of complaint, and the tradition of complaint both within it and about it; and finally 5) building upon all of these elements, the conceptual representation of parliament as a unified body "with one voice," at the same time that it is represented as fractured and discordant. Naturally each of these elements is not temporally limited to any particular period or reign, and their elements overlap. For the sake of clarity and organization – and with some faith in the implicitly developmental model providing a trajectory for the changes outlined here – these points are arranged chronologically, beginning, for our purposes, with Edward I. To start this exposition with a better understanding of parliament in the later fourteenth century, it is useful to have a look at some of the earliest images and imaginings of a parliament's opening session.

I THE IMAGE OF PARLIAMENT AND THE ESTATES OF THE REALM

The famous Wriothsley portrait (see below, Figure 1), often reproduced, was made over a century after the period in focus here, but it still accurately captures many elements of the late fourteenth- and early fifteenth-century parliament. In its arrangements the manuscript picture reveals important clues to the development and function of the assembly, its origins and conceptual boundaries. It is also revealing when compared to later portraits made in the same style.

The working room of parliament was generally the White Chamber of the Lords in Westminster Palace, but the formal meeting place for opening

Figure 1. Parliament 15 April 1523, by or for Sir Thomas Wriothsley (c. 1460–1534),
Garter King of Arms. Wriothsley Garter Book. The Royal Collection © 2006 HM
Queen Elizabeth II

and plenary sessions was the Painted Chamber (*Camera Depicta*), which is the room these portraits present, recognizable by its pattern of checkered floor tiles. The portrait depicts a specific meeting of parliament and it has been explicated in some detail by Powell and Wallis: many of the individuals can be identified.[3] The artist accurately portrays the position, orientation, and personnel of parliament in an arrangement that had remained largely the same for about two centuries. Although parliaments could meet anywhere in the kingdom and not all of these constituents would have been present, the overall disposition was probably uniform regardless of locale.[4]

Rather than beginning at the top and head, with the king seated on the throne (in this portrait, Henry VIII in 1523), it is more useful to start from the central parliamentary perspective: the middle. The chamber itself was rectangular and not square, as these early portraits imply by their symmetry. This squareness is undone in later portraits, as, for example, in the image from Elizabeth's parliament in 1584, which shows the same view but with better visual perspective and proportionality (Figure 4). The distortion of perspective in the 1523 picture accurately conveys the historical and functional centrality of the middle figures. Seated on four woolsacks facing each other are (at the top) two chief justices, (on the sides) eight junior or *puisne* justices from the courts of the King's Bench and Common Pleas, and (at the bottom) four serjeants-at-law. Behind the serjeants are two clerks, the clerk of the crown and the clerk of parliament, kneeling or seated on the floor with their writing instruments. The woolsacks themselves were symbolic of the wool trade's importance for the well-being of England. The legal personnel are arranged in a way to facilitate consultation amongst themselves and, as Pollard noted, such seating implies the early core function of the king's parliament as a law court for addressing pleas and determining judgments.[5] Around the justices and serjeants are arranged the lords spiritual and temporal. On the king's right, the "spiritual side," the archbishops of Canterbury and York (in this portrait, Warham and Wolsey), with the other bishops, abbots, and upper prelates arrayed in their mitres on the double row of benches stretching around the chamber. On the king's left, the "temporal side," in front of two councillors of the court in non-parliamentary

---

[3] Powell and Wallis, 555–7; Butt, 265–6. See also Pollard, *The Evolution of Parliament*, 247–8 and 380–3, who differs in some details.

[4] For descriptions of the usual meeting places of parliament at Westminster Palace, see Edwards, *The Second Century of the English Parliament*, 4–16; Butt, 265–7. As Pollard notes (383) this parliament in 1523 would have been at Blackfriars, not Westminster, but the accoutrements and the distinctive flooring of the chamber (compare Figures 2–4) indicate a conflation with Westminster.

[5] Pollard, *Evolution of Parliament*, 248.

robes, the upper bench remains empty (the archbishop of York would be depicted there if he had not, for reasons of office, moved to the right). The greater nobility of the realm, in distinctive parliamentary robes, are seated on the benches to the king's left. Two dukes (Norfolk, with the baton of the office of Earl Marshal, and Suffolk) are at the head, distinguished by their coronets and by the four ducal bars on their robes.[6] Below them are seven earls, and behind them, eight barons. Other baronial peers are arrayed at the bottom of the assembly on the front bench. In front of the king on the carpet (the "cloth of state") are three earls bearing symbols of office (the cap of maintenance, the sword of state, and the chamberlain with his wand). Thus the secular and ecclesial nobility are ordered by titular prominence and in the same ring or plane as the king, but beneath him in stature and below him in position. The nobility surrounds the clerkly personnel in the middle of the room in a manner suggestive of how parliament as a baronial assembly was grafted onto, and developed with, the legal functions of the royal court as a court of law.

The last layer of that growth is the Commons, barely visible at the bottom of the 1523 portrait and entirely missing from the portrait of 1551 and the Edwardian reconstruction, but gaining in prominence by the Elizabethan portrait (see Figures 2–4). The Commons as a group were restricted to standing behind a rail; an opening or gate, visible at the right, is for entering the chamber. The speaker stands in the center, probably on a platform. In the parliament of this portrait, the speaker plainly visible at center bottom would have been Sir Thomas More. The Commons' peripheral presence accurately correlates with their later arrival as a permanent part of the assembly, the last "estate" to join its structure. It also conveys their formal status as petitioners – looking from the outside in – in the procedures of deliberation. Mirroring them in some ways is the mob of figures at the upper right (on the king's left) that breaks the symmetry of the portrait. This awkwardly placed group probably represents the first-born of the noble peers, themselves future parliamentarians who are watching and learning from the proceedings.[7]

These portraits as a group, while depicting the historical and administrative arrangements within parliament as an assembly, also communicate parliament's status as an imagined assembly. It was both a national and a

[6] The rank of duke was created after 1337: see Butt, 265; on ducal coronets in parliament see Powell and Wallis, 396.
[7] This group is missing from the Edwardian reconstruction and becomes a handful of five gentlemen in the 1551 portrait. In the 1584 portrait, the figures labeled *proceres primogeniti* move from a door behind Elizabeth's throne, on the left, behind a low curtain or wall similar to the Commons' railing.

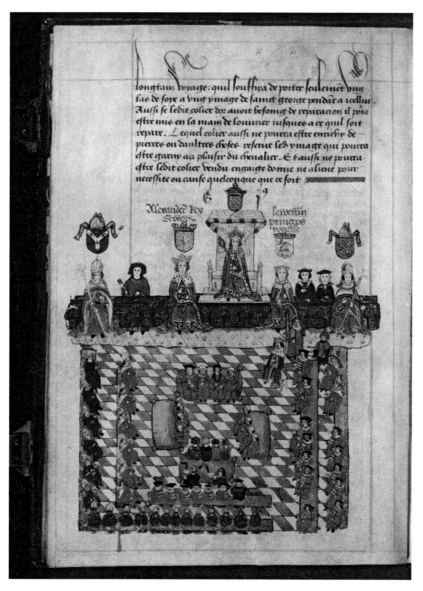

Figure 2. Imaginary reconstruction of a parliament of Edward I, including Alexander, King of Scots and Llewelyn ap Gruffydd, Prince of Wales. Wriothsley Garter Book. The Royal Collection © 2006 HM Queen Elizabeth II

Figure 3. Parliament in 1551. From the collections of Sir Gilbert Dethick (c. 1519–84),
Register of the Order of the Garter. The Royal Collection © 2006 HM Queen Elizabeth II

Figure 4. An Elizabethan parliament ("*Pompa Parliamentaris*"). From Robert Glover's *Nobilitas politica vel civilis*, 1608. © Yale Center for British Art, Paul Mellon Collection.

notional forum, a gathering of estates that is separate from, but also connected to, the community at large. The symbolic value of the portraits as
an image of community is perhaps best exemplified by the second portrait
(Figure 2), which includes Alexander, the King of the Scots and Llewelyn,
the Prince of Wales, seated to the king's right and left. These two figures
from the English *imperium* never attended the same parliament, so their
presence here is purely a representation of a political imaginary mediated
through the form of parliament.[8] While it might be a bit much to claim (following Pollard) that England had no national self-conception prior to the
development of parliament, it is also easy to see how it would have fostered
a growing sense of a specifically "English" identity.[9] As portraits of "parliament" *per se* (or of a particular parliament), all such pictures are inherently
symbolical and idealizing, especially for the later medieval period. Parliaments lasted weeks and sometimes months. Lords and Commons met
and deliberated in different and sometimes changing locales. Negotiations
between Crown and Lords, or between Lords and Commons, could be
expedited by smaller "intercommuning" committees and not only before
the entire assembly. Parliamentary business was coordinated with sessions
of the law courts, and it could itself be solely a law court for trial of cases,
with or without the presence of the Commons; the attendance of the
Lords could vary widely. As Cam noted, parliaments had to be declared or
cried "open" like a bazaar; their atmosphere could be communally festive
or uneasy and threatening.[10] Parliaments had a lot of coming and going,
energy and desuetude, representativeness and tension and sometimes violence, between constituent members and estates. They were the occasion for
official, legal, and bureaucratic work, but also for jousts, tournaments, trials, and the occasional execution; religious ceremony, feasts, and weddings;
military musters, magnate gang brawls, and personal fights. They were the
major venue for publicity and appeals to a national public, which became
an increasingly complex and important aspect of parliament's social function. So if plenary portraits such as these reveal a particular perspective on
parliament as both an occasion and an institution, they are also a static
self-imagining of a culturally vibrant event. The portraits also give visual
evidence of two essential aspects of parliament's conceptual importance for
the late medieval period: its completion and "roundness" or wholeness –
that is, its conception as an organically constituted and fulfilled whole,

---

[8] On this point see Davies, *The First English Empire*, 24–5.
[9] Pollard, *The Evolution of Parliament*, 134–5.
[10] Cam, "From Witness of the Shire to Full Parliament," 129–30; Butt, 264.

its ideal plenitude represented by its symmetry – and secondly, its ritual appearance and nature.

The estates of parliament, their identification and definitions, play an important part in parliament's institutional and political definition. But in many ways the term "estates" is itself problematic, raising more questions than it answers. The traditional tripartite feudal model of "nobility, clergy, commons" fits only loosely. As historians have noted, regular references to a three estates model in contemporary discussions of parliament were more characteristic of the fifteenth century than any period before. By that time the example of the French estates general had provided an ill-fitting analogue to English practice, and by the early sixteenth century institutional developments had led parliament decisively away from an estates framework and toward a two-houses structure.[11] Pollard went so far as not only to deny the usefulness of a three estates model for the English parliament but to argue "that parliament, so far from being a system of three estates, is the very negation of the whole idea."[12] This is an overstatement, but the basic point is worth considering. Granted that parliament represented national estates, but who(se), and how many?

Throughout the later middle ages reference can be found to a varied number of estates for parliament or in particular parliaments, and for society as a whole. They can be two (nobility and commons); three (clergy, nobility, commons); four (king, nobility, prelates, commons). In one Good Friday sermon of social criticism in 1375, bishop Brinton puts the number of estates at five: "prelates and ecclesiastics" for prayer to God and the direction of souls; "kings and princes and other temporal lords" for defense of the realm and rule of the body; "faithful merchants" for the good of the "republic"; "faithful workers and laborers" who are born to labor; and the Devil's estate of "usurers," who do no good work and who will have to answer to God at the last judgment.[13] The *Modus Tenendi Parliamentum* identifies no fewer than six degrees or grades of parliamentary peers (*grades parium*) to represent the estates of the kingdom: the king; upper prelates (archbishops, bishops, abbots, priors); proctors of the lower clergy; secular magnates; knights of the shire; and "citizens and burgesses." This arrangement, while plausible in itself, is not found in any surviving records of parliament.[14] In the two most traumatic parliamentary events of the fourteenth century, the depositions of Edward II and Richard II, specific

[11] See A. R. Myers, "Parliament, 1422–1509," 151–3; Chrimes, *English Constitutional Ideas in the Fifteenth Century*, 81–141; Elton, '*The Body of the Whole Realm*,' 18–19; Powell and Wallis, 328–9, 553–4.
[12] Pollard, *Evolution of Parliament*, 77.   [13] Brinton, *Sermons* 56, 259–60.
[14] *Modus*, sections 2–7 and 26, "De Gradibus Parium Parliamenti," 67–70, 78–9.

social and regional estates were identified for the ratification of the depositions. In 1327 the parliamentary deposition of Edward II was effected by an assembly including not only selected earls and barons, representatives of the cities, shires, boroughs, and the Cinque Ports, but also representatives called from North Wales. His deposition was announced to him, as Walsingham describes it much later, "on behalf of the entire parliament" (*de parte totius Parliamenti*) by a delegation of bishops, dukes, abbots, barons, knights, "and also by a certain number of honorable men from the cities and great towns, and the ports."[15] The idea that a parliament had the power to depose a legitimately reigning king was fundamentally contradictory; parliaments assembled only by royal authority. Nonetheless a hybrid parliament/estates-assembly deposed Edward in favor of his son on behalf of "the community of the realm," establishing an ambiguous revolutionary precedent. Seventy-two years later, his great-grandson Richard II was similarly deposed by a "parliament" called in his own name and with representatives sent to him to announce his removal. This time, the procurators were chosen on behalf of "the estates of the land" to represent the bishops and archbishops; abbots and priors; "dukes and earls"; "barons and bannerets"; "bachelors and commons of the south"; "bachelors and commons of the north"; and lawyers, speaking "for all these estates," for a total of six (or seven) specified estates.[16] In both depositions, what was sought was not a fully schematized representation of national and notional estates, such as one might find on the continent, nor just a delegation of official parliamentary personnel. Instead these revolutionary assemblies were, functionally, something in between. They were constituted by a number of agents who could carry the legal and procedural legitimacy of parliamentary representatives along with the social representativeness of the regional and class communities of the realm.

Examples such as these could be multiplied, just as, apparently, could the number of estates. Overall they point to a familiar conclusion. In parliament as in society at large, there were implicit and competing notions of estates, one limited and ideal (with only two or three classes) and the other expansive and pragmatic, more or less flexible to the context or political exigencies of a given situation.[17] While the former was certainly a part

---

[15] Thomas Walsingham, *Ypodigma Neustriae*, 265: " . . . et etiam de civitatibus et magnis villis, atque de Portibus, ad certum numerum virorum honorabilium . . ."

[16] The number changes depending on how the role of the lawyers is interpreted, as a separate estate or as legal spokesmen for the others: *RP* 3.424.

[17] For further discussion see Kaminsky, "Estate, Nobility, and the Exhibition of Estate in the Later Middle Ages"; Scammell, "The Formation of the English Social Structure: Freedom, Knights, and Gentry, 1066–1300"; Strohm, *Social Chaucer*, 190–1; Myers, "Parliament, 1422–1509," 152.

of the conceptual background of parliament as a vaguely tripartite body
that developed into bicameral houses, the latter was a greater influence
on the daily and yearly practices of the assembly, especially in the later
fourteenth century. This conclusion is reinforced by Chrimes' observation
of the parliamentary records that "from 1377 to 1400, the parliamentary
estates are named with a good deal of at least formal diversity, and with
no definite tripartite distinction."[18] It was also of fundamental importance
for the composite representativeness sought by imaginative literature. In
this regard the pragmatic disposition of parliament is comparable to the
contemporary practice of estates satire, where the "theoretical social idyll
of organically related and fixed groups," as Coleman has called the estates-
model, gives way to an inclusive and recursively reiterable framework that
tended to blur certain distinctions (especially between laity and clergy) even
as it typified them.[19] Both made use of a similar combination of ideality,
functionality, and ambiguity in the conception of a representative social
portrait.[20]

So while it is true that continental estates models "do not seem to be
really of outstanding practical significance"[21] for the development of parliament in England, the *idea* of estates was neither foreign nor without
import. Parliament did not negate it so much as complicate it and give it
a particularly miscegenated national form. Members of the lower nobility could sit with the Commons as shire representatives, and the Lords
would sometimes voice their complaints through the Commons: shire
MPs and Lords were sometimes from the same family.[22] Members of the
clergy sat with the secular baronage. Lower clerical orders were at first
included, and then excluded from parliamentary summons; certain positions (e.g. the chancellorship) could be held by clergy or laity. Regional
representatives from the shires mingled with civic ones from the towns.
And in some cases, individuals from the Commons could be appointed
to speak for all of the members of parliament.[23] If we understand "estates
representation" to include parliamentary petitioners as well, it also cov-
ers specific professional communities and guilds; towns, administrative
localities (shires), and regions; ecclesial communities; and other units of

[18] Chrimes, *English Constitutional Ideas in the Fifteenth Century*, 105.
[19] Coleman, *English Literature in History*, 47.
[20] See especially Mann, *Chaucer and Medieval Estates Satire*, 1–16.
[21] Cam, "The Theory and Practice of Representation," 174.
[22] Clark, "Magnates and Their Affinities," 135.
[23] On the bringing together of social groupings in parliamentary setting, especially in the category of shire knights, see Butt, 254; Musson and Ormrod, *The Evolution of English Justice*, 70.

community.[24] Part of the challenge in identifying *what* estates were constitutive of a parliamentary gathering thus lies in the dual nature of the English parliament as both a court of law and a legislative assembly. It was a court with petitioners and judges following precedented procedures of legal redress at the same time that it was the unique forum of the realm wherein the voices of representatives were intended to be the voice of the community at large and not just the voice of individuals or of discrete class-estates. Representation was both proportional and petitionary. As such, parliament was uniquely positioned to act as the hypostasization of a public self-conception and national identity, even as it became the target of criticism from all of the estates it putatively represented.

2 BARONIALISM, CHRONICLES, AND ROMANCE PARLIAMENTS

The relationship and tension between the courtly identities of parliament arose from early on, and there are other elements to complicate it as well, especially during the later fourteenth century. But in the thirteenth century, the "voice of the community" was expressed by the baronage both in popular opinion and political practice. A baronial model of parliamentary assembly dominated. This dominance is evident in the literary products of the late thirteenth and early fourteenth century, focused as they are on baronial politics and ethos. What is interesting from a social perspective is the fact that appeals to this ethos were not limited to the barons in either political or literary discourse. Rather, the cause of the barons in conflict with the Crown, following the baronial wars of the reigns of John and Henry III, provided an ideological focus for a wide part of the social spectrum. It is reflected in the genre-straddling accounts of chronicles and romances that also reveal important developments in the conception of parliaments.

Not only the barons and upper nobility, but other classes appealed to the baronage as *communitas regni* and as the vehicle for the expression of the popular voice.[25] In the reigns of John and Henry III, decisions and actions taken "by the counsel of the whole realm" (*consilio totius regni*) were done so effectively "by the common counsel of our barons" (*communi consilio*

---

[24] As Holt notes, for example, representatives from the Jewish communities were summoned to the king's council in 1231 and 1241: "The Prehistory of Parliament," 21–2.

[25] See Prestwich, "Parliament and the Community of the Realm in Fourteenth Century England"; Ferster, *Fictions of Advice*, 16–21.

baronum nostrum), in the wording of both Magna Charta and *Fleta*.[26] This principle developed after decades of conflict between Henry and his barons as a result of which the baronial demands for reform, and their use of parliament to press for them, entered into public consciousness.[27] By 1254 both the lower clergy and the knights of the shire make their first appearances in parliament, and it was the events surrounding 1253–8 that turned parliament "from an occasion into an institution, an institution which [the barons] used as the fundamental source of authority for the government of England and for the adoption and execution of their plan of reform."[28] Among the demands of the barons in the Provisions of Oxford of 1258 were the regular meeting of parliament and the creation of a standing baronial committee to control the Crown's expenditures.[29] The Provisions also mandated the presence of knights in the shire courts and as local administrators. In 1259 a proclamation of the provisions was published in English as well as Latin and French. Also in the later Provisions of Westminster of 1259, the reforms forced on Henry were enacted in part (or so it is represented) by the demand of "the community of the bachelors of England" (*communitas bacheleriae Angliae*), apparently referring to the lesser nobility and knights of the realm in addition to the greater magnates.[30] Similar actions motivated the Statute of Marlborough in 1267.[31] From the 1240s onward, some chronicles repeatedly declare that "all the nobility of the entire realm" (*totius regni nobilitas*) were to meet in parliament to deal with the problems of the nation, which meant, functionally, the baronage in concert with the upper clergy and, occasionally, elements from the commons.[32] During the Barons' War of the 1260s, parliament took on even greater importance as the forum in which Simon de Montfort pressed for reform. Following Henry's defeat at Lewes in 1264, de Montfort called the famous parliaments of 1264 and 1265 which explicitly and systematically included representatives from the cities, boroughs, and shires.[33]

From its earliest manifestations as a baronial assembly, parliament had a double political valence as both an afforced royal council meeting at the king's will and as a mechanism for imposing restraint on the king. In both

---

[26] Cited in Sayles, *The King's Parliament of England*, 25–6.

[27] For general treatments of this period see Holt, "The Prehistory of Parliament"; Sayles, *The King's Parliament of England*, 21–69; Powell and Wallis, 154–200; and Butt, 65–116.

[28] Treharne, "The Nature of Parliament in the Reign of Henry III," 227, 215–19.

[29] As Sayles notes, "there is no room for doubt that the year 1258 marks the date of the conception of organised parliaments in England" (*The King's Parliament of England*, 48).

[30] Butt, 102.   [31] See Guisborough, 204; Butt, 115–16.

[32] For examples from the reign of Henry III see *Flores Historiarum*, 2.219–20 (for 1237); 2.308 (for 1246); 2.336 (for 1247); *et passim*.

[33] Butt, 108–13.

scenarios, the necessity of baronial counsel – and hence a form of public voice for the community – was a fundamental ideological justification for the practice of assembly. These tensions are evident in the lyrics of the era and occasionally include specifically parliamentary references.[34] The strongest and most artistically accomplished statement of this baronialist ideology is the Latin *Song of Lewes*, probably composed at the height of the baronial movement in 1264. The poem does not adopt a parliamentary stance (parliament is nowhere mentioned), but it unwaveringly supports the barons as the voice of *communitas*.[35] It is a remarkable statement of provincial communal identity in contrast to royal power, locating that identity in the specific class and oppositional struggle of the baronage as the traditional counsellors of the king. Baronial grievances were communal grievances. Their expression was a public matter, and hence parliament developed in part from this conflated perception of interests and the right to voice them in an authoritative context.[36]

In this sense, then, the barons were the "public." They were the identifiable voice of oppositional power, and the identity of parliament as a baronial court of grievance underlies the long-term practice of parliament as a plenary court expressing the voice of the community. Although the role of an oppositional baronage predates the bulk of the development of parliament as a petitionary court under the Edwards, its importance cannot be overemphasized. When Edward I acceded to the throne in 1272 he inherited this conflict and redirected it. During his reign parliament became the premier court for auditing complaints, which was a development in no way necessitated by its origins but that fitted into the increasing pattern of petitioners seeking justice in the king's centralized courts.[37] The start of this "tradition of complaint," as Musson and Ormrod have called it, was crucial not just for the legal identity of the court of parliament but for its literary conceptualization as well.[38] From a subordinate point of view, complaints and the

---

[34] See for example "De Provisione Oxonie," in *Anglo–Norman Political Songs*, 56–66. See also (in Anglo-Norman, English, Latin, and even Spanish) the "Song of the Peace with England," "The Song of the Barons," "Song Against the King of Almaigne," "Song Upon the Divisions among the Barons," and others collected in *Thomas Wright's Political Songs of England*, 19–127.

[35] See *The Song of Lewes*, 765–81, *et passim*.

[36] A well-known example is found in a 1265 petition of the villagers of Great Peatling (in Leicestershire), which justifies an attack against the retainers of a royalist magnate because "they (i.e. the retainers) were against the welfare of the community of the realm and against the barons" (*contra utilitatem communitatis regni et contra barones*). Cited in Cam, "Theory and Practice," 174–5; Ferster, *Fictions of Advice*, 17; Prestwich, "Parliament and the Community of the Realm," 5.

[37] Sayles, *Functions of the Medieval Parliament*, 11–23; Edwards, "'Justice' in Early English Parliaments," 279–97.

[38] *The Evolution of English Justice*, 86.

hearing of complaints were the reason for holding parliaments. From the vantage of the Crown, redress of grievances or the creation and enforcement of statutes were exchanged for subsidies, sometimes quite directly, as in 1290 when Edward expelled the Jews at parliamentary request in direct exchange for the grant of a fifteenth and a tenth.[39]

In addition to this development of parliament as a court of redress, Edward I's reign was also notable for the new tone of chivalric ethos entering the discourse of the assemblies and inflecting this exchange relationship. While the tradition of magnate resistance did not wane, to it was added the quasi-literary and quasi-historical traditions of romance parliaments and Arthurianism. These are especially prominent in the context of Edward's military ambitions. Baronial and judicial magnate assemblies were typical in works such as *The Song of Roland*, so the literary representation of the king-in-council was certainly nothing new by the late thirteenth century. During Edward I's reign some chronicles make clear the continued importance of the baronial magnate parliaments, which could be, as we might expect, just as conflictual and combative as his father's. To them are added the veneer of romantic and chivalric practices and attitudes centered on the person of the king. There are indications that the king himself was the impetus for this new English involvement with romance conventions. Edward was an Arthurian enthusiast and, as Roger Loomis has shown, "he evidently liked to think of himself in the role of *Arthurus redivivus*."[40] In 1278 Edward relocated the supposed remains of Arthur and Guenevere to a magnificent new tomb. In 1279 he held the first of several feasts of the "round table," the most significant one in 1284 to celebrate the conquest of Wales.[41] Around 1299 he held another Arthurian feast to celebrate his second marriage to Margaret, the sister of Philip IV of France. The knighting of Prince Edward (the future Edward II) and the elaborate banquet and avowal ceremony that followed, performed in 1306 in anticipation of a campaign in Scotland, was carried out with the chivalric pomp and theatrical solemnity reminiscent of a scene from Chrétien or the prose *Lancelot*. In other contexts, some chronicles portray Edward as a headstrong leader who governed his assemblies and parliaments in an occasionally histrionic manner. In 1294, for example, Edward convened his barons and sought aid yet again to recover his Gascon lands:

---

[39] For a frank account see Guisborough, 226–7.

[40] Loomis, "Edward I, Arthurian Enthusiast," 126; see also Denholm-Young, "The Tournament in the Thirteenth Century."

[41] Similarly Edward III held an Arthurian feast at a great Tournament at Windsor in 1344 and began the abortive project of building a Round Table for 300 knights: see Butt, 303.

And directly, having called together his magnates with John the king of the Scots, he held his parliament in London; and in their presence, with the whole matter laid out, he asked for their counsel and aid, vowing for himself that even if he had no more retinue than one page and one horse, he would pursue his right unto death and vindicate his injuries in this matter.[42]

This rousing statement elicits a similarly rousing declaration of fidelity from his nobles, who vow to follow him in life and death (*At illi vnanimiter responderunt ei dicentes se eum velle sequi in vitam et in mortem*). The actual sequence of events was more complicated. Later in 1295–7, Edward's war expenditures provoked a crisis and resistance among the barons that was as strong as this gesture of unanimity.[43] But the ideal pattern of a strong king meeting with his barons in parliamentary assemblies is clear in records like this, and his romantic historiographers sometimes appear captivated, if not necessarily seduced, by the force of Edward's Arthurian self-presentations.

A good example of this mythical–historical dynamic, and of its importance for parliamentary representations, is the Arthurian flavor of the contemporary metrical history of Peter Langtoft's *Chronicle*, and of Langtoft's English verse translator, Robert Mannyng.[44] Langtoft's Anglo-Norman *Chronicle* is a hybrid combining the early mythical history of Britain, derived largely from Geoffrey of Monmouth, with a historical record from the Norman Conquest to Henry III and a contemporary record of Edward I's reign up to his death in 1307. It includes accounts of every major contemporary parliamentary event, especially those related to the king's wars. Throughout the latter part, Edward is put forward as a new Arthur. According to Langtoft, he fulfills Merlin's prophecies that the territories of Britain, especially England and Scotland, will be united under one king; Arthur himself never controlled so many fiefdoms (2.266–7). His historical claim to Aquitaine/Gascony is partially justified through Arthur's bestowal of the region on his butler, Beduer (Bedevere) (2.278–9). The Whitsuntide feast of 1306 is extolled as the greatest celebration in Britain "except Caerleon in ancient times, / When sir Arthur the king was crowned there" (Forpris

---

[42] Guisborough, 243: "Moxque vocatis magnatibus suis cum Johanne rege Scotorum tenuit parliamentum suum London' et in ipsorum presencia toto processu recitato consilium eorum peciit et iuuamen, attestans se eciam si maiorem non haberet sequelam cum vno puero et vno equo ius suum prosequi velle vsque ad mortem et super huiusmodi iniuriis vindicare."

[43] For fuller treatment of this crisis during 1295–7 see Butt, 155–63; Powell and Wallis, 232–41; and Prestwich, *Documents Illustrating the Crisis of 1297–98 in England*, 1–37.

[44] *The Chronicle of Pierre de Langtoft*, 2 vols., ed. Wright; Robert Mannyng of Brunne, *The Chronicle*, ed. Sullens. The verses are not numbered in Wright's edition of Langtoft so references are by volume and page. For a good discussion of Langtoft's romance style of history see Gransden, *Historical Writing in England c. 550 to c. 1307*, 476–86.

Karleoun en antiquitez, / Qaunt sire Arthur luy reis i fust corounez) (2.368).
At his death, Edward is compared to Arthur as an exemplar of chivalry: "Of
chivalry, after king Arthur, / Was king Edward the flower of Christendom"
(De chevalerye, après ly reis Arthure, / Estait ly reis Edward des Cristiens
la flure) (2.380).[45]

Perhaps surprisingly, the most prominent example of Langtoft's Arthurianism is not an accolade but a comparative criticism of the king in the
account of the 1296–7 conflict over the barons' refusal to provide military
muster for the king's wars in Gascony. Edward "goes to the parliament,
bearing down on them like a lion" (et vait al parlement abataunt cum
leoun) (2.288), but when the barons continue to resist he is compelled to
go unaided to France. The chronicler blames Edward's inability to satisfy
his magnates. He then appeals to the *ensaumple du noble rei sire Arthur* as
a king who dealt successfully with his barons:

> En gestes aunciens trovoums-nous escrit
> Quels rays et quels realmes ly rays Arthur conquist,
> Et coment sun purchace largement partyst.
> Roys suz ly n'avoit ke ly countredist,
> Counte, duc, e baron, qe unqes li faillist,
> En guere n'en bataille ke chescun ne suyst.
> Ly rays sir Eduuard ad doné trop petyt;
> Par quai à sun aler, quant en mer se myst
> Vers ly roys de Fraunce, fet ly fu despit,
> Ke nes un de ses countes of ly le aler emprist.
>
> (2.296)

[In ancient histories we find written what kings and what kingdoms king Arthur
conquered, and how largely he shared his gain. There was not a king under him
who contradicted him or failed him in war or battle, earl, duke, or baron; but each
followed him. The king sir Edward has given too little; whereby at his departure,
when he put to sea against the king of France, the affront was shown to him that
not one of his earls undertook the expedition.]

Again, the actual course of events was not so straightforward. The charge
that Edward – unlike Arthur – was simply too stingy with his "gain" (*pur-
chace*) is misleading. The demands Edward demurred to meet, as summarized in the "Remonstrances" put forward by the barons in July 1297, were
for the regulation of writs and tallages, observance of traditional wool taxes,
reaffirmation of the Charters, and other matters for which the baronage was

---

[45] Other passages include the monitory list of kings, including Arthur, as examples for avoiding
treachery and unwise conduct (2.282–5), and the reference to Arthur and Gawain as conquerors
(2.378).

again assuming the voice of the community.[46] So the chronicler's recasting
of this conflict into digestible Arthurian terms reveals more about the public expectation of how a king should deal with his parliamentary baronage
than it does about the specific conflict itself. Edward has a recalcitrant or
rebellious nobility, but this is due to his failure to properly cultivate them
in assembly and consultation, and in this he contrasts poorly with the historical example of Arthur. A similar comparison is made by Mannyng, who
translates the latter section of Langtoft's *Chronicle* closely.[47] At one point
in the account of the conflict over a proposed judicial perambulation of
1301, Mannyng adds his own comparison to Arthur's skillful cultivation of
his barons. Again, Arthur is portrayed as an ideal king:

> Of Arthure, men say þat rede of him in pas,
> alle tymes in medle euer more first he was,
> mornyng & euenyng sobre & honest,
> felons þat wild him greue, or enmys þat mad chest,
> als he was worþi had he iugement.
> Had he of non merci, for praiere no present,
> at conseil & at nede he was skilfulle kyng;
> so curteis of non, men rede, ne prince of more praysing,
> was non in cristendam als he was in his tyme,
> ne suilk on ȝit non cam þat man may mak of ryme.
>
> (2.7593–602)

These accolades of Arthur's kingly qualities are immediately contrasted with
Edward's failure to perform the judicial perambulation he had promised
at the previous parliament in 1299. If he had fulfilled his parliamentary
oath, the chronicler avers, "þe lond had bien alle his / long tyme or now
þat now in auenture is" (2.7607–8). This Arthurian criticism is then followed by a lengthy account of the ensuing Lincoln parliament of 1301
(2.7609–87).

From a later perspective these historical accounts necessarily have a fic-
titious quality about them because of their appeals to Arthur. But they do
not stand alone, and they are part of a wider tendency. The intersections
of these Edwardian examples with the romance historiography of the early

---

[46] These complaints were put forward on behalf of "the archbishops, bishops, dukes, barons, and the
entire community of the land": see Prestwich, *Documents*, 115–17: "Ces sunt les monstrances qe
le . . . . . . ercevekes, eveskes, countes, barons e tote la comunalte de la terre monstrent a nostre
seygnur le rey . . ." (115). The petition continues to speak in the voice of "(tote) la comunalte de la
terre."

[47] On Mannyng's adaptations from Langtoft see Johnson, "Robert Mannyng's History of Arthurian
Literature"; Turville-Petre, "Politics and Poetry in the Early Fourteenth Century: The Case of Robert
Manning's *Chronicle*."

chronicle tradition are augmented by a larger pattern of parliamentarism
in the rewriting of historical events, one that may or may not have been
entirely conscious. That is to say, "parliaments" as assemblies – both baronial and quasi-popular – are introduced into the chronicles at new points,
and these representations present a subtly but significantly altered image
of the assembly. Arthurian historiography thus acts as an important bridge
between baronialism and later populism.

Mannyng's *Chronicle* combines the latter part of Langtoft's text with earlier sections from Wace's *Brut* because, as he tells us, Langtoft had cut out
too much of the Arthurian narrative for his taste (1.63–70). Although Mannyng's history had limited circulation (only two manuscripts and a fragment
survive), it nonetheless stands as a revealing indicator of how early chronicle
accounts were rendered, both in narrative and historiographical terms, into
a specifically English text. In the pre-Edwardian part of Mannyng's history there are numerous references to baronial councils and parliaments,
particularly in the context of royal successions and ceremonies of fealty
and homage. Mention is made of parliaments in post-Saxon England and
Wales; parliaments of William the Conqueror; at the crowning of Cnut;
parliaments in Scotland and France; and at particular periods of conflict in
England.[48] All of these appear prior to the numerous references to Henry's
and Edward's parliaments in the last three thousand lines of the history.
None of these refer to what would later be technically termed a "parliament," nor do they appear to be used restrictively. That is, they refer to
councils, discussions, *parlements* as parleys. But they are still anachronistic
applications of the term by Mannyng, who was writing in the late 1330s,
and several carry clear overtones of formal governmental assemblies where
the source-texts have no such implication.

The most interesting of these references come in the earliest parts of the
history adapted from Wace's *Roman de Brut*. Parliaments are introduced
by Mannyng at points where Wace uses a different term, or nothing.[49]
Early on, Mannyng simply repeats Wace when Mempricius and his brother

[48] The term *parlement* for royal or baronial assemblies is used for the reigns of Cuthred (2.147),
Aethelwulf (2.360), Edward the Elder (2.552), Eadwig (2.767), and Cnut (2.1149); a parliament in
Wales (2.1547); assemblies of William the Conqueror (2.2030–1, 2.2149–51); assemblies in Scotland
(2.2192, 2.2758); assemblies in France before the French king (2.2015, 2.3296, 2.3502, 2.3513, 2.3607);
and assemblies of Richard I (2.3581, 2.4939).

[49] *Le Roman de Brut de Wace*, ed. Arnold. Wace's passages are also cross-referenced with his source,
Geoffrey of Monmouth, *Historia Regum Britanie*, Vol. 1, Bern Burgerbibliothek MS. 568, and Vol.
2, The First Variant Version, ed. Wright. References to Monmouth's *Historia* are by text section
numbers, which are the same in both versions. These specifically Arthurian-era parliament scenes
also are not found in Langtoft, who makes no references to parliaments anywhere in the first part
of the *Chronicle*.

Malin meet at a *parlement* (in which Malin is subsequently killed), and again when Belinus and Brennius hold a *parlement* at London to decide on their campaign against France.[50] Elsewhere Mannyng uses *parlement* for Wace's *conseil*, as when Brutus consults with his crew before setting sail for Albion.[51] At other points Mannyng introduces parliaments where they have a distinctly formal and institutional resonance. Enniaunaus, brother of Marganus, becomes king but is deposed because of his tyranny: "þan mad þei a Parlement / & chese a kyng þorgh alle assent" (1.3938–9). The new king chosen by the parliament is Idvallo. Similarly Asclepiodotus, the Earl of Cornwall, is made king by a baronial parliament, and later so also is Cadvan (1.5926–9; 1.14791–4). In these instances Wace has the kings "chosen" (*par electiun*) or crowned "by everyone's agreement" (*par le los de tuz*), but there is no specification of any assembly.[52] Most notably, after Uther Pendragon's death and burial, Arthur is summoned to Silchester (variously mis-identified as "Chichester" or "Chirenchester" in Mannyng and Wace) and is raised to the kingship by a parliament called by archbishop Dubricius:

> Whan sir Vter, our kyng,
> was dede & don his endyng,
> at stonhengis als he said,
> beside his broþer men him laid.
> þe Archbisshop his conseile held,
> erles, barons, knyghtes of scheld,
> ilkon after oþer sent
> to com to þe comon parlement,
> & after Vter sone, Arthure,
> to com to Cecestre burgh
> & bitauht him þe croune
> þorgh comon graunt of ilk baroune.
> (1.9596–607)

This detailed description – summons of "earls, barons, knights," a parliament, and a baronial "common grant" of the Crown – is unique to Mannyng. It expands on the bare accounts in Wace and Monmouth.[53]

---

[50] Mannyng 1.2123–6, 1.3233–6; Wace 1463–8, 2833–6.

[51] Mannyng 1.1720–3; Wace 1045–8.

[52] Neither are there any references to parliaments at these points in Monmouth's *Historia*, which simply notes the overthrow of Enniaunaus and that Asclepiodotus was raised to the kingship: see Wace 3637–8, 5493–6; Monmouth §§ 52, 76.

[53] In Wace the scene takes up only four lines: "Li evesque s'entremanderent / E li barun s'entr'assemblerent; / Artur, le fiz Uther, manderent, / A Cilcestre le corunerent" (9009–12). Langtoft follows Wace in brevity but has Arthur "elected" by "the people of the land" (le pople de la terre, en

Mannyng appears to have introduced this formal procedure in the most sensible place, at least from the perspective of the 1330s, and it makes the greatest British king sovereign as a result, at least in part, of a parliamentary act of baronial recognition and coronation.

Another of Mannyng's subtle innovations is found in his account of the raising of Stonehenge by Merlin at the request of King Ambrosius Aurelius. Wace repeats the detailed account of the origin of the stones in Ireland and the trouble of getting them transported and raised. The stones are intended as a burial monument for the British nobles treacherously killed by the Saxons under Hengist during a peace conference. As Mannying describes the monument,

> Within þe compas of þe stones
> er biried all þe lordes bones
> þat Hengist at þe parlement slouh
> here beforn ȝe herde wele how.
> (1.8814–17)[54]

Here Mannyng's use of *parlement* picks up his earlier description of the fatal meeting with the Saxons (following Wace) as the "dai of þe parlement / opon þe plain of Salesberi" (1.7728–9). The idea that Stonehenge commemorated a fallen baronial parliament, as a formal assembly, was probably suggested by its roundness. This association of Stonehenge with a parliament is Mannyng's innovation, but one that makes sense in the context of a general association of Arthur and the ancient Arthurian era, both with the glories of the Edwardian regime and with the necessity of a baronial and parliamentary framework of legitimation. We might wonder if Edward himself looked at Stonehenge as another Arthurian monument on the landscape like the tomb of Arthur and Guenevere. Travelling along with the historical glories of Arthur, then, is the association of his rule with a proper cultivation of his baronage: "he conseils with his baronage / & his gode knyghtes him redde / þat he had fostred & forth fedde" (1.10422–4). This association carries forward to the contemporary example of Edward I as a new Arthur and as a king uniquely worthy of praise "in romance & ryme" (2.8318–24).

---

grant devocioun, / Sount alez à Sicestre, pur fere eleccioun . . . Arthur est eleu, e doné la coroun . . .) (1. 146). The two versions of Monmouth's *Historia* note the gathering of knights at Silcester, that archbishop Dubricius crowned Arthur (Arturum diademate regni insignuit), and (in the Variant Version only) that Arthur was accepted by "the people and princes of all the realm" (unde populo ac principibus tocius regni gratus et acceptus erat) (§ 143).

[54] Compare Wace 8159–78; Monmouth, § 130; also see Wace 7220 ("De parlement unt assis jur"). Another specific and unique reference to the fatal assembly as a "parlement" is made later by Mannyng at 1.8218; contrast Wace 7633–40.

What these details suggest, from a social and literary perspective, is not only the historical exemplarism of Arthur, but more fundamentally the importance that these baronial-romantic narrative topoi had for the representation of political forms as well. What I am calling here romance baronialism specifically in its Arthurian iteration has the unexpected but direct result not only of stressing the importance of "parliament" in a baronial sense, but of historically back-projecting it and thus endowing the quasi-formal practice of parliaments with the authority of tradition.[55] Both Langtoft and Mannyng consistently associate Arthur's ideal rule with the participation of, and in, parliaments. This association was apparently strong enough to lead Mannyng to see parliaments in the mythical past – giving them the power to elect and depose sovereigns and making Arthur a parliamentary king – and indeed, to project them onto the present-day landscape at Stonehenge. If there is little textual sanction for these changes in the sources, we can probably ascribe them to the ideological changes evident, as we have seen, in the growing importance of parliament after the 1260s. Further, although they are the most resonant, the chronicles' Arthurianisms and Arthurian narratives are not the only examples of this baronial-parliamentary dynamic in the literature of the early fourteenth century. In the romance *Sir Orfeo*, roughly contemporary with Mannyng, a parliament is charged to choose a new king when Orfeo decides to search for his wife Heurodis.[56] In *Athelston*, from the later fourteenth century, the conflict between King Athelston and his supposedly traitorous earl Egeland is arranged to be decided in the court of a "plaine parlement."[57] And in *Havelok the Dane*, discussed below, parliaments and assemblies provide key elements in the narrative. Elaborate council and parliament scenes remained a staple of Arthurian narratives well into the fifteenth century, down to the time of the *Alliterative Morte Arthure* and later romances. This combination of elements in chronicles and romances thus presents a recognizable pattern: an Arthurian ideal of a strong king working in concert with a strong baronage, meeting in parliaments and assemblies that are both "noble" and communally representative. The baronage is idealized as the public voice of the *communitas regni* that explicitly speaks on behalf of all estates, just as the king is idealized as a national hypostasis of communal identity. A good nobility serves a good king, and a proper parliament is the combination of the two.

---

[55] On the tendency in this period to create legitimating back-projections of constitutional practices see also Given-Wilson, *Chronicles*, 179–80.

[56] *Sir Orfeo*, in *Middle English Romances*, ed. Shepherd, 204–18.

[57] The declaration is made twice: *Athelston*, in *Middle English Verse Romances*, ed. Sands, 265–6; 445–9.

In later literary works this romance baronial ideal also underlies many standard representations of parliaments. A concluding example from Walsingham's abbreviated chronicle from the early fifteenth century, the *Ypodigma Neustriae*, illustrates how these quasi-historical, quasi-romantic elements of Arthurianism and parliamentarism were viewed in historio-graphical retrospect. In the record for 1283 Walsingham notes,

> The king held parliament at Acton Burnell after the feast of St. Michael; in which was declared the statute which gets its name from that place. The son of the king was born at Carnarvon in Wales on the day of St. Mark, and he was named "Edward." And king Edward made the English laws to be observed through-out Wales, assigning a sheriff there. During that same time, at Carnarvon, the body of the father of emperor Constantine was found – that is, of the senator Constantine – and, by the king's orders, it was placed honorably in a church. And the crown of Arthur, formerly the famous king of the Britons, was rendered to the king of the English along with other precious objects, and thus the glory of the Welsh, by the providence of God, was transferred.[58]

In this context, it is significant that given the choice of events to select for 1283, Walsingham chose these. He neglects to mention, for example, the trial and execution of the rebellious Welsh prince David, which also occurred during the 1283 parliament. Walsingham's obvious point (at least to his English audience) is that Edward transferred (or "returned" *reddebatur*) the glories of Arthur to his dynasty. Each event selected by Walsingham reflects the historical and political legitimacy of Edward's rule, both back-wards and forwards in time, in distinct historiographical traditions. The discovery of the bones of Constantine the Senator connects England to imperial Christian Rome and its greatest ruler (indeed, makes England the father of it, and him). Arthur's crown appropriates the erstwhile glory of the indigenous Welsh to the English. The birth of his son secures the legit-imate succession of the Plantagenet dynasty and the legitimacy of English domination of Wales. And along with these sanctions, the statutes of Acton Burnell and the extension of English law into Wales reflect his assertion of rule specifically through parliament, which stands coordinate to all the

---

[58] *Ypodigma Neustriae*, 176: "Rex Angliae apud Acton Burnell tenuit Parliamentum, post festum Sancti Michaelis; in quo editum est Statutum quod a loco cognominatum est. Natus est Regi filius, apud Carnervan in Wallia, die Sancti Marci, et vocatus est Edwardus. Et Rex Edwardus fecit leges Anglicanas per Walliam observari, Vicecomites ponens in ea. Sub eodem tempore, apud Karnervan, inventum est corpus patris Constantini Imperatoris, scilicet, Constantii Senatoris, et, Rege jubente, honorifice in ecclesia collocatum. Corona etiam quondam famosi Regis Britonum, Arthuri, Regi Angliae, cum aliis jocalibus, reddebatur, et sic ad Anglos gloria Wallensium, Dei providentia, est translata." The statute is also called the Statute of Merchants. See Butt, 135–9.

rest. An English king in parliament here takes his place as the legitimate heir of both a Roman and an Arthurian legacy.

In sum, Walsingham's history reflects the ideological nexus of these elements for the early fourteenth century as much as for his own day, as Arthurian history underwrote parliamentary legitimacy – understood in this baronial context – and vice versa. And might this backward–forward historical interplay of romance and history have had an influence in its own day? Historians have sometimes puzzled at the rapid development of parliament under Edward I into a regular and prominent court of public petition, a development which seems to have arisen from no strong administrative precedent.[59] Although impossible to prove, the literary–historical conflation of romance Arthurianism and baronial parliamentarism could suggest that in this regard, Edward was simply fulfilling what he perceived to be another aspect of his Arthurian legacy. If, as chroniclers and romancers insistently told him, a good king holds his parliaments regularly and openly, and if his historical–mythical exemplar Arthur listened to appeals and judged his subjects in public court – with "conseil" and "worþi jugement," as Mannyng says – would it not have been natural for Edward to exploit this ideal for his own purposes, as he did the rest of the Arthurian ethos? The developing technology of documentary writing would have fostered this change as well. It is entirely speculative, but not beyond possibility, that the vigorous development of parliament in the early fourteenth century – and, as a result, its entire subsequent history down to our own day – owed some of its initial impetus to these Arthurian historiographical anachronisms which put "parliaments" in places that Geoffrey of Monmouth never imagined them, with powers he could not have foreseen.

3   PARLIAMENT AND PENTECOSTALISM: SPIRITUAL IDEALS OF ASSEMBLY AND SPEAKING "WITH ONE VOICE"

Moving away from the strong baronialism of the late thirteenth and early fourteenth centuries we approach an idea of the *vox publica* that has a wider social valence, but one predicated on an even greater level of abstraction or ideality. The next major element of the conceptualization of parliament, its status as a spiritual assembly, is closely related to this foundational

---

[59] See Richardson and Sayles, *Rotuli Parliamentorum Anglie Hactenus Inediti*, viii–ix; Sayles, *The Functions of the Medieval Parliament of England*, 21; Brown, *The Governance of Late Medieval England*, 161–162; Harriss, "The Formation of Parliament," 30; Cam, "Stubbs Seventy Years After," 196–7; Butt, 117–18.

baronialism. It is also reflected in the literary sources, both historical and popular, of the early fourteenth century and beyond. A good starting point is the story *Havelok the Dane*.[60] This northern romance, the best early middle English example of the genre, was also taken as history. Mannyng noted the story's absence from his sources and a shortened version is supplied in one manuscript of his *Chronicle*.[61] The full romance version, dating from the first quarter of the fourteenth century, provides another perspective on parliament partaking of the baronialist tradition while it also reveals the spiritual and communal ideals of assembly that reached beyond it.

The story of *Havelok* tells a parallel plot in which Goldeboru, the beautiful orphaned daughter of the English king Athelwold, is dispossessed by her scheming guardian, the Earl Godrich of Cornwall. Similarly Havelok, the rightful but orphaned heir to the Danish throne of King Birkabeyn, is disinherited by the earl Godard. Godard gives the child-prince Havelok to his servant Grim to be drowned. When Grim and his wife see a holy light around the boy, they decide to take him and flee to England with their family. They settle north of the Humber in the Lindesey region, in the town that would eventually carry Grim's name, Grimsby. Havelok, in true *bel inconnu* fashion, is reared as a commoner and taught the habits of good work. Everyone is impressed with his beauty and noble bearing. Havelok comes to Lincoln to work as a porter and quickly earns renown for his strength. Then a parliament is declared by Godrich, which meets in Lincoln:

> Jn þat time al Hengelond
> þerl Godrich hauede in his hond,
> And he gart komen into þe tun
> Mani erl and mani barun;
> And alle þat liues were
> Jn Englond þanne wer þere
> þat þey haueden after sent
> To ben þer at þe parlement.
> With hem com mani chambioun,
> Mani with ladde, blac and brown . . .
>
> (1000–9)

The parliament, at which "þere was sembling inow" (1019), is also a great festival with public contests of strength. Havelok defeats everyone in these

---

[60] Citations are from *Havelok the Dane*, ed. Smithers.

[61] Mannyng seems to be genuinely confused by its absence when he notes, "Bot I haf grete ferly þat I fynd no man / þat has writen in story how Hauelok þis lond wan" (2.519–520); see 2.499–502, and 2.712.

games and everyone talks about how "strong," "hey," and "fri" he is (1072–3). That is, he is the strongest, the tallest, and the most noble of bearing, despite being a lowly porter. This gives Godrich the idea of marrying off Goldeboru to Havelok, because he has sworn an oath to marry her to the "fairest" and "highest" man in the kingdom. Since Havelok is supposedly a "þral" or a serf (1098), he will be unable to inherit any land and the inheritance of the kingdom will revert to Godrich by default.[62] After bringing the young princess to Lincoln and threatening her with death, Godrich forces Goldeboru to marry Havelok in a public wedding presided over by the Archbishop of York:

> þe messe he dede, eueri del
> þat fel to spusing, an god clerk -
> þe erchebishop uth of Yerk,
> þat kam to þe parlement
> Als God him hauede þider sent.
>   (1177–81)

The deeper significance of these events is suggested by the hint that the Archbishop's presence at the parliament is God-ordained. Of course Goldeboru *is* marrying the highest man of the kingdom insofar as she is wedded, despite Godrich's machinations, to an actual but unacknowledged prince. The parliament thus provides the legitimate setting for a royal wedding (and the archbishop is the appropriate ecclesial figure for the nuptials) with the dramatic irony that no one realizes that it is, in fact, a royal wedding.[63] Shortly thereafter, Havelok's adoptive family and new wife learn that he is a prince and they all urge him to recover his patrimony. When Havelok returns to Denmark and, with the help of his new retainer Ubbe, reasserts his claim to the throne, Ubbe calls together "Erles, barouns, drenges, theynes, / Klerkes, knithes, burgeys, sweynes" (2195–6) to swear allegiance to the new king. They all do homage, as does Ubbe himself (2252–66). After Havelok is dubbed and crowned, the usurper Godard is defeated and then sentenced to death by an assembly of estates – "Hise erles and his barounes alle, / Dreng and thein, burgeis and knith" (2466–7).

With his Danish kingdom in order, Havelok returns to England and defeats Godrich. The people of England now see that Goldeboru has been lawfully wedded to a king, so they gather to do him homage and cry mercy to their sovereign:

---

[62] The oral-folkloric aspects of this legal literalism are analyzed by Green, *A Crisis of Truth*, 61–2.

[63] On the collocation of parliaments and marriages, see further the discussion in Chapter Four.

He comen alle to crie 'merci',
Vnto þe king at one cri,
And beden him sone manrede and oth
þat he ne sholden, for lef ne loth,
Neueremore ageyn him go
Ne ride, for wel ne for wo.

(2773–8)

This declaration of fidelity or trothplight is the community's recognizance of licit authority.[64] Shortly after this Godrich is hauled back to Lincoln, condemned, and executed, and the oaths of allegiance or "manrede" are taken "of brune and of blake . . . of alle Englishe" (2817; 2848–52) in a direct parallel to the "brown and black" commoners of the earlier Lincoln parliament (1009). The later scenes of recognition and justice thus directly parallel the opening marriage parliament, except that now the rightful positions of Goldeboru and Havelok have been restored. The tale ends with other marriages and lands distributed to loyal retainers, and with the royal couple living happily ever after.

The parliaments in this narrative are largely peripheral, but despite that – indeed, partly because of it – they are revealing examples of the quasi-religious ideal of deliberative assemblies. *Havelok* is usually dated to the end of Edward I's reign. The marriage ceremony at Lincoln may have been suggested by the parliament at Lincoln in 1301 when the Archbishop of York was present, or later by the parliament at Carlisle in 1307, Edward's last parliament, in which the Archbishop of York was also present and the marriage of the Prince Edward and the Princess Isabella of France was proposed and agreed (but not performed).[65] The details of the first parliament may therefore be lightly allusive. But the thematic importance of this and the other gatherings in the poem comes more from their legitimating role. They provide the sanction for the inadvertent royal marriage as well as for the resolution of the political conflicts at key points in the story. In *Havelok* the assemblies are traditional magnate court gatherings at the same time they are occasions for the entire community to witness the dynastic marriage and then, later, to acknowledge its legitimacy through public assembly. The estates of the realm swear fidelity by proclaiming "at one cry" their recognition of their sovereigns. While this is somewhat different from the Arthurian model of parliaments, it is similar in as much as

---

[64] See generally Green, *A Crisis of Truth*, 41–77.
[65] See Smithers' commentary, p. 125 n. 1179–80, who notes the 1301 parliament. On the Lincoln parliament of 1301 and Carlisle parliament of 1307, see Butt, 163–6, 173–4; Powell and Wallis, 241–5, 249–63.

the body of the *communitas* speaks through noble gatherings that are both broadly representative – made up of nobility, knights, clerks, burgesses, and "swains" – as well as spiritually idealized, providing the God-ordained punishments for the royal usurpers.

As this particular narrative would suggest, there was a distinct strain of specifically religious justification behind the practice of parliaments, and it became stronger as the fourteenth century progressed. Parliament was a form of civic spiritual ritual. Assemblies could be idealized as inspired gatherings. Like the clerical convocations they imitated and paralleled, part of their ideological sanction came from a pentecostal model of apostolic assembly. They were opened and concluded by religious observances, usually a mass and a sermon, which were standard practice by the end of the fourteenth century.[66] In 1401, in an extended closing speech, speaker Arnold Savage compared the performance of the parliament to the celebration of the mass.[67] Parliaments were often the site of religious spectacles as well as secular. Sometimes they were associated with extraordinary portents, as in 1382 when an earthquake struck on the closing day of parliament, or during the sessions of the Merciless Parliament of 1388, when a wheel of fire was seen in the sky, a wax head was heard to speak, and part of the Thames dried up.[68] During parliaments, excommunications were declared, reaffirmations of charters and liberties were performed with ritual religious solemnity (as they were in 1365), and meetings of clerical convocations were often coordinated with secular parliamentary sessions.[69] While all of the king's courts participated in this "quasi-religious aspect" of legal performance, parliament was unique for the heights of its ritual emphasis.[70] The physical layout of parliament itself suggested a church service. The Commons stood behind a rail like communicants while the priestly classes, the men of law and the nobility, attended in front, dressed in special parliamentary robes in the presence of the king himself with his regalia. The Lords were seated in places analogous to the choir and apse of a church.[71] Parliaments were usually held at the time of high feasts, Michaelmas, Easter or,

---

[66] The *Modus* specifies the preaching of a sermon by "an archbishop or a bishop or a higher clerk, who is discreet and eloquent . . . ought to preach on one of the first days of parliament and in the King's presence" (Unus archiepiscopus, vel episcopus vel unus magnus clericus discretus et facundus . . . debet predicare uno istorum primorum quinque dierum Parliamenti et in presentia regis . . .) (71, 84).

[67] *RP* 3.466.   [68] See *Westminster Chronicle*, 26–9, 234; *Knighton's Chronicle*, 428–9, 430–1.

[69] On the collocation of clerical convocations and parliaments see Butt, 261; Denton, "The Clergy and Parliament," 98–100; Clarke, *Medieval Representation and Consent*, 125–53.

[70] See Musson, *Medieval Law in Context*, 18–21.

[71] When not held at Westminster, parliaments were sometimes convened in churches, as in the 1378 parliament held in the nave of the abbey church of St. Peter in Gloucester (*RP* 3.32). See Butt, 363;

occasionally, Pentecost or Whitsuntide, further reinforcing the association of the assembly with the scriptural ideal of divine guidance and eloquent speaking drawn from Acts 2:1–4, the scene of the Pentecostal arrival of the Holy Spirit upon the assembled apostles.

The idea of parliament as a time when the Holy Spirit descended upon the assembly was a durable one. It underlies the cheeky comment made by John Paston the Younger to his elder brother who was sitting as an MP for Norfolk in 1473 when he remarked in a letter, "I pray God send you the Holy Ghost among you in the parliament house, and rather the Devil, we say, than ye should grant any more taxes."[72] Almost two centuries earlier, Langtoft's *Chronicle* includes a few scenes appealing (much more seriously) to the same notion of divine guidance in assembly. Concerning the 1296 parliament at Bury St. Edmunds, Langtoft declares,

> Sire Deus omnipotent,
> A saint Edmoun al parlement
> Li counsayllez;
> Et sur li faus Phelippe de Fraunce,
> Par ta vertu, aver vengaunce
> Li grauntez.
>
> (268)

[Lord God almighty, at St. Edmunds at the parliament, give him counsel! And upon the false Philip of France, by your virtue, grant to him to have vengeance!]

Later, a similar appeal to God's intervention – that God "interposed his counsel" in the tumultuous 1301 parliament at Lincoln (Deus i mist counsayle [332–3]) – makes explicit the connection between Edward, his barons, and God's blessing in parliament: "The Prince who died on the mount of Calvary / Loves king Edward and his barons" (Le Prince ke morust en mount de Calvarye / Ayme li rays Eduuard et sa baronye [286–7]).

The associations are thus the same as they are in Walsingham's later history, as we have seen: Edward was the regent of God's rule, a new Arthur, and his kingship is sanctioned by divine providence and the counsel of the Holy Spirit. The Pentecostal ideal adds the hortatory notion that the assembly can, and indeed should, rightly speak with the "voice of the community" or *vox populi* at the same time that it adopts the functional identity of the *vox Dei*, and that the two can become mixed in the particular setting of parliament. One of the most unique examples of this biblical

---

Powell and Wallis, 383–5. The *Westminster Chronicle* notes that during the Merciless Parliament of 1388 the hall was decked out in churchly vestments (343).

[72] Cited in McFarlane, "Parliament and 'Bastard Feudalism'," 10.

influence comes from the record of Edward I's last parliament at Carlisle in 1307. A papal collector of taxes had been attempting to collect money from the English clergy, a tenth of clerical income for five years, and he met stiff resistance. A papal legate came to the parliament to deal with this and other issues (among them, peace between England and France and the marriage of Edward and Isabella), when during the deliberations there appeared a "cedule from heaven." According to Guisborough,

> During the foresaid parliament, when many things were spoken by many people about the oppressions the lord pope had brought against the English church, behold!, suddenly there descended a certain document (*talis cedula*) into the open council, as if sent from heaven, and it was read immediately in the hearing of the king, cardinal, and all the prelates and others who had gathered.[73]

The mysterious bill, written by "Peter, son of Cassiodorus," is transcribed in the chronicle. In florid scriptural rhetoric it complains of the oppressions suffered by the English Church from the papal pursuit of money. The parliamentary record also includes a petition against the papal tax collector "put forth by the community of the realm" on behalf of the clergy.[74] While not purporting to be the direct voice of God, this complaint from heaven obviously appeals to a Pentecostal ideal of the Holy Spirit descending upon the assembly. Its "miraculous" introduction allowed the charges to be voiced but not localized, and thus to become a different sort of common complaint by virtue of its heavenly (or at least altitudinous) origins. The end result was a parliamentary declaration voiding the papal collector's license to collect taxes, a restriction that was lightened after the dismissal of the parliament.

As we will see in Chapter Five, the strongest and most politically important expression of this Pentecostal ideal occurred at the end of Edward III's reign during the Good Parliament of 1376 when the parliament viewed itself, and was seen by the public, as uniquely charged with God's grace for the reform of the realm. In the case of this petition from 1307, its un-localizability stands out as its salient point. By this time parliament had become important enough in the public consciousness that reports of events at the assembly were being circulated in separate newsletters.[75] The concerns of the community, as put forward in parliament by the *countes et*

---

[73] Guisborough, 371: "In predicto parliamento cum multi multa loquerentur de oppressionibus domini pape quas inceperat in ecclesia Anglicana, ecce quasi subito in pleno consilio descendit talis cedula quasi celitus emissa, legebaturque statim audiente rege cardinale et vniuersis prelatis et aliis qui conuenerant."

[74] Powell and Wallis, 261–3; Butt, 173–4.

[75] See Richardson and Sayles, "The Parliament of Carlisle, 1307 – Some New Documents."

barons e la comunaute de la terre, were thus finding an increasingly public and critical voice as parliamentary controversies became ever more important to the ecclesial and civic communities they affected, particularly through taxation.

However, the public expression of criticism and complaint also courted the danger of retribution and royal censure. In 1301, in one of the most important early displays of parliamentary forwardness, a bill was submitted to parliament listing a series of public grievances and requiring that the demands be addressed before a subsidy would be granted. Edward gave generally capitulatory responses as his needs compelled him. Five years later – not long before the 1307 parliament – the king ordered the arrest and imprisonment of the submitter of the bill, Henry Keighley, a shire knight from Lancashire who had entered the bill on behalf of the entire community. As Butt notes, Keighley stands out as a predecessor of the later medieval MPs and speakers of the Commons who challenged the Crown at their own personal risk.[76] "Keighley's Bill" was an early example of what later developed into the practice of common petitions. The strange method of submission for the "heavenly" bill in the 1307 Carlisle parliament was thus probably employed in order to avoid provoking the kind of retaliation that the earlier bill had brought down on Keighley. To do so, the natural maneuver was to exploit the spiritual and ideological trope of Pentecostal assembly upon which parliament was partially founded in the first place, since presumably the king could not punish the Holy Spirit.

This complex series of events indicates the convoluted way in which political practice, ideological assumptions, and the institutional forms of parliament interacted in the development of a wider public sphere. An integral part of the Pentecostal ideal of inspired assemblies was the further ideal of "speaking with one voice," of expressing consensus in parliament by way of unified communal gesture. "Unity" as both a spiritual and political ideal was certainly not unique to parliament as an institution.[77] But again, at key points it was expressly through parliament that social and political pressure for *unitas* was manifested. Scriptural examples of assemblies and groups speaking *uno ore* are found in both the Old and New Testaments, and they were cited by parliamentarians and ecclesial

---

[76] Butt, 164; Powell and Wallis, 243.

[77] See, e.g., Isidore's *Etymologiae*, Book 5, "de legibus et temporalibus"; Aquinas' *Summa theologiae*, Ia IIae, 90–1 (from the Treatise on Law), and *Summa contra gentiles* 3.63 (on the unity of human felicity), *et passim*. The strongest statement of a conflated ideal of political and religious *unitas*, combined in the divinely ordained unity of one monarch and one law, is in Dante's *Monarchia*, esp. sections 1.5–9, 14–15, *et passim*.

convocants.[78] In the sermons of Thomas Brinton, the bishop of Rochester who was an important parliamentarian from 1376 to 1380, *unitas* is an insistent theme.[79] Following 1 Corinthians 10:17 and Ephesians 4:4–7, he exhorts his audience in convocation in 1373 to "seek to keep unity," *sollicite seruare vnitatem*, by analogizing the estates of the nation to the various parts of the body. The sermon directly addresses the laity as well as the clergy, and the word *ciuitas* is etymologized as the combination of "citizens" and "unity" (*verum, ciuitas quasi ciuium vnitas solet dici*).[80] The most resonant biblical passage for understanding this ideal of a commmunity voice appears in Exodus. Having escaped from Egypt and come to Sinai, the Israelites, led by Moses, receive the law from God in a public assembly which agrees, as one, to abide by it: "Moses came, and calling together the elders of the people, he declared all the words which the Lord had commanded. And all the people answered together (*responditque universus populus simul cuncta*): 'All that the Lord hath spoken, we will do.'"[81] The scene represents not just an archetypal moment of scriptural history but also, for a medieval audience, a political ideal of receiving and affirming a transcendent law with community consensus expressed through assembly. In biblical exegesis this episode from Exodus, and the law-giving immediately following it, were read as a prefiguration of the Pentecostal reception of the Holy Spirit. Moses was interpreted as a *mediator*, a Christ-figure who performs the role of a speaker for the community and for God.[82] Similarly in Judges

---

[78] For examples of these themes of communal unity, in addition to the key texts from Acts, Exodus, and Judges, see Deuteronomy 18:15–17, 31:30; Samuel (1 Kings) 8:4–7, 11:4, 12:19, 14:40–5; 2 Chronicles (2 Paralipomenon) 18:12; Psalm 47:5 (LXX: "Quoniam ecce reges congregati sunt, convenerunt in unum"), 48:3 ("quique terriginae et filii hominum in unum dives et pauper"), 132:1 ("Ecce quam bonum et quam iucundum habitare fratres in unum"); Daniel 3:51; Luke 23:18; John 18:30, 18:40, 19:15; Acts 19:34; Romans 15:6.

[79] On Brinton (Brunton), c.1320–89, see Devlin, "Bishop Thomas Brunton and his Sermons"; *DNB* "Brinton, Thomas (d. 1389)", and *DNB* online (http://www.oxforddnb.com/view/article/3442).

[80] Brinton, *Sermons* 28, 109–17. This sermon was preached at the Convocation of the province of Canterbury in October 1373 immediately following the parliament of November, which resisted the king's request for a subsidy. See Butt, 335; Powell and Wallis, 371.

[81] Exodus 19:3–8: "venit Moses et convocatis maioribus natu populi exposuit omnes sermones quos mandaverat Dominus responditque universus populus simul cuncta quae locutus est Dominus faciemus." *Biblia Sacra, iuxta Vulgatam Versionem*; translation from *The Holy Bible, Douay Rheims Version*.

[82] The typological conflation of the lawgiving in Exodus with Pentecost is made by Augustine and Bede. See Augustine (Augustinus Hipponensis), *Sermones de Scripturis*, Classis prima, Sermo 155 "De verbis apostoli Rom. VIII 1–11" cap. 6, and Sermo 156 "De verbis apostoli Rom. VIII, 12–17" cap. 13 (*Patrologia Latina* 38, cols. 843 and 857); *De spiritu et littera*, cap. 17, sec. 29 "Legis Mosaicae et novae comparatio" (*Patrologia Latina* 44, col. 219); Auctor incertus (Augustinus Hipponensis?), *Quaestiones Veteris et Novi Testamenti*, el. 95, "Unde orta sit observatio Pentecostes, vel qua ratione?" (*Patrologia Latina* 35, col. 2289–90). For Bede (Beda), see *Expositio super Acta Apostolorum*, cap. 2 (*Patrologia Latina* 92, col. 946A-D), and *Homiliae*, lib. 1, "Homilia XI in vigilia Pentecostes"

20, the community of Israel responds "as one man" (*quasi vir unus*) in public assembly in the war against the tribe of Benjamin, gathering "in the assembly of God's people" (*in ecclesiam populi Dei*) and speaking with one voice in the muster.[83] In a way consonant with this conflated scriptural ideal, parliament was viewed as the specific forum in which God's voice could come down. It was also the forum for God's voice to speak *up* and through the community, and for the community to bear witness to its own, divinely-ordained identity as a unified body.

This ideology of unity was strongly but not exclusively clerical, as the overarching desire for *unanimitas* was manifested in the basic procedures of parliament. In general practice, members of parliaments did not vote in the modern manner. Approval or disapproval of proposals was expressed only by voice acclamation with the ideal of unanimous assent or denial. On occasion, separate groups – nobility, clergy, Commons – would deliberate among themselves until a unifed position or answer could be brought forth. While there may have been tallying by division in the separate deliberations, when parliament was brought together, the appearance of unity and unanimous assent was expressly sought.[84] In the first recorded instance of a voice-vote in 1354 over the possibility of a peace treaty with France, the king's chamberlain and negotiator Bartholomew de Burghersh brought the question before the Commons, *Donqes Vous Voillez assentir au Tretee du Pees perpetuele si homme la puisse avoir?* The roll records the response, *Et les dites Communes responderent entierement & uniement, Oil, oil.*[85] Without doubt this was a spontaneous expression of unanimity from the war-weary Commons, but it also fitted the general pattern of univocal speech implicitly sought both within and from parliament. Repeatedly the parliamentary rolls record the assembly as speaking *a une voice* and *uniement*, particularly at times of stress.[86] The desire to be seen as speaking unanimously

---

(*Patrologia Latina* 94, cols. 194A-195D). For Moses as Christ-mediator, see Hugo de S. Victore (auctor incertus), *Miscellanea*, Lib. 1 Tit. 36 "Quod Moyses typus fuit Christi, inter Deum et homines futuri Mediatoris" (*Patrologia Latina* 177, col. 492D-493A); and the anonymous *De promissionibus et praedictionibus Dei*, Pars 2 Cap.1 "In monte leges datae, et Christi Domini mandata in monte. Praedictio facta et figurata. In Exodo credita et visa" (*Patrologia Latina* 51, col. 767A-D).

[83] Iudices 20:1, 2, 8, 11: "egressi sunt itaque omnes filii Israhel et pariter congregati quasi vir unus . . . omnesque anguli populorum et cunctae tribus Israhel in ecclesiam populi Dei convenerunt . . . stansque omnis populus quasi unius hominis sermone respondit . . . convenitque universus Israhel ad civitatem quasi unus homo eadem mente unoque consilio." For Brinton's use of Judges 20:1–11, see *Sermons* 44, 199.

[84] For extended discussion of this point see Edwards, *The Second Century of the English Parliament*, 71–9.

[85] *RP* 2.262; Butt, 319–20.

[86] Examples include the naming of Richard as heir apparent to the throne in 1376 (*RP* 2.330, item 50), the controversy over the accusations against Gaunt in 1377 (*RP* 3.5, item 14), and during the

was undoubtedly the motivation in the Good Parliament of 1376 when the speaker of the Commons, Peter de la Mare, refused to proceed with his demands to the Lords until every member of the Commons was allowed to stand with him in the chamber. Speaking assent "with one voice" was an actual, physical goal of the assembly, which was, as we can recall from the portraits, still unicameral throughout the medieval period. There were no "houses" of parliament, only *the house* of parliament. Division was at best a fault, at worst an evil. Unanimity was the surest defense against accusations that one was speaking or acting for private or singular interests. It was also an implicit index that the assembly as a whole was operating with the guidance of the Holy Spirit, and that its decisions were divinely sanctioned.

4 VOX POPULI, VOX DEI: THE DEPOSITION OF EDWARD II

As these examples from the mid- and later fourteenth century suggest, unanimity became an ideal particularly associated – or, as we shall see in the next chapter, negatively associated – with the Commons. Throughout this period the parliamentary Commons occupied an increasingly liminal space, both in concept and political practice, as a formal and bureaucratized assembly as well as the voice for the *communitas regni*. Ironically enough it was one of the most blatant and far-reaching acts of baronial power, the deposition of Edward II in 1327, that was essential for the development of the identity of the Commons as the *vox communis*. The deposition was also (again, somewhat ironically) the most radical expression possible of the ideal of a divinely inspired assembly. As such, Edward II's misrule was a turning-point in the administrative development of parliament, as it was also for the growing sense of communal power generally evident during his reign.

The outline of this development requires some historical summary. As with his father and grandfather, many of the conflicts of Edward II's difficult reign occurred in or around parliament. Edward II showed himself unable to manage his barons as well as his father had.[87] In 1309 the barons refused to attend "the normal meeting place of our parliament" (*ad locum*

post-Uprising deliberations of the 1381 parliament (*RP* 3.100, item 13). Other examples from across the fourteenth century can be found through the keyword search function of *PROME* (s.vv. *unement, uniement, unanimiter, d'un assent, d'un accord*, et al.).

[87] For the details of what follows, see Butt, 175–230; Powell and Wallis, 264–302; Fryde, *The Tyranny and Fall of Edward II;* and especially Clarke, "Committeees of Estates and the Deposition of Edward II," in *Medieval Representation and Consent*, 173–95.

consuetum parliamenti nostri uenire differrent) because they opposed the king's favorite, Piers Gaveston; instead they held a private colloquium.[88] In 1310, the baronage forced the king to accept the control of a baronial council appointed by the magnates, the "Ordainers," who were to formulate binding provisions to control the king's expenditures and the membership of the royal household. The Ordinances established a permanent council for control of the Crown.[89] The proposals they drafted were put to the magnates and the king for approval in parliament in August 1311. These included explicit provisions, for the first time, that parliament was to be a "necessary and routine instrument in government," meeting at least once a year.[90] Gaveston was removed from the court, but by early 1312 he and others had returned. The baronage, led by Thomas of Lancaster, revolted. Gaveston was captured and condemned to death by Lancaster and the other magnates. After he was executed, according to the chronicler, "and the voice of the people (*vox publica*) had dinned his death into the ears of all, the country rejoiced, and all its inhabitants were glad."[91] Parliamentary conflicts over the enforcement of the Ordinances continued. Following the defeat of the English by the Scots at the battle of Bannockburn in 1314 and severe food shortages due to disastrous rains in 1314 and 1315, the realm suffered greatly from the effects of shortage, disease, social unrest, and war. Attempts to mediate in the conflicts had few lasting results and tensions increasingly spilled over into parliament. In 1312, as later in 1318 and 1321, nobles and the king brought armed retinues to the assembly, "so that you would have thought they had come not to parliament, but to battle."[92] In 1321 Lancaster called his own gathering of magnates to oppose the power of the king and his new favorites, the Despensers. Following their defeat and capture in battle, the Despensers were then tried and condemned in parliament by the "Peers of the Land, Earls and Barons"; they went into exile.[93] In 1326, after Queen Isabella had fled to France and organized opposition

---

[88] *Vita Edwardi Secundi*, 7–8.

[89] On the importance of the Ordinances see especially Sayles, *The King's Parliament of England*, 94–108.

[90] See Butt, 188–9. Representatives of the commons were present at this parliament and were involved with all of the conflicts until 1327.

[91] *Vita Edwardi Secundi*, 28–9: " . . . cum uox publica mortem eius auribus singulorum inculcasset, letata est terra, gauisi sunt omnes habitantes in ea."

[92] *Vita Edwardi Secundi*, 86–7: " . . . ut reputares eos non ad parliamentum uenisse, sed potius ad bella."

[93] This was the first time that the concept of a distinct "peerage" was formally invoked in parliament: see Butt, 207–9, 213; Powell and Wallis, 284–6; *Vita Edwardi Secundi*, 111–12. Later in 1322 when Lancaster himself was defeated, he too was tried before an assembly of magnates and condemned as a traitor.

with Roger Mortimer and others, the king was defeated and compelled to abdicate in parliament in 1327.

Through all the violence of these years and through all the back-and-forth struggles between baronial parties and the Crown, the unexpected but undeniable result was the growth of the authority and power of parliament. There developed not only a concept and practice of a noble peerage – that is, the principle that certain members of the nobility were summoned to parliament by hereditary right, not just at the pleasure of the king – but also the notion that the Commons in parliament were the voice of the community. This occurs almost by default. The Statute of York of 1322, passed in parliament that year, outlawed the prior Ordinances of 1311 but also granted that good government required proper consultation in parliament. In effect the king tried to remove the Crown from liability to baronial controls while reassuring the realm that royal parliaments would remain the legitimate forum for determining governmental policy.[94] The Statute distinguished between the baronage and the "commonalty" of the realm, so that the parliamentary Commons were now recognized, at least on parchment, as the voice of the *communitas regni* in matters of public import.[95]

A few years later when events turned against Edward, the Commons' new voice of the *communitas*, now a formally integral estate of parliament, was used against the king with even greater effectiveness. When Edward was deposed by the baronial faction led by Isabella and Mortimer, they convoked a parliament with the king's writs. The assembly as a whole, not just the peerage, was positioned as the authoritative voice of the community. It included elected members from class estates and regional communities, as well as representatives from the clergy and from the city of London in particular. Westminster Hall was crowded with the London mob.[96] The Archbishop of Canterbury, Walter Reynolds, read out a list of complaints against the king. After the charges were read,

Because of this the people agreed and cried out that he should no longer reign, but that his son the duke of Guyenne should be king; therefore certain bishops, abbots, priors, earls, barons, knights and burgesses were sent to the king at the said Kenilworth castle to give back to him their homage and to find out whether he would assent to the coronation of his son.[97]

---

[94] Butt, 216–17.   [95] Butt, 219; Clarke, "Committees of Estates," 176.
[96] Clarke, "Committees of Estates," 178–9.
[97] *Anonimalle Chronicle, 1307–34*, 132–3: "par quei le poeple graunta et cria qil ne deveroit plus reigner, meis qe son fice duk de Guyenne seroit roi; pur quei evesqes, abbes, priours, countes, barouns, chivalers, et burgeis furent maundez au roi al dit chastel de Kenilworth pur rendre a li sus homage et pur saver sil voleit assentire al corounement de son ficz."

Edward was effectively deposed before he renounced the throne, but his renunciation was needed for legitimacy. Far from assenting to his fate as this version would suggest, he was eventually compelled to accept his dethronement as a *fait accompli*. Nonetheless most chronicles record the tumultuous events of the parliament as the effective deposition, one achieved "with the whole commonalty of the land" and "by common assent of all."[98] The outcry of the Londoners in particular played a large role in the events; chronicles note that magnates were forced by the mob to swear fealty to the commonalty against Edward.[99] Other accounts are even more insistent in attributing the events to the "unanimous will" of the community as expressed in the parliament, and that the deposition was performed during the parliament by "the unanimous assent of the bishops and of the nobles and of all the people."[100] This "common cry" of the mob and the deputation of estates thus presented the appearance of a unified community voice even as the actual deposing authority was unclear, as it would be later in 1399, and even as there were significant dissenters from the proceedings. The Archbishop of Canterbury preached in French on the "text" *vox populi vox Dei*, [101] asking if the gathered audience assented to the removal of the king in favor of his son:

Which hearing, the whole community, with unanimous consent and raised hands so that they were extended forward, cried, "Let it be! Let it be! Let it be! Amen!"

In a scene directly and ironically echoing the Old Testament presentation of the Mosaic law before the community in 2 Esdras – when the Israelites had come together "as one man" (*congregatusque est omnis populus quasi vir unus*) for the reestablishment of the law – this popular–parliamentary assembly is called on to ratify the deposition of Edward by acclaiming his fall.[102] This

---

[98] Pipewell Chonicle, cited by Clarke, "Committees of Estates," 183; the Lichfield Chronicle records that the deposition was proposed "in the assembly at the unanimous and persistent clamor all of the people" (*ad clamorem tocius populi unanimiter in ipso clamore perseverantis*) (184). See also Powell and Wallis, 298.

[99] Both the Lichfield Chronicle and the *Gesta Abbatum* note this; cited by Clarke, "Committees of Estates," 180–1. But of fifty-four magnates present, only twenty-eight are recorded as taking the oath; see Butt, 228.

[100] From the account of the deposition given in MS. Trinity College, Cambridge R.5.41, fos. 125r-126r, printed in Fryde, *Tyranny and Fall of Edward II*, 233–5: "In isto parliamento ex unanimi assensu Episcoporum et procerum et totius populi depositus est dominus Edwardus Rex Anglie secundus a gubernacione terre sue et filius suus primogenitus Edwardus dux Acquitannie subrogatus est" (233).

[101] On the long and particularly English history of the pseudo-biblical proverb *vox populi vox Dei* (similar to Isaiah 66:6–7), see Boureau, "L'adage *vox populi, vox Dei* et l'invention de la nation Anglaise."

[102] Fryde, *Tyranny and Fall of Edward II*, 234: "Quod audiens populus universus unanimi consensu rursus manus ut prius extendentes clamabat Fiat, fiat, fiat, Amen." Compare 2 Esr. 8.1, 5–6

sermon was repeated later in the week and other prelates preached similar sermons against Edward.[103] Whatever the initial intent of the primary participants, by the time the deposition committee visited Edward at his castle at Kenilworth on January 20, all the "estates of the realm" had been enlisted into the deposition specifically through the manipulation of parliamentary assembly in what had become a ecclesially licensed revolution.

Over the course of the deposition several important shifts are evident: from baronage to populace, will of God to the voice of the people, individual grievances against the king – of which there were many – to the generalized *vox publica* of outrage. This, then, was the *vox populi* as *vox Dei*: the crowd, both parliamentary and public, gave its own benediction to the deposition with the raised hands of a negative blessing (*fiat* and *amen*) that was also a universal vote, but a voice-vote of, putatively, one acclamation. According to Archbishop Reynolds, the voice of the people had been heard and their prayers answered by Edward's fall, if they would consent to it together (*si unanimiter consentitis*).[104] The dynamics of the whole deposition thus combined most of the elements we have seen in parliament's conceptual development, but in an inverted manner. The parliament, led and afforced by the magnates, was a baronial assembly and a deeply biased one at that; Isabella and Mortimer sent summonses primarily to those sympathetic to their cause. But as an assembly it both gave voice to, and got its power from, the commonalty as mob, to which public appeal was expressly made by the Lords and assembled representatives. Between the baronial magnates and the wider populace, in a mediatory position, was the *idea* of parliament as much as the Commons themselves.

The true liminality of the parliamentary Commons is best exemplified in the formal ceremony of renunciation, which reveals the desire for an actual, physical unity of voice. The final act of speaking was given neither to the gathered assembly or crowds, nor to the elected parliamentary representatives, nor even to the smaller deposition committee, nor to a bishop or magnate. Rather, it was given to a single representative drawn from the commons, Sir William Trussell. Speaking with *plein et suffisant*

(Neh. 8.1, 5–6): "Et venerat mensis septimus filiiantem Israel in civitatibus suis, congregatusque est omnis populus quasi vir unus ad plateam quae est ante porte Aquarum . . . et aperuit Ezras librum coram omni populo super universum quippe populum eminebat, et cum aperuisset eum stet it omnis populus et benedixit Ezras Domino Deo magno et respondit omnis populus Amen, Amen, elevans manus suas . . ."

[103] Clarke notes that Orelton, the Bishop of Hereford, preached on *Rex insipiens perdet populum suum* (Eccl. 10:3), and Stratford, the Bishop of Winchester, preached on the theme *caput meum doleo* (cf. 4 Rg. 4:19, "caput meum, caput meum") ("Committees of Estates," 181–4).

[104] Fryde, *Tyranny and Fall of Edward II*, 200, 234.

pouer, Trussell delivered the final renunciation of homage on behalf of the clergy, nobility, and *autres* represented by his procuracy.[105] The choice of Trussell instead of a baronial representative may have been strategic so as not to give the appearance that a particular magnate had staged a *coup d'état.* But the implications of his representativeness go deeper. He was a dependent of Lancaster and a clear partisan of the contrariants, but he was not himself noble. He was present and active at the parliament but he was not, at least officially, a parliamentarian. He had been one of the judges delivering sentence against Hugh Despenser the younger in October 1326, although his status as *justiciarius* is unclear.[106] Trussell was, in short, as ambiguously liminal as the parliament itself. Only thus could he act as the figure, as another chronicle puts it, "in whose mouth the entire parliament put its words" (*in cuius ore universitas Parliamenti sua verba posuerat*).[107] The whole process of the deposition and all the events leading up to it, *and* the choice of a representative "speaker" from the commons, served to reinforce the position of the Commons-in-parliament as the authoritative voice of the community.[108] This position was made all the more accessible by the scriptural tropes and historiographical traditions which had underlain parliament at this point by upwards of a century. As a result, a sitting king could be deposed, with the grace of God, through the one voice of a commoner.

5 CONCLUSION

Without too much difficulty, this parliamentary perspective also allows us to see Edward II as a sort of anti-Havelok. Where the romance ideal of kingship in *Havelok* depicts a sovereign who is at first disinherited but then recognized "at one cri" by the estates as the true and legitimate king, the exact reverse befell Edward. The one voice of the *communitas regni* not only rejected him, it was politically constituted and institutionally legitimated *by* that rejection, an act bestowing upon parliament the kind of power it never had before and in practice never really had at all – except in the representations we find, contemporaneously, in romantic chronicle and literature. Like the deposition of Richard II in 1399, whose major actors

---

[105] For the text see *Rotuli parliamentorum Anglie hactenus inediti,* 101. On Trussell's role as a type of speaker, see Roskell, *The Commons and their Speakers in English Parliaments,* 5–10.

[106] He had been a justice deputed for the purpose of the judgment, but his prior judicial status is not recorded anywhere; see Powell and Wallis, 299; McKisack, *The Fourteenth Century,* 86–7.

[107] MS. Bodley, Roll 23, cited by Clarke, "Committees of Estates," 191.

[108] Prestwich, "Parliament and the Community of the Realm," 5–10.

would look back at 1327 for inspiration and procedural forms, the deposition of Edward II was carried out by a concerted group of magnates exploiting extra-constitutional procedures and the vicissitudes of popular rebellion. But even Edward himself may have judged the "false faith of parliament" as the decisive blow, as recorded in the lament he supposedly composed thereafter:

> Pener me funt cruelement,
> E duint qe bien l'ai deservi.
> Lour faus fai en parlement
> De haut en bas me descendi.
> Hay sire de salu jeo me repent
> Et de toutz mes mals vus cri merci!
> Ceo qe le corps soufre de torment
> Soit a l'alme joie et merci.[109]

[They make me suffer cruelly, granted that I have well deserved it. Their false faith in parliament has brought me down from the heights to the depths. Ah, Lord of salvation, I repent and beg thy mercy for all my sins! May the agony which my body endures be to my soul joy and mercy.]

Having been victimized by one set of romance tropes, "Edward" turns to others: he laments his lost kingdom (and queen) in the spiritual and erotic terms of Provençal lyric. As we have seen, during this period Robert Mannyng's *Chronicle* revised its sources to include the historical possibility of parliaments both electing and deposing kings, making even Arthur himself the royal product of parliamentary acclamation. Since he was writing in the 1330s scarcely a decade after Edward of Caernarvon's fall, we might wonder if Mannyng's parliamentarizing representations were motivated by the more immediate and monitory example of Edward II, a king who was, for all public appearances, a *rois abatu* through the exercise of parliament.

---

[109] "Lament of Edward II," *Anglo-Norman Political Songs*, 96–102, ll. 17–24. On the probability that this lyric was written by Edward shortly after his deposition, see Aspin's analysis, 95–6.

CHAPTER 2

Parliament, criticism, and complaint in the later fourteenth century, 1330–1400

* * *

As politically disastrous as it was, the reign of Edward II and the period from roughly 1300–30 were pivotal for the development of parliament's power as an assembly unique from both the king's *curia* and the baronial context of the contrariants.[1] The deposition of Edward II brought about a shift in the identification of the community of the realm, a change for which William Trussell could stand symbolically – as he did during the deposition – as an actor and spokesman. The office of speaker of the Commons did not formally develop until several decades later, but there is justification for thinking of Trussell, like Keighley before him, as a prototype of a speaker. [2] It is also important to recognize the major difference, namely, that he was not a speaker of the Commons but rather *totius populi*, and by extension, of the entire realm, not just the shire knights and burgesses. In this manner Trussell hypostasized, in an early form, the changing personification of communal action and a fantasy of univocal voice. With the nobility having developed into a distinct peerage, their traditional role as the representatives of the community was largely ceded. Drawing further into the fourteenth century, we see that role increasingly adopted by the Commons at the same time that the centrality of parliament led to increasingly trenchant criticisms of its performance.

This tradition of parliamentary criticism grows out of the longer tradition of courtly satire and the familiar genre of courtier's trifles. We have already noted how certain genres of storytelling and history-writing made important contributions to a growing sense of *parlement* in communal governance and self-awareness. In this second historical chapter, we will see

---

[1] As Butt notes, "the reign of Edward II appears, in retrospect, as a kind of watershed in political behaviour, after which the tacit contract of a king's acceptance by his people could more easily be broken, especially if a Parliament (which was thereby assisted towards a new sense of its corporate importance) could be brought to have a hand in the change" (232).

[2] Another William Trussell, probably his son, was the spokesman of the Commons for the consideration of a truce with France in the parliament of 1343: see Butt, 300.

that while baronialism of the earlier period continues to mutate into more communal forms – mediated through chronicles and petitions – the identification of parliament as a *vox communis* leads to conflicts of representation. Accordingly, our critical focus shifts to the developing forms of common complaint that parliament both produced and was the object of, particularly from clerical writers, and to the conceptual image of parliament as a forum of unified voice. In some ways the desire for *unanimitas* was the ideological undoing of the point with which we began, the enumeration of parliament into various and competing estates. It was both an implicit and impossible expection that parliament should represent both the diversity and the unity of the nation, its multiplicity and singularity. Where complaint and division would be submitted, unity was the desired but impossible result. While this persistent fantasy motivated much of the public poetry of the Ricardian era, the express inability of parliament to meet such representational demands also motivated some remarkable images of division, houses and bodies that figured forth the contemporary desire for representation and voice in all of its contradictory power.

I   REPRESENTING THE NATION AND THE *COMMUNITAS PARLIAMENTI*

Following the revolution of 1327, the parliamentary Commons increasingly took on the hitherto baronial role of the *vox communis*, which was partly a result of the judicial developments surrounding Edward's deposition. If the barons and earls were to be judges in parliament – a role they increasingly adopted as the century progressed – then they could not also be petitioners, at least not to the same degree or in the traditional manner. As foreign wars came to dominate politics during the reign of Edward III, the role of the baronage as the carriers of domestic complaints receded against their more vigorous role as the prosecutors of war.[3] This shift was also implicitly divisive, as the older ideology of baronial representation of the *communitas regni* gave way to a view of the noble peerage as a legally distinct class, set apart with less investment in domestic justice.[4]

This shift also points to more than the changed spheres of interest for the parliamentary estates. In addressing the question of granting aids to the king, the *Modus Tenendi Parliamentum* puts the case most strongly for the communally representative role of the elected members of parliament.

[3] See Musson and Ormrod, *The Evolution of English Justice*, 86–7; Clarke, *Medieval Representation and Consent*, 154–72.
[4] See particularly Prestwich, "Parliament and the Community of the Realm," 18–20.

The *Modus* itself could stand, historiographically, for the shifts and vicis-situdes in the ways parliament has been conceptually co-opted and re-cast for different political ends. It is a bureaucratic manual, possibly influenced by the French *Stilus Curie Parliamenti* (c. 1330), which became a quasi-authoritative text on the operation of parliament and was later cited (by John Hooker and Henry Elsyng especially) in the developing literature of parliamentary procedure and history. It was cited and extensively circulated during the later fourteenth century, but its date of composition remains unsettled. Proposals range from shortly after the deposition of Edward II to the reign of Richard II; all surviving manuscripts are extant from the time of Richard II, which makes its textual circulation directly contemporane-ous with the time of greatest parliamentary foment before the seventeenth century.[5] In it, for the first time the representative role of the Commons is made the focal justification for parliament's authority, especially in tax matters. This is so, it asserts, because,

. . . two knights who come to parliament for the shire, have a greater voice in granting and denying than the greatest earl of England, and in the same manner the proctors of the clergy from one diocese, if they are agreed, have a greater voice in parliament than the bishop himself, and this in everything that ought to be granted, denied, or done by parliament . . .[6]

Like the *Modus*'s description of the estates, this assertion of the power of the lower clergy and Commons, as opposed to the bishops and magnates, is simply fictional. There never was a mechanism for ensuring the "greater voice" of the lower estates nor any procedural recognition of their greater importance. What evidently motivates it is the further point that specifically the elected members of parliament are its representative element. They stand for the nation *totaliter* and not just for individual interests:

---

[5] For analysis, see especially the introduction by Pronay and Taylor, *Parliamentary Texts of the Later Middle Ages*, 13–63; Weber, "The Purpose of the English *Modus Tenendi Parliamentum*," who argues cogently for an early date, around the period of the Statutes of York, circa 1311–22; and Kerby-Fulton and Justice, "Reformist Intellectual Culture in the English and Irish Civil Service: The *Modus Tenendi Parliamentum* and its Literary Relations," who revise the texts' stemmatics and argue for a later date, circa the Good Parliament of 1376. See also Powell and Wallis, 285–6, and Butt, 219–20 for brief assessments; and the earlier research of Galbraith, "The *Modus Tenendi Parliamentum*," and Clarke, *Medieval Representation and Consent*. For my interpretive purposes, I assume only the *Modus*'s demonstrable textual currency during the later fourteenth century.

[6] *Modus* 77, 89: ". . . quod duo milites, qui veniunt ad Parliamentum pro ipso comitatu, maiorem vocem habent in Parliamento in concedendo et contradicendo, quam maior comes Anglie, et eodem modo procuratores cleri unius episcopatus maiorem vocem habent in Parliamento, si omnes sint concordes, quam episcopus ipse, et hoc in omnibus que per Parliamentum concedi, negari vel fieri debent . . ."

And therefore it is necessary that all matters which ought to be confirmed or annulled, granted, denied, or done by parliament, ought to be granted by the community of parliament, which is composed of three grades or orders of parliament, that is to say the proctors of the clergy, the knights of the shire, the citizens and burgesses who represent the whole community of England, and not the magnates because each of these is at parliament for his own individual person, and for no one else.[7]

The magnates do not represent (*representant*) the realm, the shire knights and burgesses (and clerical proctors) do. The magnates stand only for themselves. This claim may seem self-evident to us (and was probably evident to contemporaries), yet it registers a profound change in the understanding of parliament's representativeness. In one sense it would be satisfying if we could pinpoint this bald assertion to a particular date or contextualizing event. But in another, the *Modus's* claim is all the more resonant because of its illocatability and generality. It could have been applied, or denied, at almost any point after the accession of Edward II. It is a radical change from the baronialism of the thirteenth century when it was precisely the magnates who "spoke" for the *communitas regni*. It further signals the developing conception of the realm as represented by the *communitas Parliamenti*, that parliament itself did – or should – mirror the nation at large. This change was not immediate or total but it was nonetheless real, and it influenced the concrete practices of parliament as well as its notional identity.[8]

This communalized characterization of collective action also brings about a shift in the tradition of criticism paralleling the changes of parliamentary consciousness. It introduces a much stronger tone at the same time as parliament itself was growing into the premier forum for voicing public complaints and for attempting to manipulate public opinion. Of course it is necessary to remember that in its public and literary representations during the reigns of Edward III and Richard II, parliament was still very much a meeting of magnates. But even as the quasi-popular constituency of parliament increased in authority, it was de-romanticized, and it appears in this period for the first time as the discrete object of criticism and scorn.

---

[7] *Modus*, 77, 90: "Et ideo oportet quod omnia que affirmari vel infirmari, concedi vel negari, vel fieri debent per Parliamentum, per communitatem Parliamenti concedi debent, que est ex tribus gradibus sive generibus Parliamenti, scilicet ex procuratoribus cleri, militibus comitatuum, civibus et burgensibus, qui representant totam communitatem Anglie, et non de magnatibus, quia quilibet eorum est pro sua propria persona ad Parliamentum et pro nulla alia."

[8] See Harriss, *King, Parliament, and Public Finance in Medieval England to 1369*, 75–85.

Again, this is a matter of degree. Early in Edward II's reign, for example, the *Flores Historiarum* notes the many "quibbling and altogether ridiculous parliaments" (*sophistica parliamenta et satis ridiculosa*) of the day that good men of the realm, following the advice of the Psalms, avoided.[9] No doubt similar criticisms went unrecorded. The early years of Edward III's reign saw a flurry of judicial reform emanating from parliament, most of it only partly successful. At about the time that the structure and constituencies of parliament were stabilizing, the Commons' control over taxation was formally established by statute.[10] After 1337 the war with France ensured the king's dependency upon parliament for funding. Edward's later military successes, as well as his success cultivating parliament for his goals, meant that there were fewer occasions for serious conflict between the Crown and the estates in parliament after 1341. Especially after the issue of military funding was resolved in the 1340s, the middle decades of Edward III's reign were notably lacking in parliamentary conflicts.[11] The decades from 1330 to 1360 were a period of vigorous development by the Commons in particular. Frequent re-election of shire knights also solidified parliament's corporate identity as a unique body of experienced and semi-professional councillors.[12]

Contemporaneously, the massive growth in legal petitioning and the "bill revolution" of the late thirteenth century became a veritable flood, much of it directed to parliament. Much of the reign's legislation arose from, and was based on, parliamentary common petitons, and it was during this period that parliament emerged as "the primary political and legislative institution in the kingdom."[13] This primacy was also manifested in parliamentary laws and statutes signalling a new intrusiveness. The Ordinance of Laborers and Statute of Laborers, the Statute of Treasons, sumptuary ordinances, ordinances on the trades, staples, and licenses, the judicial and legal reactions to the Uprising of 1381, restrictions on maintenance, and others, all bear witness to the readiness of parliament to legislate aspects of social life. Later, the most controversial political battles were fought in parliament as a judicial body in 1376, 1386, 1388, 1397, and 1399. From a

---

[9] *Flores Historiarum*, 3.143–4 (for the year 1308).

[10] This occurred in the January 1340 parliament at Westminster: see Butt, 285–7, *PROME*, Edward III 1340, January, "Introduction."

[11] This characterization holds, of course, only prior to the tumults of the last decade of Edward III's reign. See Butt, 231–354; Ormrod, *The Reign of Edward III*, 13–34.

[12] Maddicott, "Parliament and the Constituencies," 75, notes that experienced MPs were a majority of the Commons at three-fifths of Edward's parliaments, as opposed to about one-third during the years 1290–1307.

[13] Musson and Ormrod, *The Evolution of English Justice*, 159; Brown, *The Governance of Late Medieval England*, 169–76.

socio-lingual perspective, the year 1362 marks a turning-point when the Statute of Pleading changed the official language of pleading in the law courts from the vestigial (and baronial) French to English. The following year, parliament opened for the first time in English, signalling the cultural as well as political centrality of the king's high court for a widened national audience.[14]

The fourteenth century has been rightly called an "age of complaint," as it was the procedural and documentary developments of complaint and petition that fostered much of the growth in legal as well as literary expression.[15] The expansion of parliamentary competence meant the expansion of access to parliament as the chief avenue for petition and redress. As a public event, parliament was a court of courts, or a fair of courts. The various judicial benches were assembled at the same time in roughly the same place. Petitioners brought their documentary submissions to panels of "receivers," who vetted bills and then forwarded them to "triers," who rendered judgment or directed the petition to the proper venue for hearing. Ideally all petitions would be heard before the end of a session of parliament. Sometimes sessions were extended to accommodate the large number of petitions. By 1348 the procedural groundwork had been laid for the development of common petitions, which were bills of redress submitted in the name of the entire Commons sitting as the representatives of the community. As much as anything else, common petitions offer further evidence of the ideal of univocal speech. It was a procedure the Commons eventually had to regulate in an effort to prevent individuals or groups from submitting bills in the name of the Commons that in fact had not been endorsed by them.[16] But as important as they were, common petitions are only a part of a discernible pattern of communal representation associated with the tradition of complaint that had become the domain of the Commons. Where the *Modus Tenendi Parliamentum* assigned formal and authoritative representativeness to the members of the Commons, it was the identity of parliament as a venue for public petition that opened the way for its ascendance as a representative forum. This, in turn,

---

[14] *RP* 2.273 (it is the last item recorded for the 1362 parliament); see Butt, 324; *Statutes of the Realm*, 375–6 Edw. III, I. c.15. In 1344 Edward had appealed to parliament for war funds on the grounds that the king of France intended "to destroy the English language and to occupy the land of England" (*a destruire la Lange Engleys, & de occuper la terre d'Engleterre* [*RP* 2.147, also 152]), a claim also indicating the importance of a growing vernacular audience.

[15] Musson and Ormrod, *The Evolution of English Justice*, 189.

[16] See Maddicott, "Parliament and the Constituencies," 76; Brown, "Parliament, c. 1377–1422," 126–9; Butt, 268–72; Rayner, "The Forms and Machinery of the 'Commune Petition' in the Fourteenth Century"; Cam, "The Legislators of Medieval England," 144–8; Brown, *The Governance of Late Medieval England*, 215–24; Edwards, *The Second Century of the English Parliament*, 44–65.

was facilitated by parliament's participation in the growth of documentary culture.

The importance of parliamentary documents can be demonstrated in the two senses of "document": parliament was both *documented* as it never had been before – it came to be a focus of reportage and public attention – and it produced documents, especially bills, that were a part of the overall growth of documentary practices. Reportage of parliamentary events (usually sketchy and sometimes inaccurate) was also consistently practiced throughout the fourteenth and early fifteenth centuries. Reports of burgesses to their constituencies were particularly common.[17] Two well-known documents from across the decade of 1376 to 1388, one a chronicle narrative and the other a formal bill, help to contextualize the importance of these trends. They also provide good examples of the kinds of storytelling that could be practiced, within and around parliament, as quasi-literary exercises in narrative. The artistic merit of these works is not the point so much as their workaday use of elements that might surprise us: a defined plot, allegory, and implicit appeals – especially through vernacular language – to a popular audience.

The first, from the Good Parliament of 1376, is the first recorded account of the Commons' deliberation during a parliament, which is found in the Anglo-French narrative of the *Anonimalle Chronicle*.[18] This account provides invaluable testimony for the early procedures of the Commons since it is the only detailed witness to their deliberations prior to the Tudor and Elizabethan era. In addition to its unique historical testimony, it also tells a good story, and a well-structured one. The parliament of 12 February 1376 had been called to secure funding for military preparations to counter the threat of a French and Castilian naval offensive. It turned into the most critical (and longest) assembly to date, bringing forward multiple accusations of royal malfeasance and mismanagement.[19] Edward's military failures and financial exactions – and the excesses of his court, which had gone out of

[17] For examples see McKisack, *The Parliamentary Representation of the English Boroughs During the Middle Ages*, 139–45.
[18] *The Anonimalle Chronicle 1333 to 1381*, ed. Galbraith. The translation is provided in Taylor, *English Historical Literature in the Fourteenth Century*, 301–13.
[19] On the Good Parliament see the analysis provided by Butt, 337–51, and the extensive history by Holmes, *The Good Parliament*.

control in the king's old age – led the Commons to attack the ministers held responsible. While criticism of the king's advisors was nothing new, the vehemence and organization of the Commons was. The *Chronicle* records how the assembled representatives of the Commons gathered and began their discussion:

And the chapter house of the abbey of Westminster was assigned to the knights and Commons, in which they could deliberate privately without being disturbed or being bothered by others. And on the said second day all the knights and Commons aforesaid gathered and went into the chapter house and sat around (*en viroune*), each close to the other, and they began to talk of the substance of the causes of parliament, and they said that it would be desirable at the beginning to be sworn one to the other, to hold counsel as to what was spoken and ordered among them, and loyally to treat and ordain for the welfare of the kingdom without concealing anything; and to this they all unanimously assented and took an oath to be loyal one to the other. And then one of them said, "If any of us knew of anything to say for the welfare of the king and kingdom he should lay his knowledge before us", and after that, one after another [said] what was on his mind.[20] (302)

In order, three speakers are recorded as standing up, going to a central podium, and declaring their accusations and counsel. Two of these three speakers (who are recorded in the first person) begin their addresses with short prayers. They are described as coming forward, speaking at the lectern, and then retiring back to their companions. Others are described as coming forward "in the same manner in twos or threes, one after the other" (*bien a deux ou troys*), speaking their knowledge; the group as a whole then "took counsel together, what was the most profitable course to pursue" (*pristrent lour conseil ensemble coment serrast profitable affair en celle cause*) (303).[21] Peter de la Mare, the steward of the Earl of March, then speaks publicly, summarizing their points. Sir Peter is said to have spoken "so well and so wisely," formulating matters so clearly, that he is asked to be their spokesperson in parliament before the Lords: "and the said Sir Peter for

---

[20] *Anonimalle Chronicle*, 80–1: "Et fuist assigne a les chivalers et communes le chapiter del abbeye de Wymouster, en quel ils purrount lour conseil privement prendre saunz destourbaunce ou fatigacion des autres gentz. Et en le dit secunde iour toutz les chivalers et communes avauntditz assemblerent et entrerent en chapiter et ses assistrerent en viroune, chescune pres de autre; et comenceront de parlere de lour mater de les poyntes de le parlement, disoyunt qe bone serroit al comencement destre iurrez chescune a autre de tener conseil ceo qe fuist parle et ordine entre eux et loialment treter et ordiner pur profit de la roialme saunz conselement; et a cestez choses parfourner toutz unement assenterent et firent bone serement pur estre loialles chescune a autre. Et donqes une de eux dist qe si ascune de nous sciet ascune chose dire pur profit del roy et roialme qe bone serroit de moustrer soun sceue parentre nous, et apres, une apres autre ceo qe lour gist au coer."

[21] *Anonimalle Chronicle*, 82.

the reverence of God, and his worthy colleagues, and for the profit of the kingdom undertook this responsibility" (304).[22] The Commons deliberate for another week – to the chagrin, apparently, of the king, who asks them to hurry up – during which time they confer with the Lords and organize their accusations for impeachment. The narrative then summarizes the proceedings of the parliament especially as it prosecuted Richard Lyons and Lord Latimer, the two ministers held most responsible for the Crown's military and financial lapses.

A great deal has been said about the processes of the Good Parliament and the *Anonimalle*'s account of the Commons' procedures. For my purposes here, I want to stress those aspects of the assembly's record that both derive and depart from their narrative antecedents. Whatever else this account provides and however else the Good Parliament affected the course of politics, the story of the assembly captured the attention of a public audience as never before. The *Anonimalle Chronicle* account in particular is evidence of this, but the official record also demonstrates its perceived importance.[23] The roll accumulated a whopping one hundred and forty-six petitions of complaint about practically every aspect of governance in the realm. As Holmes notes, over three hundred men had a voice in the assembly.[24] The chronicle gives a clear sense of this communal reaction by skillfully reducing it to a digestible literary form. It is not a gathering of nobles nor a round table of knights, nor is it a public assembly and quasi-mob such as extolled Havelok and brought down Edward II. Rather, the knights and burgesses of the Good Parliament are presented, artfully, as a sort of halfway-point between court and community, and as an implicitly inspired gathering – a point made even more strongly in Walsingham's account. The Anonimalle chronicler emphasizes the roundness (*en viroune*) and closeness of their separate assembly, which was no doubt fostered by the small and roughly round octagonal shape of the Westminster chapterhouse. We hear the specific voices of only the first three speakers, but the narrative makes clear that everyone had the chance to contribute to the deliberations before they settled on de la Mare as their univocal – and

---

[22] *Anonimalle Chronicle*, 83: ". . . en quel trete et conseil par commune assent par cause qe le dite sire Peirs de la Mare fuist si bien parlaunt et si sagement rehersaunt les maters et purpose de ses compaignouns et les enfourmaunt pluis avaunt qils mesmes ne savoient, prierent a luy qil vodroit prendre la charge pur eux davoir la sovereinte de pronuncier lour voluntes en la graunt parlement avaunt les dit seignours coment ils furount avysez defair et dire en descharge de lour conscience. Et le dite sire Peirs al reverence de Dieu et ses bones compaignouns et pur profite del roialme prist celle charge."

[23] *RP* 2.321–60. The procedures against Latimer and Lyons actually occupy only a small portion of the record, 2.321–7. The bulk is taken up by the massive number of complaints submitted.

[24] Holmes, *The Good Parliament*, 108; Butt, 338.

Godly – spokesman. It also stresses that what he spoke was the single voice of the commons: "what one of us says, all say and assent to" (*ceo qe une de nous dist touz diount et assentount*) (83, 305). The representatives swear loyalty and secrecy – a fact reported, ironically enough, in this public account of their deliberations – and de la Mare himself later speaks only by their common grant. Later he makes the famous first "Speaker's protestation" that he stands to be corrected by his peers. When they move back to the parliament house (the White Chamber of the Lords), they move as one; when they are limited in their entry, they demand to present their case as one; and when they impeach Lyons and Latimer, *toutz les comunes crierent a une voyce* (90). Later the Commons form a unified block with the Lords and the entire parliament proceeds *unanimiter*, if not without conflict.

This account of the Commons thus stresses unity and consensus in a narrative form that is itself a unified and univocal gathering of multiple voices. It was probably redacted from a contemporary eyewitness account given by one of the attending clerks and circulated for public consumption.[25] To a large degree the spotlight was on Peter de la Mare, who later paid for his forwardness with imprisonment (like Keighley before him) before also serving as the speaker for the first parliament of Richard II's reign in 1377. Other chronicles record the public adulation he received for his actions and eloquence.[26] As Kathryn Kerby-Fulton and Steven Justice have emphasized, the "broadly reformist enthusiasms" of the parliament were its real legacy, however short-lived were its specific efforts.[27] It provided a communal focus for national sentiment as well as an individual figure of unified speaking that were both re-represented in the developing expressive capacities of clerical record and documentation. They (and he) could complain for the nation as a whole, and the account of that voice could be circulated and reported back to the public.

---

[25] The *Anonimalle*'s account was probably composed independently and incorporated into the chronicle as a unit. A possible author was John Scardeburgh, Clerk of Parliament and prebend of St. Mary's Abbey, York, the source of the chronicle. He may also be responsible for the chronicle's accounts of the later Gloucester parliament and the Uprising of 1381. He is probably the same John Scardeburgh who later became a deputy to the chief butler, Thomas Chaucer: see Pollard, "The Authorship and Value of the 'Anonimalle' Chronicle." If so, Scardeburgh could have been acquainted with Thomas Chaucer's father during the 1370s and 1380s, as two of the thirty-four mainpernors for Richard Latimer were known to Geoffrey Chaucer: John Clanvowe and Philip de la Vache (*RP* 2.326–7).

[26] When he was released from prison, de la Mare was given a hero's welcome by the Londoners; an errant priest who had dared to denigrate de la Mare was beaten to death (*St. Albans Chronicle*, 90, 130). De la Mare was also praised in contemporary ballads, none of which survive: see Wilson, *The Lost Literature of Medieval England*, 201.

[27] Kerby-Fulton and Justice, "Reformist Intellectual Culture," 153.

The events of the Good Parliament also demonstrate how, by the end of the 1370s, the parliamentary Commons in particular had a much stronger political role than previously, but that this role was adapted from the traditional parliamentary duty to present public complaints. It could be manipulated to devastating effect, as the events of the Merciless Parliament of 1388 later showed. Parliamentary reportage had expanded well beyond the kind of session summaries and progress reports that accompanied parliaments earlier in the century.

Along these lines, my second example of vernacular documentary practice is more focused in provenance, and it provides a good example of the kind of petitionary form that becomes extremely important for literary use. The "Mercers' Petition" of 1388, submitted during the Merciless Parliament, is a unique example of the genre of bill complaints in several respects. It is the earliest surviving petition written in English for which the date is certain. It also shows how Latin and Anglo-French documents of the courts, and of parliament in particular, sometimes had English documents along with or behind them.[28] The complaint is addressed to the Lords on behalf of "the folk of the Mercerye of London," that is the Mercers' guild, which was deeply enmeshed in the conflict between Richard II and his nobles. During the parliament of 1388 the party of John Northampton, the mayor of London, was probably compelled by the Appellant lords to bring forward a bill of complaint against the former Lord Mayor Nicholas Brembre, Richard's ally and a primary target of the Appellants' wrath.[29] Where most complaints and petitions were relatively short (usually on a small piece of parchment written in one long paragraph) this one is physically large – almost two feet long – and more like a substantial broadside than a legal bill. It has twelve separate paragraphs with room left for later additions. While it has the form of a complaint, the content makes clear that this document's real use was as a piece of propaganda, which also justifies its composition and presentation in English (Figure 5).

In a mode similar to the different stories told in the *Anonimalle Chronicle*, this bill recounts Brembre's attempts to fix recent London mayoral

---

[28] National Archives SC 8/20/997; the text is taken from "A Petition of the Folk of Mercerye," in *A Book of London English, 1384–1425*, eds. Chambers and Daunt, 33–7. The earliest English petition is dated circa 1344, a petition of John Drayton and Margery King, his wife (National Archives SC 8/192/9579), from Gloucestershire; see *A Book of London English*, 272. See also the English and French petitions discussed in Chapters Four and Six.

[29] The processes of the 1388 parliament are recorded extensively in the roll: *RP* 3.228–56. See Saul, *Richard II*, 176–96; McKisack, *The Fourteenth Century*, 454–9; Clarke, "Forfeitures and Treason in 1388"; Butt, 394–9; Powell and Wallis, 404–11. These events are discussed more fully in Chapter Four.

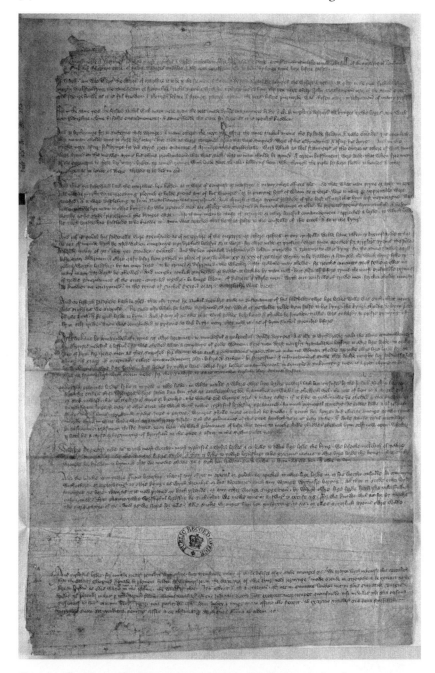

Figure 5. The Mercers' Petition. National Archives SC 8/20/997 (reduced, approx. 13 × 22 inches). © 2006 The National Archives

elections and to manipulate the king's favor through political intimidation and violence. The account of Brembre's second mayoral election (probably referring to his re-election in October 1385) is particularly notable as a narrative complaint:

And so ferthermore, for to susteyne thise wronges & many othere, the next yere after, the same Nichol, ayeins the forsaide fredam & trewe comunes, did crye openlich that no man sholde come to chese her Mair but such as were sompned, & tho that were sompned were of his ordynaunce & after his auys. And in the nyght next after folwynge he did carye grete quantitee of Armure to the Guyldehalle, with which as wel straungers of the contree as othere of with-jnne were armed on the morwe, ayeins his owne proclamacion that was such that no man shulde be armed; & certein busshmentȝ were laide, that, when free men of the Citee come to chese her Mair, breken vp armed cryinge with loude voice 'sle! sle!' folwyng hem; wherthourgh the peple for feere fledde to houses & other [hidy]nges as in londe of werre, adradde to be ded in comune. (34)

Even through the rather tortured English (which imitates the style of legal French) the story comes forward in engaging detail, with Brembre's thugs chasing the other London citizens away from the guildhall. In such a manner the "true commons" were supposedly kept from exercising their liberties of election and franchise. Brembre was blamed for destroying city records and for violating statutes prohibiting the victuallers from holding office. Because he was a confidant and advisor of the king, he was also accused of manipulating the king and slandering his political opponents. The petition presents a picture of Brembre that is both uniformly condemnatory – the author of "common wrong" – and mildly allegorical, punning on his name to characterize him as a briar or bramble-bush,[30]

. . . for sithen thise wronges bifore saide han ben vsed as accidental or comune braunches outward, it sheweth wel the rote of hem is a ragged subiect or stok inward, that is the forsaid Brere or brembre, the whiche comune wronge vses, & many other, if it lyke to yow, mowe be shewed & wel knowen bi an indifferent Juge & Mair of owre Citee . . . (36)

The plaint calls for the Lords to act as judges and "grecious menes to owre lyge lorde the kyng" in this case, because Brembre had illegally restricted petitionary access to the king (37). The petition thus thematizes the conditions of its own access and operation, another durable aspect of petitions we shall see in other bills and literary contexts.

---

[30] *MED* sv. *Brēmbel, brember,* "a thorny shrub or prickly plant; a bramble or brier," specifically blackberry or dewberry, or dog rose.

Here also the gestural force of the vernacular was strategically deployed for the publicity of parliamentary acts. Parliament was fundamentally multilingual, a fact that gives unique valence to its documentary record and to its claims to speak with a public voice. This English bill – which, fascinatingly enough, was composed by Chaucer's own scribe, Adam Pinkhurst[31] – also provides a good example of parliament's use as a forum for circulating propaganda. To a degree, bill writing *was* propagandizing. Thomas Usk, for example, was employed by Northampton as a bill writer, and his documentary products became potent tools in the factional struggles.[32] From a historical distance it is hard to judge the probity of the Mercers' charges because they appeal to an ideal of the king-in-parliament that was itself ideologically manipulable. That is, if the king was doing the wrong things, then he must be misled by the wrong counsellors with personal access; he must not be working in concert with his baronage and "true advisors." So an opposing action or view of policy becomes treason, which in turn falls within the particular orbit of parliamentary jurisdiction. The legality of the accusation is lost, or run roughshod over, by the relative lack of procedural safeguards since parliament was, in practice, beyond the reach of appellate review by any other court. Thus the high court of parliament could be turned against the very source of its authority – the king – in the name *of* that authority. In accusing the "ragged stock" Brembre in parliament, the framers of the petition attempted to open more space for the Lords to make their attacks on the mayor specifically by manipulating the procedure of common complaint, even though the partisanship of the document is scarcely concealed. Eventually Brembre was condemned and executed by the *viva voce* of the parliament, as the chronicler Thomas Favent calls it, "to the great joy of all."[33] Although it is not clear how much weight was given to evidence of this sort, the petition and its circumstances offer a grim demonstration of how the procedural and legal bases of parliament could just as easily be turned for partisan purposes and violence not despite, but because of, its unique appeal to be the common voice.

3 THE CRITIQUES OF PARLIAMENT IN THOMAS BRINTON AND JOHN BROMYARD

The performance both documented and enacted in the Mercers' Petition was the inverse of the ideal of a parliamentary common voice idealized by the

---

[31] See Mooney, "Chaucer's Scribe," 106–12.

[32] See Strohm, "Politics and Poetics: Usk and Chaucer in the 1380s"; Galloway, "Private Selves and the Intellectual Marketplace in Late Fourteenth-Century England: The Case of the Two Usks."

[33] Favent, *Historia*, 16, 19: ". . . et gaudium magnum erat in populo."

performance of the Commons in 1376 and recorded in the *Anonimalle* and elsewhere. As much as it could be a voice of the Commons or the *communitas regni*, parliament could also be strong-armed by the powerful or silenced by the reticence of a community too afraid and too insecure in its procedural protections. Even as critics and chroniclers recognized these shortcomings, the ideological ideal of a unified voice trumped the realization that, in such circumstances, the very desires for "truth" and "unity" were not just difficult to reconcile, they might in fact be incommensurate. To get at the truth, some discord must be not only allowed, but cultivated. Opposing voices must be tolerated and heard *within* the legal framework of commmunal assembly and not just against it. At the same time, the desire to see or to represent the community as *one*, as a *universitas*, is both idealized and pejorized by thinking of it as "one voice," since vocal singular interests supposedly oppose the communal interests of the speaking assembly. The assembly itself, when it acts in unity, can become the very thing it is supposed to avoid: a singular interest.

The *de facto* kangaroo court that parliament became in 1388 (and again in 1397, and 1399) serves as an extreme endpoint of this kind of ideological manipulation.[34] There are lesser examples, and other clerical writers broached the problem in different terms. Recounting the parliament of 1382 held during Richard's wedding, the St. Albans *Chronicle* criticizes the uselessness of parliaments in which laws are passed but not enforced. The tone of the criticism is less of condemnation than exasperation that the assembly does not live up to its own promises. A major source of the problem is that parliament fails to control its own record and voice:

> With the royal nuptials completed, the parliament was re-assembled . . . in which many articles were proposed and decreed . . . and there were many and various statutes made at that time. But what does it help to write parliamentary statutes, when later they give rise to no effect at all? Indeed the king, with his privy council, was accustomed to change or delete everything that by parliamentary preference the entire kingdom – not only the commons (*communitas*), but also even the nobility (*nobilitas*) – had established.[35]

Although parliament speaks and decrees statutes – too much, it seems – the effect is nothing, or is perverted. Both *communitas* and *nobilitas* have their

---

[34] For a similar analysis of manipulated documents during the Revenge Parliament of 1397 and the deposition parliament of 1399, see Giancarlo, "Murder, Lies, and Storytelling."

[35] *St. Albans Chronicle*, 576–8: "Expletis nupciarum solemniis reincipit parliamentum . . . in quo plures articuli sunt propositi et decreti . . . Multa sunt et alia que statuta sunt ibidem. Set quid iuuvat statuta parliamentorum [scribere] cum penitus ex post nullum sortiantur effectum? Rex nempe cum priuato concilio cuncta vel mutare uel delere solebat, que in parliamentis antehabitis tota regni non solum comunitas set et ipsa nobilitas statuebat."

wishes thwarted by the privy council. Similar accusations of parliamentary malfeasance and procedural abuse followed Richard to the end of his reign. Nor was it only the king who could undo what had been done by the highest legal authority of the land. After the Good Parliament, the reforms and banishments imposed on members of the royal court were either curtailed or negated by John of Gaunt, the Duke of Lancaster. He dissolved the parliament's governing council and declared the parliamentary actions null and void:

> After this, so that he might attach some appearance of legitimacy to his acts, he [i.e. Gaunt] said that it ought not be called a "parliament" that was lately celebrated, nor in true fact to have been a parliament, and therefore nothing ought to be observed of those things which had been instituted there. And thus, by the will of one (*unius libidine*) the hope of the community (*spes communis*) was frustrated, and the profit of the community (*universitas*) gave way to him alone, while alone he deleted (*delevit*) what the community established.[36]

The contrast between the *universitas* and the *unius libidine*, the "desire of one" (that is, Gaunt) versus the community or the whole of the realm, as expressed in parliament, is established as a one-to-one struggle, unity versus unity. The language is also overtly documentary: Gaunt's actions delete or blot out (*delevit*) the statutes that had been established (*statuit*) by the assembly in formal parliament. To a large degree, control over writing and documentation *was* control over public voice. Framed in this way, the conflict comes across as an example of singular versus common interests in the unique documentary environment of parliament. At the same time we can see the conflict as inherent in the *form* of parliament as an idealized individual voice of univocal speech. If parliament can write statutes, then Gaunt can erase them. And if Gaunt and the parliament are opposed, they are also mirror images of each other. The deliberative multiplicity in some sense wishes it could be reduced to univocal conformity, but in this case it can hardly stand against the embodiment of powerful magnate identity that Gaunt "represents." This is probably the rationale behind Gaunt's cryptic assertion that the Good Parliament was not a "true" parliament at all. Without the assent of the king or his greatest magnate, in a sense parliament could not *be* a parliament in the older model of noble assemblies meeting at the king's command. Without royal assent it was no unity, no true *universitas*. Here and a little later, when Walsingham derides the

---

[36] *St. Albans Chronicle*, 54: "Post hec, ut colorem suis factis apponeret, dixit non uocandum esse parliamentum ultimo celebratum, nec in rei ueritate parliamentum fuisse, et ideo nihil debere obseruari eorum que ibidem fuere statuta. Sicque unius libidine et frustrata est spes comunis, et comodum uniuersitatis sibi soli concessit, dum solus deleuit quod universitas statuit."

undoing of the Good Parliament as being done "without the cognizance of the common people" (*praeter conscientiam communis plebis*), we see the conflict of a traditionalist notion of baronial parliaments running headlong into the newer communal understanding.[37] But the nobility as a class was neither unified nor any longer representative, in a traditional sense, in the ideological scheme of the estates. The opposition of the baronage itself had undone the strict necessity of royal will for parliamentary action. Having become a separate peerage, the magnate use of parliament became one more manifestation of a singular interest. In this case it was made all the more blatant by Gaunt's supposedly unilateral rewriting of events.[38]

Similar complaints were made by Bishop Brinton. In the previous chapter we have seen how Brinton voiced some of the strongest expressions of the ideal of social unity with both a scriptural and secular political foundation. His preaching is almost unremittingly critical but not without its own subtleties in observing the behavior of men in assembly, and the connection between communal and individual representation. In his sermon to the convocation of the clergy during the Good Parliament, probably delivered on 18 May 1376, he rails against the same faults of uselessness and fecklessness, in both clergy and laity, that trouble the St. Albans chronicler. Brinton exhorts the clergy to be fearless critics of sinners regardless of their position or standing, and he too derides parliaments – prelates, Lords and Commons – that identify and condemn wrongdoers but will not follow through with punishments.[39] Temporal lords are to blame for keeping quiet out of fear of offending the king (*tacent domini temporales quia timent offensam regis*); confessors and preachers are to blame for keeping quiet when they should correct wrongs. Brinton says they should be called not *confessores* but *confusores*, not "doctors" (*doctores*) but "traitors" (*proditores*). He concludes,

> . . . it is confirmed concerning these men – as says the Psalm (52:4), *All have gone aside, they are become unprofitable together, there is not one who doth good, no not one*, that is, no community – who effectually support the kingdom and parliament like the foundation of the republic. Do not so, reverend lords, lest our parliament be compared to the fable of the parliament of the rats and the mice . . .[40]

[37] *St. Albans Chronicle*, 100.
[38] However, many of Gaunt's undoings were re-established in the following parliaments. See the further analysis in Chapter Five.
[39] Brinton, *Sermons* 69, 316–7.
[40] Brinton, *Sermons* 69, 317: ". . . vereficetur de eis quod dicit psalmus, *Omnes declinauerunt simul inutiles facti sunt. Non est qui faciat bonum non est vsque ad vnum*, scilicet, communitatem qui tamquam rei publice fundamentum effectualiter supportant regnum et parliamentum. Non sic, domini reuerendi, sed ne parliamentum nostrum comparetur fabuloso parliamento murium et ratonum . . ."

After this follows the famous parable of the "Parliament of the Mice and the Rats" and the belling of the cat, which probably inspired Langland's version added to the Prologue of the B-version of *Piers Plowman*.[41] What stands out here – the shift Brinton makes subtly but firmly – is his unique gloss of the passage from Psalms 52:4. He mixes singular and plural terms, and persons. The Psalm laments the lack of one good man (*non est qui faciat bonum non est vsque ad vnum*), that is, "one" good individual who will follow God's commands. This lament of moral default becomes a lament about the lack of *unum bonum* specifically as *communitatem*: there is no group or community willing to stand up as a bulwark of the *res publica*, the political community of the nation as a whole. Brinton mixes the scriptural lament for a lack of a good *person* with the political lament for the lack of a good *community*, a virtuous group or estate (clerical or lay) that would effectively support the public good as a whole and not just a singular interest. "These men" (*de eis*) of his critique, the classes who are called to assembly, thus become corporate individuals whose singular interests work to the detriment of kingdom and parliament. The assembly itself cannot rely on the individuals that make up its constituencies; unities confound unity. This shift is characteristic of Brinton's desire, in this sermon and elsewhere, for a singular voice of the community, even as he recognizes the threats that individuals and individual communities face when they stick their necks out, like mice and rats among cats. What results is silence, but not just the silence of a toadying courtier or illegitimate prelate. It is the silence imposed upon the *communitas* by the very system and forum in which it is supposed to find voice and representation.

From his role as a clerical *vox clamantis*, Brinton gets to the heart of the paradox of a unified political voice drawn from the disparate communities of England at the same time that he relates the practice of a particular parliament to the tropes of curial complaint. The forum of parliament is both the best and the worst place for speaking with one voice, because it has the dynamic of a court in which "mum" – silence – will often triumph over truth-telling. A similar critique appears in Brinton's predecessor and occasional source, John Bromyard's massive *Summa Praedicantium*. Bromyard was a Dominican friar who probably studied at Oxford and eventually became the chancellor of Cambridge in 1383.[42] His *Summa*, composed between 1330 and 1352, provides encyclopedic articles used as aids for

---

[41] For further analysis, see Chapter Five.

[42] On Bromyard, see most comprehensively "Bromyard[e], John (*d. c.*1352)," *DNB* online, http://www.oxforddnb.com/view/article/3521; also Emden, *A Biographical Register of the University of Oxford to A.D. 1500*, 1.278; Boyle, "The Date of the *Summa Praedicantium* of John Bromyard."

composing sermons but that are not sermons themselves. His comments on parliaments are in the article on *consilium*, which bridges two distinct but related traditions in the medieval writing on counsel. [43] It repeats many familiar nostrums of the *Fürstenspiegel* genre and also draws heavily from the ecclesial traditions of scriptural commentary about counsel which align *parlement* with the practice of confession and ideas of prophecy and divine influence. As such it was natural to associate the theological virtue of *consilium* – one of the seven gifts of the Holy Spirit – with the practice of parliaments.

Also like Brinton, Bromyard associates parliamentary practices with an enforced and bad-faith silence of fraudulent consensus imposed by the threat of violence or retaliation. Such parliaments are called sick, the lord who relies on them one-eyed; even if there are good counsellors, often lords will not follow them; "modern parliaments" (*parlamenta moderna*) are rightly so-called because while they are full of speech (*merito vocatum est nomen eius parlamentum, quia ibi multa loquuntur*), they have little action; what is spoken there is later falsified.[44] He also describes a more subtle strategy of manipulation in which the form of common voice and the supposed representativeness of communal deliberation are retained but subverted by the actual performance of parliamentary assembly:

Therefore the root of bad counsel is in the seeking of counsel, because in recent times many do not actually seek counsel but rather determine their own counsel before seeking it. For they make up their own minds by themselves, or decide with one person secretly, what the counsel will be; and afterwards, according to plan, they call others to their councils and parliaments (*ad consilia, et parlamenta sua*), and then the business is proposed as if the lord wished to receive counsel while in doubt. But in making the proposal he adds circumstances and conditions which make one side appear worse. In this way it becomes known to which side the lord inclines, and what he determined beforehand, and what he finally wishes to have. As a consequence the prelates and the other counselors – who ought to conduct themselves there as they did in ancient times according to the fashion of priests, saying "The Lord be with you," and giving sound counsel according to God and reason – instead conduct themselves in modern counsels and parliaments in the fashion of clerics who answer, "Amen." Because in this case they see what the lords wish to be done, they reply, "Amen, so be it." And so those free men, who reproved and censured the deeds of the lords while they were in their own dwellings, before

---

[43] Unfortunately the *Summa Praedicantium*, like the rest of Bromyard's surviving oeuvre, does not have a modern edition or translation. Citations are taken from Bromyard, *Summa praedicantium omnibus Dominici gregis pastoribus* . . . (Antwerp, 1614), article s.v. "Consilium," by numbered article-distinction.

[44] Bromyard, *Summa Praedicantium*, "Consilium" 3.4–5.

they took part in the counsels of the lords, now, after they have become counselors or confessors to them, agree with them.[45]

This example of a toadying council does not refer exclusively to what we would call a "parliament" with king, Lords, and Commons, but to the general dynamics of councils and deliberation wherein the actual relations of power subvert the ostensible reason for gathering in the first place. If a lord wishes to hear good counsel, he must be open to hearing opposing viewpoints. However, in this setting the "free men" whose opinions are being solicited are actually not free, but misled and coerced. Theirs is not counsel but flattery. Extending the metaphor of a wind-blown weather-cock, Bromyard likens the assemblymen to birds in a cage. The details of the criticism also align it closely with the institutional practices of parliament and the Commons:

It is with these men in this case just as it is with birds who sing freely in the forest according to their natural inclinations, but in a bird cage (*cauea*, "place of assembly") they sing and speak just as they hear men speak there, English or French. So it is with these others who also learn the language of the country, even down to certain words. Therefore they are not birds of heaven, but of hell. They congregate on both sides, and when a plea is made by a leader or powerful man, asking how he can obtain money for wars, or for the marriage of a daughter, or of this sort, one of those – who, as chance would have it, has the first voice in the hall of the prince, and with whom the lord has conspired before they convened in counsel – responds, saying, "It is fitting that you either put a tax upon your people, or have a tenth from the church, for in your needs it is fitting that you should have recourse to your subjects." Then the lord is urged on by a second, and then a third, and all say the first man spoke well, for no one wishes to offend the lord. And finally he is even urged on by his own confessor, who says "It seems to me that they have spoken well," who, if he were not in that cage/assembly, would sing otherwise. But there, that clever bird learned to speak just as he heard the others.

---

[45] *Summa Praedicantium*, "Consilium" 8.29: "Est ergo radix mali consili in petente consilium. Quia reuera moderno tempore multi non petunt consilium, sed potius consilium determinant, antequam petant. Determinant enim apud seipsos, vel fortè cum vno secretius, quo modo erit: et postea, propter modum alios conuocant ad consilia, et parlamenta sua, et tunc negotium proponitur quasi vellet de dubio consilium accipere, sed tamen in proponendo circunstantias, et conditiones adiungit, vnam partem aggrauantes per quas cognoscitur ad quam partem dominus inclinatur, et quam prius determinauit, et quam vult finaliter habere. Praelati ergo, et alij consiliarij, qui se ibi habere deberent, sicut antiquitus solebant ad modum sacerdotum, dicentes. Dominus vobiscum, sanum consilium dando, secundum Deum et rationem, facti sunt in modernis consilijs, et parlamentis loco clericorum respondentium, amen. quia ad illud quod vident dominos velle fieri, Respondent amen: ita, fiat. Et sic illi, qui libere repraehendebant, et detrahebant factis dominorum in hospitijs suis, vel antequàm essent de consilio dominorum, postquàm fiunt consiliarij, vel confessores, eis assentiunt."

Of such a person, says Nehemiah (2 Esdras 13:24), *He [Vulg. they] spoke according to the language of the people.*[46]

"He spoke the language of the people": the example is clearly parliamentary since only parliaments (and convocations) could vote for grants of subsidy and taxation. Military funds and marriage-aids for the king's daughter were also traditional feudal dues of parliament. Critics have noted the similarity of this scenario to Chaucer's *Parliament of Fowls*.[47] While the similarity is there, Bromyard is both more caustic and more probing. It is not that the assemblymen (or the confessor, who is the particular focus of disdain) are simply stupid, bull-headed, or self-serving, but that the whole dynamic of communal voice is etiolated by the inability to speak freely. In this setting, the *cavea* of assembly, freedom becomes mere parroting and deliberative unity is false. Deliberation and language are in fact predetermined, and diabolical. Beyond this, Bromyard reaches an even deeper insight in his deployment of a unique exemplum about the "house of Provence":

Hence also it is the case with these like with those in the house of Provence in which, according to fables, there are some ring-dancers of all men's statuses. Close by this house, men passing by and looking in despise the dancers, in as much as they are behaving against their status. But those who judge them from outside, entering into the house out of curiosity or for whatever cause, dance with them, compelled by the house and by the condition of those in the house. For the house is of this nature, that everyone entering dances in the same way, and thus many, while they are poor – while they are out of offices, and councils, and dignities, and powers, and prelatures, like those outside of the house of Provence – judge those who are inside; but when they arrive at that position, they are necessitated, as they themselves say and others inform them, who say, "It is fitting for us to do so-and-so, because all our predecessors did thus, and thus our position requires": thus compelled, they dance with others whom before they judged. Concerning

---

[46] *Summa Praedicantium*, "Consilium" 8.30: "Et est de eis in hoc casu, sicut de auibus, qui in nemore libere cantant, secundùm consuetudinem naturarum, sed in cauea cantant, vel loquuntur, sicut audiunt homines ibi loqui, Anglicum, vel Gallicum, et sic de alijs: discunt enim linguam patriae, quo ad aliqua verba. Ita tales non volucres coeli, sed inferni, congregati ad inuicem, quando quaestio fit à principe, vel potente, vbi potest habere pecuniam pro guerris, vel pro matrimonio filiae, vel huiusmodi: vnus illorum qui fortè habet primam vocem in atrio principis, cum quo fuit dominus confoederatus, antequàm ad consilium conuenirent. Respondit, dicens: oportet vos habere taxam populi vestri, vel decimum denarium ecclesiae, quia ad illos subditos vestros oportet vos habere in necessitatibus vestris recursum, postea petitur à secundo, et tercio, et omnes dicunt, quòd primus benè dixit, quia nullus vult offendere. Vltimo petitur à confessore, qui dicit mihi videtur, quod benè dicunt, qui si non esset in cauea illa aliter cantaret, sed ibi auis illa ingeniosa didicit loqui, sicut alios audiuit. de quo Neae. 13. *loquebatur secundùm linguam populi.*"

[47] See McCall and Rudisill, "The Parliament of 1386 and Chaucer's Trojan Parliament," 279–81, who note this passage and its pun on *cavea*.

this, Romans 2:1 says, *for wherein thou judgest another, thou condemnest thyself. For thou dost the same things which thou judgest.*[48]

What sets this exemplum apart from the one preceding is the implicit argument, conveyed by its allegorism, that the very *structures* of assembly compel conformity. They dance (*tripudiant*) in a manner induced by the "house" where the individuals and estates gather. The dance itself is another ring-image of a gathering, like the parliamentarians of 1376 sitting around the Westmister chapterhouse or even the stones of Stonehenge. It implies a certain unity and harmony while it also plainly represents exclusion, disconnection, and solipsism, a blithe unconcern for the world outside from which the dancers come and of which they are presumably meant to be representatives. The dancers in the house of Provence are not quite like the Dancers of Kolbeck (from Mannyng's *Handlyng Synne*), insofar as they choose to enter the house and even when they are dancing, they retain their presence of mind. It is strongly reminiscent of the many enclosed structures common to medieval imaginative literature: temples and houses of glass and brass, gardens of *deduit* and delight, houses of fame and rumor that, like this one, are fundamentally ambivalent in their structured community. What happens to the counsellors and parliamentarians is co-option: outside the system they critique it, inside the system they reinforce it. It is all the more remarkable that an ecclesial figure like Bromyard would come up with such an image that is also, in a manner, a negative version of the Pentecostal ring of apostolic inspiration descended from the Holy Spirit. A demonic parody of divine assembly seems to be implied. As an image of a household, the house of Provence is both a criticism of the noble *familia* (as Bromyard later says, *qualis Dominus est, talis familia*) and a critique of foundational assumptions about harmony and unity at the national level, where the dance in the king's parliament-house could become nothing more than an empty ritual.

[48] *Summa Praedicantium*, "Consilium" 8.31: "Vnde est de eis, sicut de illis in domo Pruuinensi, in qua secundùm fabulas sunt de omnium hominum statu aliqui choreisantes. Iuxta quam homines transeuntes, et introspicientes choreisantes, vtpotè contra statum suum facientes, contemnunt. Sed illi, qui extra eos iudicant ex curiositate, vel quacunque causa domum intrantes, ex domo, et conditione illorum de domo compulsi, cum alijs tripudiant, domus enim illius est naturae, quod omnes intrantes simili modo tripudiant, ita multi dum sunt pauperes, dum sunt extra officia, et consilia, et dignitates, et potestates, et praelaturas, quasi extra domum Pruuinensem illos, qui intra sunt iudicant; sed cum ad statum illum peruenerint, necessitantur, vt ipsi dicunt, et alij eos informant, qui dicunt oportet nos sic, et sic facere, quia sic fecerunt omnes predecessores nostri, et sic status noster requirit: compulsi sic, cum alijs tripudiant quos prius iudicauerunt. Iuxta illud Ro. 2. *In quo enim alium iudicas, teipsum condemnas.* eadem enim agis, quae iudicas."

4 CONCLUSION: SPEAKING WITH ONE VOICE

Reflecting on this critical image, we can look back to the pictures of parliament in Chapter One to see them in a darker aspect. The ordered and rounded gathering of estates, supposedly representative as a forum for true speech in its social symmetry and plenitude, is also an image of the power of mum and a dangerously coercive *tripudium*. Taken together, Brinton and Bromyard offer a critical perspective on the possibilites of communal representation and collective action available through the formal structures of council and parliament. Brinton's *canes muti* and Bromyard's toadying sycophants and self-satisfied dancers resonate with such figures as the ill-counselled and incorrigible (and eventually blinded, and unblinded) January of Chaucer's *Merchant's Tale*; the headlong and ill-advised Trojan parliament of *Troilus and Criseyde*; the large-speaking but little-doing parliament in *The Parliament of Fowls*, as well as the parliament of the mice and the rats in *Piers Plowman*; and the parliament of devils in John Gower's *Mirour de l'Omme*. The criticism of councils and parliaments as ideologically manipulative also contextualizes the bureaucratic visions of later parliament-poems such as *Mum and the Sothsegger*, where we find another competing image of a house or *familia* in the freehold of the Franklin beekeeper. By the time of these later poems, the events of parliaments such as 1376 and 1388 had demonstrated just how problematic and conflictual parliaments could be, but at the same time, how important and effectual.

What these critiques thus also demonstrate – however negatively – is a brief period, in between the earlier representation of councils and parliaments as predominantly magnate affairs and the later literary representations of "council" and counsel in the *Fürstenspiegel* genre, when the discourse of *parlement* focused on the possibilities of communal representation in the framework of a specifically parliamentary voice. From baronialism to princely advices, there was, in short, a brief period of parliamentarism proper. Nothing demonstrates this so strongly as the critiques, criticisms, and abuses that parliament itself was subject to for the first time. This process of conceptual development, which brings us to the last quarter of the fourteenth century, was thus in large part a *literary* development as well, using "literary" as a cover-term for the lively intersection of the chronicles and poetry, scriptures and exegesis, political events and documentary records, that were involved in the public development of parliament, both as an idea and as an institution.

Of all these sources and examples reviewed here, most of which can be securely dated, the last passage I want to consider is the most emblematic and enigmatic. To again turn to the *Modus Tenendi Parlia-mentum*, its seventeenth chapter, *De Casibus et Judiciis Difficilibus*, outlines a process for arriving at a decision when parliament deliberates on some difficult or intractable matter. In it we can see the fantasy of univocal voice combined with the ideal of a personified and individualized collective in a manner that is utterly fictional but still historically representative of the dis-cursive tradition I have outlined here. For best understanding, the section requires quotation in full:

When a dispute, doubt, or difficult case arises of peace or of war, within or without the kingdom, that case is to be referred and recited in writing in full parliament, and debated and discussed there among the peers of parliament . . . And if there is discord between the King and some magnates, or perhaps between the magnates themselves, whereby the King's peace is undermined, and the people as well as the land is afflicted, so that it seems to the King and his Council that it would be expedient for the matter to be considered and settled by the advice of all the peers of the realm; or if the King and the kingdom is afflicted by war, or if a difficult case comes before the chancellor of England, or a difficult judgement pending before the justices needs to be rendered, and such like – if by chance in these matters all or even the greater part are not able to agree then the earl steward, the earl constable, and the earl marshal, or two of them shall elect twenty-five persons from all the peers of the kingdom, that is to say two bishops and three proctors for all the clergy, two earls and three barons, five knights of the shire, five citizens and five burgesses, which make twenty-five, and these twenty-five can elect twelve from among themselves if they wish and reduce into them, and these twelve can reduce into six, and these six into three and reduce into them, but these three cannot reduce themselves further unless they obtain leave from the Lord King, and if the King agrees, these three may become two, and of these two one can decline into the other, and in that case only his ruling will stand above the whole parliament, and so by the reduction of twenty-five persons to one person only, unless the greater number have been able to agree and decide, then this one person, as stated, who cannot disagree with himself, shall decide for all; reserving only to our Lord the King and his Council the power to examine and amend these ordinances after they have been written, if they know how and so wish, so that it shall then be done in full parliament, and with the consent of parliament and not behind the back of parliament.[49]

---

[49] *Modus*, 74–5, 87–8: "Cum briga, dubitatio seu casus difficilis pacis vel guerre emergat in regno vel extra, referatur et recitetur casus ille in scriptis in pleno Parliamento, et tractetur et disputetur ibidem inter pares Parliamenti . . . Et si per discordiam inter regem et aliquos magnates, vel forte inter ipsos magnates, pax regni infirmetur, vel populus vel patria tribuletur, ita quod vidatur regi et eius consilio quod expediens sit quod negotium illud tractetur et emendetur per considerationem omnium parium regni sui vel si per guerram rex et regnum suum tribulentur, vel si casus difficilis coram cancellario Anglie emergat, seu iudicium difficile coram iusticiariis fuerit reddendum, et huiusmodi, et si forte in huiusmodi deliberationibus omnes vel saltim maior pars concordare non valeant, tunc comes

This entire scenario calls for comment and explication. It should be stressed that the bizarre mechanism of the "committee of twenty-five," which Kerby-Fulton and Justice have called the "self-abolishing committee," resembles nothing ever put into practice in any recorded parliament.[50] Very generally, the desire to distill a committee or representative panel (a small group of elected representatives with the power to determine policy or to set an agenda) does resemble the repeated efforts to establish ruling or advisory baronial councils throughout the thirteenth and fourteenth centuries. Such efforts were made in various forms, with almost clock-like regularity, in 1215, 1258, 1297, 1311, 1316, 1341, 1376, 1386, 1388, and 1406. The idea of a council drawn from parliament (directly or indirectly) was thus nothing new or striking. The number of councillors, twenty-five, is also approximately the number for a legally recognized jury or quorum. What *is* striking, as has been noted, is, first, the preponderance of weight given to representatives of the lower estates on the committee (fifteen out of twenty-five positions), which would potentially provide a numerical quorum against the magnates and upper prelates. Second, the mechanism for distilling even this small council further, "the reduction of twenty-five persons to one person only" whose "ruling will stand above the whole parliament," is both strange and strangely logical. It seems consciously evocative of a sorites paradox wherein by degrees of reduction, the representativeness of the committee is asymptotically focused while its identity, and its ability to speak for the *communitas regni* and *communitas parliamenti*, remains. The reluctance to impose division – for if there are twenty-five committee members, why not simply submit the *casus difficilis* to a majority vote? – is the implicit reason for continually reducing it to the point where, as a single man, the representative can no longer even *threaten* to divide, as

senescallus, comes constabularius et comes marescallus, vel duo eorum, eligent viginti et quinque personas de omnibus paribus regni, scilicet duos episcopos, et tres procuratores, pro toto clero, duos comites et tres barones, quinque milites comitatuum, quinque cives et burgenses, qui faciunt viginti quinque; et illi viginti quinque possunt eligere ex seipsis, si velint, duodecim et condescendere in eis, et ipsi duodecim sex et condescendere in eis, et ipsi sex adhuc tres et condescendere in eis, et illi tres se in paucioribus condescendere non possunt, nisi optenta licentia a domino rege, et si rex consentiat illi tres possunt in duos, et de illis duobus alter potest in alium descendere et ita demum stabit sua ordinatio supra totum Parliamentum; et ita condescendo a viginti quinque personis usque in unam solam personam, nisi numerus maior concordare valeat et ordinare, tandem sola persona, ut est dictum, pro omnibus ordinabit, que cum se ipsa discordare non potest; salvo domino regi et eius concilio quod ipsi huiusmodi ordinationes postquam scripte fuerint examinare et emendare valeant, si hoc facere sciant et velint, ita quod hoc fiat ibidem tunc in pleno Parliamento, et de consensu Parliamenti, et non retro Parliamentum."

50 Kerby-Fulton and Justice, "Reformist Intellectual Culture," 162. Clarke, *Medieval Representation and Consent*, 189–90, attempts to relate this procedure to the deposition proceedings of 1327, a view that has not gained much support.

one person who "cannot disagree with himself." Whatever the date of the *Modus*, from this remarkable passage it is clear that the substrate desire for consensus still drives its vision of the assembly, especially in matters where "all or even the greater part are not able to agree."

Of all the representations of representation and of all the procedural expressions of communal voice we have encountered, this is perhaps the most striking, and the most ideologically revealing. The twin ideals of multiplicity and unity, of *communitas* and *unitas*, are made to meet in the impossible but single voice of the parliamentary representative who stands both *over* parliament and across from, or opposite, the king. This "speaker" is therefore not reducible to the king himself nor to the abstraction of sovereign power. It is, by design, an other of the king, a figure – like an Earl Simon, Henry Keighley, William Trussell, Peter de la Mare, or (men we will meet later) Thomas Haxey, or Arnold Savage – who could speak to the king with the authority of the community and with a voice authorized by the sovereign by virtue of the mirrored authority of the king's parliament. As both an image and a fiction, the *Modus*'s committee-to-one is a perfect (and perfectly imaginary) objective correlative for the entire ideology of late medieval parliament and *parlement*, the desire to speak and be heard with one voice. The parliamentary representative as an ideal figure – if not necessarily as a single idealized person – would stand as the embodiment of communal will and as the single form or body, to return to the images with which we started, for enveloping all of the disparate voices gathered into one place as regional representatives. Indeterminately baronial, clerical, communal, and royal, this voice would be a final hypostasization of community beyond which there would need be no other.

Again it is necessary to emphasize that what we have here is a fiction or a dream. But in form, this fiction is commensurate with, and in some ways indistinguishable from, the artistic images of unity-in-multiplicity that populate all of later medieval poetry in its most accomplished forms: a community desperately seeking its representative speaker and leader in the elusive voice of a single Plowman; the disparate and noisy estates alternately speaking, and then falling silent, before the voice of an authoritative Parson; and the insistent but troubled voice of a single *vox clamantis* that speaks out in a multitude of identities and that stands both within and outside of the world that is its target of complaint. In proceeding forward to Langland, Chaucer and Gower, it is the changed image of communal voice that stands out as the most important legacy of the baronialist and scriptural roots of the parliamentary tradition. Each of these poets chose to write about parliaments real and fanciful, but more fundamentally they also chose (or were inclined) to write with this parliamentary form in mind, in a manner unique to the environment of late medieval English public discourse, where a new communal perspective had decisively taken shape. Understanding the background of this change helps us appreciate why, at this point in literary history, the best poets were occupied with the artistic representation of complaint, common voice, and parliamentary practices that had become so important for the nation as a whole. To these poets we can now turn our attention.

CHAPTER 3

Property, purchase, and parliament: the estates of man in John Gower's Mirour de l'Omme *and* Cronica Tripertita

In the middle of the *Mirour de l'Omme*, in his explication of the virtue of Charity, Gower refers to a proverb that emerges, over the course of his career, as one of his favorites:

> Ly sage ce nous vait disant,
> Solonc que pueple vait parlant
> L'estat de l'omme s'appara:
> Escript auci j'en truis lisant,
> Au vois commune est acordant
> La vois de dieu . . .
>
> (12721–6)[1]

[The wise man tells us that as people speak, so the state of man (*l'estat de l'omme*) appears; and I also find written that to the common voice is accordant the voice of God . . .] (174)

The *sage* or "wise man" is indeterminate. It could be either King Solomon, who provides the exemplum preceding this, or Cato, who comes after and advises his son not to praise or blame himself; or it could be neither, the impersonalized voice of moral authority. The proverb here, however, is clearly a version of *vox populi vox Dei*, the voice of the people is the voice of God, the pseudo-biblical proof-text preached at Edward II's deposition. Fittingly Gower makes this bit of folk-wisdom illocatable, not saying precisely *where* he finds it written. But the crux of this small passage hinges less on this than on its questionable applicability to the topic at hand. Why should a version of *vox populi vox Dei* – an impersonal sentiment if there ever was one – crop up in the *Mirour*'s analysis of charity, and specifically in

---

[1] All citations of Gower's works are from *The Complete Works of John Gower*, 4 vols., ed. Macaulay. Translations of the *Mirour* are from Wilson, trans., *Mirour de l'Omme (The Mirror of Mankind)*; translations of Gower's Latin works (*Vox Clamantis* and *Cronica Tripertita*) are from Stockton, trans., *The Major Latin Works of John Gower*. I have made occasional changes to the translations.

the matter of moral praise and blame? Ostensibly it comes at the moment of personal (and interpersonal) examination, at the point in the catalog of vices and virtues when the subject of individual self-exploration meets external criticism, and at the point of its public expression. This is when *l'estat de l'omme s'appara*: the state or estate of "Man" – a single individual but also *l'omme* of the entire work's title, man as image of society – comes forward in the realm of speech, *parlant* (12722). In this *parlement*, this speaking, man surfaces for praise or blame, benediction or detraction. Gower's juxtaposition of this almost phenomenological appearance with the *vois commune* thus joins the estate of *l'omme* with the voice that would judge it. It is a voice that is itself both singular and communal, simultaneously mundane and sacral.

For the reader of his poetry, each of these thematic elements is recognizably Gowerian. He was, of all his contemporary poets, the one most overtly concerned with the public voice and moral use of his verse. Individual moralism is everywhere combined in his works with public comment and criticism. In this regard it is both fitting and frustrating to begin with John Gower as a "parliamentary" poet – certainly not a title normally ascribed to him – precisely for the reason that his work is so self-consciously the labor of a public poet, but one with such a vexed relationship to the very idea of the "public." Most criticism of the last thirty years has rightly stressed the troubled *conjointure* of political and personal ethics in Gower's works, particularly in Gower's framing of kingship and the poet's own public voice.[2] Indeed the two can hardly be separated. As Russell Peck has succinctly summarized it, Gower's engagement with political forms provides the basis for exactly those moments of personal examination that loom so large in his works: "when exploring man's individual psyche he turns to metaphors of state; when criticizing the state he conceives of a common body."[3] Gower's dissections of the "estate of man" thus always have at least two valences: an inquiry into the moral condition of man and also into the nature of *estate*, of political and hence propertied arrangement. The poet himself is both

[2] In this line of criticism see Peck, *Kingship and Common Profit in Gower's Confessio Amantis*, and more recently "The Politics and Psychology of Governance in Gower: Ideas of Kingship and Real Kings"; Coffman, "John Gower, Mentor for Royalty; Richard II"; Porter, "Gower's Ethical Microcosm and Political Macrocosm"; Stow, "Richard II in John Gower's *Confessio Amantis*: Some Historical Perspectives"; Stillwell, "John Gower and the Last Years of Edward III"; Galloway, "Gower in His Most Learned Role and the Peasants' Revolt of 1381"; Scanlon, *Narrative, Authority, and Power: The Medieval Exemplum and the Chaucerian Tradition*, 245–97; Grady, "The Lancastrian Gower and the Limits of Exemplarity".
[3] Peck, *Kingship and Common Profit*, xxi; see also Yeager, *John Gower's Poetic*, 265–79.

within and without the social dyad he critically represents, introducing a third element that is both conjunctive and disjunctive. In his analysis, the "voice of God" is never far from the poet's own voice. But the complex amalgam of the three – divine guidance, poetical art, public significance – meshes elements that can join only in tension, and, as here in this small moment in the *Mirour*, somewhat obliquely.

That oblique relationship is the focus of this chapter, in the context of two of Gower's relatively understudied but important works: the Anglo-French *Mirour de l'Omme* and the Latin *Cronica Tripertita*, from the start and the end of his literary career respectively. Although parliamentary elements do also appear in his other major works – especially the *Confessio Amantis*, which has several stories with parliaments prominent in them – in the interests of both focus and space, I will limit my analysis to these poems and to the records of Gower's involvement with parliament. These texts and contexts speak to one another, and there are thematic and structural elements connecting them and their uses of parliament.

Of the known poets of this study, John Gower has the dubious distinction of being the only one whose name actually appears in parliamentary rolls. The context of that appearance is both intriguing and troubling. He was involved in a legal case in 1365–6 that made its way to the high court of parliament and trial before the Lords. For many years (since his involvement was first confirmed by his modern editor, G. C. Macaulay), the case has been a blot on the poet's reputation. Like the infamous records of the rape quitclaim involving Chaucer and Cecily Chaumpaign, the records of Gower's involvement in the "Septvauns affair" are ambiguous, legally and ethically. And as with Chaucer and the Chaumpaign case, the Septvauns affair touches on elements of enduring concern to Gower's work. In all probability the events unfolded before Gower's major works were written and before he embarked on his career as a public poet, beginning with the *Mirour de l'Omme*. The date of this large work can only be conjectured to have a *terminus ad quem* of about 1377, and it may have been composed in several stages.[4] Although not in English (it was the last major work written in Anglo-French), the *Mirour* is important to the English literary tradition for inaugurating the prototypically Miltonic scene of the "Devils' Parliament." The *Mirour* served as a template for Gower's later projects, and in turn the *Cronica Tripertita*, Gower's

---

[4] See Wetherbee, "John Gower"; Yeager, "Politics and the French Language in England During the Hundred Years' War," and "John Gower's French."

career-concluding account of the downfall of Richard II, provides a fascinating contrast because it exploits, decades later, many of the same foundational tropes.

For this analysis, both the *Mirour* and the *Cronica* stand out not just because of their representations of parliaments, but more because of the way Gower uses parliaments to structure these texts of personal and political criticism. This aspect of his poetry has gone unremarked, although as we shall see, it in no way contradicts his generally elitist bourgeois perspective and his frank disdain for the very "commons" he presumes to speak for. Indeed, much the opposite: as I will argue here, Gower's subtle but insistent use of the tropes of parliament and *parlement* underlies his representations of a noble *proprietas* or *propreté*, "property" in the root sense of "self," a figuration of sovereign and ethical individuality. For Gower, parliamentary form is a way to speak – successfully or not – to the crisis of a *lack* of "proper" communicative ability, both within and between the conjoined and disjoined members, the *propre*, of a body politic. Parliaments are, in short, the allegorical form of the very individuals he wants to critique, *and* the metonymical form of the voice, the *vox publica*, he adopts to do so.

A close look at the Septvauns affair helps to enrich the terms of this formulation, and so I will proceed from the law-case to a reading of the *Mirour*. The *Mirour* shares not only the Anglo-French language of parliament and the law; it also exploits the specific legal-parliamentary terms and concepts of the courts for its troubled allegory and overall argument about social reform. My reading proceeds from back to front, analyzing the castigations against lawyers in the estates' criticism of the second part against the Devil's Parliament of the first part. From there, the *Cronica Tripertita* provides a challenging coda to Gower's attempt to speak, critically, with the one voice of an authoritative moral vision for the nation of England. As the *Mirour* and the *Cronica* make clear, Gower's search for a proper voice, one that was both personal and public, led him both to adopt and to critique a form of parliamentary *vox communis*, to the point in the *Cronica* of collapsing his own writing with it. But even to the end of his career, Gower's poetry is haunted by the threats of division and *debat*, social and personal, inherent in his vocational practice as the representative speaker of the *vox populi*. This sense of a fractured self – or of an alienated *propria* – comes to characterize Gower's poetry as much as its desire for resolution and unity, as both are dependent not upon "kingship" but upon his quasi-parliamentary position as a common speaker.

I THE SEPTVAUNS AFFAIR OF 1365–6

The controversy was a property dispute, and the details of Gower's involvement can be briefly summarized.[5] In 1351 Sir William de Septvauns, the lord of Aldington Septvauns manor (adjacent to Aldington Cobham manor in Kent) died and left his property to his minor son, William, who was a royal ward.[6] Thirteen years later, at the time of his mother's death in September 1364, young William established his age in escheat proceedings in Kent, asserting that he was twenty-one years old and thus of full age to possess and sell his properties. This he did, selling his Aldington property to John Gower (among others) in 1365. The sale was part of a large and quick liquidation of some of the Septvauns assets.

However, that same year, John de Cobham of Cooling, the third Baron Cobham and the owner of neighboring Cobham manor, initiated a legal inquiry into William's majority. It was asserted that in fact he would not be twenty-one until May 1366 – that is, that William was three years younger than he asserted himself to be – and that his alienation of the properties, including the Aldington property, was therefore illegal. Because it involved the alienation of crown lands held by a tenant *in capite*, potentially in derogation to the king, the case was brought before a royal commission of inquiry and eventually before parliament. The commission was charged to determine the ward's true age, and if proved to still be a minor, "to ascertain by whom the previous proof was made and by whose procurement, imagination, and information, who had been in possession of the lands since the said proof, in whose company the heir has been and by whom he has been counselled and led . . . and what profit the king has lost by reason of the incorrect proof of age."[7] In other words, the commission was to determine who had put the idea into young William's head to prematurely (and hence illegally) sell his lands. Once his age had been definitively determined by new witnesses, the Septvauns lands would be reassessed and, if necessary, reseised into royal wardship. Any contracts made would

---

[5] The details and documents of the affair have been treated editorially by Macaulay in *Complete Works*, 4. xi–xv; and biographically by Fisher, *John Gower, Moral Philosopher and Friend of Chaucer*, 51–4 and 313–18.

[6] For a full family genealogy see Tower, "The Family of Septvans."

[7] Fisher, *John Gower*, 51–2. See the translation of the *Calendar of Inquisitions Post Mortem, Edward III*, given by Fisher, 314; and the transcript entered into the parliamentary rolls, *RP* 2.291: ". . . per quos vel per quem probatio etatis sue predicte facta fuit, & ad quorum vel cujus procuracionem, imaginacionem, seu informacionem, & quis vel qui terras & ten' predicta a tempore probacionis etatis predicte occuparunt . . . & in cujus comitiva dictus heres a tempore predicto extitit, & per quem vel per quos consiliatus & deductus fuit."

be nullified, and any losses to the king or wastes of the property would be recovered.

Ultimately it was determined that William Septvauns Jr. had in fact been a minor, and the sale of his lands and properties was voided. Of the several people involved in the matter, one of the names most frequently mentioned is John Gower's. He was not the only man involved in the purchases – he bought about half of the property in question – but he figures prominently because he was adept at maneuvering his way through the maze of documentation. A "sale" of this sort, which was really an exchange of royal property between two leaseholders, was a highly formalized affair, one susceptible to problems of bad documentation or ill-executed procedure. Gower appears to have anticipated this. In March 1365, at the time of the sale, he made a Chancery inquisition (an *inquisitio ad quod damnum*) into whether his purchase would be to the detriment of the Crown and thus probably illegal. A while later he received clearance for his purchase after paying a nominal fine. He also had the writs and charters of his purchases enrolled in Chancery, helping to ensure the formal legality of the sale. As Fisher notes dryly, all of this parchment-shuffling and documentation was done with "more than the usual formality" because Gower apparently realized that "this was a sticky wicket."[8] These Crown-authorized preemptions would stand him in good stead if the sales were later challenged.

About a year later, in the records of the parliament of March–May 1366, the official account of the Septvauns affair takes up about half of the entire roll, and it does indeed indicate just how sticky this wicket was. On 11 May, the Septvauns case was presented to the Lords and Commons by Thomas Ludlow, the Chief Baron of the Exchequer. In full parliament, Ludlow summarized how the Septvauns "lands and tenements were delivered out of his (i.e. the king's) possession, to his deceit and great damage," because the heir William had been under-age, as demonstrated by the new inquest.[9] The assembly rendered judgment against the sales which were reversed by parliamentary decree.[10] There is a brief statement that all of the "charters, writs, and obligations" resulting from the unlawful alienation are quashed and annulled (*cassez & adnulleez*). After recording the parliament's adjournment, the roll records the pertinent commissions to determine "by whom he [Septvauns] was counseled and misled" (*per quem vel per quos consiliatus et deductus fuit*). Gower is named as one of the men enfeoffed

---

[8] Fisher, *John Gower*, 51 and 334 n. 53; *Complete Works*, 4.xi.
[9] *RP* 2.291: ". . . & par une proeve de l'age le dit William meins verroi faite mesmes les Terres & Tenementz mys & liverez hors de la possession le Roi, a grande damage & deceite de lui . . ."
[10] *RP* 2.292–3.

with Septvauns' tenements and, more pointedly, as one of his counselors in the affair:

... at which time the said William, son of William, enfeoffed in the said tenements one John Gower, to hold to him and his heirs for ever ... by virtue of which feoffment the said John Gower has occupied the said tenements, from the said Feast of the Nativity of our Lord until now, and still occupies them ...

And they say that, after the foresaid feoffment made to the foresaid John Gower, the said William, son of William, was continuously abiding in the company of Richard Hurst and the said John Gower, at Canterbury and elsewhere, until the feast of St. Michael last past, and throughout the whole of that time the said William, son of William, was there led away by them, and counselled to alienate his lands and tenements ...[11]

Records of this tone outline the case, both in the parliamentary documentation and the enrollments in the Exchequer. From them we learn that Gower acquired a significant stake in Aldington Manor, other properties and rents plus some cash owed him, and – in a homely detail – "13 hens, one cock, and 140 eggs in Maplescompe."[12]

So while the legal parameters of the Septvauns affair are relatively clear, the ethical implications are more complex. These records are fairly damning of Gower and the other men involved with young William. While ultimately no real harm was done to the noble estate of William Septvauns, this episode appears in the record much as it must have appeared at the time, as a problematic case of exploitation and misappropriation involving a fatherless young nobleman. Macaulay, with late Victorian dudgeon, declared it impossible that John Gower the "grave moralist" was the same John Gower, "the villainous misleader of youth who is described to us in the report of the above commission, as encouraging a young man to defraud the Crown by means of perjury, in order that he may purchase his lands from him at a nominal price."[13] And indeed it appears, as Fisher admits, "to

[11] See "L. B. L." [Lambert B. Larking], "'Probatio tatis' of William de Septvans," 129–30; *RP* 2.291–2: "... quo tempore idem Willelmus filius Willelmi quendam Johannem Gower de tenementis illis feoffavit, tenendum sibi & heredibus suis imperpetuum ... Virtute cujus foeffamenti idem Johannes Gower eadem tenementis occupavit a dicto Festo Natalis Domini usque nunc, & adhuc occupat, & exitus & proficua inde continue percepit ... Et dicunt, quod post predictum feoffamentum factum predicto Johanni Gower, dictus Willelmus filius Willelmi continue morabatur in comitiva Ricardi de Hurst, & ejusdem Johannis Gower, apud Cantuariensis & alibi usque ad Festum Sancti Michaelis ultimo preteritum, & per totum tempus predictum idem Willelmus filius Willelmi ibidem pers ipsos deductus fuit & consiliatus ad alienacionem de terris & tenementis suis faciendum ...". See also Fisher, 314–15.

[12] Fisher, *John Gower*, 317 and 334 n. 53.

[13] *Complete Works*, 4.xv; Fisher, *John Gower*, 53. Macaulay's disapproval was exacerbated by his misreading of the purchase price as 24 marks and not, properly, 80 marks (*quater-viginti marcas*): *RP* 2.292 (the error is noted by Fisher, 53 and 318.)

be something of a mess."[14] Fisher offers a more defensive view, arguing that other factors militate against interpreting Gower's role as a nefarious one. First, his purchase was only part of what appears to have been a veritable Septvauns fire-sale. William liquidated large portions of his family assets in order to make good on a debt of over a thousand pounds: £1000 owed to one Nicholas de Loveyne and a further £60 owed directly to Gower. Leaving aside the question of how the young Septvauns fell into this debt, it, not manipulation by the purchasers, appears to have been the reason for the sale. Second, the legal inquisition was motivated primarily by the question of the Crown's rights and the loss of income from escheat holdings, not (as Fisher puts it) "to ascertain whether the heir had been defrauded."[15] Lastly – and most interestingly – Gower's own purchases were so well executed, and so thoroughly documented, that they eventually withstood all challenges. At the end of the parliamentary record there is a rider, missing from the Exchequer exemplifications, making exceptions for those purchasers who could prove in Chancery that they had due legal right to the land despite the sales' nullification.[16] Gower's prudent inquisitions, preemptions, and documentary enrollments stood him in good stead: his claim was eventually awarded to him in 1369.

These points notwithstanding, a more critical view of the proceedings could be taken that, while not condemning Gower as a villainous misleader of youth, is still sensitive to their ambiguity. While it is partly correct to assert that the inquiries were taken on behalf of the Crown rather than Septvauns, the parliamentary record makes it clear that fraud against both the Crown and the heir was very much the issue. William is repeatedly described as having been misled and ill-counseled, and the king as "deceived" (*decepti eramus*) and "falsely informed" (*falso informatam*).[17] The purchasers under inquiry were thus liable for a double breach: personally against the heir, with whom they are depicted as having kept company in a deliberate attempt to misguide; and publicly, against the estate of the king, whose income was affected by the awarding of wardships and the collection of escheat revenues. It was, clearly enough, a case involving both personal tort and the public weal – public and private estate – and it was presented in parliament as such. The Lords in parliament in 1366 were thus putatively speaking "for" the king and Septvauns by protecting the royal demesne and the inheritance of a noble family, as the Crown's loss of such sources of revenue was a constant topic of parliamentary anxiety. But also, as the records suggest,

---

[14] Fisher, *John Gower*, 53.   [15] Fisher, *John Gower*, 53.
[16] Fisher, *John Gower*, 53–4, 318; *RP* 2.293.   [17] *RP* 2.291.

the purchasers come across as tempting devils, pernicious agents working for the derogation of the king by trying sinfully to defraud and disinherit one of his loyal tenants.

We have no way of knowing what Gower's reaction was to all of this, nor if he was present during the actual judgment of the case. But he was undoubtedly aware of what was happening, because his name was being publicized in unwelcome ways. Whatever the actual disposition of the principal purchasers, one of the most revealing aspects of the whole affair is, with regard to Gower, the ultimate ineffectiveness of the parliamentary ruling. Because he had performed his own prior inquisition and documentation – effectively beating the commission to the punch – he was eventually awarded his purchases. Later he was able to sell them for a healthy sum.[18]

So while it is true that Gower and the others were men of station and reputation (some, like Cobham, also associated with Chaucer[19]), this was precisely the problem. Skillful lawyers and bureaucrats knew how to work the system because the system largely depended on them.[20] This intense moment of antagonism against the Septvauns purchasers looks, from a distance, like an example of someone being made an example of. The case is presented, and scrupulously documented, as a public demonstration of parliament's readiness to protect both king and noble subject – neither of whom speak for themselves during the whole process – and the subject positions of victim, victimizer(s), and protectors are studiously constructed by the parliamentary record.

This theatrical dimension is also reinforced by other events in this otherwise unremarkable assembly. The record notes parliament's showy refusal, *par commune Assent*, to submit to the Pope's demand for homage of one thousand marks annually.[21] And on the same day as the presentation of the Septvauns case before full parliament, the king presented, for full parliamentary assent, his daughter Isabella's marriage to Enguerrand de Coucy of France. This was purely a formal matter, but one well within the feudal traditions of parliamentary ritual. The assembly "accorded with one assent" to the marriage (*d'une assent acorderent*) and left the king to bestow appropriate lands on de Coucy. He was awarded the earldom of Bedford.[22]

---

[18] Fisher, *John Gower*, 53–4 and 334–5 n. 56; Macaulay, vol. 4, xiv–xv.

[19] John de Cobham was an MP for Kent starting in 1355, later a JP for Kent with Chaucer in 1385 and 1386: see *Chaucer Life-Records*, 348–63. also *DNB* 4:611–12.

[20] See Musson and Ormrod, *The Evolution of English Justice*, 139–60.   [21] *RP* 2.289–90.

[22] *RP* 2.290–1. See Powell and Wallis, *The House of Lords*, 365–6, who downplay the importance of the Commons' presence during the Septvauns proceedings.

In this context, the Septvauns case takes on a richer significance, not as just a property dispute or problematic purchase but as a public spectacle. Like the refusal of papal exactions and the ritual solemnification of a royal marriage, the reseising of the Septvauns properties was another example of parliament working for the "common good," protecting the fiscal interests of nation, Crown, and nobility alike. It was an act well within the familiar but already dated framework of feudal property customs. But this action comes at the expense of other money-and-mercantile-minded figures, John Gower one among them, and with the foregrounding of one man, William Septvauns, as the subject of misdirection, communal inquisition, and royal judgment.

2 DAMNED LAWYERS AND DEVILISH PURCHASES IN *MIROUR DE L'OMME* PART II

We will return in a bit to the feudal ideological overtones of the Septvauns affair. As Fisher notes, the case also reveals a Gower who was, in practice and apparent disposition, similar to Chaucer's Sergeant of the Law, that "noble purchasour"; the allusion to Gower by the Man of Law may have been motivated, however distantly, by the memory of Gower's own dexterity at purchasing.[23] Certainly the larger issues suggested by this affair are not simply questions of technical legal procedure but of speaking and voice, and of the proper or improper purchase of this noble inheritance. The commission's inquisition, as well as the legal record, focuses on the question of who was speaking for Septvauns and who was leading him to misrepresent himself. Correlatively, the parliament is presented as making the final, authoritative judgment on the matter and as speaking for the public good. And yet the ultimate disposition of the subject-positions of the affair – victim(s), exploiter(s), and defender(s) – is anything but clear. Interpreted with different sympathies, each of the principal actors could plausibly occupy any position, and the purchasers no doubt felt they were doing young Septvauns a good turn by providing him the means to get out of debt. With this complexity in mind, it becomes clearer how Gower's *Mirour* raises similar problems of licit voice and speaking position. Not only these specific concerns of manipulation and misrepresentation, but also the forms of representation themselves, emerge as central and conflicted elements.

[23] Fisher, *John Gower*, 56–7, 287.

While the Septvauns affair demonstrates Gower's dexterity with the bureaucracy, it also hints at his own liminal and potentially ambiguous status as a lawyer, or, possibly, as a clerk of the Chancery where property cases were treated.[24] If he was in fact a lawyer, then in the *Mirour* he denounced, with characteristic severity, the same professionally murky behavior he practiced as a younger man. In the second section of the *Mirour* devoted to criticism of the estates, condemnation of the "legal estate" – judges, lawyers, sheriffs, bailiffs, jurors – occupies an outsized proportion of the portraits overall: 996 lines, compared to 587 for knights and men at arms, 323 lines against merchants, 479 criticizing artificers and vitaillers, and so on. He rails against the abuses specific to each position, but from the beginning he views the legal professions as one estate uniquely positioned to offend everyone:

> Une autre gent y ad, du quoy
> L'en poet oïr murmur en coy,
> Par les paiis communement
> Chascuns se plaint endroit de soi;
> C'est une gent nomé du loy,
> Mais le noun portont vuidement . . .
> (24181–6)

[There is another set of people of whom one can hear quiet murmuring. Throughout the country everyone is complaining about them. They are called the men of law, but the name they bear is an empty one . . .] (316)

The legal professions are all tarred with the same brush of covetousness and dishonesty. They offend both the high and the low and provoke common complaint: "The common people of the country are crying out and complaining of this, and so do the lords and ladies" (Dont font lour plaintes et lour cris / La gent commune de paiis, / Si font le seignour et la dame [25162–4]). Although all of Gower's estates-criticisms are habitually framed as "the common complaint," the complaints against the legal estate are particularly notable for their offense to, and outcry from, the commonalty. The lawyer will not advocate for the poor, "no matter how loud they clamor" (pour null clamour escoulte pas [24222]); pleaders and advocates enrich themselves from "the common good" (se font richir / Del bien commun [24340–1]); and sheriffs, who should protect "the common law" for "the profit of the community" (la loy commune . . . au proufit de

---

[24] On Gower's probable status as a lawyer see Fisher, *John Gower*, Ch. 2; Hines, Cohen, and Roffey, "*Iohannes Gower, Armiger, Poeta*: Records and Memorials of his Life and Death."

communalté [24818, 24823]), have become corrupt oppressors and exploiters of the system.

In particular, law-men offend against the community by offending against the king with their ill-gotten gains of *pourchas* (et leur maltolt et leur pourchas), which the king should rectify by taking from the takers and reverting it to the "common good" (au bien commun doit revertir) (24343–5). Throughout the portrait of the legal estate, *pourchas* stands forth as a characteristic evil: if lawyers are particularly offensive, purchasing is their particular offense.[25] But purchasing *per se* is not always evil. There are examples in the Mirour where *pourchas* and the activities of the *pourchaçour* are presented indifferently.[26] What exercises Gower is "purchasing" as *fraude* or *tricherie* (24932, 24934), that is, as the acquisition of other people's property (or wealth) by manipulation. These sorts of legal shenanigans are repeatedly figured as machinations or *engins* (24505) and damnable deceptions. The most prominent example is a case of disinheritance arranged by a sheriff (*visconte*) manipulating a jury to testify about the age of an heir, a scenario that sounds remarkably close to the Septvauns affair:

> O le conspir, o le brocage,
> Dont l'en requiert, prie et brocage,
> Qe le visconte aider voldra
> A luy qui d'autri l'eritage
> Demande avoir de son oultrage!
> Car il les larges douns dorra,
> Dont le visconte avoeglera,
> Qui le panell ordeinera
> Des fals jurours a l'avantage
> De luy q'ad tort. O quoy serra,
> Qant homme ensi pourchacera?
> Dont n'est celly qui n'ad dammage.
>
> (24889–900)

[O the conspiracy, O the intrigue (*brocage*) with which one requests, begs, and bribes the sheriff so that he will help the man who is trying outrageously to get someone else's inheritance! For by giving generous gifts it is possible to blind the sheriff so that he will set up a panel of false jurors to the advantage of the dishonest man who is doing wrong. O what shall happen when a man thus procures something dishonestly (*pourchacera*)? There is no one who is not thereby injured.] (326)

---

[25] On this see Fisher, *John Gower*, 56–7.

[26] For compartive examples, see *Mirour* 5839–44; 23750–1; 23817–20; 5441; 7217–18; 14431–3. Generally *pourchacer* is the negative or ambiguous counterpart to *marchander*, the verb used more often for positive aspects of the estate of Merchants. For this contrast note the diction at passages 7309–12, 6946–56, and 25177–500.

A false jury return like the one described here – presumably the result of manipulation or bribery – was the offense of the first inquisition *De aetate probando* in the Septvauns inheritance case, and it was the specific legal instrument overturned by the parliamentary decree. Here Gower appears to be going out of his way to condemn the kind of legal manipulation and misrepresentation that he himself was a party to in 1365, which is specifically an example of bad *pourchas*. Yet he goes on, subtly, to modify the strict condemnation of the purchaser to make him out, in this case, as a victim as well:

> Primerement est dammagée
> Cil q'est au tort desherité,
> Mais c'est en corps tantsoulement;
> Et l'autre encore est pis grevé,
> Q'ensi la terre ad pourchacé
> De son malvois compassement . . .
>   (24901–6)

[The man who is wrongly disinherited is injured first, but this is in body alone; the other party, who has secured lands (*pourchacé*) by his evil contrivance, is hurt still worse (*pis grevé*) . . .] (326)

Here, plainly the purchaser is not blameless. But he is not so much blamed as harmed – *pis grevé*, "harmed worse" than the heir himself – by the scheme. This is a curiously defensive arrangement of offenders and victims in which the offender is also defrauded. Even knowing as little as we do about the Septvauns affair (and without reducing this to a merely topical aside), it is not hard to read this as a subtle identification of the "purchaser" with the victim, both of whom, as he goes on to claim, have been manipulated by the sheriff. This would lend deeper meaning to his use of *brocage* or "brokerage" as a specific term for the manipulation.[27] It is the sheriff who causes the juror to commit perjury (ensi font l'autre perjuré [24909]) and who makes his gain from both sides of the bargain, which is also a form of purchase: *ensi se pourchace a despendre* (24921).

On the whole, Gower is at pains to present "bad" purchasing as an evil temptation, a form of fraud specific to the legal estate. These sorts of stories provide Gower with his story, *mon conte*, of what the "common voice" says, *sicome la vois commune conte* (24937–8), about the evils of lawyers. The focus on misrepresentation, *pourchas*, and law thus slides into

---

[27] See sv. *brocage*, "brokage, brokerage, jobbing (often in the sense of taking bribes for procuring offices etc.)," Baker, *Manual of Law French*; sv. *brocage, brog(g)age, Anglo-Norman Dictionary*, fasc. 1.76. Compare also the uses of *brocage* at 15699 and 18725.

an assertion of what the "common voice" says about justice. As this passage also hints, the scenario fits into the overall characterization of law-men as devilish manipulators of language, and this in turn reinforces the sins of *pourchas*.[28] The offenses are legion. Lawyers protect each other by refusing to plead against other lawyers, and they are deaf and dumb until they are paid. Through their machinations they are exempted from taxes and tallages. The estate of the law is in fact the most degenerate of the secular estates, and they make profits – again, *pourchas* – regardless of the situation: "whoever sells, they make profits; from the ills of others, they breathe in their good" (car quique vent, ils font pourchas, / Del autry mal leur bien respire [24812–3]). *Pourchas* is first figured as an excess. The lawyer gains so much from his craft he cannot reasonably purchase for himself alone (luy semble a estre trop estroit / De pourchacer soulein a soy [24539–40]); *fals pourchas* wins the *maisouns gay* that God will take away from them in his "court" or assize (a celle assisse tout perdras [24555–6, 24562]). Judges who "build fine manors" (les beals manoirs edifiez) only end up lodging devils (tu le deable as herbergez / En tes maisouns comme tes amys), and they themselves will be lodged forever in hell (24733–44). Lawyerly purchasing is a specifically devilish exercise. The traditional image of the Devil trying to establish his own *beal manoir* in opposition to God is here transmuted into the acquisitive property purchasing of the ones who should be honoring the property of others. Evil *pourchas* is, it implies, an etiolation of a prior divine exemplar. For their trickery, fraud, perversion, outright lies and subtle manipulations, the men of law resemble nothing so much as a gang of devils – *vei la du deable les vassals!* – who use fraud, *fraude*, to "beat down" the good, *pour faire abatre loyaltés* (24973–6; 24984; 25052–6). These insults are directed at bailiffs and juries who commit perjury and sell their verdicts, but they apply to the entire estate of the law. By the end, "the law" comes across as one big criminal and infernal enterprise. It is *la plus greveine*, "the most grievous thing," to the people (25176).

If this was Gower's opinion in the later 1370s, we can imagine, as Fisher has suggested, that he was speaking from the recollection of his own experiences with the law and, as some of the details might indicate, of his specific experience in the Septvauns affair. But if we posit these historical connections, the ethical disposition of the matter is still difficult to read. He recounts the offenses of the legal estate with the knowledge and pique of an insider, and as the Septvauns case shows, at one time he profited

---

[28] On Gower's presentation of lawyerly hypocrisy see also Landman, "Pleading, Pragmatism, and Permissible Hypocrisy," 153–4.

from the system. There is in fact no reason to suspect that Gower held any deep grudges about the matter. After the revolution of 1399, he included a portrait of John Cobham in the *Cronica Tripertita* that is uniformly flattering.[29] So if his work reflects a negative re-appraisal of his own prior actions (or those of his contemporaries), its criticisms are artfully displaced.

In turn, Gower's devilish characterization of the legal estate also resonates revealingly in a contemporary context. Certainly lawyers are not the only estate portrayed as having truck with the devil in the *Mirour*.[30] Even so, the intensity and specificity of this characterization is notable. His condemnations echo similar anti-legal satires and complaints (especially in *Piers Plowman*), and they have some contact with parliamentary developments. In 1372, not long after the Septvauns affair, an attempt was made to disqualify lawyers from membership in the Commons on the grounds that "they exploited this position to advance the causes of their clients" – and doubtless their own as well – "to the neglect of public business."[31] This exclusion was limited to lawyers sitting as shire knights with active cases in the king's courts. It was complained specifically that lawyers submitted petitions "in the name of the Commons, which do not at all concern them (i.e., the Commons), but concern only the private persons."[32] That is, lawyers were accused of manipulating the documentary procedure of the common petition: they claimed to speak in court with a "common voice" when in fact they were speaking only on behalf of private or individual interests. Despite this restriction, lawyers continued to form a large contingent of the MPs returned from both the boroughs and the shires.[33] Unsurprisingly, given their documentary and legal expertise, lawyers were an indispensable but problematic presence in the high court of parliament.

From this perspective – and keeping in mind the strident efforts at governmental reform put forward in parliament in the later 1370s and 1380s – the ambiguous position of lawyers in the body politic thus mirrors the ambiguity of Gower's own position. Lawyers attempted to manipulate another court, the king's high court of parliament, into rendering felicitous

---

[29] See *Cronica Tripertita* 2.212–32, where he calls Cobham "dignus, paciens, pius atque benignus, / Prouidus et iustus, morum virtute robustus, / Non erat obliqus, regni set verus amicus . . ." (213–15). His praise (also at 3.262–4) is perhaps studiously laudatory.

[30] See, for example, *Mirour* 20335, 20905–7, 25860, and elsewhere, where primarily members of religious estates are overtly aligned with devils.

[31] Butt, 254 and 333. See *RP* 2.310.

[32] *RP* 2.310: ". . . [ils] procurent & font mettre plusours Petitions en Parlementz en noun des Communes, qe rien lour touche mes soulement les singulers persones ove queux ils font demorez."

[33] Musson and Ormrod, *The Evolution of English Justice*, 149–50, note that during the 1380s and later about 10% of the Commons were lawyers, a figure that rises to 20% and higher in the fifteenth century.

judgments (or statutes) in situations like the Septvauns affair. At the same time, parliamentary representatives – as a class of nobles, upper commons, and professional men alike – made themselves out to be the protectors of the Crown and community and the licit voice of public interest, and not entirely without justification. In this historical fact we can find another ironic aspect to Gower's self-presentation. Just as lawyers attempted to manipulate the common petition for private interests, in the *Mirour* Gower maneuvers himself into the poetical stance of "the common voice" for his own, rather idiosyncratic ends, with only limited success. Lawyers in parliament apparently could spell trouble. The particular form of this trouble – the crafty misuse of documentary procedure and public authority – exercises Gower in his particular and potentially self-condemnatory obsession with the legal estate's devilish extraction of wealth from the commonwealth.

3 THE DEVILS' PARLIAMENT AND THE PROPERTY OF MAN IN *MIROUR* PART I

With these elements in mind, we can turn to the more resonant parallels in Part I of the *Mirour*. In the first large section of the *Mirour* Gower introduced to England (but alas, not to English) the continental tradition of the Devils' Parliament. This tradition was rooted in the topos of the *concilia deorum* stretching back to Homer.[34] Gower's is clearly a formal parliament conceived as a baronial assembly with contemporary elements mixed in its representation. Of all the estates criticized in the second part of the *Mirour* – all the ranks of the clergy (popes, cardinals, bishops, priests, friars, and more), the secular nobility (emperors, kings, lords, knights, men-at-arms), the men of law, the merchants, artisans, victuallers, and retailers – there is no estate of "parliament" *per se*. Parliament is not a class or estate, nor is it yet the discrete target of criticism. Rather it is, of course, a gathering of estates, and so for Gower's purposes it provides an important structuring principle in the opening allegory of Part I, the parliament of demons gathered to tempt Man.

It is clear from the details that Gower had in mind a contemporary form of parliament as a model. Fisher has noted how Gower's use of the terms of legal practice (*plaidour, client, tort, deslayment, cas, advocat,*

---

[34] On the history of the *concilia deorum* and its mutation into the Devil's Parliament, see Moore, "The Infernal Council"; Hammond, "*Concilia deorum* from Homer through Milton"; and Marx, *The Devils' Parliament and the Harrowing of Hell and Destruction of Jerusalem*, and *The Devil's Rights and the Redemption in the Literature of Medieval England*, 126–39.

president, apprentis, attourné) shows his technical familiarity with it.[35] There is a similar display of familiarity with parliamentary practice and language. The parliament itself is not strictly necessary for narrative progress. After a perfunctory account of Satan's fall, the temptation of Adam and Eve, and the expulsion from Eden, the story begins with the Devil autocthonously begetting his "daughter" Sin. The Devil and Sin then incestuously beget Death, and Death and Sin give birth to seven daughter sins. The Seven Deadly Sins are anatomized later in the poem in a traditional scholastic order largely repeated in the confessional structure of the *Confessio Amantis*.[36] Before that, following the begetting of the sins and their subsequent enumeration, Gower interposes the parliament. Satan calls the assembly after having made a pact with the World:

> Mais pour son purpos achever
> Communement volt assembler
> Tous ses amys, et pour cela
> Un parlement faisoit crier,
> Par queux se pourroit consailler
> Comme son purpos achievera.
>
> (331–6)

[. . . but to achieve his purpose he decided to call together all his friends, and therefore had a parliament proclaimed, through which he might take counsel on how he might achieve his end.] (8)

The Devil "cries" a parliament in a traditional manner. Insofar as the actual deliberations are concerned, it is superfluous. He has already determined his end and has plotted with the World to bring Mankind into sin. Since this is after the fall has already occurred, man is already in a state of sin. Thus Gower's parliament does not deal with the usual subject of the Devils' Parliament tradition, namely, deliberation over the significance of Christ's incarnation or the plotting of his temptation in the desert.[37] The *Mirour* uniquely employs the parliament as an allegorical expression of the everyday temptations of the post-lapsarian secular world, making it, significantly, the first imagining of a corporate political body in all of Gower's works.

The ethical and spiritual issue of temptation is central to Gower's altered scheme of parliament, and we get a bureaucratized version from the start. The assembly is called by royal writs of summons or *bries* (les bries tantost

---

[35] Fisher, 57; also "colour" (Landman, "Pleading, Pragmatism," 153), and the terms discussed here.
[36] See Peck, *Kingship and Common Profit*, 35–7.
[37] See the work by Marx on the *Devils' Parlament* (supra) and the devils' council in *The N-Town Play*, ed. Spector, 111–19 and 213–20.

furont escris [337–40]).[38] The MPs are figures we have already seen: Sin and her seven daughters, the World, and Death. Once assembled, the Devil solicits their counsel on how to bring about the further ruination of Man. Three well-spoken representatives step forward and declare their plans in turn. Sin says she and her daughters will "trick human Flesh" (je fray tricher la char humaine [368]); the World will deceive with riches and landed property or *manantie*[39] (de la richesce et manantie [377]); and Death will take care of the body. The Devil then proposes to issue a summons to "Man." They send Temptation, who calls man before the assembly "where the nobles were assembled" (u sont ensemble ly baroun [417]). Man comes to learn the cause of the summons, and all of the assembled parliamentarians work their temptations, flattering and cajoling him, except Death, who "by common assent" (par commun assent [489]) is hidden away. All of the demons work their wiles in turn, and Temptation makes the final decisive gesture for "the flesh of Man" (la char de l'omme [517]):

> Mais cil qui lors ust bien oï
> Temptacioun come il blandi
> Par la douçour de sa parole,
> Il porroit dire bien de fi
> Que ja n'oïst puisqu'il nasqui,
> Un vantparlour de tiele escole:
> Car plus fuist doulce sa parole
> Que n'estoit harpe ne citole.
>
> (505–12)

[But anyone hearing how Temptation cajoled by the sweetness of her speech would certainly swear that never since he was born had he heard such a persuasive boaster (*vantparlour*), for her speech was sweeter than the harp or lyre . . .] (10)

The word *vantparlour* used here for Temptation is noteworthy.[40] The word translates Latin *prolocutor*, "fore-speaker," and was used as an early term for the office of the Commons' speaker, as in the roll record of the tumultuous

---

[38] See sv. *Brief/brefe*, n. pl. *bries*, "writ," Baker, *Manual of Law French*; sv. *bref, bre(f)s, Anglo-Norman Dictionary*.

[39] See sv. *manauntie/maynauntie* "dwelling, household," Baker, *Manual of Law French*; also sv. *manant/ie* "bien, possession, domaine," Greimas, *Dictionnaire de l'ancien français*; "wealth, riches, possessions, property, lands," *Anglo-Norman Dictionary*. Compare the use of *manantie* and *franchise* at 6786, 14494–8, 15869, 16198, 18048, 18262, 18834, 22297–300, 22346, 25249.

[40] See sv. *vantparlour*, Baker, *Manual of Law French*; svv. *vanter* "to praise highly, to boast about, claim (falsely); to boast;" *vantparlour, vaunt-* "spokesman," *Anglo-Norman Dictionary*. This usage compares with the more common terms *parlour* and *commune parlour*. Compare also the description of *Orguil*, "Pride," at 2497–8: "Orguil vantparle en toute assise, / Et quiert qu'il soit primer assise."

parliament of November–December 1381, in which the candidate for speaker, Richard Waldegrave, is titled *vant-parlour*.[41] The word itself is rare enough for us to note the congruence, and its appearance in the parliamentary record is not, on the face of it, sarcastic. Given the relative newness of the office of speaker – formalized only since 1376 but probably practiced informally for some time – this use of the term may be Gower's way of adding another small but recognizable bit of institutional currency to his allegory. Here in the *Mirour*, however, things are artfully mixed. It is an assembly of demonic "barons" or a bunch of noble devils who are tempting Man. Thus they are not "Commons," although by the end they act as a rabble of evildoers working their blandishments through their representative mouthpiece, Temptation, in parliamentary assembly.

The specific temptation or problem that emerges is a property dispute. All of the contriving, and the parliament itself, is explicitly put forward *pour l'omme enginer*, the deceptions of the Devil are repeatedly characterized as *engins*.[42] This fact alone does not make the demons of Part I like the lawyers of Part II so much as does the actual focus of their efforts. They are tempting man to his disinheritance, to the alienation of Man as a holder of property and *as* property, as himself a contested "domain." Theologically speaking, this metaphorical complex is not new. But Gower's Anglo-French diction and setting make it a unique combination of the language of land tenancy and the bureaucratic structure of parliament. The devils are, in effect, attempting to bring off a *pourchas* in much the same spirit as the damnable men of law. It is the Devil's first point of honor that he has already dispossessed or "beaten down" Man (*l'omme abatu*) from his dwelling in Paradise (352–6). Like the men of law, here the devil has "beat down" Man in the same legal terms, *abater-abatement*: Man has been vacated from his land in a case of forcible entry.[43] Immediately following this, his daughter Sin assures the Devil that through her efforts Man will be *malbailli* (372) by her seven daughters: not just "brought to evil," but specifically "maldelivered" as a piece of property or legal surety.[44] The Soul chides the

---

[41] *RP* 3.100: "ITEM le Lundy proschein ensuant la tierce semaigne de Parlement, que fu le XVIII jour de Novembre, les Communes revindrent en Parlement, & illoeques Monsieur Richard de Waldegrave, Chivaler, q'avoit les paroles de par la Commune, s'afforceast de lui avoir excusez de cel Office de vant-parlour . . ."

[42] See the headnote at 276; 291; 490; 550–2; headnote at 757.

[43] See sv. *abater/abatir*, "to cast down, to knock down . . . to abate (*i.e. quash or declare void*) a writ . . . *abatement en terre*, abatement (*i.e. wrongful intrusion*) in land; *se abater*, to intrude." Baker, *Manual of Law French*; sv. *abatre*, "to abate," *Anglo-Norman Dictionary*. Compare also 313–15.

[44] See svv. *bail(l)e, bail(l)er*, Baker, *Manual of Law French*; sv. *bailler*, "to give, entrust, hand over . . . to grant, lease . . . to deliver seisin of," *Anglo-Norman Dictionary*. Compare *malbailly* at 9039, 15982, 17483–4, 22179–80, 23586–7, 26400.

Flesh, accusing Flesh of having fallen into "such false company" (tiele false compaignie [566]), and that through "barratry" he has been cast out of the high joys God had given Man. But if he reforms, he will "re-ascend" to the place he has lost (543–6; 566–8). The loss to Man is thus presented, in a complaint by Soul, as a loss of *franchise* that is also a loss of Man's proper inheritance:

> Car s'il avient que d'autre guise
> No cause soit deinz soi devise,
> Lors devons perdre la franchise
> Q'au nostre franc pooir attent;
> C'est de monter par bon aprise
> En paradis, dont par mesprise
> Susmes cheeus si folement.
>
> (594–600)

[For if it happens otherwise, that our interests be internally divided, then we must lose the freedom (*franchise*) to which our free strength is destined: this is to go up by good teaching to Paradise, from which, through offense, we have fallen so foolishly.] (11)

"Franchises" or liberties were properly granted by the Crown. So the analogy here is neither difficult nor over-subtle: Man has been tricked out of his property by *deablerie* (703) and only through appeal to the sovereign can he regain his former "possession," which is really a grant from God.

The broad similarities to the Septvauns case are obvious, but so are the differences. Man, like Septvauns, has been defrauded of his property through his own stupidity and ill-advisedness. But here it is a parliament that is doing further tempting, not protecting, and the whole scene comes off as both a court drama and a theatrical representation. While the Devil and his parliamentary minions speak like lawyers, so also do the allegorical figures charged with protecting Man and Flesh: Reason, Fear, the Soul, and later Conscience. The parliamentary allegory allows these legal and deliberative elements to be combined in a naturally dramatic manner, one appropriate for a contest that is simultaneously internal and external, private and public.

The fact that the struggle is both internal and external in two senses is the more subtle part of Gower's allegorical arrangement. That is, the conflict over Man is figured first as something external to him: he is summoned to a parliament where he must submit to a court deliberation. But all of its elements are internal to Man, and in fact the speakers are serially speaking "for" Man who himself never says a word *in propria persona*. Similarly, the whole metaphoric complex of property ownership is split between the initial presentation of Man as having lost property (Paradise) and his more extensive role *as* lost property. When Reason and Fear try to bring the Flesh back from the Devil's service, the Devil complains to Sin and the World:

> Du ceste chose je me pleigne,
> Car s'il eschape moun demeine,
> Lors ay perdu tous mes essais.
> (766–68)

[Of this thing I complain, for if he escapes my domain (*demeine*), I have lost all my efforts.] (14)

Here the word *demeine* is more accurately translated as demesne.[45] The Devil makes a legal plaint, *pleigne*, not because Man will exit his domain like a traveler crossing a stretch of property, but because Man himself will *be* lost property or an alienated holding. He will no longer be part of the Devil's property "domain." This detail in itself provides a further implicit motivation for the parliamentary allegory, as prior to the full development of the court of Chancery in the fifteenth century, parliament had final jurisdiction in matters of land inheritance and tenancy in cases such as the Septvauns affair. In presenting the loss of Man as the problematic alienation of property, the appropriateness of a parliamentary setting would have been immediately recognizable to his contemporary audience.

Gower maintains this parliamentary allegory for almost ten thousand lines and returns to it after the wedding of the World to Sin and the lengthy enumeration of their various progeny. After this, the Devil re-convenes the parliament (9749–56) and immediately returns to the trope of property possession in the deliberations. The Devil was "seised," *saisi*, of Man (9770); but this seisin has been threatened by the interventions of Reason and Soul (9769–76).[46] Again there is an implicit contrast here between the property of Paradise that Man himself has lost and Man as potentially lost property under the Devil's control – hence the need for the reconvened parliament to re-ratify his plans. At no point does Gower explicitly state that the Devil is engaged in an act of *pourchas*. But all of the fundamental elements – particularly the legal setting and the manipulations of speech and

---

[45] See svv. *demesne, demeigne*, Baker, *Manual of Law French*, and especially sv. *demeine, Anglo-Norman Dictionary*; compare *demeine/se demeine* meaning variously "(self) control" and "property," at 6767, 7493, 7588, 8787, 9158, 9952, 10541, 13229–30.

[46] This standard legal use of the term (as property possession) contrasts with a punning use a little further on, when Sin is said to have "seized" man in her Prison (Pecché l'omme avoit saisi/ En sa prisonne [10034–5]). Compare also 6516.

procedure – reinforce this sense of a property purchase gone bad. Thus what will be called the *malvois compassement* (24906) of the purchases of men of law in Part II is directly anticipated in the false *compassement* of the World and the Devil (796–8).

These false contrivances, diabolical and legal, have a similar liminal nature. Just as the law-men are uniquely positioned to offend against all estates, high and low, and to profit from the discord between social estates and within them, so also the devilish forces of Part I in the *Mirour* are positioned to tempt and to manipulate Flesh against Soul and Reason and to act, as it were, as the disjunctive element at the seams of Man's unitary identity and self-possession. The Devil's temptations to alienation are an alienation from the self as much as from the community, but also from the community-as-self, as a communal body. The significant result is a shift in "governance": the World and his alliance, defeating Man with sins, gain control in a manner that specifically restricts Man's connection with others:

> Ore ad le Siecle ove s'alliance
> De l'omme tout le governance,
> Q'ascuns ne puet parler a luy,
> Si ce ne soit par l'aqueintance
> Du Pecché, qui celle ordinance
> Sur tous les autres ad basty . . .
> (9853–68)

[Now the World with his allies has complete rule over Man. No one can talk to man except through the intermediary of Sin, who has built up this control over all others.] (135)

Similar terminology is used further by Reason and Conscience, who complain to God *par quoy ne furont mais puissant / A gouverner l'estat de luy*, "because they were no longer able to rule the estate of him" (10043–4). By the end of the Devils' Parliament section, the overall effect has been not only to lead Man into sin, but to deny access to Man by the voices that would licitly "govern his estate." The parliament has, ironically, destroyed the ability to *parler a luy*. At first glance this may look like a curious way to stress Man's sinful condition. But it makes sense in the larger context of the allegory and its emphasis on speech and public representation. As the contemporary setting makes clear, this is the kind of thing law-men supposedly do, and, in the specific case of Septvauns, what Gower and his confederates supposedly did: mislead, hijack speech and access, adopt a wholesome, "common" voice when in fact they speak only for illicit or singular interests. The question of ethical and moral governance here in Part I is, at heart, the same issue that will be dealt with obliquely in the complaints against the law in Part II. Ultimately the question under adjudication – who can speak to, and who can speak for, this Man, this purchased and thus alienated bit of "property"? – is the root issue at stake here, as it was in the case of Gower's purchase from Septvauns. Legal metaphors naturally lend themselves to the ethical allegory, and Gower further specifies them through his innovative use of a parliamentary setting and the lexis of property.

4 PARLIAMENT AND *PROPRIA*: SPEAKING WITH ONE VOICE

In this manner the lawyers and devils play a structurally similar role in the degradation of the body politic. The parliamentary allegory allows Gower to bring these elements together even as the two parts of the poem stand in contrastive juxtaposition. Before moving outward from these numerous lexical observations toward a broader synthesis, a few more connections are worth pausing over. We can recall that the parliament where the Septvauns case was judged also included the public announcement of a royal marriage, the wedding of Edward III's daughter Isabella to Lord de Coucy. The record of the parliamentary acceptance of that marriage –

Queux Grantz chescun par soy, & les Communes, d'une assent acorderent . . .

[To which the Lords each individually, and the Commons, agreed with one assent . . .][47]

– is echoed in the *Mirour*'s marriage of the World to the seven daughters of Sin with the stock phrase, "to accord with one assent":

> Et pour voirdire courtement,
> Tous s'acorderont d'un assent,
> Le mariage devoit prendre.
> (829–31)

[And, to tell the truth briefly, it was agreed with one assent that the marriage should be accepted.]

This basic trope of speaking with one voice is combined with the collocation of marriages and parliaments, which is a recurrent element in the literary representations of parliament.[48] It arises again in the parallel presentation of "God's court" later in Part I, which continues the metaphors of legal

---

[47] *RP* 2.290   [48] See the analysis in Chapter Four.

property exchange in the marriage of Reason with the Seven Virtues. When Reason is awarded the marriage with the Virtues, he rejoices over his new wealth in similar property terms. Where the Devil was disseised of Man (and proud to have put Man out of Paradise), Reason rejoices at his own gain as a good and legal acquisition replete with terms of land law: *heritage, manoir, franc mariage* (*liberum maritagium*) (10088–92). The wedding of Reason and the Virtues will, in another legalism, restore the Soul *a son droit plit*, "to her right estate" (10175). After the correlative (and equally lengthy) enumeration of the Seven Virtues (10177–18372), at the end of Part I, the brief *recapitulacioun* of the vices and virtues brings together many of the same terms of property and law:

> Ore est a trere en remembrance
> Comme je par ordre en la romance
> Vous ai du point en point conté
> Des vices toute la faisance;
> Primerement de la nescance
> Du Pecché, dont en propreté
> Mort vint . . .
> Et puis apres vous dis auci
> De l'omme q'en fuist malbailli,
> Dont l'Alme a dieu se compleigna . . .
> L'un claime avoir la seignourie
> De l'omme ove tous ses propretés,
> Et l'autre dist qu'il n'avera mie;
> Ensi la guerre est arrainié,
> U q'il y ad peril assetz.
>
> (18373–9; 18385–7; 18404–8)

[Now it is to be brought into remembrance how I have told you the story in order, from point to point, all about the doings of the vices. First about the birth of Sin, from whom Death came into his own (*en propreté*) . . . And then afterwards I told you also about Man, who was brought to evil (*malbailli*), of which the Soul complained to God . . . The one claims to have the control (*seignourie*) of Man with all his properties (*propretés*), and the other says that he should have nothing; and so war is declared, in which there is much peril.] (252–3)

Even as the subject-positions remain labile, the terms of property and personal identity merge in Man. The sins control his properties and his property, the *seignourie* and the *seignour*.

In sum, at the end of the narrative proper (and before the concluding hymn to the Virgin Mary), we find the allegorical expression of one of the fundamental ideological tropes of medieval feudalism: the metonymy of landed nobility. The landed noble was at once an individual and a piece of property, a piece of land: Lancaster, York, Northumberland, Gloucester, Buckingham, and so on. "Septvauns" was not a toponymic landed title, but for a royal tenant *in capite* the fundamental assumptions were no different.[49] Loss of property was tantamount to a loss of noble identity; willful and improper alienation of *propreté* was a sinful abnegation of *seignourie* to, among others, villainous misleaders of youth. In contrast to this deeply embedded feudal notion, the very unfixity of "property" in late medieval England – the fact that it *could* be purchased and hence alienated, even at the highest levels – makes the noble subject a figure for both the stability and variability of the subject-positions, the *propre*, in the text. The legal challenge of *pourchas* here is, as it was in society at large, a challenge to the largely archaic ideological foundations of the noble "person" much in the same way that the devils challenge the unitary identity of *l'omme*. This, then, is the core connection between a property law case like that of William Septvauns and Gower's imaginative representation of a social identity under siege. In taking his land, they were taking *him*. If the *Mirour* only indirectly relates to the specific events of Gower's own purchasing crisis and parliamentary inquisition, nonetheless the same fundamental terms and anxieties resurface in it, artfully recast but ideologically recognizable.

For a man like Gower, who was both a class parvenu attempting to enter into a landed identity (and hence, unavoidably, to destabilize its class assumptions), and a social conservative who held to the inviolability of those traditional social roles, these conflicting desires necessitated a mediating term or framework. This ideological tension thus practically forces Gower to assume the representative identity of "the common voice" in Part II. As he proceeds to enumerate the proverbial parliament of evils that infects the world, these malices remains internal to *l'omme*, and so the allegory both collapses to a unity of subject and remains multiple; they are the property of both one and many. In turn, this unity-of-multiplicity characterizes his

---

[49] For historical and legal background on this point see Holt, "Politics and Property in Early Medieval England"; Musson and Ormrod, *The Evolution of English Justice*, 117; and more generally Lyon, *A Constitutional and Legal History of Medieval England*. With only slight modification for the environment of post-conquest England, we can apply the assessment of Bloch, *Etymologies and Genealogies: A Literary Anthropology of the French Middle Ages*, 74: "The affiliation between the proper and the paternal strikes to the core of the medieval concept of property, for land that is inherited – whether over the course of many generations or only once – becomes a *propre*, the possession of ancestors (*terra aviatica, avitins*). A *propre* is an *immeuble* owned by one partner at the time of marriage, or that is inherited after marriage. It belongs, in essence, to a lineage rather than to the individuals through whom it descends. And not only is the *propre* the equivalent of *heritage*, but it is synonymous with ancestry (nobility) itself . . . The history of the noble family is, at bottom, the history of its land."

adopted position as authoritative speaker for the common voice. He makes this clear from the beginning of Part II:

> Ce que je pense escrire yci
> N'est pas par moy, ainz est ensi
> Du toute cristiene gent
> Murmur, compleinte, vois et cry . . .
>
> (18445–8)

[What I intend to write here is not from myself only, but is rather the murmur, complaint, voice, and cry of all Christian folk.] (253)

This speaking position of the common cry – and all of the attendant terms, "complaint," "cry," "murmur," "clamor," "voice," "testimony," "speech" – is repeated insistently through Part II of the *Mirour*.[50] It becomes a defining characteristic of his poetry in the *Vox Clamantis* and, to a lesser degree, the beginning of the *Confessio Amantis*, as it is key to the narratorial stance of his social criticism.[51] That is, the way to assume a licit voice of critique, one to which the care and concern of the realm is a *proper* concern, is to assume the parliamentary position of speaking *for* the land, on behalf of the "public estate," as the voice of both a singular noble or baronial subjectivity, and simultaneously, the voice of the public, as it was assumed as the *vox communis* of the divided commons. It is crucial to recognize – both for the *Mirour* and for his later poetry – that if he is assuming the role of a public *vox clamantis*, he is also a *vantparlour*, a fore-speaker of an ambiguous assembly that both is, and is not, coterminous with his proper self. The divisions of the social estates mirror the *divisioun* within Man, and it is the rancorous expression of that disunity which betrays *l'estat de l'omme*.

At the end of Part II, having roundly criticized each estate, the narrator gives his lengthy assessment of the melancholy situation:

> Ore est q'om de commun usage
> Despute, argue et se fait sage,
> Chascuns son argument sustient;
> Tu dis que c'est le seignourage,
> Je di que c'est le presterage,
> Du qui no siecle mal devient;

---

[50] For additional examples see 21776–80; 22247–8; 24007–9; the famous "prophecy" of the Rising of 1381 at 24097–108; the complaints of *la gent menour* against the *errour* of knights at 24169–80; the complaints against the *gens du loy* discussed above; 25237–9; 25573–7; 26125–7; 26180–2; 26305–9; and the passages discussed in the following.

[51] See generally Middleton, "The Idea of Public Poetry in the Reign of Richard II"; and Galloway, "Gower in his Most Learned Role"; Peck, *Kingship and Common Profit*, 13; Fisher, *John Gower*, 105; Coleman, *English Literature in History*, 148–56.

Et l'autre dist, mal se contient
La gent commune et point ne tient
La dueté de son estage:
Mais qui du reson soy sovient
Puet bien savoir que c'est tout nient
D'ensi jangler sanz avantage.
    Quant pié se lieve contre teste,
Trop est la guise deshonneste;
Et ensi qant contre seignour
Les gens sicomme salvage beste
En multitude et en tempeste
Se lievent, c'est un grant errour;
Et nepourqant la gent menour
Diont que leur superiour
Donnent la cause du moleste,
C'est de commune le clamour:
Mais tout cela n'est que folour
Q'au siecle nul remede preste.

(27217–40)

[Nowadays men by common custom dispute, argue, and pretend to be wise men, each upholding his own argument. You say it is the fault of the nobles, I say it is the priests, through whom our world is becoming evil. Someone else says the common people behave badly and do not fulfill the obligations of their estate. But whoever thinks reasonably must well realize there is no advantage in chattering idly like this.

When the foot rises up against the head, this is very dishonorable; and likewise when the people rise up like savage beasts in a multitude and a tempest against the lords, it is a great error. And yet the little people say that their superiors give cause for the disturbance; that is their common clamor. But all this is only folly, which gives no remedy to the world.] (357)

This passage reprises a similar one, about a thousand lines earlier, stating that "each estate makes clamor against the other . . . and so the whole world is at odds" (Chascun sur autre fait clamour . . . et ensi tout le mond combat [26563, 26568]). It is not just that each estate is sinful, but that each is in conflict and *debat* (26557) against the other. At this point, as elsewhere, communal "debate" is Gower's great anxiety. The actual substance of the debate is not highlighted so much as the simple fact *of* it. Thus here and in what immediately follows, the narratorial voice sounds like nothing so much as a speaker, in a rowdy assembly, trying to call everyone to order and to summarize what everyone is saying. There is, and has been throughout, only one speaker, but now it is a voice simultaneously singular and multiple, a unity figured as the conflicting voices of the disjointed body politic. *You blame the nobles, I blame the priests, someone else blames the commons. This is the common usage. But,* he goes on, *this is useless debate. We aren't solving anything by talking like this.* More than any specific issue or complaint, the point of the talk *is* the talk, the debate, and the public voice that Gower is trying to give to his earnest if ideologically simplistic formulation of present evils. Far from actually unifying or reconciling the various subject-positions at work in the poem, this newly authoritative (or self-authorizing) voice emerges as at once both among them and above them.

Thus the assumed framework, the social model not far behind the poetry, is one of a quasi-public debate, of a social parley where each estate blames the others and excuses itself – in a word, a contemporary parliament. In the structural subject-position or role of speaker or tempter, we now have instead that of reconciler. The poet's role becomes that of a moderator, a common voice among and above the voices trying to direct the discussion and common clamor toward some form of *remede*. At the same time Gower is keenly aware of the temptations of hypocrisy, and so, in a surface paradox, he justifies himself as authoritative only because he has been the worst offender. He collapses the positions of victim, victimizer, and protector for the last time, offering the inevitable turn to self-examination and self-correction as the true remedy.

> Mais je di que tout bien serroit,
> Si chascun de sa part voldroit
> Mais q'un soul homme corriger:
> Car ja n'estuet plus loins aler
> Forsq'a soy mesmes commencer;
> Et si chascuns ensi ferroit,
> Je suy certains sanz nul doubter,
> Plus q'om ne sache diviser,
> Le siecle amender l'en verroit.
>
> (27280–8)

[But I say that everything would be well if each one were willing to correct one single person, for it would never be necessary to go farther than to begin with oneself. And if each one would do so, I am certain without any doubt that one would see the world improve more than anyone can tell.] (358)

The "world" collapses, via corrective focus, into one, into the single individual. As Arthur Ferguson has noted, this ethical turn reflects both Gower's characteristic moralism and his general inability to conceptualize the functioning of a social order independent of a moral order.[52] Although the "man

---

[52] Ferguson, *The Articulate Citizen and the English Renaissance*, 56–7.

as microcosm" topos makes surprisingly little appearance in the *Mirour*, this alternative conceptual framework is very important for Gower's overall social ideology.[53] Man, *l'Omme* of the title, is both society as a whole and everyman, *un soul homme* who must engage in self-examination, and, at the same time, the poet in his identity as *l'omme peccheour* (headnote at 27360). But these representative individuals – "Man," society, sinner, poet – are also a veritable congeries of multiple voices – vices, virtues, classes and estates – that have alternately threatened and enabled Gower's voice of correction. This traditionalist ethical gesture marks the final conflation, as the tempting devil, noble subject, and voice of correction are all rolled into one. In the historical context of Gower's own experience – like Septvauns before the court – we can now also see why a form of communal assembly would represent *both* the epitomization *and* the demonic pejorization of precisely this ideal of a unified and sacralized voice. Gower's voice, implicitly but formally, *must* assume the position normally granted to the unified-but-multiple *vox populi* of a true assembly if it is to achieve anything like the authoritative representativeness he so desires. Yet it also represents the very division he so profoundly fears, in society as in himself. Thus for all his focus on kings and kingly correction, it is instead the conflicted forms of parliaments and *parlement* which allow Gower's speaking subject, and subjectivity, to stand forth, as both a projection of himself, and as an accusatory account of the devilish ways in which men like Gower could behave.

5 PARLIAMENTS OF THE *CRONICA TRIPERTITA* AND THE PROPERTY OF KINGSHIP

The *Mirour* thus presents an early and particularly conflicted example of the complexity involved in the adoption of a *vox populi*. To place Gower in the subject-position of a parliamentary "speaker" is perhaps a curious identification, but it is necessary to stress that his attempts at reconciliation are themselves conflicted from the very start. Embodiments of reconciliatory and mediatory plenitude abound in Gower's works. As Wetherbee has noted, the ideal of the "whole man" or *plenus homo* is foundational to his entire vision of "the ideal relationship of human dignity and divine order."[54] And as Copeland has expertly demonstrated, precisely the kind of social *divisioun* that the poet laments in the *Confessio Amantis* – "debat,"

---

[53] See the passage discussed above (27229–40) and at 26389–400, where it is used to describe the relation of the mayor (head) to the city (body). See Porter, "Gower's Ethical Microcosm and Political Macrocosm."

[54] Wetherbee, "John Gower," 597.

"divisioun," "werre," "dissencioun," "comun strif," "discord," "argument" –
is enacted by the very form of a vernacular poem that employs *divisio* as
its basic hermeneutical and rhetorical procedure.[55] In the parallel context
of contemporary bureaucratic discourse, we can see how Gower's desire to
bring a fractured society to a proper unity above or beyond such *divisioun*
and *debat* is precisely analogous to the wish, so fascinatingly represented in
the *Modus Tenendi Parliamentum*, for a single unified voice of a communal
representative *quae cum se ipsa discordare non potest*, "which cannot disagree
with itself."[56] Where the *Modus* dreamt of reducing a parliament to a committee and a committee to an individual, Gower poeticizes a society that
organically reconciles its discords and divisions in the reductive metonymy
of a single noble identity, the conjuncture of *propre* with the property that
is both its own care and its true inheritance.

But these claims of a noble unitary *proprietas*, overt and implict, were
also increasingly antithetical to the very form Gower chose for representing
his critique of a society in crisis. As we have seen and as the historical record
makes clear, noble or "baronial" representativeness was simply no longer
the vehicle of communal representativeness. In the contentious reigns of
Edward III and Richard II, neither were kings themselves very good figures
for the embodied correlative that Gower so desperately wanted to stand
as a representative image of the nation. If this older style of communal
speaking and representation was no longer available for Gower's critical
project, what then? After a fashion, the only *homme* left is the poet. Toward
the end of the *Vox Clamantis*, Gower identifies himself with the land of
England, physically and viscerally, as his origin and *propriam terram*:

> Singula que dominus statuit sibi regna per orbem,
> Que magis in Cristi nomine signa gerunt,
> Diligo, set propriam super omnia diligo terram,
> In qua principium duxit origo meum. . . .
> Hec si quid patitur, mea viscera compaciuntur,
> Nec sine me dampna ferre valebit ea . . .
>
> (7.1289–92, 1297–8)

[I love all the kingdoms which the Lord has established for Himself throughout
the world and which bear standards in Christ's name. But above all I love my own
land (*propriam terram*), in which my family (*principium meum*) took its origin . . .
if she suffers anything, my innermost feelings (*mea viscera*) suffer with her, and she
shall not be able to suffer her misfortunes apart from me . . .] (284)

[55] Copeland, *Rhetoric, Hermeneutics, and Translation in the Middle Ages*, 202–20.
[56] See Chapter Two.

While England is his motherland, "she" is also *him*: inseparable, his own, with a bodily connection to the poet's past and present. The identity of his *principium*, his familial origins in England, are combined with his personal suffering for the nation in a manner that can only be read as "noble." This is not "as if" England were his. It *is* his, and him, in this metonymical formula, as much as, or more than, Septvauns' lands were of the *gens Septvauns*, or (as becomes evident in the *Cronica*) as much as the land belongs to either Richard or Henry. At the same time, shortly after this comes one of the numerous declarations in the *Vox* that Gower's voice of lament is *not* just his own: *clamor vbique, vide, non solus conqueror ipse* ("See, there is clamor everywhere; I do not complain alone" [7.1335]). Even – or especially – at the moments of greatest personal identification with the land, Gower claims the *vox communis* is precisely not-just-him, not just a singular interest. His *estat* is not just a noble or isolated one, but the voice of all. These conflicted positions are, of course, devilishly difficult to maintain, especially when it was the clamor of the community that he wanted to embody and reflexively abhorred, as he did the outcry of the rebellious commons in 1381.

In the terms that have been the focus of analysis here, the last representation of Gower's *vox populi* is surprising but sensible: the *Cronica Tripertita*. The *Cronica*, a Latin addendum to the *Vox Clamantis*, was probably Gower's last major discrete work, but it was apparently never intended to stand by itself. As an addition to the *Vox* written after the Lancastrian revolution of 1399–1400, the *Cronica* provides a conclusion parallel to the *Vox*'s similarly tacked-on account of the Uprising of 1381 in Book I. In this way "chronicles" both begin and end the *Vox Clamantis* (which is itself titled a *Cronica*, although rarely referred to as such). The *Cronica Tripertita* thus complicates the overall trajectory of Gower's works as a triad of coherent compositional units. It belatedly completes the second work while also capping his oeuvre as a group, providing a final historical overview of the end of Richard's rule and the beginning of Henry's. It provides an end in the middle; and like the *Mirour*'s representation of *l'omme* as a counterpart to the estates, it brings a narrative of historical singulars – *les hommes*, Richard and Henry – into contrast with the systematic critique of the estates in the *Vox*'s central part.

Along with this temporal complexity, the *Cronica Tripertita*'s structural similarity to the parliamentary elements of the *Mirour* is striking, in so far as both works use parliaments as the scaffolding for narratives of judgment, loss, and recovery. The *Cronica* is divided by the events of the Merciless Parliament of 1388, the "revenge" Parliament of 1397, and the deposition parliament of 1399. As in the *Mirour*, the major legal issue that emerges is the disposition of property rights and land: in this case it is the land of the kingdom, as it is *represented* well or badly, licitly or illicitly, by the noble claimants to its title. The metonymy of noble property is thus made to subsume the fate of the entire nation as the *Cronica*'s parliamentary narratives clearly exploit the differing representational traditions Gower had available to him. In this way Gower's first use of parliaments in the *Mirour* is rewritten by his last use of them, in historical-chronicle form, to structure a parting gesture of social critique that also takes the aesthetic shape of a contemporary political *commedia*.

A brief summary bears this out. In Part I of the *Cronica*, the parliament of 1388 is presented as a communal manifestation of public law and right legal procedure. The parliament is the assembly of the land according to the law, and the "common voice" speaks in the safety of its concord (*terra covnata fuerat de lege vocata; / Rex sedet, et tutum fuit os commune locutum* [1.131–2]). It is explicitly the common voice of parliament that "speaks" the sentence of banishment, which is *also* the voice of the "nobles" (*dicit . . . procerum sentencia* [1.133–7]). The two are rolled into one with no functional distinction. The political complexity (and actual illegality) of the Appellant's maneuvers are never mentioned by Gower, who presents not a merciless parliament but an orderly assembly with the open approval of "the voice of people" for its punishments (*et hoc certe vox plebis dixit aperte* [175]).[57] In Gower's decidedly partisan representation, the parliament struggles for the "purging" and "emptying" of the royal court's baleful influences (*purgetur . . . euacuetur* [1.205]), but more importantly, for the individual reformation of the king himself, who is altered and "renovated" in his very person (*Sic emendatum Regem faciunt renouatum, / Cercius vt credunt, et sic cum laude recedunt* [1.210–1]). This is the end sought by the Appellants, but it is explicitly the parliament that achieves both the legal and personal reform of the king by ostensibly protecting Richard – again as the 1366 parliament "protected" Septvauns – from the evil counsellors misleading him.

In contrast to this virtuous assembly, in Part II parliament is deformed by the return of the king's evil favorites and by Richard's continued bad behavior. Where the 1388 assembly is presented as legal and legitimate, in Part II the 1397 parliament – assembled against Gloucester, Warwick, and Arundel – is represented as nothing more than tyrannical machinations working through a manipulated assembly. Parliament is cursed, darkly,

[57] See especially the analysis by Galloway, "The Literature of 1388 and the Politics of Pity in Gower's *Confessio Amantis.*"

as a "hundred parliament" – *milia quo Centum maledicunt parliamentum* (2.150) – which may mockingly compare it to the lower (and presumably worse) Hundred Courts of the shires.[58] Parliament is now associated with the king's parasites (who illegitimately dissolve the parliament [2.272–3]); with the voice of the fickle mob, *vox variata*, which has turned against the Appellants whom before it praised (2.284–5); and with the "voice of the fatuous crowd" in the city (*sic fatue turbe vox conclamabat in vrbe* [2.317]) that sings mocking songs about the nobles. This debased *vox* of the mob is distinguished from the legitimate *populus* who dare not speak and who "do not hear a voice proffered" to defend the accused nobles (*intra se flebat populus, qui dampna videbat; / Cum non audebat vocem proferre, tacebat* [2.324–5]). So the assembly of a public *vox* in Part II is characterized not only as a mere communal mob, but also as the weapon of silence forcefully imposed upon the very community it supposedly speaks for.

Gower's partisan contrasts to the parliament of 1388 are blatant, and of course the text of the *Cronica* was written well after Gower had become a committed Lancastrian. But his concern for the manipulation of parliament in 1397 is not mere Henrician hackery. The functional significance of this abuse becomes clear at the start of Part III. Parliament is made by Richard not just into an illegitimate court (a charge brought against him during the deposition) but into an actual extension of his physical person:

> Per prius optentum semper sibi parliamentum
> Per loca conseruat, in quo mala queque reseruat;
> Est vbi persona regis residente corona,
> Corpore presenti stat ibi vis parliamenti . . .
>
> (3.27–30)

[From the beginning, he bound 'parliament' joined to himself wherever his location, through which he unleashed all kinds of evil; where there is the person of the king residing with crown, present in body, there stands the force of parliament . . .]

Gower refers to the supposedly illegal commission instituted by Richard to exercise lawmaking authority after the dismissal of parliament. But it is described here (and later) not as a *commissio* or *concilium* but simply as the parliament itself, illegitimately joined to Richard's very body, moving wherever he moves, crushing dissent (3.37–8). Rather than renovating the king, Richard has instead made parliament in *his* image; it now is an extension of the tyranny and rage of this *rex pestifer* (3.43). The providential reversal of this abuse is also signalled at the start of Part III. The introductory headnote asserts that the return of Henry was greeted with the

---

[58] Noted by Stockton, *Major Latin Works of John Gower*, 477 n. 17.

universal and nigh-biblical joy of the community which "praised God as if with one voice" (*deum quasi ex vno ore collaudantes* [13–17]). The trope of *unanimitas* is joined, as we might expect, with the lexis of property. After his father's death, Henry Bolingbroke had legally petitioned for the inheritance of his properties – *sua propria* – as a full adult (*et sic consultus velut heres Miles adultus, / Que sua cognoscit post patrem propria poscit* [3.105–6]). When Richard summarily disinherited him, it was with Christ's direct injunction that Henry pursued *sua propria* (3.128–9). The property is, at this point, not just the Lancaster duchy but England itself. So when Henry disembarks in England, it is "his earth," *humo sibi,* he goes to and kisses, and his native land, his *patria,* that welcomes him (3.150, 154, 158). Bolingbroke's reassumption of his patrimonial inheritance is mirrored by Richard's slinking away, practically under the ground itself, as a "contemptible mole" (*quasi talpa reiectus* [3.223, and previously 3.17]); Richard is not a true owner of the land, just a mean digger and scrabbler in it.

The forum for the universal voice of Henry's reception is parliament; the legitimating manifestation of Henry's natural right to ascendance is his reception by the realm and the parliamentary acclamation of him as the land's destined sovereign. This marks the final comedic upturn in Part III. Parliament is first established in safety as the proper forum for God's intervention; what "fate has in store" in the parliament (*sunt parliamenta statuta . . . que sors sibi fata rependit*) is the communal overthrow of Richard and the acclamation of Henry as king (3.268–71). Richard is dethroned, his court is disgraced, and Henry is chosen in a ceremony "held" or "beheld" (*tulit*) by parliament – a studiously ambiguous term – which then recesses (3.299–301). These events are not just political necessities. They are, explicitly, the predestined will of God, and Henry is the sovereign chosen by both God's will and the people's unanimous voice:

> Predestinauit deus illum quem titulauit,
> Vt rex regnaret sua regnaque iustificaret.
> Quem deus elegit, regali laude peregit,
> Vnde coronatur in honoreque magnificatur . . .
> Marsque sequens terre dat parliamenta referre:
> Rex sedet et cuncti proceres resident sibi iuncti,
> Stant et presentes communes plus sapientes;
> Tempus erat tale communeque iudiciale . . .
> Tunc de consensu Regis procerum quoque sensu,
> Plebe reclamante, stant parliamenta per ante;
> Sic procedebant super hiis que gesta videbant
> Ad commune bonum, recolentes gesta baronum . . .
> (3.318–21, 343–6, 360–3)

[God predestined him whom he entitled, so that the king should rule and should justify his rule (*sua regnaque iustificaret*). He whom God chose, proceeded to the regal honor; hence he was crowned, and magnified in honor . . . and following Mars permitted the land to re-call parliament: the king took his seat and all the nobles sat joined to him, and also standing present were the wiser Commons; such was the time and the common judgment . . . Then by the king's consent and the approval of the nobles, with the people calling out, parliament stands as before; recalling the barons' deeds, thus they proceeded concerning these acts they witnessed . . .]

Henry's kingship is destiny, but it is parliament – here, we can note, explicitly represented as both baronial and popular – that, like Gower's poetry, gives one voice to that destiny. Where in the first part of the *Cronica*, parliament was a court of formal process and law, and where in the second part it was an illegitimate and irrepresentative assembly of exploitation and disappropriation – both, as we have seen, images of parliament with long histories – here at the end we have the final act in which parliament is divinely ordained and inspired, the kind of communal, politico-religious assembly not too distant from the fictionalized versions found in romances and chronicles. The tropes at play here consciously exploit the Pentecostal tradition of parliament as a God-directed assembly in which the *vox populi* harmonizes with the *vox Dei*.[59] Especially in the case of the judgment of Gloucester's murderers, the voice of the *populus* comes forward in parliament – in a direct allusion to Judges 20:1 – *quasi vir foret vnus*: "as if it were one man" (3.371). Again later, when Henry is threatened with revolt, the people "surge" forward as one to protect the king: *Ecce dei munus! populus quasi vir foret vnus, / Surgit ad omne latus, sit vt H. ita fortificatus* (3.418–19). Having restored proper kingship to the throne, Henry becomes the catalyst for the rebirth of the realm and the healing of social division. But he has done so by the processes of both an *individual* effort of self-assertion and recovery, and a *communal* representation of collective voice that Gower, here as elsewhere, can both claim and disclaim as his own.

Indeed it is only through this putative unity of voice that Gower can hope to represent the nation as a whole, and so at the end the *Cronica* asserts, remarkably, that this record of events has itself been spoken, like the judgment, *by the people*, –

> Cronica Ricardi, qui sceptra tulit leopardi,
> Vt patet, est dicta populo set non benedicta:
> (3.478–9)

---

[59] They also reinforce the ideologically loaded "threefold right" of Henry's usurpation. See especially Strohm, "Saving the Appearances."

[This chronicle of Richard, who bore the sceptre of the lion, was spoken by the people, as is clear; but it is not blessed . . .]

Having given his biased account of the events, he represents a *vox populi* that is the voice of God's predestination and the voice of a baronial nobility exercising its ambiguously traditional political role, as well as the voice of the people. Gower tries to blend all of them, and all of their speaking positions, into the one voice of the chronicle's text, while he himself fairly vanishes behind the mirror or *speculum mundi* that it represents (3.480). Gower can thus dissolve into the very voice of mediated authority declaring that "he who is a sinner cannot be a ruler" (*est qui peccator, non esse potest dominator* [3.486]), with the figure of Richard as its proof. Where Richard fell, the *Cronica* itself will stand – *cronica stabit ita* (3.489) – itself reflecting all the fixity of the kingdom's land and property as it is now refounded by Henry. At the end of the chronicle, parliaments give way to the voice of the poet, having given voice *to* him, first.

6 CONCLUSION: GOWER'S UNCOMMON VOICE

As the *Mirour* and the *Cronica* demonstrate, from the start of his career to the end of it, Gower represented a collective voice in his poetry that bore a complicated relation to the specifically parliamentary tropes of his contemporary social environment. It was not just the problems of "kingship," but the conflicted role of parliament and *parlement*, which stand at the formal base of the poet's efforts to speak. As I have argued here, the Septvauns affair reveals, in the arrangements of its elements, the same sort of positional and structural dilemmas of voice and representation that emerged in his poetry, in both moral and political allegory. In his efforts to assume the common voice, and in the effort to present a unified noble subjectivity, Gower actually aligns his own voice with the voice that had been, in 1365–6, aligned against him. To bring this investigation back around to the point where it started, from this analysis it becomes clearer why, for Gower, the ethical or "charitable" *estat de l'omme* should appear specifically *que pueple vait parlant*, and with a focus on *la vois commune*: the ethical disposition of the individual can *only* appear, in this arrangement, when Man's "estate" and *proprietas* take on this dual aspect of unity-in-multiplicity, private and public, that was a special property of parliament.

As I stated at the beginning, I have refrained from approaching the *Confessio Amantis* from this parliamentary perspective even though it contains many individual tales with parliaments in them. The *Confessio* is Gower's most accomplished and intricate work (much more so than those discussed here), and I would be reluctant to reduce its complexities to any single rubric, parliamentary or otherwise. And yet it too displays some of these points of parliamentary form. In instances, the parliaments within the tales of the *Confessio* – like the council of "The Tale of Mundus and Paulina," the court assembly of "The Tale of the Three Questions," that of "The Tale of Constance," the ineffectual and troubling parliament of the "Tale of the False Bachelor," the doomed parliaments of the "Tale of Jason and Medea" and the "Tale of Paris and Helen," the deliberations on governance and the common profit in Book VII, the parliaments of "Apollonius of Tyre" and others – could all be read, in various ways, as manifestations of this dynamic of proper *parlement*, of the voice of assembly that is individual and multiple, as each individual both belongs to, and is, an assembly of enfranchised estates. As the emperor Constantine says at the moment of his ethical decision in the "Tale of Constantine and Sylvester,"

> 'For every man his oghne wone
> After the lust of his assay
> The vice or vertu chese may.
> Thus stonden alle men franchised,
> Bot in astat thei ben divised . . .'
>
> (2.3260–4)

At the moment when he must choose whether to kill innocent children to obtain the blood he needs to cure his disease, Constantine's own ethical dilemma is presented, explicitly, as an interior debate precisely about "estate" –

> And thus this worthi lord as tho
> Sette in balance his oghne astat
> And with himself stod in debat,
> And thoghte hou that it was noght good
> To se so mochel mannes blod
> Be spilt for cause of him alone.
>
> (2.3280–5)

The conclusion of Constantine's own interior *debat* is the correct one (in a tale exemplifying "Charity" and "Pity") and he shows pity on the children. In turn he receives divine mercy for his bodily affliction and is cured by the intervention of Christ through Pope Sylvester. At the very end of the *Confessio*, the same terms are used to declare Amans' own final decision to leave the desires of *his* body and to give over his estate, as confused and conflicted as it has been:

Wher as the wisdom goth aweie
And can nought se the ryhte weie
How to governe his oghne estat,
Bot everydai stant in debat
Withinne him self, and can nought leve.
And thus forthy my final leve
I take now for evere more . . .

(8.3147–53, my emphasis)

Another sovereign individual, a figure of an emperor or a king – Amans – thus fulfills the ethical injunction of properly governing his *proprietas*, his own self, as the Confessor Genius has already made explicit the analogy of princely rule and personal ethics. Each individual, as Genius has told Amans, must seek good counsel and justify his kingdom, "that is to sein, his oghne dom" (8.2109–13). Every man *is* a king, a noble proprietor, of the realm of his own judgment. In this way, for the last time the political evil of *divisioun* of the land and the abuse of the "comune right" (8.3013) are allied with the division of the self. It should therefore come as no surprise that Amans' amorous division – his self-deluding desire to obtain his lady-love – is negated and put beyond legal claim ("ther was no recoverir" [8.2443]) specifically by a parliamentary judgment:

Me thoghte I sih tofor myn hed
Cupide with his bowe bent,
And lich unto a Parlement,
Which were ordeigned for the nones,
With him cam al the world at ones
Of gentil folk that whilom were
Lovers . . .

(8.2452–8)

Like the parliament of demons and the heavenly assembly, this concluding assembly of Venus becomes the forum of the lover's agon. Amans, *l'omme*, must submit to its judgment and ministrations. Unlike the parliament of the *Mirour*, it is not clear that this is an interior assembly. It is more allegorically exterior and literary, populated by an assemblage of history's lovers. Nonetheless the subject-positions at the end of the *Confessio* lend themselves to an ironic analogy to the embarrassing affair of Gower's past. Where Septvauns was judged in parliament and legally prohibited from his desire to alienate his *propria* because he was too young, at the end of the *Confessio*, "Gower"/Amans is judged in parliament and is prohibited by "law" from pursuing his lady – which, like the *propria* of England, and perhaps as an allegory for it, has come to define his very self – because he is too *old*. Amans is made to stand before a "mirour" (8.2821) to witness his own body, how it is faded, dimmed, and "thinne" with age (8.2824–31). As he must face and accept himself, this act of unification quickly leads to the end of his poetry and the end of his *vox communis*. No doubt he is still a sovereign self. But as *l'estat de l'omme s'appara*, in a gesture that is as melancholy as it is peaceful – and without further *debat* – he must bow to another common voice and accept the parliament's judgment that the estate of lovers is not properly his. In this way, the frame of the *Confessio Amantis* recapitulates some of the same gestures of parliamentary form that have informed Gower's poetry from the start. But for once, and finally, he soberly acknowledges the limits of his labors as a representative speaker, and he leaves the talking to somebody else.

CHAPTER 4

"Oure is the voys": Chaucer's parliaments and the mediation of community

Chaucer's books, by act of parliament, shall in these days prove more witty than ever they were before; for there shall so many sudden, or rather sodden wits, step abroad, that a flea shall not frisk forth, unless they comment on her.

"The Pennyless Parliament of Threed-bare Poets: Or, All Mirth and wittie Conceites." London, 1608. [1]

* * *

Whatever the opinion of this anonymous pamphleteer about Chaucer's books – and even if he really thought an act of parliament was needed to declare Chaucer "witty," which seems doubtful – both the poet and his work have more connections to parliament than any poet before Milton. Gower and Langland probably composed their allegories of parliaments before Chaucer composed his. The *Mirour de l'Omme* probably was started in the 1370s, *Piers Plowman* in the 1360s and 70s, while the *Parliament of Fowls*, a centerpiece of the Chaucerian canon, was probably composed around 1380, on the occasion of the betrothal and marriage of Richard II and Anne of Bohemia. [2] Although he was not working alone in this regard, Chaucer nonetheless stands out for the overt parliamentary elements in his poetry, and it seems sensible to connect them to his own life experience. Chaucer served as an MP for Kent in the important "Wonderful Parliament" of 1386, and this fact has been used for hunting topical elements in his verse. Beyond this single appointment as a parliamentary representative there lies a career of assignments and bureaucratic appointments that brought Chaucer within the sphere of parliamentary politics. [3] As the

---

[1] *The Harleian Miscellany: A Collection of Scarce, Curious, and Entertaining Pamphlets and Tracts, as well in Manuscript as in Print*, ed. Oldys and Park, Vol. 1, 185.

[2] See the now standard analysis of Benson, "The Occasion of *The Parliament of Fowls*." All citations of Chaucer are from *The Riverside Chaucer*, 3rd edn., ed. Benson et al.

[3] On Chaucer's term as MP see *Chaucer Life-Records*, 364–9; Galway, "Geoffrey Chaucer, J.P. and M.P."; For an aggressively Marxist assessment of Chaucer's professional history as a royal retainer and bureaucrat, see Carlson, *Chaucer's Jobs*, especially 1–31.

controller of the wool customs from 1374 to 1386, Chaucer was responsible for the single largest source of royal revenue controlled by parliament.[4] As a JP from 1385 to 1389 he sat on the bench in Kent with some of the most important law-men and nobles of his area who were also parliamentarians, including Baron Cobham, Gower's erstwhile parliamentary adversary, and Sir Arnold Savage, twice speaker of the Commons.[5] The JP appointments were also under parliamentary oversight. As a long time bureaucratic member of the royal household, Chaucer's professional activities as controller, clerk of the King's works, deputy forester, commissioner *de wallis et fossatis*, and his earlier appointments as a diplomat would have brought him into contact with parliamentary personnel and occasionally, as in 1386, under parliamentary scrutiny. Chaucer's elder son, Thomas, followed his father into public service and became one of the most important parliamentarians of the early fifteenth century. He served as an MP for Oxfordshire in fourteen parliaments between 1401 and 1431, five of them as speaker. We would not want to make too much of the father-son connection, given that Thomas Chaucer was a substantial landowner and political figure in his own right.[6] But proceeding from the principle that the fruit doesn't fall far from the tree, it makes sense that the son of a parliamentarian-poet became one of the most important (and occasionally truculent) parliamentary representatives of the following generation.[7] Nor should we expect that during his own lifetime, Geoffrey Chaucer's various appointments had only a functional or practical impact on his mind. It would hardly be surprising if the poet, appointed to these posts of both public importance and direct accountability to the Crown, were led to muse on the *bonum commune* and the duties that made him a member of this select professional community.

Chaucer's parliamentary connections also contextualize his artistic interest in representing his social environment. Much of his professional life – as MP, JP, bureaucrat, and diplomat – was spent speaking and working

---

[4] *Chaucer Life-Records*, 148–270; for explanation of the customs for which Chaucer was responsible as the accountant (the "ancient custom" of wools, wool-fells, and leather, the parliamentary wool subsidy, the "petty custom" and the parliamentary petty subsidy on wines) see 150–2. See also Pearsall, *Life of Geoffrey Chaucer*, 99–102.

[5] *Chaucer Life-Records*, 348–63; Galway, "Geoffrey Chaucer, J.P. and M.P.," 7–13.

[6] Roskell, "Thomas Chaucer of Ewelme"; Pearsall, *The Life of Geoffrey Chaucer*, 276–84.

[7] Roskell notes the hints of a pointed exchange between the aging Henry IV and speaker Chaucer in Henry's last parliament in 1411, where the king stated he would tolerate "no sort of innovation in this parliament" ('nulle manere de Novellerie en cest parlement') on the part of the speaker ("Thomas Chaucer of Ewelme," 162–3). Thomas Chaucer was a vigorous participant in the factional maneuverings of the 1410 parliament: see Clark, "Magnates and their Affinities in the Parliaments of 1386–1421," 140.

for the interests of others, usually the king. His electoral representativeness as an MP is another key element in his community engagements, one that has been relatively understressed by scholarly inquiries into late fourteenth-century *communitas*. Paul Olson's analysis of the *Canterbury Tales* as a model of a Christian commonwealth, a "perfective society" or a "rejoicing society," hints at the significance of parliamentarism in concluding that "the perfective society depends not only on the perfected king but on a perfected *parlement*, on 'parfitness' in each estate."[8] Paul Strohm's *Social Chaucer* aligns "Chaucer's *aesthetic* enterprise of defining a literary space that permits free interaction of different forms and styles . . . in reciprocal relation with the *social* enterprise of defining a public space hospitable to different social classes with diverse social impulses."[9] Both Olson's stress on *parlement* and Strohm's "commonwealth of style" identify some parliamentary aspects of Chaucer's aesthetic practice that are central but difficult to pin down. Additionally, David Wallace's investigation of the guild-structure environs of late medieval Europe argues for the influence of "associational forms" of *felaweshipe* or *compagnye* on Chaucer's works that are at once institutional and practical while also ideational and broadly ideological.[10] Other analyses have investigated the communal and nationalist self-imaginings of late fourteenth-century England, but usually (if at all) describing parliament as "that group of usurping and self-aggrandizing middlemen who [had] ironically claimed the very title of commons, those rural landowners and urban entrepreneurs who were constituted as the commons of Parliament."[11]

These studies in particular are closest to a parliamentary reading of Chaucer (for lack of a better phrase), but at the same time tend to avoid or dismiss it. The terms of this dismissal are significant, for it is through the styles of mediation – of go-betweens, "middlemen," or medial figures – that we can better understand parliament and *parlement* as central aspects of Chaucer's formal practice. They also help to explain why the middle strata of society loomed so large in his art's purview.[12] As we have seen in the first two chapters, parliament became medial in the sense that at this point in history, its actions and interventions were reaching further than they ever had. Its role as "the mouthpiece of the political community" put it right in

[8] Olson, *The Canterbury Tales and the Good Society*, 295; see also 46, 296–7.
[9] Strohm, *Social Chaucer*, 164.   [10] Wallace, *Chaucerian Polity*, 65–103.
[11] Scanlon, "King, Commons, and Kind Wit: Langland's National Vision and the Rising of 1381," 214, quoting Strohm, *Hochon's Arrow*, 41–2. For examples see the essays collected in *Imagining a Medieval English Nation*, ed. Lavezzo.
[12] See especially Strohm, *Social Chaucer*, 64–71.

the midst of national debates on justice, wealth, war, and society in a way that was hardly avoidable, especially for a poet briefly accounted one of its number.[13] As an assembly devoted to the politics of talk and the tensions both within and between social classes, parliament provides a uniquely analogous formation to the communal structures of Chaucer's poetry for exploring communicative exchange in settings that are at once conflictual and consensual, self-interested and public-oriented. In this regard Chaucer parts ways with Gower. While both poets exploit parliamentary forms for poetical structure and thematic development, Chaucer moves decisively beyond baronialist roots to a securer and frankly more entertaining look at the parliamentary practices of his day.

One of Chaucer's most important innovations – indeed one of his signature elements in the use of parliaments and *parlements* – is the alignment of talk against violence: parliaments are settings where force can be met, and sometimes mastered, by talk. This is not necessarily an ideal or a self-evidently good thing. As early complaints make clear, one of the biggest perceived problems of parliaments was their propensity for talk and no action, or that licit or needed actions were drowned out by talk. This is not simply a case of virtuous pens or voices, so to speak, being mightier than illegitimate swords. Parliament itself could be (and was) the occasion for violence, and for ritualized judicial violence, as Chaucer must have been aware. But taken on its own terms and in its documentary context, Chaucer's use of parliamentary form reveals a characteristically insightful exploration of the assumptions and procedural investments in a forum that tries to reach communicative resolutions in place of blows.

In this regard, two distinct social elements emerge as central and are reflected in accompanying literature. First, always associated with parliaments – for all of these poets, not just Chaucer – is marriage. My analysis begins with the collocation of parliaments and marriages and a limited consideration of marital sovereignty in a specifically parliamentary context. Second, also central is the procedural practice of petitions and bills, and of bringing bills before a sovereign figure for redress. From these points of inquiry, we can approach the *Parliament of Fowls* as a unique representation of parliamentary practice, the resonances of which go beyond its status as a topical poem. To a large degree this enriched context solves the "problem" of the *Parliament* by helping us to better see how its political–theoretical and allegorical–romantic moieties are closely related. The *Parliament* is certainly one of Chaucer's richest and most literarily accomplished works.

---

[13] Musson and Ormrod, *The Evolution of English Justice*, 159.

Almost fifty years after J. A. W. Bennett's magisterial survey of the poem's artistic sources and philosophical influences, it still seems somewhat churlish to suggest that the poet was engaged, in any extensive way, with the mundane bureaucratic details and governmental forms of his daily life.[14] But this is precisely what I want to suggest, and my approach returns to the poem some of the tensions that Bennett's study elides.

Chaucer's participation in the Wonderful Parliament of 1386, and the Merciless Parliament of 1388, thus provide useful if anachronistic contexts that must be read back in time, and against, the presumably prior *Parliament*. If it was in fact written at about 1380–1, the *Parliament* is the product of a brief period when silly birds and amorous gardens would have been a more comfortable set of images for the highest court of the land. By 1388, that court had become England's deadliest. This temporal juxtaposition also proves useful for teasing out the significance of what was, by the later 1380s, a typical stance for parliament as a whole: namely, the impotence of being a middleman, the potentially feminized – what has been recently called the "hymeneal" position – of mediatoriness.[15] With this mediatory aspect of parliamentarism in mind, I will conclude by considering parliament's importance for the structure of the *Canterbury Tales* as an expression of this mediational dynamic.

I   MARRIAGES AND PARLIAMENTS: THE CASE OF ELIZABETH DE BURGH

To understand the procedural and documentary context of parliamentary petitioning and the relationship between marriage, politics, and parliamentary actions, we can begin with the story of Elizabeth de Burgh, widow of John de Burgh, inheritor of the extensive de Burgh estates in Ireland and de Clare estates in Wales. She was member of one of the most powerful Anglo-Irish families from the thirteenth century onward.[16] During the

---

[14] Bennett, *The Parlement of Foules: An Interpretation.*

[15] Davis, "Hymeneal Alogic: Debating Political Community in *The Parliament of Fowls.*"

[16] On the de Burgh family see the entries in *DNB*, *sub nominibus* "Burgh", *et al.*, 3.315–31, especially Walter de Burgh (d. 1271), Richard de Burgh (d. 1326), and William de Burgh (d. 1332), the first, second, and third earls of Ulster respectively. The clan of de Burgh settled in Ireland in the early thirteenth century. Elizabeth de Burgh, *née* de Clare and later D'Amory, was a co-heiress of Gilbert de Clare, Earl of Gloucester and Hertford, and one of the largest landholders in England at the time of his death in 1314. See Holmes, "A Protest Against the Despensers, 1326." There is an indirect link between this Elizabeth de Burgh and Chaucer. Elizabeth was the mother of William de Burgh, third Earl of Ulster, who in turn was the father of Elizabeth, Countess of Ulster and wife of Prince Lionel, the second son of Edward III. As a boy, Chaucer served as a page in the household of Elizabeth and Lionel from 1356 to 1359. So Chaucer was a servant to the granddaughter (and namesake) of

period of the "Despenser regime" from 1321 to 1326, Elizabeth (also named Elizabeth D'Amory after her last husband) was subjected to remarkable oppressions by Edward II and the Despensers in an effort to obtain control of her lands.[17] The machinations of the elder and younger Hugh Despenser resulted in Elizabeth's imprisonment and effective disinheritance, as they dispossessed her of large tracts of property in Wales through a complicated and factitious chain of legal schemes. Elizabeth resisted as best she could and made repeated entreaties to parliament to no avail; the king was allied with the Despensers and permitted not only her disendowment but that of several other prominent landholders, especially widows and heiresses.[18] Following Edward's deposition in 1327, Edward III immediately set to work with his council (essentially under the control of Isabella and Mortimer) to undo the damage wrought by the deposed king and his favorites.[19] In the first parliament of his reign (really a continuance of Edward II's last), the new king systematically reinstated many of the nobility who had been disinherited, most notably Thomas, Earl of Lancaster.[20] Appropriately there was a particular concern that wives of noblemen who had lately been attainted should be returned to their marriage-rights and dowers.[21] Among the scattered records of this remediatory assembly, the case of Elizabeth de Burgh is recorded in Anglo-French and Latin petitions, as well as an English adaptation (probably composed later). The English version of her process in parliament begins, "Elizabeth, which was the wife of John de Burgo delivered in this Parliament a certain Petition, as followeth":

To our Lord the King and his Councell Elizabeth de Burgh sheweth, That whereas our Lord the King, father of our Lord the King that now is, commanded her by his Writt, that shee should come to Everwick [ie., York] to stay with him upon the Feast day of our Lord's Nativity in the XVIth yeare of his Raigne, our said Lord the

the woman pillaged by the Despensers. See *Chaucer Life-Records*, 13–22, and Pearsall, *Life of Geoffrey Chaucer*, 34–5.

[17] For fuller explication of the case, see Holmes, "A Protest Against the Despensers," and Fryde, *The Tyranny and Fall of Edward II*, 34, 106–18. As Fryde notes (106–7), "no other royal favourite in English history was ever able to take such liberties with the properties of the king's subjects and with the laws of the realm" as the Despensers did in the period 1321–6. On the administration of the Despenser rule see Saul, "The Despensers and the Downfall of Edward II."

[18] Fryde, *Tyranny and Fall of Edward III*, 112–17. These victims, some of whom were threatened with violence, included Elizabeth de Burgh; Thomas of Lancaster's widow Alice de Lacy and her daughter, who was imprisoned; Mary de St. Pol, Countess of Pembroke and her niece, Elizabeth Comyn; and others.

[19] *RP* 2.3–12; see Butt, 231–5.

[20] See Holmes, "A Protest Against the Despensers," 209–10; *RP* 2.22, 411; and the petitions collected in *Rotuli parlimentorum anglie hacetenus inediti*, 141–79.

[21] *RP* 2.8, petition 13.

King by the abetment and ill councell of Hugh de Spencer, Mr. Robert de Baldock, and Sir William de Cliffe, caused the said Elizabeth to bee arrested, and caused her to make a bond obligatory, that if shee took any contrary to the King's liking; that if shee allyed herself by marriage to any body without the King's licence; or that if shee gave away lands or tenements which shee held in Fee or in Dower to any man living without his licence; or if shee did contrary to any of these three points; all her lands, goods, and chattels should bee forfaited to the King, as appeares more plainly by the transcript of the said obligation tackt to the said Bill.[22]

Robert Baldock was the Chancellor and William Cliff was a clerk of the Chancery, both co-conspirators with the Despensers.[23] The restriction on her property and marriage must have been particularly galling to Elizabeth, as her last husband, Roger D'Amory, had been killed, probably executed, during the conflict in 1322.[24] The details of the account in this petition are verified by other enrollments in the Exchequer and Chancery, as well as by a remarkable account given in a "notarial act of protest" that Elizabeth drafted secretly in 1326 while being pressed to give up more land.[25] The parliamentary petition continues that she "prayes remedy of the said imprisonment, and acquittance by our Lord the King of the said Bond, or that the said Bond bee given againe to the said Elizabeth."[26] In another royal writ, the king orders that the offending bond be delivered in parliament for review:

And at the delivery of the said Script in ful Parliament, because it was advised by the Archbishops, Bishops, Earles, and Barons, and other of the Nobility, and by all the Commons of the Land, that the said Writing was made against law and against all reason, they caused the said Writing by the award of Parliament to bee damned, and to bee delivered to the said Elizabeth.[27]

Thus by act of parliament the forced acquisitions of the Despensers were undone for Elizabeth and others who flooded to the parliament to get back the lands they had lost. The English of this record indicates that it was

[22] The English record of the bill from Harleian MS. 252 (and British Museum MS. Add. 36824) is extracted in *RP* 2.440, from which these excerpts are taken. The corresponding Latin and Anglo-French versions, taken from Cotton MS. Titus E.I, are recorded in *Rotuli parliamentorum anglie hactenus inediti*, 151–3, 177–8.

[23] Fryde, *Tyranny and Fall of Edward II*, 110.

[24] Holmes, "A Protest Against the Despensers," 208. The Despensers' machinations against her Welsh estates were for properties held in her dower of de Clare, not by right of her husband who was attainted with treason.

[25] The protest, in Latin and Anglo-French and written in Elizabeth's own voice, is transcribed by Holmes, "A Protest Against the Despensers," 210–2.

[26] The Anglo-French version makes the same reference to the *escript obligatorie*, but understandably the bond itself is not recorded: *Rotuli parliamentorum anglie hactenus inediti*, 177.

[27] *RP* 2.440.

composed later than the time of the petition. Other records also display a mixture of vernacular and formal documents, again showing (as we have already seen in the case of the Mercers' Petition) how English-language documents travelled along with the Latin and French parliamentary records, occasionally rising to the surface.[28] As with John Gower's parliamentary law-case, we have no way of knowing whether Elizabeth was physically present at Westminster for the decision, but it seems likely. The "damned" bond was handed over and she was therefore free – within limits, one assumes – to choose her own marital partner and to legally dispose of her properties as the common law allowed.

The de Burgh petition is part of a particularly compelling account of how closely the issues of marriage, property, and legal and parliamentary petitioning could stand, especially in the cases of women who inhabited the upper echelons of the socio-economic scale, and who stood to lose or gain greatly by controlling their own marital dispositions within the web of dynastic and familial concerns that bound them. Since the rules of inheritance were comparatively generous under English common law, unmarried women could control substantial amounts of land. Their marriages and remarriages were therefore of paramount political concern.[29] In attempting to gain access to her lands and dowers, Edward and the Despensers proscribed Elizabeth's marriageability. Correspondingly, the capacity of parliament to void the obligation hints at the concerns of marriage as a parliamentary issue. The award of parliament in this case provided her with documentary control over the legal instument of her indenture at the same time that it presented a bit of drama. Edward does a good turn to "our beloved kinswoman" (*dilecta consanguinea nostra*)[30] and frees her in a regal display of parliamentary indulgence, one that had been denied her for several years but which, even in the granting, still underscores how limited her marital self-determination could be in practice.

[28] Other examples of French, Latin, and English records – sometimes mixed within the same petition – are given in the texts from MS. Titus E.I in *Rotuli parliamentorum anglie hactenus inediti*, 141–79.

[29] See Payling, "The Politics of Family: Late Medieval Marriage Contracts." As Payling explains, "By the middle of the thirteenth century, a widow's common-law dower entitlement had come to comprise a third of all those lands of which her husband had been seised at any time during their marriage, rather than the more restricted entitlement that had prevailed in the late twelfth century. A rule so generous to widows was an important factor in determining the structure of landed society, ensuring that a significant part of the kingdom's wealth was always in their hands, and from the point of view of landed society in general, could only be tolerated because of the tendency of widows to remarry" (25). The developments of jointure and dower account for "what McFarlane described as the 'new and sometimes disproportionate weight' of widows in late medieval society" (29), a situation certainly evident in the case of de Burgh.

[30] *Rotuli parliamentorum anglie hactenus inediti*, 178.

Authority over marriages was in fact a long-standing element of parliament in several ways, not just in the possibility of equity judgment or, as in this case, the voiding of a prior judgment. Parliaments were often the occasions of weddings, and the marriages of royalty or high nobility were subject to parliamentary acknowledgments and ratifications. One of the traditional feudal aids of parliament was an award to the king for the marriage of his daughter; in 1290 one such aid was awarded to Edward I, and his daughter, Joan, was married during parliament.[31] In 1323 it was proposed to obtain the consent of the prelates and nobility in parliament for the marriage of Edward II's son.[32] A similar marriage grant for the king's daughter was made in 1348, and later, the marriage of Edward III's daughter Isabella was presented for approval before a full parliament in 1366.[33] In 1382 Richard II's marriage to Anne of Bohemia took place between the sessions of parliament.[34] The marriage arrangements of Edward III's several sons necessitated parliamentary grants of taxation as well as the awarding of noble titles in parliament.[35] Parliamentary statutes affirmed the king's prerogative over marriages and wardships; and parliamentary complaints were made that the Crown should not carelessly alienate its control over royal wards and marriages as a source of revenue.[36] Parliament could also force the confirmation of a marriage covenant, and the violation of marriage laws (especially bigamy) were repeated concerns of parliamentary statute-making.[37] As early as 1248 nobility were complaining in parliament that the king was marrying off his nobles "to the unknown and ignoble" (*ignotis ignobilibusque maritavit*).[38] Marriage controversies of high politics would occasionally surface in parliament, as in the complex annulment case of Marjory Nerford and Sir Robert Howard of 1378, and down to the fifteenth century and beyond, as in 1428, when the marital

---

[31] *RP* 1.25; Butt, 145, 148.

[32] Richardson and Sayles, "The King's Ministers in Parliament, 1272–377," 549 n. 2; see Rymer, *Foedera*, 2.524.

[33] *RP* 2.201; 2.290–1. *Knighton's Chronicle*, 90–1, 192–3.

[34] The parliamentary session began in November 1381 (with the post-Uprising conflict between Lancaster and Northumberland). The Queen arrived in England before Christmas and the marriage took place on 20 January 1382. Parliament adjourned for the wedding festivities and reassembled on February 25, for a total session of three months. See Butt, 377–80; *Westminster Chronicle*, 21–5; Saul, *Richard II*, 89.

[35] Especially in the parliament of 1362: see Tout, *Chapters in the Administrative History of Mediaeval England*, 3.252.

[36] On the *prerogativa regis* regarding marriages, wardships, and primer seisin, see *Statutes of the Realm* 1.226; for the 1376 bills, see *RP* 2.341, 355–56 ("Qe gardes & mariages ne soient donez legerement").

[37] On marriage contracts, see Harding, *Medieval Law and the Foundations of the State*, 175; see also the complaints regarding bigamy in 1344 (*RP* 2.151–2) and 1376 (*RP* 2.333).

[38] *Flores Historiarum*, 2.346.

shifts of Humphrey, Duke of Gloucester became a public issue and were protested by London women submitting a petition of complaint to the Lords in parliament.[39] In the sixteenth century Elizabeth I famously butted heads with her parliaments over the question of her own marriage, and by the seventeenth century, the submission of mock bills to parliament on behalf of women in search of husbands – and mock responses from men avoiding them – were a playful extension (and defusing) of this documentary trope.[40] What the case of Elizabeth de Burgh helps to make clear, for the fourteenth century in particular, is the way this ostensibly personal and familial issue could be a matter of serious public concern, not just of the law-courts but of the highest court in the realm. A specific noblewoman's marital status could in effect be determined as a matter of public policy.

In this light, the repeated collocation of marriages and parliaments in all of our literary sources makes more sense. As we have seen, the parliament of *Havelok the Dane* involves a clandestine (or inadvertent) royal marriage; the parliament of demons as well as the parallel heavenly assembly in *Mirour de l'Omme* celebrate a group of "royal" marriages. The parliament of Langland's Visio in *Piers Plowman* involves the question of Mede's espousal to False, and the *Parliament of Fowls* centers on a marriage-debate. At the end of the *Knight's Tale*, Theseus declares, "with al th'avys heere of my parlement" (3076), an end to the mourning for Arcite and the nuptials of Palamoun and Emelye:

> Bitwixen hem was maad anon the bond
> That highte matrimoigne or mariage,
> By al the conseil and the baronage.
> And thus with alle blisse and melodye
> Hath Palamon ywedded Emelye.
>
> (3094–8)

Theseus' parliamentary declaration slides into the actual marriage, which appears to take place at the same time. It also harmonizes with Theseus' presentation of the cosmic order and "Great Chain of Love" as its natural human expression of concord.[41] Correlatively and negatively, the parliament in Book IV of *Troilus and Criseyde* decides to send Criseyde to the Greeks and effectively to terminate the clandestine marriage of the lovers, and in so

---

[39] On Nerford and Howard see *RP* 3.39–40; on Humphrey, Duke of Gloucester, see the summary in his entry in *DNB*, 28.241–8, for contemporary references.

[40] Examples are collected in *The Harleian Miscellany*, vol. 4, 326–9; 400–3; 437–41; 504–7.

[41] On marriage as a "symbol of concord" see especially Bennett, *The Parlement of Foules*, 125–30.

doing, to seal the doom of Troy. In another late example, the second book of John Capgrave's *Life of St. Katherine* has an assembly of Katherine's vassal nobles who are "calle[d] to parliament" and who exhort her unsuccessfully to marriage.[42] In the Arthurian narrative tradition any number of marriages in assemblies could stand as examples, and even in highly aristocratic literary contexts the baronial assemblies often take on the air of popular gatherings and public festivals.[43] In each case the specific issue may be slightly different, but taken together these literary examples reveal a strong and long-lasting association of parliamentary assemblies with the festivities and conflicts of marriages. Like the case of de Burgh, they reveal the fundamental political association of proper social order with licit marriage, both of which are to be ratified, or set straight, in a parliamentary assembly. This association would also lend itself to the metaphor of parliament *as* a wedding, as the "spouse" of a sovereign, and there is evidence of medieval kingship understood as a marriage to the nation through parliaments and assemblies.[44] But for later fourteenth-century England, the stronger view was of parliament as a forum for the investigation of marriage, as marriage was jurisdictionally and metonymically associated with the legal controversies of parliament. It is therefore fitting that one of the most sober and searching narratives about the extent of marital freedom and obligation in the *Canterbury Tales* is told by a parliamentarian, the Franklin; and another parliamentarian of

---

[42] Capgrave, *The Life of Saint Katherine*, 2.73.

[43] Examples from the Arthurian tradition are varied but generally exhibit the close connection of baronial councils and marriages. In Chrétien, for example, in *Erec et Enide*, Erec and Enide are married at a gathering of Arthur's baronage at Pentecost; in the first part of *Le Chevalier au lion*, Yvain and Laudine are wedded at the urging and assembly of her nobles in a public ceremony after Laudine has sought their counsel. In the English adaptation *Ywain and Gawain*, Yvain and Alundyne are similiarly married in "thaire parlement" with the assent ("with an [one] acord" and "with a [one] voice") of the barons (1180–3, 1245–8). In Malory, the festive aspects are downplayed. At the beginning of the narrative, Uther's wedding to Igrayne is urged "by one assent" of his barons, and the royal marriage is followed immediately by the baronial marriages of Lott to Margawse and Nentres to Elayne. Later Gareth and Gaheris are married to Lyonesse and Lyonette, and Aggravain to Lawrell, in Arthur's plenary court. More significantly, the wedding of Arthur and Guenevere is the occasion for Leodegreans' gift of the round table, so the marriage and the creation of Arthur's baronial assembly – very much a parliament in the traditional sense – are coterminous, even as the wedding itself is de-emphasized. Even Arthurian parodies connect marriages and public assemblies. In *The Weddyng of Syr Gawen and Dame Ragnell*, the loathly lady demands of Arthur that she be wedded to Gawain "before alle thy chyvalry" (529) and requires that "there were made a krye in alle the shyre, / Both in town and in borowe" (558–9), effectively requiring that the marriage be "cried" or announced like an assembly or parliament. And in the "The Wife of Bath's Tale", part of the pathos of the tale lies in the fact that the rapist-knight weds the old lady "prively" and hastily without public acknowledgement or communal assembly, the opposite of the usual public festivities of Arthurian marriages.

[44] However, as Kantorowicz noted, this metaphor was almost completely absent from the political theology of medieval England: see *The King's Two Bodies*, 223.

sorts, the host Harry Bailly, is particularly voluble about his own marriage woes.

2 BILLS AND PETITIONS: THE CASE OF CECILIE DEUMARCZ

A second aspect of the de Burgh case also helps to illuminate later literary practice: the operation of petitions and bills. What we know of Elizabeth de Burgh's claim comes to us not in a legal narrative or roll summary but largely from a series of petitions and responses preserved in separate enrollments. Parliament was first and foremost a court of petition. The chance for display, for the public "showing" of complaints in the technical sense of *to shew* a bill or petition, was the court's aspect that attracted petitioners most strongly.[45] Parliament was the highest court where petitions for redress could be submitted. An elaborate system of receivers, vetters, and triers was put in place to receive petitions from all parts of the realm. That is, any petitioner with a bill could submit it to the receivers for consideration by the triers for a particular region.[46] Once vetted by the Chancery clerks as receivers, the bill would be directed to the proper triers, who were judges and peers (usually bishops, dukes, and earls), and by them directed to the proper court for judgment (King's Bench, Common Bench, Exchequer, and later the Chancery.) Or a petition would be forwarded for consideration to the clerk in parliament and submitted either to the king in council or to the king in full parliament. By the mid-fourteenth century, petitions submitted to the Commons could be directed immediately to the king and council in parliament, a much speedier route to royal consideration.[47]

---

[45] *MED* s.v. "sheu(e)," def. b, "attendance at Parliament," with reference to *Mum and the Soothsegger*; but a better sense is given by the *OED* s.v. "show," V.23.c "to set forth, allege (in a legal document). Often in petitionary formulae," and in the following related definitions with examples from the *RP*. See Musson and Ormrod, *The Evolution of English Justice*, 146–51; Harriss, "The Formation of Parliament," 49–52; Maddicott, "Parliament and the Constituencies," 62–8.

[46] As the roll puts it in ideal terms at the opening of the parliament in 1414, *RP* 4.34: "Insofar as our Lord the King wishes that right and equal justice be done to all his lieges, to the poor as well as the rich, if there be any who wish to complain of any wrong or tort done to him, so that there might be remedy for it at the common law, let him bring forth his petition . . . to the receivers assigned to the petitions." (qe purant qe nostre dit Seigneur le Roy voet qe droit & ouele justice soit fait a toutz ses Lieges, si bien povers come riches, si ascuny soit qe voet compleindre d'ascun mal ou tort a luy fait, quell ne purra estre remedie par la commune leie, q'il mette avaunt sa Petition . . . as Resceivours des Petitions assignez.)

[47] For descriptions of these procedures see particularly Brown, "Parliament, c. 1377–1422," 121–7; Harding, *Medieval Law and the Foundations of the State*, 178–86; Edwards, *Second Century*, 44–65; Harding, "Plaints and Bills in the History of English Law"; Sayles, *The King's Parliament of England*, 118; Rayner, "The Forms and Machinery of the 'Commune Petition' in the Fourteenth Century"; and Richardson and Sayles, "The King's Ministers in Parliament, 1272–1377." For the fourteenth century it is necessary to remember, as Edwards explains, that "during the time of a parliament, 'the

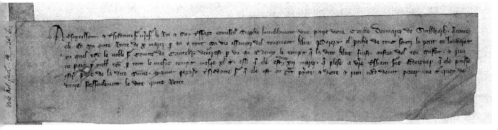

Figure 6. Petition of Cecilie Deumarcz, November 1381. National Archives SC 8/20/962
(reduced). © 2006 The National Archives

Parliament acted as a sort of clearing-house and court of afforcement for
lower courts, often requiring action on petitions and cases before the ending
of a particular parliamentary session. By the later fourteenth century, the
flow of private petitions to parliament had waned as it became dominated
more by public political matters. But at no time did parliament lose its
fundamental identity as a court of justice, either in practice or in the public
imagination.

The process of submitting a bill before parliament, like submitting a
bill or a plea to any court of law, was therefore a practice open to a wide
social range of participants, from the high nobility like de Burgh on down
to the lower classes of free men and women, and even, as we shall see in
Chapter Six, to "villeins" challenging their status as unfree. Another bill
submitted by a woman, this one from November 1381, can stand as a small
but completely typical example of the kinds of petitions submitted to parliament. This petition was probably put forward by one Cecilie Deumarcz
(Figure 6):

To the most excellent and most redoubtable lord, our Lord the King, and his
most wise Council, supplicates a poor widow, Cecilie Deumarcz of Southwark,
who, as she has a quit-rent of ten marks per year for all her life, arising from
the tenement [of] Alice Perrers, the one next to All Hallows the Less in London,
in which tenement the noble lord the Earl of Cambridge has dwelled for a year
and a half, [from] the time that the said Alice was put out of the aforementioned
tenement, and [he] has not paid anything for this tenement during the entire
meantime except forty shillings, so that she is due twelve marks. May it please
your most high Lordship to ordain, that she should be paid the said sum, having regard, most redoubtable Lord, that she is in great poverty and debt, and

King and his council' meant 'the King and his council in parliament' i.e. the King and his council
meeting in the White Chamber in company with the prelates and barons who had been individually
summoned to attend the parliament" (*Second Century*, 48).

has nothing from which to pay, nor on which to live, excepting only the said quit-rent.[48]

The back of the petition is endorsed *sue a la commune ley*, "Let her sue at common law." This example is selected more or less at random, but we can make a few observations from it. First, we can note its structure. It begins with the politeness and deference common to all such petitionary formulae. The king and his council are addressed for redress from a suppliant, frequently in the hyperbolic terms more common to parliamentary petitions than to other legal bills. It is not uncommon, particularly in petitions from individuals, for a bill to be addressed to the sovereign as *tres-redoute, tres-puissaunt, tres-exsellent, tres-graciouse, vostre Hautesce, tres-soveraigne, tres-sage*, and so on.[49] Then the specific appeal is laid out. It ends with a plea for grace, often with reference to the life or livelihood of the petitioner. Second, in this case we can note that the petitioner is a woman, specifically a widow, who like Elizabeth de Burgh has certain rights at law in her status as a widow and who has entered this petition under her own cognizance. While the majority of bills submitted in parliament are clearly from men, there are also enough of them submitted by men and women, and some by women alone, to indicate that the experience of legal petitioning in parliament was common enough to both sexes. Third, also like the petition of Elizabeth de Burgh some fifty years prior, this petition ultimately concerns a property dispute. This is overwhelmingly the subject of most disputes among private petitioners. Whatever the specifics of this case, Cecilie Deumarcz asserts a legal claim to a dwelling in London which has been transgressed. In all likelihood Cecilie had sought redress from a lower court, but finding none there, brought her petition to the high court of parliament in an effort to get her case heard. The endorsement to "pursue

---

[48] *RP* 3.130: "A T'S EXCELLENT & t's redoute S'r n're S'r le Roi, & son tres sage Counseil, supplie humblement une povre veve Cecilie Deumarcz de Suthwerk, q' come ele ad une quite rente de x marcz p' an a tout sa vie, issauntz del tenement Alice Peres el proche de Tous-Seintz le petit en Loundres, en quel ten' le noble S'r Counte de Cantebr' demeurast p' un an & demy, le temps q' la dite Alice fuist oustee del ten' sus dit, & rien ne paia pur ycell ten' par tout le mesne temps mes qe XL s. issi q' ele est duez xii marcz. Qe plese a v're t's haut S'rie ordeigner, q' ele puisse estr' paye de la dite summe, eyaunt regard, t's redout S'r, q' ele est en g'nt pov'te & dette, & rien n'ad dount paier, ne sur quey de vivre, fors soulement le dite quite rente." [Sue a la co'e Ley.]

[49] For example, in 1378 one particularly deferent petitioner, Paul Odbek, addressed his bill thus: "A notre exsellent, tres-puissaunt, & tres-graciouse Seigneur le Roy & a son Counseil supplie tres-humblement un povre Marchaunt Paull Odbek, Marchaunt de Brugges . . ." (*RP* 3.54). On the increasingly grandiose addresses to Richard II in parliamentary petitions, see especially Saul, "Richard II and the Vocabulary of Kingship"; also Ormrod, "A Problem of Precedence." The earliest extant English petition, the Drayton petition c. 1344, is even more obsequious, beginning: "Wiþ the grace of god, leue sire, worþi louered ful of grace, Edward kyng of Engelond, þe heie kyng of heuene þe blesse wiþ his holinesse . . ." National Archives SC 8/192/9579.

it according to the common law" was not therefore a summary dismissal but probably an afforced direction. The fact that this small petition actually survives in the records of the parliament – among the many, sometimes hundreds that could be submitted during the course of a session – may indicate that it held some importance.[50]

In its size, concerns, and form, this petition is very much like thousands of others which still survive in the records of parliament. Petitions or "bills"[51] of this sort could be submitted or "shown" by practically any person or corporate entity: a nobleman or private person, a town, professional guild, shire, monastery, church, just about any individual, group, or community. It was in the name of the "community of the realm," the commons *qua* the nation, that the practice of submitting common petitions developed in the fourteenth century.[52] Petitions were addressed directly to the Commons, and over time the Commons became an intermediary between petitioners and the Crown as the ultimate source of justice.[53] The opportunity for a sort of showy display was also open to individual petitioners. In 1339 during the parliament at Westminster, a bill was submitted on behalf of one John Maltravers appealing his banishment from the realm, arguing that it was irregular, "saunz loi et reson," and that the banished had not had the opportunity to defend himself by due process. The case is exceptional as it appears to have been submitted not by Maltravers (who was out of the kingdom), nor by the Commons, but by his wife, who accompanied the Commons to the king and presented her bill personally to the king, probably pleading on his behalf.[54] In other cases, exceptional petitions were submitted in parliament directly to the king for

---

[50] If "Alice Perers" was in fact Alice Perrers, Edward III's erstwhile mistress stripped of her possessions by parliament in 1376 and 1377, the Deumarcz petition is probably related to the disposal of the properties following that judgment. See *PROME*, Appendix, November 1381, petitions 14 and 17.

[51] In the later fourteenth century, the word "bill" entered the English language from Anglo-French *bille*, from Anglo-Latin *billa*, from Latin *bulla*. Technically a "bill" was the actual physical document of a petition or plaint, but the terms are often used interchangeably. See the *OED* s.v. "bill" n. 3, esp. definitions 2a-c, "a formal document containing a petition to a person in authority; a written petition"; "a supplicatory address (not necessarily in writing); a prayer, supplication, request"; "*to put (up) a bill*: to present a petition"; and 3, "the draft of an Act of Parliament," the first citation for which is from *Piers Plowman* (discussed next chapter) but which became regular only in the fifteenth century. See also *MED* s.v. "bille."

[52] On the development of common petitions and the identity of the "commons" in this petitionary capacity, see especially Edwards, *Second Century*, 44–65; Cam, "The Legislators of Medieval England," 142–58; Rayner, "Forms and Machinery of the 'Commune Petition'."

[53] See Maddicott, "Parliament and the Constituencies"; Butt, 268–72.

[54] *Rotuli parliamentorum hactenus inediti*, 285–6; for a discussion of Maltravers, who had been on the continent since 1330, see Edwards, *Second Century*, 57–9.

review.[55] In the record of the 1355 parliament, the lady Blanche de Wake brought a petition directly to the king in her property dispute against the Bishop of Ely. It is recorded at the end of the roll with the request that the king take up the case *en sa tres graciouse main*, "in his most gracious hand," which, according to the record, Edward did explicitly.[56]

This last point also gets to the reason for displaying this example of a bill in its textual form. When we think of people submitting bills, we need to think of them in these material terms, that is, as the little (or large) scraps of parchment that circulated in a pre-print manuscript culture. Submitting a bill was a textual exercise, literally. Parliament was the highest court in the land where such bills could be submitted, vetted, heard, and judged. This fact helps to account for the strong hold that such bills had on the literary imagination of the time, in court contexts in general but parliamentary ones in particular. As Burrow and others have noted, the conditions of "petitionary dependence" were central to the very self-conception of poets in their artistic practice, and for clerkly poets the petition was profoundly important as both a bureaucratic instrument and a literary form.[57] In this context, what I want to stress is not just the subjective disposition of petitioning, but the actual, material practice of submitting a bill. In this regard, petitionary form did not signal only (or exclusively) a relationship between a subordinate and a singular lord. Petition-poems also represent courts and parliaments as necessary elements and in fact sometimes come to be dominated by them. A few later examples demonstrate this. In John Lydgate's dream-vision *The Temple of Glass* (c. 1420), two lovers submit a series of formally structured petitions to the court of Venus. A lady first offers "a litel bil / Forto declare þe somme of al hir wil / And to þe goddes hir quarel forto shewe" (317–9). A knight then submits a similar bill, and later the lovers submit petitions for grace directly to one another. All this happens in the court, where Venus renders her decision to aid the lovers and a gathered assembly sings praises to the goddess. Throughout, the narrative centers more on the process of petitioning itself – in the rather overwrought exchange of pleas and bills – than on any one petition or person. Similarly,

---

[55] Two similar examples of direct petitions for restitution following disinheritance are found in the roll for 1354, *RP* 2.255–7: a bill on behalf of Roger Mortimer and another on behalf of Richard, Count of Arundel.

[56] *RP* 2.267: "Quelle Petition entendue, notre Seigneur le Roi ottrohi a la darreine clause de sa Petition, & dist overtement, Jeo prenk la querele en ma main." See Butt, 320. We can compare the similar treatment of a petition listed for John Cornwall and his wife Elizabeth, Countess of Huntington, in 1402, which Henry IV received *de sa grace especiale, en plein Parlement. RP* 3.483.

[57] Burrow, "The Poet as Petitioner." For the contemporary example of Thomas Hoccleve's petitionary poetry, see Knapp, *The Bureaucratic Muse*, 17–43.

the anonymous *Assembly of Ladies* represents no fewer than eight short bills submitted to the court of "Lady Loyalté" by an assembly of "ladies" and "gentlewomen" who are said to speak on behalf of a larger gathering (395). After the assembly is described and the bills are presented, Loyalté refers the women to "oure court of parlement . . . and in al this wherein ye fynde yow greved / There shal ye fynde an open remedy" (720–3). Both *The Temple of Glass* and *Assembly of Ladies* are written in rhyme-royal stanzas echoing Chaucerian themes, particularly the typically Chaucerian lament of amorous frustration and constraint: "for I am bounde to þing þat I nold; / Freli to chese þere lak I liberte" (*Temple*, 335–336). As bill-poems they are also comparable to Chaucer's "Complaint Unto Pity," which in turn is similar to the *Parliament of Fowls* in its rhyme-royal style and phrasing. The "Complaint" is not a parliament-poem *per se* as the setting is never specified, nor need we think of it as allegorically depicting anything but a generalized court. In it, the narrator describes his desire to submit a bill to Pity ("a compleynt had I, writen in myn hond, / For to have put to Pite as a bille" [43–4]), but that he is frustrated by enemies and, as he discovers, by the death of Pity herself. He nonetheless goes on to read his complaint, which has the organization of a formal bill replete with the legal terms of property and dispossession.[58] The poem as a whole is notably inconsistent, as the narrator finds Pity dead and then later refers to Pity in the bill – supposedly composed earlier – as *already* dead. This inconsistency reflects Chaucer's characteristic complexity in representing courtly love and textual-legal forms.[59] It may also suggest that the "bill" in the poem was at one time a discrete unit that circulated – or was even handed to a lady – on a small piece of parchment, like a real bill, only later to be reworked into the longer narrative. In each case, the contemporary model of documentary bills is clear. Submitting a bill was a concrete legal exercise common to various strata of society, and largely through Chaucer's influence it became part of the formal repertoire of poets composing in the particular idiom of verse that was "courtly" in both senses, amorous and political. In this regard, the textual exercise of an individual like Cecilie Deumarcz before parliament would have been a direct analogue, both personal and public, to the kinds of contemporary literary discourse that drew its currency from the forms and terms of public documentary petitioning.

[58] See Nolan, "Structural Sophistication in 'The Complaint Unto Pity.'"
[59] Simpson, for example, reads the poem as an example of Chaucer's self-cancelling Ovidianism in which "the very formulation of the means to legal redress insists upon the impossibility of redress": *Oxford English Literary History*, 128.

3 FEMININE POSITIONING: "MELIBEE" AND MEDIATION

These examples suggest the general observation that in addition to being linked with the issues and ideology of marriage, parliamentary narratives were also intimately connected to the textual exercise of petitioning. Petitions in general – from the Wycliffite petition to parliament and the Lollard *Twelve Conclusions*, to the petitionary political broadsides that were posted in public in the 1380s and 1390s – were exploited and imitated for a range of expression.[60] In the next chapter we will see another example of this literary bill-practice in *Piers Plowman*, Peace's submission of a parliamentary bill against Wrong. In this courtly context, as suggested by the comparison of the bill-poems with the bills of de Burgh and Deumarcz, there is the potential for gender reversal in the literary appropriation of the bill *topos*. I have chosen the examples of de Burgh and Deumarcz in part because they were women, and also to show the availability of the practice to both men and women. There is a way in which the act of petitioning itself, for both men and women, was to assume a culturally determined "feminine" stance. To plead was to act like a woman; even the queen herself could submit a petition to the king in parliament as an *humble suppliant* to her *tressoveraigne seignur*.[61] But pleading was also an act of potential authority and power, and a position from which to voice licit demands. The practice of billing was therefore inherently liminal, a means of gaining access or opening a door to the avenues of power towards which the pleader hoped to move, or from which a plaintiff hoped to gain some remedy. Often the submission of a bill is an appeal for intervention or mediation. We can compare Chaucer's *ABC*, where an appeal to God through the Virgin Mary is framed as a petition by way of a bill:

> From his ancille he made the maistresse
> Of hevene and erthe, oure bille up for to beede.
>
> (109–10)

This conjuncture is slightly ambiguous because although Mary herself may be the object of petition here, it is more likely that she takes up the bill to God on mankind's behalf. She takes the role of "pity" from courtly complaint. The liminality of a queen – her role as advocate and intercessor,

---

[60] On the Wycliffite "Petition to Parliament" and the Lollard *Twelve Conclusions*, see Somerset, *Clerical Discourse and Lay Audience in Late Medieval England*, 3–9 and 103–6. They are similar to the bill of "Libel" against Archbishop Neville of York, posted outside parliament at Westminster and Saint Paul's Cathedral, probably from 1387–8: see the transcript by Illingworth, "Copy of a Libel against Archbishop Neville."

[61] *RP* 4.532–3: petition from Queen Joan to Henry IV, January 1404, for confirmation of her dower.

and as a partaker of the royal identity – was a common cultural trope that would have been readily understood in spiritual, erotic, and political registers.[62] In the same poem, Christ is figured as the author and text of a bill of acquitance for mankind: "And with his precious blood he wrot the bille / Upon the crois as general acquitaunce" (59–60). In becoming a man, Christ has "vouched sauf" (57) in the legal claim against mankind, in effect becoming humanity's legal advocate or intercessory as well as the bill of appeal himself. It is thus the figure of the mediator – alternately figured as Christ the Savior or Mary the intercessor – who carries the bills forward. We could compare this to the examples of specifically feminine intervention in a story like the *Knight's Tale,* where the petitions of women at key points (at the start, with the plea of the Theban widows, and in Part Two, when the royal women plead for mercy on behalf of Palamon and Arcite) are the efficient cause of the narrative's progress.

In the courtly tradition the receiver of the bill is the sovereign woman, the figure of the *domina* who acts as lord. This was, of course, one of the gender-reversals of courtly poetry that gave it both a political resonance – since men must "plead" to their ladies – and a piquancy of some complexity. But in actual political practice (as in religious settings), the lord who received appeals for grace and mercy from both men and women was almost always male. In a very real sense, bills and petitions were the everyday textual equivalent of mash-notes to the king. "Billing" the king was an act of subordination and, to a certain extent, of feminization, of consciously and formally submitting one's self to the grace of the sovereign in an almost marital appeal.[63] At the same time it was an appeal on behalf of what was assumed to be a fundamentally licit demand, a bill for something owed or sought deservedly, through a formal process, and hence not easily or lightly denied. Courtly and political assumptions in this regard were thus exactly congruent. Just as a woman was, presumably, not supposed to lightly turn away a proper appeal from a deserving claimant to her "pity," so too a sovereign could not peremptorily deny the licit appeal of a subject, submitted in the proper form and forum, through which his "grace" might be sought or effectively compelled.

The complexities of this petitionary dynamic and its political implications, especially for the control of violence, are central to Chaucer's other

---

[62] See Strohm, "Queens as Intercessors," in *Hochon's Arrow.*

[63] As Strohm notes, "In the thirteenth and especially the fourteenth centuries, a flood of commentaries, sermons, meditations, chronicles, ceremonials, and poems modeled and celebrated female subordination and self-marginalization as a source of characteristically feminine power" (*Hochon's Arrow,* 96). See also Davis, "Hymeneal Alogic," 171–4.

parliamentary narrative, the one he gives to himself: the "Tale of Melibee."
As a political narrative the "Melibee" resides in an uneasy space somewhere
between mere workaday translation, bland allegory, and serious practical
writing that Chaucer may have assigned to his own character with some per-
spicuity. The text descends from the *Liber consolationis et consilii* of Alber-
tanus of Brescia by way of the French translation of Reynard de Louens,
the *Livre de Melibée et de Dame Prudence*, which Chaucer translated. It
is a prominent example of the *Fürstenspiegel* genre of political education
and counsel.[64] But as Wallace has argued, especially in the context of the
Canterbury Tales it stands out less as an example of a traditional mirror
for princes than as "a handbook for go-betweens."[65] The other characters
of the pilgrimage reinforce this mediatory focus since Prudence (and not
Melibee himself) is the center of their attention in their comments on the
story. Through her actions as both a petitioner and mediator – not only
between Melibee and his attackers, but also between Melibee and his own
parliamentary assembly – Dame Prudence manages to waylay the threat of
Melibee's retribution into an equitable settlement.

The assembly in the "Melibee" is nowhere called a parliament but plainly
it participates in the practices of *parlement*. The "greet congregacion of folk"
(1004) called to counsel Melibee offers up another example of an ill-guided
council. At points Prudence's advice is plainly counter to the authority
of the opening assembly, and she criticizes Melibee's inability to make a
"division" by calling together "a greet multitude of peple, ful chargeant
and ful anoyous for to heere" (1243). She observes that they would tell him
only what they think he wanted to hear in the first place, but this claim's
validity is less narrative than thematic, since there is nothing in the story
(nor in Chaucer's sources) to indicate that the crowd tailored its cries for
war to meet Melibee's desires or "affeccioun." It is, rather, a stock aspect
in an exemplum of a parliament *mauvais fois*, like the parroting *cavea* or
assembly criticized in Bromyard's *Summa*.[66] Prudence not only denounces
the "hochepot" (1257) assembly but comes to *be* Melibee's parliament, his
best interlocutor and advisor-spouse, fulfilling the role it was called for. She
notes that the wise men of his council had "seyden alle by oon accord" (1296)
that Melibee should keep himself and his household, which effectively

---

[64] For comprehensive treatments of Chaucer's "Tale of Melibee" in the context of the *Fürstenspiegel* genre see Scanlon, *Narrative, Authority, and Power*, 206–15; Ferster, *Fictions of Advice*, 89–107.

[65] Wallace, *Chaucerian Polity*, 221. A similar observation is made by Askins, "*The Tale of Melibee* and the Crisis at Westminster, 1387," 106–7: "the evidence suggests that, whatever else it might be, the *Melibee* is an object lesson in how a mediator might handle a hard case." See also Collette, "Heeding the Counsel of Prudence: A Context for the *Melibee*."

[66] See the discussion of Bromyard and Brinton in Chapter Two.

means to obey order and to "accorde to resoun" (1377) in his reaction to the crime against him. This means he should forego vengeance, and Prudence counsels Melibee "after the ordre of right; that is to seyn, by the lawe and noght by excesse ne by outrage" (1529). This plea is fundamentally legalistic but also gently petitionary. She is counselling him to follow the common law. We are meant to contrast this position explicitly with the lawless blood thirstiness of the opening assembly. In general, the whole of Prudence's strategy for guiding Melibee depends upon her subtle ability to place herself between Melibee's passions and his actions, in an allegory of both individual and communally prudential advisement. Speaking as one with only the non-coercive authority of "law and reason," Prudence must in effect assume the simultaneously subordinate and authoritative stance of a rightful petitioner and queenly intercessor, one who wants to move the sovereign to her ends but for his own good as well.

So while Prudence replaces the parliament, she must also assume its role. In turn she must look back to it for authorization, as both the woman and the assembly hold similar positions in relation to the lord. By the time Melibee agrees and puts himself completely in Prudence's "disposicioun and ordinaunce" (1725), the roles have been reversed: the lord is now governed or covered, and his wife has the authority to determine the legal process of the conflict. She acts as an intermediary for the accused men, who all speak "with o voys" by placing themselves under her direction (1765). After this she further ratifies her own role by acquiring the consent of "hire kyn and . . . olde freendes which that were trewe and wyse" (1784), that is, by seeking the ratification of a true parliament as opposed to the false and ill-advised one from the narrative's beginning. The offenders petition for grace through her, and in so doing they submit to the "comandementz" (1822) of Melibee and his wife.

During this second assembly, the allegory comes closest to the contemporary dynamic of petition, mediation, and parliamentary action that would have been very familiar to Chaucer's audience. After the offenders submit to Melibee with a plea for mercy, he dismisses them, and Prudence asks Melibee what he plans to do:

To which Melibee answerde and seyde, "Certes," quod he, "I thynke and purpose me fully / to desherite hem of al that evere they han and for to putte hem in exil for evere." (1834–5)

At first glance Melibee's response appears to be a complete retrogression from everything Prudence has advised. Indeed it is, as Patterson has called it, a "devastating moment" in the narrative, for despite Prudence's long explanations and admonitions, Melibee still appears fixated on retaliation.[67] But as severe as it may appear to us, a sentence of disinheritance (or disappropriation) and banishment was, repeatedly, the normal and in some ways more temperate legal response to political upheaval and "treason" in the period. It was also just as frequently the subject of parliamentary judgment and reversals, as in cases like those of Thomas of Lancaster in 1327, John Maltravers in 1339, Mortimer and Arundel in 1354, Alice Perrers and her husband William Windsor in 1384, the numerous victims of the parliamentary judgments of 1388 and 1397, the descendants of Richard Fitzalan the Earl of Arundel in 1399, Henry Percy the Earl of Northumberland in 1404, and many others.[68] Melibee's decision is similar in context to the kind of punishments suffered by de Burgh and Deumarcz, who then had to sue for grace in parliament for the restoration of disappropriated properties. As much as the opening allegorical attack on Melibee's household was an attack on his lineage and patrimony, the move to "deherite hem of al that evere they han" is fundamentally a legal claim on the offenders' patrimonies and properties. A large part of Prudence's accomplishment thus derives not just from her ability to sway Melibee with her counsel, but to get the entire conflict moved into a proper court of adjudication in the first place, and to reconstitute the assembly in a manner fulfilling its proper role as a forum for reconciliation. Melibee's initial gesture towards disinheritance – as opposed to outright baronial war – shows that he too understands this legal context, even if his answer is not the one Prudence wants to hear.

The initial mediatory image of the single surgeon curing two men who have wounded each other (1013) is thus fulfilled in the second assembly through her efforts. Prudence enables Melibee to receive his enemies and grant them mercy because he is *constrained* to do so by their petitions, as he says: "yet for as muche as I see and biholde youre grete humylitee / and that ye been sory and repentant of youre giltes, / it constreyneth me to doon yow grace and mercy." (1878–80) They have abased themselves publicly, so he must respond with public mercy. This is a judgment that will, presumably, restore order and unity, as Melibee's readiness to be reconciled under the guidance of a single advisor signals a further readiness of the body politic to be healed by its proper "phisicien" (1004–34). The intervention of Prudence

[67] Patterson, "'What Man Artow?': Authorial Self-Definition in *The Tale of Sir Thopas* and *The Tale of Melibee*," 157.
[68] On Lancaster, Maltravers, Mortimer and Arundel, see above; on Alice Perrers and William Windsor's petition to have Perrers' properties reinstated, see the analysis next chapter; on the dispossessions of 1388 and 1397, see Butt, 395–401, 430–9; on Fitzalan, who was executed in 1397, and others reinstated to their patrimonies after the revolution of 1399, see *RP* 3.418; on the judgment of Northumberland, see Butt, 458–60.

thus constrains violence. Through her petitionary position the sovereign must recognize the power of the licit submission of his subordinates, as the offenders, through their "lowe submyssioun" (1823), highlight the double sense available in reading a "submission." It is to put something forward and to put one's self low, but also to make a strong demand precisely *through* putting one's self low. This success has been enabled only through the mediatory action of one who confounds the borders of high and low, and multiplicity and unity, by her very figure; and in whom petition, marriage, and communal authority all reconcile felicitously at the end of the allegory.

4 "OURE IS THE VOYS": THE *PARLIAMENT OF FOWLS*

The contemporary suggestiveness of the *Tale of Melibee* thus seems less likely to reflect particular events than it does a wider ideological environment where the interaction of mediation and petition were cathected in parliamentary assembly.[69] With this complex amalgam of elements in mind – the collocation of marriage and parliament; the dynamic of petitioning as simultaneously subaltern and compelling; the mediation of violence and discord through figurations of discussion and unity; and the figuring of unity in a single, representative, and prudential voice – we can approach the *Parliament of Fowls* as a paradigmatic example of Chaucer's own representation of the mediatoriness of parliamentary form.

As we might expect, the *Parliament* reveals a complex understanding of the social elements involved in the practices of a court that was uniquely located between bureaucratic, aristocratic, and loosely popular registers. To note that Chaucer was in the middle of these competing social positions is not to assert his disinterestedness nor the "universality" of parliament, even as the Commons explicitly petitioned on behalf of the *universitas*. As Margaret Galway has noted, "in all his recorded employments the poet was in one way or another looking after the king's interests," and his overlapping assignments as MP and Controller are cases in point.[70] Even in these jobs, the dangerous complexity of those interests would have been all too obvious. For example, among the various efforts put forward to restrain royal spending in the parliament of 1385, the Commons explicitly refused to grant the wool subsidy for a month between 24 June and 1 August 1386 as a demonstration of its authority over the tax. This denied the king access

---

[69] I would therefore be less likely to align the "Melibee" with any specific sequence of events as topical references, such as Askins identifies from the start of the Appellant conflict: "*The Tale of Melibee* and the Crisis at Westminster"; also Ferster, *Fictions of Advice*, 89–107.

[70] Galway, "Geoffrey Chaucer, J.P. and M.P.," 16.

to his most important source of revenue for a crucial period.[71] In response, Richard imposed an embargo on wool exports and then allowed merchants to trade only if they purchased a license to evade his own ban. Thus through a manipulation of the law, the king squeezed the merchants for the revenue denied by parliament. The official responsible at the time for collecting the revenue – and who would have been squarely in the middle of the conflict – was Chaucer, whose job it was to collect the wool levy.[72] He was literally the man in the middle, since the funds were authorized only by decree of parliament but were collected on behalf of the Crown. In this case he would have been responsible for overseeing that parliament's ban was evaded by the sale of an evasion of another ban. In all of his jobs Chaucer appears to have taken his work seriously, but administering the "king's interests" probably put him in a difficult position more than once.

Situations and conflicts such as this, occurring with increasing regularity after the 1370s, offer a different context for understanding the *Parliament*'s opening focus on an abstract and neo-Stoic analysis of the "commune profit" (47, 75). As Bennett has shown, there was ample poetical and philosophical precedent for the combination of Macrobius' Ciceronian text with French courtly allegory, and with the tradition of visions and debate-poems. In the context of Chaucer's personal environment, these texts also would have made sense in conjunction with a satirical portrait of an English parliament. Put simply, these narrative forms are all *medial*. Chaucer begins the poem with an account of the dream of Scipio the Younger focusing on the *Somnium*'s message of political anagogy.[73] The way to "heaven" is the goal, and working for the *bonum commune* is the means for achieving it:

> "Know thyself first immortal,
> And loke ay besyly thow werche and wysse
> To commune profit, and thow shalt not mysse
> To comen swiftly to that place deere
> That ful of blysse is and of soules cleere."
>
> (73–7)

The text gestures to an afterlife, asserting that "oure present worldes lyves space / Nis but a maner deth" (53–4). The observance of "the lawe" is also necessary to avoid the infernal or purgatorial punishments of purification imposed on unruly souls (78–84). But in fact the real focus of Scipio

---

[71] *RP* 3.204. See Palmer, "The Parliament of 1385 and the Constitutional Crisis of 1386," 487.
[72] Galway, "Geoffrey Chaucer, J.P. and M.P.," 14–5; Pearsall, *Life of Geoffrey Chaucer*, 202–5. He resigned his position at the wool custom on 4 December 1386, following his appearance in the Wonderful Parliament of October-November 1386.
[73] See particularly Bennett, *The Parlement of Foules*, 25–61.

Africanus' lesson to his descendant is the "harmony" of the present world, which he lets him hear:

> And after that the melodye herde he
> That cometh of thilke speres thryes thre,
> That welle is of musik and melodye
> *In this world here*, and cause of armonye.
>
> (60–3, my emphasis)

In between heaven and hell is the middle space of our existence (32–3). The point is to gain a better perspective on how to live virtuously "in this world" (70) for both individual and communal good, for "commune profit" and – for the disposition of the single soul – singular profit. Harmony and well-being are the point, but in the terrestrial sphere as much as the transcendent one; it is the reason why Africanus makes his appearance in the first place.

Thus for all its transcendentalism, the dream-lesson of Scipio Africanus to Scipio the Younger is a distinctly mundane patrimony, one that requires a certain level of mediation and interpretation in order to have effect in the world. When the narrator falls asleep and experiences his own dream-visit from Africanus, this mediation shifts humorously. Africanus now derides Macrobius' text as a poor trot ("myn olde bok totorn, / Of which Macrobye roughte nat a lyte" [110–11]) and decides, willy-nilly, that the narrator will become his new *interpres*. Africanus grabs and shoves him through the gate or *limen* of the dream "park" into the middle of the new environment, the *locus amoenus* and temple of Venus.[74] His assignment is to see and "t'endite" (167–8) what goes on there. For our purposes, we can note that the delightful richness of Chaucer's version of a garden of *deduit* is inflected by parliamentary elements. First, although the narrator is presented in the Chaucerian idiom as one who "of love hast lost thy tast" (160), the beginning of his dream-travels is framed with the declaration that became, as we have seen, a catchphrase of petitionary desire: "for bothe I hadde thyng which that I nolde, / and ek I ne hadde that thyng that I wolde" (90–1). Regardless of his self-deprecatory positioning, the narrator is clearly looking for *something*, and so he comes forward as a petitioner and "sek man" (161) seeking remedy. His unwitting progress towards the assembly of birds is consonant with the social framing of the high court of parliament as the court with unique prominence and province, the one (or last) place to go to get petitions heard and, with luck, answered. Toward this end, the park, garden, and temple are themselves a congeries of assemblies,

---

[74] For analysis of sources and analogues see Bennett, *The Parlement of Foules*, 62–133.

a sort of natural *communitas communitates*. They include a catalogue of trees and flowers (173–86); the harmony of birds "on every bow" (190) and animals "of gentil kynde" (196); "every holsom spice and gras" (206); the easy assemblage of gods and allegories such as Cupide, Wille, Plesaunce, Aray, Lust, Youthe, Flaterye; and the gathering women dancing around the "temple of bras" (231). Around the temple are more figures of classical gods (Venus, Priapus, Bacchus, Ceres), lovers submitting their pleas to "Cypride" (277–9), and within the temple, images on the walls of fated lovers from myth and history, "peynted overal / Ful many a story" (284–5). These various gatherings prefigure the major assembly of the birds, which apparently takes place not within the *camera depicta* of Venus' temple but in the open garden of Nature.[75] This garden is represented not as a single space but as an assemblage of halls and rooms, probably evocative to anyone familiar with the environs of Westminster Palace and its clutch of chambers (including the *chambre depainte*) that filled with people at parliament-time:

> And in a launde, upon a hil of floures,
> Was set this noble goddesse Nature.
> Of braunches were *here halles and here boures*
> Iwrought after here cast and here mesure;
> Ne there nas foul that cometh of engendrure
> That they ne were prest in here presence
> *To take hire dom and yeve hire audyence.*
>
> (302–8, my emphasis)

The gatherings, dancings, and arrangements, both natural and artful, all converge in the plenitude of Nature and the birds, which are given the fullest catalogue (323–64).

As Bennett has demonstrated, overall the introductory sequence of the *Parliament* is similar to Guillaume de Lorris' garden of *deduit* and the images of nature in Alain de Lille's *De planctu naturae*. But it also is like stepping into Bromyard's house of Provence, with a much lighter touch. We are entering a rarified and refined environment that has the delights of a courtly dream-world but that is also tinged with hints of institutional solipsism. The progress of the poem to its focal scene, the parliament of the birds, prepares the reader for a grand gathering that takes part in the traditions of baronial and popular assemblies. As Nature the "vicaire of the almyghty Lord" declares, with "esy voys,"

---

[75] But as Bennett notes (115), there is no clear division between the Temple and the Garden or glade.

> "Ye knowe wel how, Seynt Valentynes day,
> By my statut and thorgh my governaunce,
> Ye come for to cheese – and fle youre wey –
> Youre makes, as I prike yow with plesaunce;
> But natheles, my ryghtful ordenaunce
> May I nat lete for al this world to wynne,
> That he that most is worthi shal begynne."
> (379, 382, 386–92)

This quasi-bureaucratic presentation of the assembly is signalled by the diction – words like "statut," "governaunce," "ordenaunce" – as well as the overt identification of the quadripartite classes of birds. They are "foules of ravyne," worm-fowl, water-fowl, and seed-fowl, reflecting the quadripartite division of the English parliament (323–9). As we have seen in other contemporary divisions of the social estates in parliament, a strict enumeration of classes was less the rule than the exception.[76] The nobility of the Lords obviously makes them the "top birds" of the assembly, but the identification of the lower three classes of fowl (perhaps representing the prelates, shire knights and burgesses, for example) is both possible and, in this context, apparently not too strict.[77] Instead, the poet's allegorical point of interest is the early and insistent description of the assembly as a deliberative one with a full range of representatives, "of foules every kynde" (365), not just from the "baronage" or the sovereign's noble council. The identity of the sovereign is also unclear, but intentionally so. Nature acts as "vicaire" or deputy and she speaks as a Chancellor would, in the name of the king to declare the cause of the summons but not in the *propria persona* of the king. This is an important procedural distinction, because although Nature claims the authority of the law in the assembly ("*my* statut" and "*my* governaunce"), it is evident that she herself is not the "almyghty Lord" in whose name the parliament has been gathered.[78] The deliberation proceeds under her guidance and command, but the power behind that command lies elsewhere.

Indeed much of the narrative's tension comes from the challenge of determining just where that guiding or commanding power lies, and from pinning down the vacillating identities that the assembly threatens to assume in the course of its deliberations. The charge to the royal tercel eagle to

---

[76] See the analysis in Chapter One.

[77] Bennett nonetheless makes some useful comparisons, *Parlement of Foules*, 170–3.

[78] It is certainly correct to identify Nature as the *vicaria Dei auctoris* but it is probably too much to call her a "monarch," as Bennett suggests (140, 174). Rather, in the English manner she acts as the "speaker" of the king, ie., a Chancellor-figure, while the sovereign, God, remains regally silent throughout.

choose first and to speak "in his gyse" (399) to his mate, after which all the other birds shall choose, is framed as a procedurally formal exercise:

> "But natheles, in this condicioun
> Mot be the choys of everich that is heere,
> That she agre to his eleccioun,
> Whoso he be that shulde be hire feere.
> This is oure usage alwey, fro yer to yeere . . ."
> (407–11)

Whatever the historical origins of this Valentine's Day ritual, the "choice" – the most insistently repeated word of the assembly – is presented as yearly and familiar. The patterned regularity of the event probably had less to do with the yearly occurrence of any such love-festival (for which there is little evidence in Chaucer's time beyond Chaucer himself) than it did with the tradition of annual parliaments, held in the late winter and early spring.[79] *Eleccioun* in this context is erotic "choice," or the expression of it, as the three tercel eagles immediately engage in a humorous bird version of the most familiar activity in parliaments: they submit pleas in the form of spoken bills. The opening of the first petition is a good example:

> With hed enclyned and with humble cheere
> This royal tersel spak, and tariede noght:
> "Unto my soverayn lady, and not my fere,
> I chese, and chese with wil, and herte, and thought,
> The formel on youre hond, so wel iwrought,
> Whos I am al, and evere wol hire serve,
> Do what hire lest, to do my lyve or sterve;
>
> "Besekynge hire of merci and of grace,
> As she that is my lady sovereyne;
> Or let me deye present in this place.
> For certes, longe may I nat lyve in payne,

[79] For contemporary analogues, see Bennett, *The Parlement of Foules*, 138–9; and *Chaucer's Dream Poetry: Sources and Analogues*, ed. Windeatt, 84–124. On the origins of Valentine's Day rituals, see the comprehensive study by Kelly, *Chaucer and the Cult of Saint Valentine*. Kelly suggests that Chaucer, as well as Gower or Graunson, may be the originator of the love-cult of St. Valentine, and that Chaucer's poem may reflect a celebration in May and not February, as the date of Valentine's Day had not yet been firmly established. The general timing of parliamentary sessions around Michaelmas and Easter (a context not considered by Kelly) would fit for either late winter or early spring. See Brown, "Parliament, c. 1377–1422," 111. During the fourteenth century, sessions of parliament were held anywhere from November to the following May, with some preference for January-February: See the calendar of parliamentary sessions given in Musson and Ormrod, *The Evolution of English Justice*, 194–205. The establishment of annual parliaments, frequently requested by the Commons, had been petitioned again in 1376: see *RP* 2.355, "Qe le Parlement soit tenuz chescun an."

For in myn herte is korven every veyne.
Havynge reward only to my trouthe,
My deere herte, have on my wo som routhe."
(414–27)

The royal tercel, first and best in this "gentil ple in love" (485), goes on the
longest in his petition for about four stanzas (416–41), as opposed to two
for the second tercel (450–62) and three for the third (464–83). The pleas
are never called bills, nor are they as discrete or textually formal as the later
examples we have seen. Nonetheless they have the form of bills and they
contain all the requisite elements, especially the first plea: an application to
the sovereign for "mercy" and "grace," a statement of wants (and extenuating
circumstances), appeals for the life of the petitioner, declarations of fidelity.
It is not immediately clear at first who "my soverayn lady" is supposed to
be, Nature or the beautiful formel eagle on her hand, until it is clarified
that "she that is my lady sovereyne" is the formel, who remains silent.
This opening sequence has less the format of a *debat d'amour* than of a
petitionary submission; in fact the three noble suitors never argue amongst
themselves at all. The stately courtliness of this procedure (which is said to
last a whole day [489–90]) is then disrupted by the impatient clamor of the
other classes of birds:

> The noyse of foules for to ben delyvered
> So loude rong, "Have don, and lat us wende!"
> That wel wende I the wode hadde al toshyvered.
> "Com of!" they criede, "allas, ye wol us shende!
> Whan shal youre cursede pletynge have an ende?"
> (491–5)

Here, when the story threatens to extend into a high-styled but very tedious
exercise in courtly love-lyricism, the other classes of the assembly interrupt
with an avian version of the *murmur, cri & noyse* for which parliaments,
especially the Commons, were notorious. Far from respecting the lofty
"pletynge"[80] of the nobles, the common birds just want them to leave off
and shut up, and they are not reticent in saying so. The scene is entirely
foreign to the *Parliament's* continental analogues in its inclusion of the lower
orders, and it is unique in its focus on the procedural aspects of assembly

---

[80] The *Riverside* text glosses *pletynge* simply as "argument," but it shares its etymon with *ple* and means
just as well "pleading, suing of a case" or, as I am interpreting it here, the submission of petitions or
pleas in a formal court context. The birds want them to leave off their pleading and "plea-ing." See
MED s.v. "plē."

formation.[81] The lower birds want the parliament concluded and themselves "delyvered" because the love-conflict between the nobles neither involves nor interests them. As it is going, the debate only delays and frustrates their own desires.

At this point the *Parliament* becomes most resonant with contemporary institutional form and most vigorous in the energy of its allegory, and most challenging. An individual steps forward to speak for each estate of birds, and in the case of the Cuckoo, to speak for the whole –

> "For I wol of myn owene autorite,
> For comune spede, take on the charge now,
> For to delyvere us is gret charite."
>
> (506–8)

– after which Nature, "which that alwey hadde an ere / To murmur of the lewednesse behynde" (519–20), formally calls for the election of speakers from the groups "to seyn the verdit for yow foules alle" (525). This repeatedly stated desire for "deliverance" leads to an arrangement of speakers that is practically overloaded with the technical and legal terms of assembly: [82]

> *Assented were to this conclusioun*
> The briddes alle; and foules of ravyne
> Han chosen fyrst, *by pleyn eleccioun*,
> The tercelet of the faucoun *to diffyne*
> Al here sentence, and as him lest, *termyne*;
> And to Nature hym gonne *to presente*,
> And she *accepteth* hym with glad entente.
>
> (526–32, my emphasis)

If we take Chaucer's playful allegory as a semi-serious application of specific terms and language, this passage stands out as one of the earliest instances in English where the word "election" is applied to the political nomination of a representative person or figure. Possibly it is the earliest such usage in a secular setting.[83] The *pleyn eleccioun*, an "open" and "full" election, combines the term usually applied to full royal parliaments (*en plein parlement*) with the choice of speakers among individual estates.[84] The arrangement

---

[81] As Bennett observes, "to 'birds of lower kind' Graunson [in *Songe Sainct Valentin*] gives never a note" (*The Parlement of Foules*, 137).

[82] On these terms see Bennett, *The Parlement of Foules*, 140 n. 2 and 168 n. 1.

[83] *MED*, s.v. "eleccioun," def. 3a, "the action or act of choosing a person to occupy some office or position." Prior examples (back to the *South English Legendary* of c. 1290) all refer to ecclesial elections and offices. Chaucer's works are among the earliest to apply the word to secular contexts (e.g., in "To His Purse" 23), of which the *Parliament* is arguably the first.

[84] On the phrase *in pleno parliamento*, see Cam, "From Witness of the Shire to Full Parliament," 113–6.

of multiple speakers could reflect a current desire – put forward abortively in the 1381 parliament but quashed by the king – that each "estate" should choose their own speakers and deliberate separately: not just the Lords and Commons, but the secular lords, prelates, justices, and shire knights.[85] More salient here is how this prominent declaration of *eleccioun* shifts the register of the term from the erotic to the electoral. Unlike later poems (the *Assembly* and the *Temple*), and quite unlike Chaucer's French contemporaries, here the voice that gets to speak is not simply an aristocratic supplicant or a figure of courtly refinement. Nor is it, pejoratively, only the voice of an unruly mob. Instead it is an elected speaker, a representative with mediatory authority between sovereign and subjects who can use the language of petition while at the same time bearing authority as the commissioned representative voice of the assembly. Thus Chaucer's unique arrangment here probably reflects, obliquely, the contemporary development of the office of parliamentary speaker, as the "choice" is shifted from the wooing of a marriage partner to the determination of a speaking voice or voices for the members of the community.

The authority of one particular bird is signalled immediately. Fittingly it is a "little eagle," a tercelet – apparently representing a member of the minor nobility – who has the voice. When this speaker tercelet comments that deciding between the petitioners is "ful hard" and "semeth it there moste be batayle," the suitors immediately respond in belligerent noble fashion by signaling their readiness for trial by combat: "'Al ready!' quod these egles tercels tho" (534, 539, 540). It is worth emphasizing that during parliaments the threat of aristocratic violence was very real. In 1381 the dukes of Lancaster and Northumberland, John of Gaunt and Henry Percy, brought large armed retinues to parliament. Their personal conflict threatened to trigger a gang fight. In the same assembly a discussion about Gaunt's sortie to Spain and Portugal turned into a "grant disputison & altercacion."[86] In 1333 a fight broke out in parliament between the lords Zouche and Grey, and earlier in 1315 the rolls vaguely record that Hugh Despenser the Younger attacked someone in parliament.[87] In 1388, when Nicholas Brembre threw down his glove and offered to defend himself in combat against charges of treason, chroniclers account that hundreds of gages were thrown in response in the parliament hall.[88] There are other examples of threats and aristocratic readiness to leave off discussion and fight, and it seems fair to assume that

[85] See *RP* 3.100; Butt, 378; Powell and Wallis, 389.   [86] *RP* 3.98, 114; Butt, 377.
[87] Harriss, "The Formation of Parliament, 1272–1377," 44; Fryde, *Tyranny and Fall of Edward II*, 33; *RP* 1.352–3.
[88] Butt, 397; *Westminster Chronicle* 310–11; Favent, *Historia*, 16.

the normal gatherings of parliaments were also occasions for the threat of feuds, personal vendettas, and violence.[89] In the French versions of the debate-poem *Blancheflour et Florence*, analogues to the *Parliament*, violence is the solution in the birds' debate over the relative worth of clerks or knights as lovers. When they cannot agree, the nightingale and parrot fight and the parrot is defeated.[90] As in the "Melibee," it initially appears in the *Parliament* that events will steer towards communal violence with the assembly sanctioning or even encouraging it. But this does not happen when the speaker tercelet responds to the suitors:

> "Nay, sires" quod he, "if that I durste it seye,
> Ye don me wrong, my tale is not ido!
> For, sires – ne taketh not agref I preye –
> It may not gon as ye wolde in this weye;
> *Oure is the voys that han the charge in honde,*
> And to the juges dom ye moten stonde."
>
> (541–6, my emphasis)

This is, of course, an allegory, and these are birds. But we should not miss the subtle radicalism of Chaucer's parliamentary representation here. Not only is aristocratic hot-headedness defused by the polite authority of the tercelet, he makes a grand claim for the legal authority of *all* the birds, not just the nobles, as judges in this case. In a rhetorical maneuver exploiting the communal tradition of parliamentary authority, the tercelet collapses the plural into the singular in the communal ideal of speaking with one voice: "*oure* is *the* voys." It is not that the speaker tercelet wants to foreclose debate. Rather, like Prudence, his mediation opens up a space that would otherwise be occupied by physical conflict and, presumably, it will enable the assembly to find the one voice needed for resolution.

His following declaration – "And therfore pes!" (547) – thus intervenes into the marriage-debate by replacing formalized aristocratic feuding with a raucous communal debate about male-female relationships. The result is both liberatory and somewhat alarming. The debate of the birds – intense, funny, insulting, accusatory – has only a general likeness to the ordered scholastic debate-poems often cited as its exemplars. Indeed the argument of the following eight stanzas has more the tone of a heated political

---

[89] A later famous example is the "Parliament of Bats" in 1426 at Leicester: see Butt, 508. Because the conflict between Gloucester and Beaufort threatened to spill out into open violence, weapons were not allowed in the great hall of the castle where parliament was held. Parliamentarians carried small wooden clubs up their sleeves, but no violence is recorded to have taken place.

[90] See Windeatt, *Chaucer's Dream-Poetry: Sources and Analogues*, 92–9.

discussion than of a philosophical *summa*.[91] This too is almost certainly reflective of the contemporary practice of parliaments, which would sometimes dilate for weeks on end and, as we have seen, were accused of pointlessness, talk for the sake of talk. In this setting no Prudence, and little prudence, is forthcoming, which seems more asinine than threatening. So the "termyne" of the exchange comes only when Nature herself also calls for "pes" and for "conclusioun" by returning the power of "eleccioun" to the formel (617, 620–1). From a public deliberation on the nature of true love, the focus returns to the individual question of *this* female and her marriage choice. Nature benignly counsels the formel to accept the first "royal tercel" (633). In this context the formel's response deserves attention and explication:

> With dredful vois the formel hire answerde,
> "My rightful lady, goddesse of Nature!
> Soth is that I am evere under youre yerde,
> As is everich other creature,
> And mot be youres whil my lyf may dure;
> And therfore graunteth me my firste bone,
> And myn entente I wol yow sey right sone."
>
> "I graunte it yow," quod she; and right anon
> This formel egle spak in this degre:
> "Almyghty queen, unto this yer be don,
> I axe respit for to avise me,
> And after that to have my choys al fre.
> This al and som that I wol speke and seye;
> Ye gete no more, although ye do me deye!"
>
> (638–51)

In its combination of institutional and artistic elements and in its irresolute resolution of what has come before it, this response is humorously dazzling. The "voys" of the assembly has been replaced by the "dredful vois" of this lone female bird. She herself assumes the position of petitioner to Nature, explicitly asking for a boon as a supplicant. But her reply immediately reveals that she also plays the role of sovereign. Her request for "respit for to avise me" overtly imitates the documentary response of the king to rejected parliamentary petitions. These were endorsed with a regal *le roi s'avisera*, "the king would advise himself," which was a polite and dignified

---

[91] Compare Bennett, *The Parlement of Foules*, 134–45. The complete lack of ecclesial trappings in the parliament also contrasts with poems such as Jean de Condé's *La Messe des Oisiaus* (*Chaucer's Dream Poetry*, 104–19).

way to say "no" without having to say no.[92] In other words, this request is really a command, a response refusing to respond which is a refusal, simply put. The further qualification that the formel will reserve "my choys al fre" alludes to the royal reservation of dignity and freedom from compulsion, commonly expressed as the protection of royal "liberties."[93] The conclusion also inverts the usual petitionary appeal on behalf of the life of the supplicant by turning it into a staunch refusal to append or amend her decision, come what may. So from the authoritative arrangements of Nature to the stylized conflicts of the aristocrats, to the democratic but blathering logomachy of the lower birds, we arrive in the parliament at the final and in some ways frankest expression of commanding power. The formel delivers a *voirdit* that cannot be overturned, and so Nature does not even try.

Yet, at the same time and in the same forms, this is an equally frank admission of the powerlessness of a feminized petitionary position. The allegorical situation of the formel is, *mutatis mutandis*, the same as the impasse faced by Elizabeth de Burgh. The female/formel is subjected to the scrutiny and authority of a parliament – and of a control that is local-ized there and diffused throughout the entire social system – that has the power to guide and authorize her marital disposition. This is not to desub-limate the *Parliament's* thematic treatment of courtship to the calculus of class positions, nor to deny completely that the formel's demurral could be understood as the operation of what Bennett calls an "instinctive femi-ninity." But precisely where that femininity is subjected to such contraints, as when "the maiden is of such rank that her betrothal is the whole com-monwealth's concern," the tensions represented in Chaucer's allegory, both political and personal, stand in greater relief.[94] Despite her possessions, power, and status, a woman like Elizabeth de Burgh must have felt like a bird in a cage, or a formel on the hand, when the question of her marriage and property was subjected to parliamentary manipulation and control. Like the formel, she was *both* marriageable and property, with the power to petition for her "choys al fre" enabled and proscribed in the confines of a royal assembly whose material operation and well-being actually depended upon the "free" circulation of women just like her. And if we assume – as we surely must – that there were noblewomen among the textual or

---

[92] Noted by Bennett, *The Parlement of Foules*, 168. The formula of simple assent was *le Roi le voet*. Refusal could vary slightly (*le Roi se ent vorra adviser, le Roi ent prendra avisement*) with other shades of assent or reservation.

[93] See, e.g., the reservation of royal liberties at the end of the 1386 parliament, *RP* 3.224. Similar reservations of royal "liberties" were sometimes appended to specific petitions (vid. *RP* 3.266–7).

[94] Bennett, *The Parlement of Foules*, 177.

aural audience for the *Parliament of Fowls*, women not unlike Elizabeth de Burgh, it is sobering to think of how they might have identified with the particular crux of marital choice that Chaucer represents in this displaced allegorical context.

So the formel's declaration is both a statement of courtly power and a petition for grace. Perhaps fairly, our sense is that eventually, wil-she nil-she, this bird will have to come to roost. Chaucer's decision not to represent *that* decision, that action, opens up the space of mediation and delay wherein an audience can reflect on the political situation of a female placed in this framework, and on the framework itself. The unique environment of discussion and deliberation in the poem is a *parlement* where the woman's plea has been a plea for some space and peace. All that passes in the meantime is, as Nature calls it, an "entremes" (665), a between-course or middle-time, an "intermission" that sums up the poem's final gesture toward mediation. The final election in the narrative is of the fowls "chosen . . . for to synge" (673), who sing a roundel, a round-song that is courtly, beautiful, and fashionable ("the note, I trowe, imaked was in Fraunce" [677]), but that is, by the demands of its form, a song that goes nowhere, only in circles. Certainly it can fill up the time in-between with a pleasant harmony, which has been a consistent thematic focus of the *Parliament's* various parts. It returns the dream proper to the lovely regularities of an aesthetic order that the poem itself, as a whole, also imitates by ending where it had begun, roundel-like. In the end the narrator searches still for "som thyng for to fare / The bet" (698–9) among his books and reading.

What we are left with on one hand is a system, of parliament and *parlement*, that just goes round and round. The joyous mating of the lower birds – who are said to have "*re*-covered" their mates (666–72, 688) – fits the pattern of dilation and repetition and grants it some level of success. But on the other hand the lack of real closure seems equally to express a sense of failure and the absence of an authoritative voice or decision that could conclude the conundrums of the public good and the "comune spede" for the whole. Nature assumes the multiple roles of an organizing Chancellor, an intercessory Prudence, and also an intercessory "queen" of sorts, but one whose ultimate ability has been simply to convene and disperse, not really to compel a decision. The formel is similarly ambiguous in her authority both to plead and to refuse pleading. Despite the birds' complaints, ultimately the parliament has decided nothing. So it appears difficult to draw any particular conclusions about the author's own view on the matter of marital power and choice, or of parliamentary efficacy, beyond perhaps Strohm's observation in a similar context that "Chaucer shows his discontent with the whole system of female abjection and male conces-sion."[95] This is a topic that attracted and taxed Chaucer throughout his career. In this institutional context "female abjection" also comes to include not just women, but the whole system of petition in which a woman's place was, formally speaking, one that could be occupied by any and all suers for grace and "pity." In a specifically parliamentary setting, Chaucer reveals a positional sympathy for those petitioners – seekers after something "to fare the bet" – whose own roles, personal and professional, allow them a window on the operations of power and an understanding of its various voices, but whose desires were by no means assured to be satisfied. In this manner, the written circulations of a clerkly poet take on some of the qualities of that feminized position to which they bear an exterior witness, and for which they artistically exploit the institutional and documentary forms specific to parliament.

5 VIOLENCE, MERCILESSNESS, AND POWERLESSNESS, 1386–8

Chaucer's most extensive representations of parliaments in the "Melibee" and the *Parliament of Fowls* thus share the thematic and formal aspects of an inquiry into the limits and voice of *communitas* when that voice is expressed by the institutional mechanisms of petition and assembly. Both works were probably composed prior to Chaucer's participation in the Wonderful Parliament of 1386 and the long crisis that culminated in the Merciless Parliament of 1388. Nonetheless, these narratives stand to be situated in the general environment of these crisis years on account of the resonances between fiction and politics.[96] Chaucer's attendance at the parliament of 1386 has often been attributed to bench-packing by the king (or by John of Gaunt). Although his presence was almost certainly attributable to his professional relation to the king, there is in fact surprisingly little evidence to suggest that the Commons of this parliament was packed with the king's supporters, or that Chaucer's election as MP in a single parliament was anything unusual.[97] What was unusual – and what may have caught him by

[95] Strohm, *Hochon's Arrow*, 112.
[96] See also the analysis of Strohm, "The Textual Environment of Chaucer's 'Lak of Stedfastnesse,'" in *Hochon's Arrow*, on the petitions against maintenance during the Cambridge Parliament of September 1388.
[97] See Scott, "Chaucer and the Parliament of 1386"; Clarke, "The Lancastrian Faction and the Wonder-ful Parliament"; Lewis, "Re-election to Parliament in the Reign of Richard II." On the question of "packing" see also Richardson, "John of Gaunt and the Parliamentary Representation of Lancashire," and Clark, "Magnates and Their Affinities," 130–1, who notes that irregularities in parliamentary elections were usually attributable to the local gentry or sheriffs, not to the king or greater lords.

surprise – was the vehemence with which this assembly attacked the king's household. The chronicles also testify to a foreboding sense of violence that only deepened as the political crisis got worse. The parliamentary session of 1385 had set the grounds for the Commons' critique of the royal household's expenditures. In 1386, parliament met during the general anxiety of an invasion scare that set the entire country on edge.[98] When the king became recalcitrant and refused to hear the Commons' complaints, he retreated to his palace at Eltham and demanded that the parliamentarians come to him there. Knighton's chronicle records another "secret rumor" (*occultus rumor*) that the king was plotting to kill the MPs on their arrival.[99] No speaker of the Commons is recorded for this assembly. In this environment of mistrust, the representatives chosen to bear the voice of parliament were from the nobility: Thomas Woodstock, Duke of Gloucester, and Thomas Arundel, Bishop of Ely. They went to the king at Eltham "on behalf of the Lords and Commons in parliament" (*ex parte procerum et communium parliamenti*) and initiated a stern discussion.[100]

The remarkable events that ensued have been well analyzed elsewhere.[101] What stands out in this context is the way the chronicle records represent the crisis, and how these accounts grimly depict an almost completely inverted version of Chaucer's more hopeful parliamentary narratives, even as they appeal to the same ideals of unity, legality, and harmony. From start to finish, the crisis of 1386–8 was conducted as a parliamentary struggle for the power and authority of public voice. In Knighton's *Chronicle* the embassy of Gloucester and Arundel to the king is presented as a direct debate, the two nobles assuming the common voice of parliament as a single interlocutor with Richard. They inform the king of his dereliction of duty, his responsiblity to respond to the needs of the community, his need for better counsel, and the threat that, if better government were not forthcoming, "it would be lawful with the common assent and agreement of the people of the realm (*cum communi assensu et consensu populi regni*) to put down the king from his royal seat, and raise another of the royal lineage in his place."[102] This personal threat had its desired effect and the

---

[98] Palmer, "The Parliament of 1385 and the Constitutional Crisis of 1386," and *England, France and Christendom*, 67–87; Butt, 387–92.

[99] This "plot to kill the knights of the shire" (*ymaginacio mortis de militibus parliamenti*) is recorded in Knighton's *Chronicle*, 354–5 and in the charges of the Merciless Parliament in 1388 (see *Chronicle*, 470–3). It is not clear from Knighton's jumbled account if he perhaps repeated it after the fact.

[100] Knighton, *Chronicle*, 354–5.

[101] See Saul, *Richard II*, 176–96; also Butt, 394–401. For a reassessment of some sources for 1388 see Oliver, "A Political Pamphleteer in Late Medieval England: Thomas Fovent, Geoffrey Chaucer, Thomas Usk, and the Merciless Parliament of 1388."

[102] Knighton, *Chronicle*, 355–61, 361.

king capitulated. Following Richard's vigorous but unsuccessful attempts to reassert his power in the next year – an effort bringing the nation once again to the brink of crisis and civil war – the parliament of 1388 assembled as a tribunal to execute judgment against members of the king's affinity deemed "treasonous." The actions of the Appellants against Richard, particularly at the start of their campaign, are represented as a popular and univocal revolt against the oppressions of the king's favorites:

And the greater and the lesser sort of the people and the commons were made as it were one (*quasi una persona*) against the aforesaid plunderers of the realm, crying and exclaiming 'Let them be swept away, lest the unsullied honour of the English people be impaired by such traitors.'[103]

The inevitable figuration of this supposedly national and unified voice speaking *quasi una persona* is parliament, the only court where state treason trials took place.[104] But it was not the kind of reform parliament as had emerged during the events of 1376. This time, the speakers were nobility. Gloucester and Arundel were joined by the earls of Derby, Warwick, and Nottingham, and they came forward as Appellants bringing a massive "petition" of accusation by way of the Commons against the king and the royal household. This was done, as the roll asserts, for the common profit, *come loiaulx lieges nostre dit Seigneur le Roi, pur profit du Roi & de Roialme.*[105]

What resulted was the most singular abuse of parliamentary procedure ever seen. With almost every check on their power removed and with no one to countermand them, the Appellant lords engaged in a version of the aristocratic violence that Chaucer's narratives had, in art and allegory, managed to defuse and contain. The records of the proceedings are all the more remarkable for the appearances of legality they try to uphold. The judgments were asserted to be "according to the established law of parliament" (*secundum consuetudinem legis in parliamento*) and "by the common judgement of parliament" (*communi iudicio parliamenti*).[106] In fact the appeals were unprecedented and the judgments of death, banishment, and disinheritance expressly violated established statutes. The roll records the assertion that the peer judges in parliament, *come lour Libertee & Franchise*, were bound by neither common law nor civil law, which was the

[103] Knighton, *Chronicle*, 420–1: "Factique sunt quasi una persona maiores et minores plebei et comines contra antedictos regni predones, clamantes et dicentes, 'Deleantur de uita ne honor egregius Anglicane gentis per tales proditores uiduetur.'" A similar "popular" event is recounted when a great crowd met outside the Tower of London (426–7).

[104] Musson and Ormrod, *The Evolution of English Justice*, 27.

[105] *RP* 3.229–36. The petition in all thirty-nine articles is also recorded in the *Westminster Chronicle*, 236–9, as are the separate trial petitions against the accused individuals.

[106] Knighton, *Chronicle*, 432–3.

frankest statement of parliamentary supremacy and lawlessness possible.[107] The Chief Justice Robert Tresilian was subjected to a lynch mob. Lord Mayor of London Nicholas Brembre, the lawyer and courtier John Blake, and the London undersheriff Thomas Usk were all executed after perfunctory trials. Other courtiers (John Beauchamp, John Salisbury, and James Berners) were later given similarly short shrift before quick executions. The six judges of the King's Bench were condemned to death but their sentences were commuted to banishment. In the most divisive judgment, the Garter knight and devoted courtier to the king, Sir Simon Burley, was tried in protracted proceedings, condemned on flimsy evidence, and executed. This was done despite the ambivalence surrounding the accusations against him and despite the personal petitions of both the king and queen. Chronicles record that Queen Anne bowed on her knees in supplication to the Appellants to intercede for Burley's life, to no avail.[108]

What is evident from the records, and what is strongly evident in comparison to Chaucer's narratives, is that the result of the events of 1386–8 was a parliamentary assembly whose violence simply would not brook any mediation or intercession. No voice of "Prudence," no queenly intercessor, no petitionary intervention was allowed. As the Merciless Parliament dragged on over months, it became increasingly clear that the Appellants were themselves indulging in the kinds of abuses they purported to punish. Another submerged piece of textual evidence betrays the growing disenchantment of the public. As far as we can tell, this too was a petition submitted in parliament, probably drafted by parliamentarians themselves. The only surviving copy appears in Knighton's *Chronicle*.[109] The long bill, purporting to express the unanimous assent of "the humble commons" (*lez humblez comines*), is framed as yet another call to the king for good governance, but it strongly hints that the behavior of the Appellants was causing nationwide strife. Justice still is not maintained, laws are unequally executed, taxes are still oppressive to the people, the realm is not protected,

---

[107] The self-declared exemption from civil and common law appears at *RP* 3.244. See Saul, *Richard II*, 191–3, who notes wryly, "the implication of this lofty if somewhat ambivalent statement was that parliament could make up the rules as it went along: which is precisely what it did" (192). Butt concurs, "thus Parliament made a mockery of its own position as guardian of law, by inventing a 'law' of treason, and a process for implementing it, which were valid for one Parliament only" (398).

[108] See *Westminster Chronicle*, 330–1; Saul, *Richard II*, 194.

[109] For analysis (and description of the Appellant's abuses) see Palmer, *England, France and Christendom*, 136–7, 237–8, who notes that the bill was probably drafted during the second session of the parliament in May 1388, when "discontent among the taxpayers had apparently reached such proportions that the Commons were acutely nervous of the possibility of another Peasants' Revolt" (136–7).

and the commons of the realm – the popular commons of the general public – have risen in revolt, "not least [because] you and your lords have stayed so long in this parliament" (*sil a fuisse pur long tariance de uous nostre seignur et noz altres seignurs en cest presente parlyment*).[110] This restlessness may have been provoked in particular by the extended proceedings over Burley. As Favent's contemporary account indicates in his paraphrase of the petition, discontent was far wider than court circles:

> Therefore, since the said Commons is exhausted by so long a time in labors and expenses attending parliament, and as it was likely that their long expectation in parliament would not be brought to effect, they requested that the king release them so that they might freely depart from parliament for their own business, and in the future, when matters did not pertain to them, not to disturb them by giving the reason for such fatigue in future times that some misfortune had been fostered unexpectedly in the kingdom.[111]

In this, we can almost hear Chaucer's lower fowls haplessly bleating to the aristocratic tercels, *have don, and let us wende*. As in Chaucer's allegory, the fatiguing insistence upon sham formality and righteousness – the insistence upon one party's pre-eminence in valor, nobility, and true judgment – scarcely conceals the manipulative tedium and frightening penchant for violence that motivated the appellants. It is not surprising that this petition was not entered in the official parliamentary roll, which presents a uniformly Appellant perspective. The events, divisive as they were and as and far-reaching as they would eventually prove to be, required a smoothly tempered sheen in the official documentary record. The parliamentary record also indicates how close the events came to Chaucer himself, as all of the men executed were probably known to Chaucer and some (like John Blake, who had also been Clerk of the King's Works) were of a roughly equivalent social position but more factionally aligned.[112]

The parliamentary roll also records the Appellants' petitionary demand, which Richard ambiguously endorsed, that none of the "traitors" attainted and disinherited during the parliament should ever be reconciled or shown pity later.[113] Reconciliation, especially the kind of parliamentary

[110] Knighton, *Chronicle*, 442–7.

[111] Favent, *Historia*, 21: "Igitur quia dicta communitas tam longo tempore laboribus et expensis in parlamento fatigatur, et ut verisimile fuerat quod diutina eorum expectacio in parliamento nichil operaretur in effectu, pecierunt regem eos dimittere ut possint libere ad propria a parliamento recedere, nec eos in posterum inquietare cum non stetit per eos dato quod aliquod infortunium in regno pretextu huius fatigacionis futuris temporibus inopinate nouercauerit." Translation by Galloway, in Steiner and Barrington, *The Letter of the Law*, 249.

[112] On Blake, see *Chaucer Life-Records*, 411–2. He held the Clerkship from 1378 to 1381.

[113] *RP* 3.250: "ITEM, qe null des Traitours atteintz par l'Appell susdit, ou Accusementz des Communes, qe sont unqore en vie, ne soient reconseillez ne restitutz a la Ley par Pardon n'en autre

reconciliation we have seen in cases such as Elizabeth de Burgh's, or Cecilie Deumarcz's, or even of Prudence and Melibee (by the reinstatement of properties by any action, charter of pardon, or revocation of banishment) is denied on pain of execution. As Andrew Galloway has noted in Gower's presentation of the events of 1388 in the *Cronica Tripertita*, "pity here has become utterly merciless, a legal instrument of absolute power over individual subjects of a dictatorial parliament, however loudly the ethic's legitimacy is proclaimed by efforts to denounce and purge a putatively false and corrupt mirroring ethic."[114] The best pity, in effect, was to show no pity. Ironically, the very textual operations *defined by* the beseeching of pity – the feminized action of petition and submission – carried this mercilessness to its furthest extreme. In petitioning for the eternal denial of further petitions, the Appellants of the Merciless Parliament were both turning on its head, and fulfilling, the inner logic inherent to the petitionary stance of powerful powerlessness. They demanded, in a request with the force of compulsion, that their victims forever remain outside the sovereign's grace – in a perverted sense, the most powerful and graceful place of all.

6 "FROM EVERY SHIRES ENDE": MEDIATION, SPEAKING,
AND THE FRAME OF THE *CANTERBURY TALES*

These events bring us a long way from the parliamentary challenges of individuals like de Burgh and Deumarcz, and a fair distance from the courtly refinement of the love-bills in poems like the *Assembly of Ladies* and "The Complaint Unto Pity." But they help to show how all of these events and discursive practices in 1386 and 1388, and in Chaucer's earlier work, participated in a common network of assumptions, tropes, and conflicts that he successfully exploited, especially in the *Parliament of Fowls*. In this context, what the mediatory voice of art and allegory allows is a *gap*, a space not unlike the space desired by the formel, or by the meddling/middling Prudence, for things to work out, or simply for some respite. But the *différance* of a specifically parliamentary kind (all talk, little action) carries with it certain real-world threats and elisions. Even as I have called the *Parliament of Fowls* hopeful and insightful, we are just as strongly led back to the recognition that for Chaucer, "associational governance" was at heart

manere: savant la Grace & Pardon q'est fait en cest present Parlement. Et si ascun pursue de les reconseiller, ou les faire pardon avoir, ou les restituer a la Ley en ascune manere, & ceo duement & overtement & par record prove, soit ajugge & eit execution come Traitour & Enemy du Roy & de Roialme."
[114] Galloway, "The Literature of 1388 and the Politics of Pity in Gower's *Confessio amantis*," 103.

"a difficult, precarious, practical affair."[115] The 1386 parliament in particular may have given Chaucer a topical model for the least ideal parliament in all his works, the myopic and ultimately self-destructive assembly of the Trojans in Book 4 of *Troilus and Criseyde*.[116] The excesses of 1388 could only have solidified the sense that just as the system of royal advising and counsel was open to abuse and injustice, so too were communal parliaments. Then as now, speaking in the name of "*the* community" was a means of victimizing particular individuals and communities. Thus the conflict inherent in the struggle to define who gets to assume the name of *communitas*, or who should presume to speak for the guardianship of the common good, plays out in the recognizable but distanced register of allegorical voices assembled in a developing literary tradition, with a new immediacy.

Leaving allegory aside, the last such recognizable register I would like to juxtapose in this parliamentary context is the frame-tale arrangement of the *Canterbury Tales* itself. If we take it as axiomatic that "Chaucer's politics lives in the form of his fiction,"[117] we may also acknowledge that parliament provides a useful analogue for the uniquely deliberative and contentious community that comes together at the Tabard Inn in Southwark. Looking at it from both a literary and an historical perspective, the frame-tale structure of the *Tales* is plainly over-determined. Tale and *novelle* collections, the *summa* form, the scribal practice of *compilatio*, estates-satires, scholastic and rhetorical *praefationes*, sermon exempla collections: all these and more provide analogues, close and distant, for Chaucer's singular achievement in the "General Prologue." Apart from all these, certain aspects of the "Prologue" find their strongest echoes neither in contemporary literary genres nor only in the general ideological structures of associational formations, but in the specific, real-world practices of parliamentary assembly and *parlement*.

A few simple observations point in this direction. When we meet the assemblage of pilgrims, the narrator proceeds to tell "the condicioun" of each and the "degree" and "array" of their social position (38–41). But the very first specification of their social provenance is not as a group of classes or estates, but as a meeting of regions: they gather "from every shires ende / Of Engelond" (15–16). The shires – not estates – were the original and durable units of constituency that defined the representative practice of

---

[115] Wallace, *Chaucerian Polity*, 79.

[116] See McCall and Rudisill, "The Parliament of 1386 and Chaucer's Trojan Parliament"; McCall, "The Trojan Scene in Chaucer's *Troilus*"; and Patterson, *Chaucer and the Subject of History*, 155–64, for analyses.

[117] Justice, *Writing and Rebellion*, 227.

national assembly in England.[118] We move among the Wife of Bath, out of Somerset in the west; the Shipman from Dartmouth in Devonshire; the Oxfordshire clerk; the numerous Londoners (such as the Manciple from a "temple" (567), presumably one of the London Inns of Court, Madame Eglentyne from the London suburb of Stratford, the Pardoner from Rouncesval, the Host from the suburb of Southwark); the Reeve from Norfolk (and the northern students of his tale); the Merchant with his Orwell interests in Suffolk. The pilgrims are arranged not only by occupation, class, and estate, but as also an assembly of the representative regions of the nation ("fro Berwyk into Ware" [692]) that are associated with the shires, north to south, east to west. Most of the pilgrims are unlocalized in this way. The Parson, for example, is "of a Toun" (478); the Knight is identified in detail by his overseas exploits but by no region of his homeland; the Guildsmen are not specified by town or region. The parliamentarian Franklin, like the Friar, is specified only by "his contree" (216, 340). And London is over-represented, a fact which, given its outsized importance, is itself accurately representative. Nonetheless, Chaucer clearly made an effort to capture a comprehensive and geographically national "portrait" as represented by people from these units of community organization, the shires, which gathered only at parliament-time.[119]

As constituents from the shires, most of the pilgrims could not have been parliamentarians or MPs strictly understood. Parliament included no women, nor (later) members of the lower clergy, certainly no one below the status of a Franklin, or the Host or, arguably, the Merchant. The Host's probable real-life model, Henry Bailiff hosteler, and the Narrator, as Chaucer himself *in propria persona*, as well as the Franklin ("ful ofte tyme he was knyght of the shire" [GP 356]), are reasonable candidates for parliamentary representatives, as also, arguably, the Knight and eventually his son and heir the Squire would be potential candidates for the baronage or peerage. But thinking of the pilgrims in the "General Prologue" as a parliament only in this limited fashion misses the deeper significance of how the assembly acted as a model for literary form. While only a small handful of the pilgrims could have been representatives at a parliament, each and every one of them, secular and ecclesial, could have had a voice at any contemporary parliament *as a petitioner*. Indeed contemporary

---

[118] On this point see the work of Cam: "The Theory and Practice of Representation in Medieval England," "The Legislators of Medieval England," "From Witness of the Shire to Full Parliament," and "The Community of the Shire and the Payment of its Representatives in Parliament."

[119] On the historical importance of representatives from the shires and shire courts see also Butt, 92–5, 127–8, 133–5, *et passim*.

parliaments probably looked, and acted, much like this assembly of individuals. They are all gathered from one end of England to the other; they
are all of free status and privileged to sue for grace and justice in the king's
courts, just as they are going to give thanks and petition for grace at the
shrine of the martyr in Canterbury. Insofar as representation was the ability
to speak and be heard in a petitionary mode – the right to tell your tale, as it
were, and to hope for a fair judgment – the Canterbury pilgrims, each and
all, are an accurate portrait of precisely the middling and vocal classes who
were the true mainstay of later fourteenth-century parliamentary business
in its most quotidian forms.

The Host's opening speech to the assembled pilgrims indicates that he
realizes the generally petitionary nature of their trip to Canterbury, and he
takes the opportunity to nominate himself their marshal or leader. Understanding the significance of this maneuver merits some close attention to
his words:

> "Ye goon to Caunterbury – God yow speede,
> *The blisful martir quite yow youre meede!*
> And wel I woot, as ye goon by the weye,
> Ye shapen yow to talen and to pleye . . .
> And if yow liketh alle *by oon assent*
> For to stonden *at my juggement,*
> And for to werken as I shal yow seye,
> Tomorwe, whan ye riden by the weye,
> Now, by my fader soule that is deed,
> But ye be myrie, I wil yeve yow myn heed!
> *Hoold up youre hondes*, withouten moore speche."
>
> (769–83, my emphasis)

For the Martyr to "quit" them their "mede" or payment, we can fairly
assume that they will be going to make their petitions at the shrine of St.
Thomas. What is more subtle and interesting is the way the Host uses the
language of assembly to organize the pilgrimage into a coherent group. He
appeals to the "oon assent" or unified voice of the pilgrims who, presumably,
do not yet *have* one voice to give. The Host's request effectively creates it
in the act of addressing them as a community. His "juggement" sounds
authoritative and impositional, until we realize that he is asking them to
do something that has never been represented in secular literature before:
he asks them to *vote*, by way of a show of hands, for what they would
like to do. As we have seen, voting by numerical division was probably
practiced, but was never represented either in assembly records or in the
literature of the period because of the social and ideological pressure for

unanimitas.[120] The request for the pilgrims to "hoold up youre hondes" is a request for the potential manifestation of separation or disagreement at the very start, before the pilgrimage even gets under way. This is perhaps the reason why the pilgrims themselves appear reluctant to take the Host at his word and instead grant him the floor, without division, to declare his "voirdit" (787). His plan for the tale-telling contest provides the motive and organization for the narrative. The principles of assembly are reaffirmed by the repetition of certain key terms:

> "And whoso wole my *juggement* withseye
> Shal paye al that we spenden by the weye.
> And if ye *vouche sauf* that it be so,
> Tel me anon, withouten wordes mo,
> And I wol erly shape me therfore."
> This thyng was graunted, and oure othes swore
> With ful glad herte, and preyden hym also
> That he wolde *vouche sauf* for to do so,
> And that he wolde been oure *governour*,
> And of oure tales *juge and reportour*,
> And sette a soper at a certeyn pris,
> And we wol reuled been at his devys
> In heigh and lough; and thus *by oon assent*
> *We been acorded to his juggement.*
>
> (805–18, my emphasis)

This is the language of associational formation, of guilds and fraternities or maybe a *pui*. More specifically, with its legal verbiage and arrangements of petition, and because it is overtly a *talking* assembly, it is also the creation of a parliament, one reminiscent of the assembly and organized grouping of the Commons as described by the Anonimalle chronicler's account of the Good Parliament of 1376 – another assembly, we can recall, where each member was called upon to share his "tale" for the good of all.[121] The Host proposes to stand as an authoritative "judge" and "governor" with a penalty for anyone who would oppose his verdict. He is also "reportour," which in this setting is an ambiguous description since it is, as far as we can tell, the first recorded English usage of the word. It appears to mean that the Host will not only judge the tales but also carry them or bear them, "re-port" them or rephrase them, in a quasi-legal sense, for the purposes of representing the assembly.[122] Also legalistic is the exchange of "vouch-safes":

[120] See the analysis in Chapter Two.   [121] See the analysis in Chapter Two.
[122] See *MED* s.vv. "report(e)," "reporten," "reportour(e)"; *OED* s.v. "report." The earliest citations after Chaucer are c. 1410–20. Official parliamentary "reports" were not regularized until the sixteenth

each side of the deal (the Host and his group) requests that the other offer a reciprocal voucher for the agreement, which in its original sense was a petition specifically for a grant of grace or permission.[123] The establishment of a concluding feast or "soper" was a common aspect of guild assemblies and also parliaments, which usually ended with a celebratory (or reconciliatory) meal.[124] The repetition of the Host's own couplet "assent/juggement" (777–8, 817–8) signals the final acceptance of his plan for the pilgrimage and they share a drink to seal the deal. The following morning the Host wakes the pilgrims "and gadrede us togidre alle in a flok" (824), reasserts his control of the assembly, and sets in motion the tale-telling sequence with drawn straws, probably rigged. The Knight, "to kepe his foreward by his free assent" (852), begins the game.

As in the *Parliament of Fowls* with its worm-fowl and seed-fowl, Chaucer's desire to represent a representative social totality among the pilgrims has led him to create a playfully parliamentary image with a generously comprehensive membership. As Muriel Bowden observed, the Host "could easily be a lord's marshal if some of his rough edges were filed down."[125] The better analogy would be to the institution to which his probable real-life model actually belonged, since Henri Bailly, burgess and hosteler of Southwark, sat as an MP in the parliaments of 1376–7 at Westminster and 1378–9 at Gloucester.[126] Perhaps the sportive confusion of the Tabard Inn and the chaotic Commons at Westminster resembled one another to Chaucer, who surely spent time in both houses. All of this suggests that the Host is presented neither as a "king" nor as an autocratic leader of the pilgrimage. Rather, in his deployment and exploitation of basic bureaucratic procedures, he offers himself, and is accepted and ratified, as a speaker of these commons. Looking back at the declaration of the Cuckoo from the *Parliament of Fowls* when that bird tried to assert itself as a speaker –

century but were practiced in the fourteenth. See the analysis in Chapter Two; also Oliver, "A Political Pamphleteer in Late Medieval England."

[123] *OED* s.v. "vouchsafe," I.1 "To confer or bestow (some thing, favour, or benefit) *on* a person"; I.2 "To give, grant, or bestow in a gracious or condescending manner"; II.5 "To grant, permit, or allow, as an act of grace or condescension," *et al.*, with relevant citations.

[124] See Rosser, "Going to the Fraternity Feast: Commensality and Social Relations in Late Medieval England." Communal feasts including king, Lords, and Commons were held at the ends of the parliaments of 1368, 1376, 1388, and presumably others.

[125] Bowden, *A Commentary on the General Prologue to The Canterbury Tales*, 294.

[126] This fact was originally noted by Manly, *Some New Light on Chaucer*, 78–9; the identification is accepted by Bowden, *A Commentary on the General Prologue*, 296.

"For I wol of myn owene autorite,
For comune spede, take on the charge now,
For to delyvere us is gret charite."

(PF 506–8)

– we find words that could be repeated verbatim by the Host with no loss
of meaning and only a slight change in significance. In both cases, the
"autorite" being sought and granted is the authority to bear or report a
common voice. Unlike the *vox communis* assumed by Gower, Chaucer's
poetic version of this role is not the expression of a pre-existing corpo-
ratist metaphor (this is not the voice of a traditional "body politic"), and
it is hemmed in by procedural and electoral processes, even in the humorous settings of an allegorical bird-flock and the "flok" that meets at the
Tabard. The Host's rather grand plans for the tale-telling contest quickly
get out of hand when the Miller violates the estates-order by interrupt-
ing the Monk. Nonetheless, throughout the *Canterbury Tales* the Host
maintains his role as a speaker in the contemporary practice of that office,
which was a cross between a master of ceremonies, director of an agenda,
representative mouthpiece, and mediator.[127]

The best example of these conflated roles comes at the end of the *Tales*
and the end of the pilgrimage, thousands of lines later in "The Parson's
Prologue." At the point when the Host effectively relinquishes his speaking duties to the Parson, he declares that his plan is almost fulfilled ("my
sentence and my decree," "al myn ordinaunce" [17–19]) and lacks only the
contribution of the Parson. The Parson refuses to tell a "fable" (31) but
offers instead to give an upbuilding spiritual discourse. This offer comes
couched in the familiar terms of the assembly's agreement, with a new
rider:

"And if ye vouche sauf, anon I shal
Bigynne upon my tale, for which I preye
Telle youre avys; I kan no bettre seye."
    "But natheless, this meditacioun
I putte it ay under correccioun
Of clerkes, for I am nat textueel;
I take but the sentence, trusteth weel.
Therfore I make protestacioun
That I wol stonde to correccioun."

(52–60)

---

[127] See Roskell, *The Commons and their Speakers*, 3–30, 76–103.

Like the Host at the beginning, the Parson seeks another vouchsafement and consensual agreement for his contribution to the exchange. More extensively, he makes a protestation for correction that echoes the formulaic "Speaker's Protestation" that speakers of the Commons gave at the acceptance of appointment to that office.[128] If the Parson accepts the charge of telling his tale and assuming the final voice of the group, he will do so only on the condition that his discourse may be corrected for error, and with the understanding that he speaks with the approval of his *entire* group.[129] This is a gesture of both humility and good form. The pilgrims' response is mediated by the Host:

> Upon this word we han assented soone,
> For, as it seemed, it was for to doone -
> To enden in som vertuous sentence,
> And for to yeve hym space and audience,
> And bade oure Hoost he sholde to hym seye
> That alle we to telle his tale hym preye.
>
> (61–6)

More than anything else, this simple (and largely overlooked) exchange makes explicit the Host's mediatory role. Why else should they ask *him* to address the Parson, who is, presumably, right there alongside? As organizer and director, the Host thus discharges his duties for the last time. Reporting the one voice of the pilgrims – "oure Hoost hadde the wordes for us alle" (67) – he exhorts the Parson to "beth fructuous" (71) with his lesson and bring the colloquy to a good end. In doing so, he effectively hands over control of the pilgrimage. The Parson assumes the platform of final speaker, which he never relinquishes. He is the last authoritative voice of the community we hear within the *Canterbury Tales*.

Obviously these parallels are not mechanical or exact, and Chaucer certainly did not want to present his pilgrims as a traveling convention of government representatives, or to frame their exchanges as an exercise in some prototype of *Robert's Rules of Order*. Neither are they assembled to treat of a single issue, like taxes or a marriage. But nothing this un-nuanced is required to acknowledge that, in diction, organization, and themes, the framework of the *Canterbury Tales* exemplifies the contemporary dynamics

---

[128] See Roskell, *The Commons and their Speakers*, 31–58. The first such Protestation, by Peter de la Mare in the first parliament of Richard II in October 1377, is recorded in *RP* 3.5. This formula "was similar to the protestation which a party or his learned counsel was entitled to make before pleading orally in any royal court, including the high court of parliament" (31).

[129] It is left productively ambiguous whether that ratifying group is his fellow clergy or his fellow pilgrims.

of parliament and *parlement* that were so important to Chaucer's professional and political world. As it gathers characters together in an assemblage
of petitionary interests both individual and communal; organizes them by
a single authoritative speaker-figure along formal lines; "reports" the raucous and occasionally logorrheic give-and-take of competing classes, professions, and genders; and ends inconclusively with an ambiguous gesture
toward a communally unified voice, the *Canterbury Tales* bears more than a
metaphorical resemblence to the practice of parliament as Chaucer himself
experienced it.

This version and vision of community is not necessarily perfective or
idealized, but neither is it uncreative or pejorative. We should, I think,
recognize it as a form of collective voice and action. In his brilliant study
of the representations of the Uprising of 1381, Steven Justice remarks that
the narrative idiom of the *Canterbury Tales* is resolutely individualist. Justice asserts, not without reason, that for the characters of the *Tales* "it
is only as individuals that they act, and it is individuals that they act
upon":

> The *Canterbury Tales* has its political purposes (as have some of its narrators), and
> it stages scenes that it would be silly not to call political. The poem can even
> gesture metonymically to collective acts . . . but it cannot *represent* such acts: a
> collectivity of one is no collectivity, just a person. In this sense, the *Canterbury
> Tales* . . . can voice relations of power in the encounters of individual characters,
> ventriloquize discourses from many sites of social experience, engage with the forms
> and ideologies of popular cultures, but at this particular price: anyone may speak,
> but no *ones* may speak together.[130]

In the sense that the *Canterbury Tales* does not or cannot overtly inscribe
collective actions such as would topically reflect the community upheavals
of 1381 – or even of 1386 and 1388 – this is surely correct. But as a manifestation of *collective election*, as the representation of a form of communal
governance and mutual will, it is not in any tale but in the *Tales* together
where we do find just such a representation. It is, to again repeat the phrase,
as a representation *of* representation that the *Canterbury Tales* succeeds in
reflecting the developing aesthetic presence of classes, groups, and individuals heretofore unseen in art, made possible by the developing sense of
parlement and the developing institutions of parliaments. Artistic form in
this sense is not above or removed from political form; it is in tune with
it, and co-productive. Its success is all the more obscure to us precisely
because it has, in large part, made possible the world we still inhabit today,

---

[130] Justice, *Writing and Rebellion*, 230.

a world where both literature and representation are not limited *a priori* to the noble, baronial, or elite voices whose earlier socio-political forms actually provided the framework for a later and more democratic realm of aesthetic and electoral exercise, a world where different "ones" can in fact speak. If we understand Chaucer thus to be, in a broad sense, a poet of a classically liberal franchise – a member of an educated political and cultural elite whose own speech nonetheless *represents* a more diverse world of discourse – this is possible only because his "ones" *are* able to speak together, collectively, to agree upon forming a space and community for speaking in the first place. The *Canterbury Tales* thus exemplifies a style of *parlement* that is neither simply whiggish nor royalist, nor only individualist, but fundamentally aesthetic. It is given over to the uneasy but necessary acceptance of a productive space or gap where the world and its representations will have a little room, "space and audience" where we – petitioners to literature in our own ways – might find a hearing, by allowing ourselves to hear.

CHAPTER 5

Parliament, Piers Plowman, *and the reform of the public voice*

'*It behoueth vs ernestly to pray unto God . . . that he will vouchesafe to send our sayde kyng lyke ȝeale and strength to make, set furth, and cause to be kepte such good polytike lawes and statutes as this Realme may be therby replenyshed wyth iustice, equitie and wealth . . . But except many inconueniences in this realme be redressed, it is rather to be feared least that the Gospell be slaundred through vs. Neuertheles even as in the time of oure greatest errour & ignoraunce, the fatte priestes wol neuer confesse that any thing concerning our religion was amis, worthy to be reformed; even so now at this daye there be many fatte marchauntes which wold haue no reformation in the comon wealth affirming that therin al thinges be wel; but he that wyll be conuersaunt with the comen sorte of the poore comens, shal (if he stop not his eares, nor hyde not his eyes) both heare se & perceyue the case to be farre other wise . . .*
        – "Pyers Plowmans exhortation unto the lordes knightes and
                burgoysses of the Parlyamenthouse"[1]

* * *

The provenance of this black-letter pamphlet is not definitely known, or its author, although it was almost certainly published around the time of Crowley's edition of *Piers Plowman* in 1550. Like a few other contemporary pamphlets, *Pyers Plowmans Exhortation* capitalizes on the poem's renewed popularity by putting the figure of "Pyers" prominently in the title, although it contains nothing even remotely evocative of the poem. Instead, it presents a practical consideration of the challenges facing England arising from the dissolution of religious houses and new trends in land distributions, namely, that property consolidations and enclosures have left the poor with "scant any litell house to put their head in" (ii). As a self-styled address to parliament, the pamphlet's focus on the practical problems of "propriety of goodes" (v) is as revealing as, for our purposes here, the notion that Piers

---

[1] *Pyers plowmans exhortation, vnto the lordes, knightes and burgoysses of the Parlyamenthouse.* London: Anthony Scoloker, c. 1550, i–ii. See the brief description in Hudson, "Epilogue: The Legacy of *Piers Plowman,*" 259.

179

Plowman himself, its titular author, supposedly speaks these complaints and suggests solutions. He submits "certeyne rude Bylles to be exhibited to you of the Parliamenthouse" (xv) with ideas for the reform of taxes, subsidies, and land policy. Where Piers was certainly known as the relentless critic and truth-teller about the "fatte priestes" of the recent past, now he is the critic of the "fatte marchauntes" who resist reform and undermine the kingdom through their greed. For an early Reformation audience, it appears to make polemical sense that he would voice his exhortation before parliament as a petitioner and legislator. In agitating against the "cruell oppression of the pore," this pamphlet-Pyers rhetorically appeals for the godly reform of the realm, like the children of the poor who would cry to the parliament-house "with one voyce" (xxii–xxiii) for a remedy. Piers the poetical figure thus becomes Pyers, the parliamentary reformer.

As I will argue here, this change is not as odd as it might seem. The question of the relationship between parliament and Langland's *Piers Plowman* has been a recurrent issue in Langland criticism since its modern inception. Much like the various readings of the *Modus Tenendi Parliamentum* over the centuries, the shifting interpretations of *Piers Plowman*'s parliamentarism have the historiographical quality of a political barometer. In early historical scholarship, J. J. Jusserand made parliamentary allusions and Langland's supposed "passionate adherence" to the parliamentary Commons a cornerstone of his reading of the poem, going so far as to say that *Piers Plowman* "would almost seem a commentary on the Rolls of Parliament."[2] The presence of parliament in the poem was one of the sub-issues at stake in the "multiple authorship" controversy with J. M. Manly, and allusions to specifically parliamentary political controversies – especially the Good Parliament of 1376 – were central to the identification of topical allusions and to attempts to date the versions of the poem.[3] This interpretive emphasis on parliament shifted in 1949, when E. Talbot Donaldson's *Piers Plowman: The C-Text and its Poet* took a New Critical approach in denying the specifically topical significance of the word "comunes." Donaldson argued that Langland was almost always speaking of the community in general and not of the parliamentary Commons in particular, and even less of particular parliaments or secular political events.[4] While most critics

---

[2] Jusserand, *Piers Plowman: A Contribution*, 109–12.
[3] Jusserand, "*Piers Plowman*: The Work of One or of Five," "A Reply"; Manly, "The Authorship of *Piers Plowman*"; Owst, "The 'Angel' and the 'Goliardeys' of Langland's Prologue"; Cargill, "The Date of the A-Text of *Piers Ploughman*"; Huppé, "The A-Text of *Piers Plowman* and the Norman Wars," "The Date of the B-Text of *Piers Plowman*"; Bennett, "The Date of the A-Text of *Piers Plowman*."
[4] Donaldson, *Piers Plowman: The C–Text and its Poet*, 85–120.

following Donaldson have not been so quick to deny Langland's interest in secular affairs, the effect of his study was, fairly decisively, to eliminate "the Commons" and parliament as institutionally and politically significant elements. Swinging the interpretive pendulum all the way to the other side, the most extensive of recent political readings, Anna Baldwin's influential 1981 study, *The Theme of Government in Piers Plowman*, not only denies the presence of parliament *qua* parliament in the poem, it asserts that the poem betrays an ideal of "royal absolutism," which is about as far as one can reasonably go from Jusserand's passionate parliamentarism and still be talking about the same poem.[5] Studies of Langland's contemporary audience, while illuminating the clerical and professional communities that were almost certainly his primary readers, have given relatively little attention to a Westminster parliamentary context, although more recent codicological and contextual research has demonstrated that the professional environment of London was in fact quite important for the poem's early copying and circulation.[6]

However, regardless of all of this back-and-forth among critics, the parliamentary elements of *Piers Plowman* are undeniable, just as they are intrusive and challenging.[7] The best example of this intrusiveness is the opening fable-vignette Langland added to his B-revision: the assembly of the Rats and Mice. Following the introduction of "the king" in the B-text Prologue – "Thanne kam þer a kyng; knyȝthod hym ladde; / Might of þe communes made hym to regne" (B.prol. 112–13) – the topic of secular governance is addressed by three speakers: a "lunatik," an Angel, and a "Goliardeis," each presenting a different perspective on the limits of royal authority. They speak in unique idioms, Latin and vernacular, each reflecting different critical attitudes towards the king's rule. Immediately following the "commune crye" of communal acclamation in Latin – *Precepta Regis sunt nobis vincula legis* (B.prol. 143–5) – the B-text immediately shifts into the fable:

> Wiþ þat ran þer a route of Ratons at ones
> And smale mees myd hem; mo þan a þousand
> Comen to a counseil for þe commune profit . . .
> (B.prol. 146–8)

[5] Baldwin, *The Theme of Government*, 15–20.
[6] See Middleton, "Audience and Public"; Burrow, "The Audience of *Piers Plowman*"; Kerby-Fulton and Justice, "Langlandian Reading Circles," "Scribe D and the Marketing of Ricardian Literature"; Kerby-Fulton, "Langland 'In His Working Clothes'?"
[7] All textual citations are from Kane, ed., *Piers Plowman: The A Version*, Kane-Donaldson, *Piers Plowman: The B Version*, and Russell-Kane, *Piers Plowman: The C Version*.

The rats and mice, seeking relief from a rapacious cat, propose to put a bell on him "for oure commune profit" (B.prol. 169). But when it comes to actually doing the deed, no one is willing to take the risk. A small mouse counsels sufferance instead: "Forþi I counseille al þe commune to late þe cat worþe . . . for bettre is a litel los þan a long sorwe" (B.prol. 187, 191). The fable is a familiar one that Skeat, following Wright, was able to identify broadly; G. R. Owst provided a much nearer source in the sermon preached by Bishop Brinton to the clerical convocation assembled during the Good Parliament of 1376.[8] As noted in Chapter Two, the fable picks up where Brinton warns his audience about the dangers of parliamentary inaction:

> Do not do so, reverend lords, lest our parliament be compared to the fabled parliament of the mice and the rats, of which it is read that when in their parliament they had specifically ordained that a bell should be put around the cat's neck – so that the mice, forewarned by the bell's sound, would be able to flee safely to their holes – one of the mice, returning from the parliament, met a very old rat. Inquiring about the news, when the mouse had told him the truth of the business, the rat said to him, 'This arrangement is best if it is agreed in the parliament that someone should carry out the plan.' And he [the mouse] responded, 'This was not settled in the parliament, and as a result, it was useless and empty (*inualidum erat et inane*)'.[9]

Following the fable Brinton exhorts that he and his listeners should not be mere talkers but doers, *non simus tantum locutores sed factores* (317). In the context of the Good Parliament, Brinton certainly was a *factor*: he was a receiver of Gascon petitions, and one of four bishops who advised the Commons in formulating their various demands, putting him at the center of the assembly's efforts at reform.[10] Whether added contemporaneously or sometime shortly afterward, Langland's own version of this fable became a key part of his narrative, but one apparently carrying a more pessimistic moral.

---

[8] See Owst, "The 'Angel' and the 'Goliardeys'"; more extensively Kellogg, "Bishop Brunton and the Fable of the Rats," and Huppé, "The Date of the B-Text."

[9] Brinton, *Sermons* 69, 317: "Non sic, domini reuerendi, sed ne parliamentum nostrum comparetur fabuloso parliamento murium et ratonum, de quibus legitur quod cum in parliamento suo precipue ordinassent quod campanella cato cuilibet ad collum imponeretur vt mures ad campanelle sonitum premuniti ad sua possent confugere foramina satis tute cuidam muri de parliamento reuertenti rato antiquissimus obuiauit. Cui noua inquirenti cum mus veritatem negocii intimasset intulit ille rato, 'Ista ordinacio est optima si quis in parliamento est constitutus vt sit tanti negocii executor.' Et ille respondisset, 'Hoc non fuisse in parliamento diffinitum, et per consequens inualidum erat et inane.'"

[10] Kellogg, "Bishop Brunton," 63–4; Huppé, "The Date of the B-Text," 35–6.

Episodically, then, *Piers Plowman* was revised to begin with an allegory of parliamentary assembly evocative of the immediate political environment, and one almost certainly intended to recall the events of 1376. This possible allusion is strong, but as I will argue in this chapter, the Prologue's fable is only the first and most overt example of parliament and *parlement* as defining aspects of the poem's episodic form. The assembly of the rodents that, in *Piers Plowman*, is arguably as *invalidum et inane* as Brinton's counterpart, provides yet another example of the narrative's critical investigation of institutional discourses, supplementing explorations of kingship, church, and the schools, and the social practices of the laity and clergy, in multiple contexts.[11] As such, it also initiates a pattern in which the bureaucratic parameters of parliamentary assembly are exploited as a way to investigate the particularly representative dynamics of social conflict.

As I have argued in the last two chapters, both Gower and Chaucer used parliament in ways that focused on its courtly identity, and that mixed the traditions of quasi-baronial and communal assembly. Langland's overall compositional strategy is much the same, as are many particular elements. Like the *Mirour de l'Omme* and the *Canterbury Tales*, *Piers Plowman* uses parliamentary forms to begin and end a long exploratory narrative of the social estates. But Langland's concerns are different, and in many ways more real-world and policy-oriented than either of his contemporaries. A close reading of the "Marriage of Meed" episode in Passūs 2–4 reveals a strikingly accurate working knowledge of the procedures and discourse of parliament. The episode also leaves open the question of how a critical social voice is to be publicly represented for the purposes of public reform. In this regard, Langland is perhaps closer to Gower; but unlike Gower there is no idealized appeal to the *proprietas regni* as an expression of the poet's unique position as critic. Instead, the emphasis is on money – meed – and the structures of exchange that parliament represents and enables. Since parliament had at least nominal control of taxing and revenue in the kingdom, this focus on cash is accurate and sobering. Langland fits it into the traditional association of parliament with marriage we have seen Chaucer exploit in the *Parliament of Fowls*. The allegorization of money in the figure of Meed also resonates with other "fables" and stories recorded at the same time. So I will begin with a story told by one of the participants of the Good Parliament of 1376, and its small incongruity, as a means for illuminating Langland's own challenging allegorization of parliamentary discourse.

---

[11] See Simpson, *Piers Plowman: An Introduction to the B–Text*, 14–5.

I ALLEGORIES OF MONEY: SIR THOMAS HOO AND THE GOOD
PARLIAMENT OF 1376

Like Brinton's sermon, the story comes from the Good Parliament of 1376, and it resonates with a traditional, and traditionally thorny, topical parallel. Since Owst's pioneering research, the character of Meed in Passūs 2–4 has been identified with Alice Perrers, mistress of Edward III and *femme scandaleuse* from about 1360 to 1377. The similarities between Perrers' stormy public career and the overall trajectory of the Meed episode are striking. Perrers was a woman of questionable parentage and ambiguous marital status, who was able to amass wealth and power through her connections at court and who readily exercised political influence. She was accused of misleading the king, of interfering with public policy, finance, and the courts (and even of sitting on the court benches and rendering, or manipulating, judicial decisions), and of generally disturbing the realm through her "maintenance."[12] These issues all came to a head in the Good Parliament, when an initial attempt was made to banish Perrers and to reclaim some of the properties she was accused of having acquired illegitimately. In the biased chronicle accounts of Perrers' activities, a more compelling real-life figure of "Meed" could scarcely have been found. In all versions of Passūs 2–4, Meed is accused of corrupting both sacred and secular estates – clergy and commons, burgesses and bondmen – with the power of money, "custumes of coueytise þe comune to destruye" (C.3.207).

I will return later to the question of whether Langland could have had Alice Perrers in mind for his description of Meed. Another person present at the Good Parliament and a different dream-vision, one displaying similar anxieties about the circulation of money or "meed," is recorded in the St. Albans *Chronicle*, written not long after 1376–7. It is an account of a miraculous vision experienced by Sir Thomas Hoo, an MP from Bedfordshire:

And so, how pious, how holy, and how commendable was the intention with which they began was shown in the beginning of this parliament by a vision granted to a knight of their group, a man of good reputation and worthy faith, whose name was Sir Thomas of Hoo (who told me the story himself and swore that it was true.)

---

[12] Owst mentions the possible identification; it is more firmly made by Cargill, "Date of the A-Text," 360–1; Huppé, "A-Text" 48–52; Bennett, "Date of the A-Text" 566, 571; Selzer, "Topical Allegory in *Piers Plowman*," 257–9; others make passing mention (e.g., Baldwin, *Theme of Government*, 34, and "Historical Context," 80; du Boulay, *The England of Piers Plowman*, 8) and some critical use of the parallels: Aers, "Class, Gender, Medieval Criticism, and *Piers Plowman*"; Trigg, "The Traffic in Medieval Women." For the most recent assessment of the evidence for Perrers' origins and identity, see Ormrod, "Who was Alice Perrers?"

When he was lying in bed one night and thinking over the business before him –
namely, how or by what means the king could be brought back to a more upright
life and to the enjoyment of saner counsel, and also how the abuses in the realm
(up to now so common) could be dug up by the root, and how the people of the
land could enjoy justice and peace more fully – troubled by cares of this sort, he
finally fell asleep and began to dream.

And behold! He dreamt that he and the other knights I have mentioned were
gathered in the chapter of St. Paul's to discuss that business. During the discussion,
with eyes downcast to the floor, he dreamt that he found seven gold coins, the
coins we call "florins" or "nobles." He picked them up and, figuring that someone
from among some of his associates had carelessly lost them, going around to each
singly, he asked them one by one if they had lost the gold. But they all said they
hadn't, and so he went into the choir to see if anyone there had lost them. And
he dreamt that he met some monks there, good devout men, Benedictines by
their habit. He asked them, too, if they had lost the money. But they said they
hadn't, and one of them, who seemed older and more dignified in his habit and
bearing and more eminent than the rest, called the knight over to him and said,
"My son, what are you carrying around in your hands?" The knight said, "I am
carrying gold, desiring to know its lord and rightful owner." "Let me see your
gold," said the monk. When he showed him the gold he had, the monk said, "This
is not lost money, as you think. How many coins do you have?" "Seven," said the
knight. And the monk said, "My son, the seven gold coins you have in your hand
are the seven gifts of the Holy Spirit, bestowed on you and your colleagues who
are gathered now to bring about reforms for the good of the realm. For the gold
stands for the wisdom conferred on you, with which you can search out what needs
reform and express yourselves more eloquently in the presence of the princes of this
kingdom."

Then he woke up, went over the dream and its interpretation in his mind, and
he told it to his colleagues. They were all overjoyed and sure they had received
divine aid. And I have told this so that nobody can doubt that everything that was
put forward by those knights for the improvement of the kingdom was prompted
by the friendly counsel of the Holy Spirit. But I return to the material.[13]

[13] *St. Albans Chronicle*, 4–6: "Itaque, quam pium, quam sanctum, quam comendabile fuit quod
mente conceperant, patuit in ipso [initio] parliamenti per quandam uisionem factam cuidam mil-
iti de eorum collegio, uiro bonae opinionis [et] fide digno, cuius nomen erat dominus Thomas
de [la Hoo]; qui etiam iureiurando michi retulit hoc quod narro. Hic, cum nocte quadam in
stratu suo quiesceret et de instantibus negotiis cogitaret, qualiter uidelicet uel quibus medii[s]
rex ad corre[ctiorem ui]tam reduci posset et consilio per[frui] saniori, necnon quomodo abu-
siones in regno actenus usitatae ualerent radicitus extirpari, quo plenius populus terre pace
et iustitia frueretur, huiusmodi curis [a]nxius et turbatus, dimissa uigilia, sompn[ium] cepit.
[Et] ecce! uidebatur sibi in sompnis se cum predictis militibus constitutum esse in capitulo Sancti
Pauli, [ubi de predictis] negotiis tractauerunt. [In]terque [tract]andum, demissis oculis in paui-
mentum, uisum est [sibi inuenisse septem aur]eos, quos florenos siue nobiles appellamus. Quos
in manu accipiens, [et autumans eos aliquos e] soc[iis suis per in]curiam amisisse, circuiens si
aurum perdidissent a singulis re[quisiuit. Quibus cunctis negantibus, chorum] intrauit, ut sciret
si quis illud ibidem exsistentium [perdidisset. V]isumque est [sibi in] eodem [cho]ro [mona]chos

This little story is unique to the St. Albans *Chronicle*, and it can be
fruitfully read alongside Langland's own dream vision at the start of *Piers
Plowman*. Thomas Hoo of Bedfordshire was, as Anthony Goodman has
described him, a typical shire knight, "an independent-minded country
gentleman, a pillar of county society, who took his parliamentary duties
seriously and had an ambitious concept of the Commons' role."[14] He was
a man of position and influence, and he has a fairly direct historical connection to the text of *Piers Plowman* itself: MS. Harley 6041, a composite
A–C manuscript dated to the early fifteenth century, bears the arms of Sir
William Hoo, his adult son.[15] This vision, which appears to be an *oraculum*
in the Macrobian typology, is of an approximately Langlandian sort. A man,
weighted with the cares of the world, falls asleep and enters a dream-world
similar to his waking one, but with interesting aberrations. Herein lies the
potential error. The knight of the shire sees himself and his fellow secular
parliamentarians not in the environs of the Commons' normal meeting
places at Westminster, but instead at St. Paul's chapterhouse, which was
the forum for the convocations of the clergy. Historians have generally
treated this as a simple mistake, a slip of the chronicler's pen where he
meant to say Westminster.[16] But there is no indication that it is necessarily
an error, or that the chronicler (who elsewhere makes factual mistakes, but
also corrections) would have found anything deeply incongruous about

inuenisse, quorum persone honeste, ater habit[us, et religio] comendabilis u[idebatur]. Quos [etiam]
sciscitatus est de auro perdito diligenter. Quibus [aurum] perdidisse negantibus, unus eorum, [qui]
etate [prouectior], habitu et persona honestior, et ceteris uisus est e[min]entior, sibi predictum
militem aduoca[uit]. Cui [ita dixit,] 'Fili,' inquit, 'quid est quod [manibus circumportas?'] Cui
miles, 'Aurum,' [inquit,] 'circumfero, | scire cupiens ejus [dominum et] debitum possessorem.' Cui
m[on]achus, '[Vi]de[am,' ait, 'aurum tuum.'] Cui demonstranti aurum quod tenebat, 'Nequaquam,'
inquit, 'est istud [aurum] perditum, [ut tu] credis. Set quis sit numerus aureorum scire uolo.'
Cui miles, 'Septem,' [ait,] 'sunt in [numero'. Et monachus ita ait], 'Septem auri, fili, quos in
manu tenes, sunt septem Spiritus Sancti dona, collata tibi et collegis [tuis], qui in presenti congregati sunt pro utilitate et reformatione status regni. Auro sapientia designatur uobis collata,
qua indagare possitis reformanda et exprimere gratiosius in conspectu principum huius regni.'
Expergefactus autem miles secum reuoluit in animo sompnium et interpretationem eius; et uisionis
[sue seriem] sociis [inti]mauit. Vnde iidem milites leteficati fiduciam conceperunt de diuino adiu-
torio optinendo. [Hec] iccirco scripsimus, ut in dubium nulli ueniat, quin ea, que pro emendatione
regni ex parte militum [sunt] prolata, familiari consilio Spiritus Sancti sint suggesta. Set ad materiam
reuertamur."

[14] Goodman, "Sir Thomas Hoo and the Parliament of 1376," 139.

[15] See Kane, *Piers Plowman: The A Version*, 6–7. On Sir Thomas' good relations with his son and heir,
and for an account of Hoo's ecclesial and secular connections, see Goodman, "Sir Thomas Hoo,"
139–41.

[16] The editor E. M. Thompson treats it as a slip (*Chronicon Anglie*, xli n. 1); more recently so also does
Given-Wilson, who calls it "a strange slip on his behalf" (*Chronicles*, 224 n. 89; see also 52–4); Holmes
changes it silently to Westminster (*Good Parliament*, 136); and Goodman treats it as Walsingham's
error ("Sir Thomas Hoo," 139 n. 1) without considering why an experienced clerical chronicler would
make such a basic mistake.

Hoo setting his dream there. It is a *dream*, after all, and in a wider perspective the change has some logic. Though separate, convocations of the
clergy were coordinated with parliaments as the clergy were asked to provide tithes along with the taxes levied by the Commons and Lords. In the
context of parliament, clergy and laity were joined not only by the presence
of the greater prelates in the assembly, but more materially by the threat of
monetary exaction. This cash connection is allegorically suggested by the
lost seven coins. Whether it is authorially intended or a clerical error, the
simple fact of the misprision of St. Paul's for Westminster is itself revealing.
While the vision happens not in the parliament-house but in a church, it
points to the interconnection of the two that was a matter of fact in fiscal
and parliamentary practice.

This fungibility is also emphasized by Hoo's actions. The lost coins that
the dream-Hoo carries around turn out to be not a material treasure in need
of a rightful owner, but an ambiguous sign in need of a proper interpreter.
This detail invites further allegorical interpretation. Parliament's fundamental concern – and the greatest power of the Commons, and of men like
Hoo – was precisely this, control of money. By the 1370s taxation had long
been under the control of the Commons, and so the disbursement of money
was the most direct means of institutional power wielded, quite readily, for
extracting concessions from the Crown.[17] In the vision, by emphasizing
the control of cash, Hoo tacitly symbolizes the most powerful function of
the Commons' specific presence in the national assembly. Wealth becomes
words and wisdom, and the spiritual "gift" they have been given is described
in terms used for finance and taxation. The coins have been *collata*, "collected" or "harvested," and with them the knights are to *exprimere*, "to
express" or "to expound" virtuously, but also, etymologically, "to squeeze
out, to extract," or more darkly, "to extort."[18] That is to say, the terms
of the old monk's interpretation of the coins could be used to describe
the kind of overburdening, extortionate taxation for which parliaments
were roundly despised. At the same time, the hope for more "eloquent"
expression, as I have translated it, is also resonantly ambiguous. The old
monk hopes their speech will be *gratiosius*, "more graceful," and clearly
also more grace-full, a theological point also emphasized by the chronicler's

[17] On this point see also Brown, "Parliament, c. 1377–1422"; Edwards, *Commons in Medieval English Parliaments*, 19–25, and *Second Century*, 17–43; Ormrod, *Political Life in Medieval England*, 30–7; Musson, *Medieval Law in Context*, 184–216; and generally Harriss, *King, Parliament, and Public Finance*.
[18] See Lewis and Short, *A Latin Dictionary*, sv. *exprimo*, where the main sense is "to press or squeeze out, to force out"; "to squeeze or wring out, to extort, wrest, elicit"; and sv. *confero-contuli-collatum*, "to collect, gather" and also "to collect money, treasures . . . to bring offerings, contribute," etc.

concluding statement about the Holy Spirit. This account of Hoo's dream explicitly appeals to the Pentecostal tradition of parliamentary assembly; and a little further on in the chronicle, Peter de la Mare, the speaker of the Commons, is described as having been "lifted up by God" and "enriched" by the Holy Spirit.[19] As with the material coins that become spiritual riches, Thomas Hoo's dream highlights the parliament as a providentially inspired assembly. The words of the parliamentarians are thus to be turned – rather hopefully – from extortion to exhortation, to good counsel and proper reform.

Nor is this the only narrative from the chronicles of the Good Parliament centering on a quasi-allegorical reading of money. The *Chronicle* records that during the Parliament, one of the accused, Richard Lyons, sent the Black Prince a thousand pounds in cash and other gifts (*mille libras cum aliis exenniis et donativis*) in an effort to buy his help. But the Prince, "weighing his crimes in the scale of justice" (*libra justitiae ponderans ejus scelera*), refused to receive them and instead sent them back. *Libras* fail where the *libra justitiae* succeeds.[20] Later in the proceedings, the *Chronicle* records a similarly amusing story. It is announced in parliament that Alice Perrers keeps in her company a Dominican friar skilled in the medical and magical arts who uses his *maleficiis* to attract the king to Perrers. Two parliamentarians, knights of shires (*duo ex militibus de provinciis*), plot to capture him at Perrers' estate at Pallenswick. Dressing in disguise and carrying a urinal pot, they approach the entrance of the manor pretending to seek a doctor to cure an illness:

When he saw those men bearing a urinal in their hands, that friar, standing in an upper room, figured he was going to get a great deal of money (*grandem pecuniam*). So he immediately said that he was the doctor they sought. They said they would be content if he would deign to come down and provide some remedy for them. Then when he came down – caught by the disease of avarice – he was caught by them.[21]

For the greedy friar, the urinal represents a proverbial pot of gold. Instead he is caught by the parliamentarians as his desire for money (*pecunia*) is his

---

[19] *St. Albans Chronicle*, 8: "suscitavit Deus spiritum cuiusdam militis ex eorum collegio, cui nomen erat Petrus de la Mare, infu[ndens] cordi suo sapientiam habundantissimam de thesauris suis . . ."

[20] *St. Albans Chronicle*, 18–20. See also *Anonimalle Chronicle 1333 to 1381*, 92, which records the bribe was sent in a barrel of fish that the Black Prince rejects as *nyent profitable*.

[21] *St. Albans Chronicle*, 48: "Frater uero ille stans in solario, cum uidisset homines ferentes in manibus urinalia, ratus se lucraturum grandem pecuniam, mox fatetur se esse medicum quem querebant. Illi autem promiserunt se sibi satisfacturos, se descendere dignaretur et eis aliquod remedium prouidere. Qui mox ut descendit, peste captus auaritie, captus est ab eisdem." The two parliamentarians were Sir John de la Mare (Wiltshire) and Sir John Kentwood (Berkshire).

undoing. The divinely ordained nature of the events is further emphasized by the friar's supposed magic: he later laments that while he did in fact foresee the parliament (*parliamentum praescivi*), he was unable to know precisely *when* his own travails would occur.[22] Not just his capture or the opposition against him and Perrers, but specifically the parliament itself is presented again as a foreseen, God-ordained or fated event.

As diverting as these stories are, at a fundamental level we can see that they are also about *meed*: cash exchange, proper payment and equitable return. They bridge the representational gap between artful allegory and contemporary politics in the same way that the story of Hoo's coins bridges secular and ecclesiastical institutions. These accounts certainly give force to the notion, as Kerby-Fulton and Justice have said, that during the Good Parliament it was hoped "that political reform could have the force of spiritual reformation."[23] Indeed, particularly in the St. Albans *Chronicle* and the *Anonimalle Chronicle*, the prominence given to the Good Parliament makes it appear like a kind of Prague Spring. It was the sort of brief, bright moment that stands out in the memory of reformers of every age, when meaningful change through collective action seems real and achievable.[24] These stories focus on the reach and power of money, which was not just the perennial concern of parliament but the source of its *own* power, the power of taxation and funding. One telling detail from the dream of Hoo is that in it, he seeks not simply the gold's possessor but its lord and rightful possessor, *ejus dominum et debitum possessorum*, showing that proper lordship and stewardship – *dominium* – is the larger issue at stake. This too is evocative of Langland's wayward Meed, where the question of her marital lordship sets off the whole debate. Unlike the allegorical figure of Meed who circulates and is accepted by everyone, Hoo's coins are virtuously *refused* by everyone, as Lyons' illegitimate coins were also turned away. No one claims them as their own because they are the communal wealth of the Commons, and that wealth itself is sublimated into artful speech. In a fitting allegorical form, Hoo's vision in particular expresses both the hopes and the anxieties – rhetorical, spiritual, and political – that were evident during the Good Parliament and that were explicitly associated with it in the public sphere.

[22] *St. Albans Chronicle*, 48.
[23] Kerby-Fulton and Justice, "Reformist Intellectual Culture," 153.
[24] As Given-Wilson notes, "it [the Good Parliament] was very probably the event which persuaded Thomas Walsingham to begin once again to write contemporary history on something approaching the scale of Matthew Paris" (*Chronicles*, 174). On the importance of prophetic dreams and wondrous portents in chronicles as "Godwitness testimony," see generally Given-Wilson, *Chronicles*, 21–56.

2 THE PARLIAMENTARY TRIAL OF MEED IN PASSŪS 2–4

These stories suggests a thicker context in which to read the beginning of *Piers Plowman*, even as I will hasten to add that I do not want to turn Passūs 2–4 into a strictly topical allegory of the Good Parliament. Rather, the political framework of parliamentary narrative is the salient point here, since it is the assembly itself making possible that inspired and "more graceful" expression. To better understand Langland's similar attempt to squeeze out a representation of such concerns, we must attend to the details of his trial of Meed to see how it responds to similar representational pressures.

Baldwin has argued that the "marriage of Meed" and the events associated with it – the arrival and pursuit of Falsnesse, the accusation by Conscience, the summoning and questioning of Reason, her circulation among the estates – all take place in the context of "the king's prerogative court," defined (with an almost allegorical convenience) as the court of the king's conscience, and understood to consist of the king and his council sitting as a court of justice in the environs of Westminster.[25] This is fundamentally correct but potentially misleading, and it fits the details of the episode awkwardly. For while "þe kynges Court" (C.2.205) in this part of the Meed episode is quite clearly a court of the king's justice, it is not a session of the King's Bench or a meeting of the King's council *per se*. What the episode obliquely represents as its overall context is the King's justice administered in the sessions of the high court of parliament. Only in a parliamentary setting do all of the issues raised by Meed, and about her, make sense. The parliamentary character of the events hinge on three primary points. First, a parliamentary context best fits the details of Meed's pointed exchange with Conscience. Second, the entrance of Peace and the submission of Peace's bill also fit best in a parliament, as the narrative itself describes it. And third, the conclusion of the trial scene has striking resemblances to specifically parliamentary events, not just to the procedures of a lower law court.

To begin with Meed's debate with Conscience, in all versions, the beginning of the trial proper in Passus 3 proceeds with the solitary Meed "ybrou3t to þe king" at Westminster (A.3.2; cf. B.3.2, C.3.2), where she is deposited in a "chaumbre" at the king's behest (A.3.10, B.3.10; "Boure" in C.3.11). While waiting for the king she meets with, and corrupts, representatives of various estates. Later when the king finally arrives, it is specified that "þe king fro counseil com & callide aftir mede / And ofsente hire as swiþe" (A.3.90–91;

[25] Baldwin, *Theme of Government*, 40–54.

cf. B.3.101–102, C.3.128–29), indicating that the king is in fact emerging *from* his privy council to meet Meed. The two then go to a "boure" (A.3.92, B.3.103) for a private conference in an intimate setting. It is not clear that this is another session of the privy council. When Conscience is called, the explicitly expanded audience of the "clerkis & oþere" (A.3.103–4, B.3.114–115, C.3.151–52) hints that the new setting is wider: there are more people present than just the King and his privy counsellors, whoever they may be. This makes sense because what follows is clearly a public trial, and Conscience begins his attack in front of this assembly.

Conscience accuses Meed of various offenses – she teaches wantonness and lechery; she is both a bawd and a whore; she corrupts jailers, perverts the law, encourages simony, and "wiþ hir Iuelx ȝoure Iustice she shendiþ," and more (A.3.145; cf. B.3.155, C.3.194) – all culminating in her desire "þe comune to destruye" (C.3.207). This is not a single case of tort being adjudicated in one of the regular courts, but rather a multi-faceted accusation against an enemy of "the community" in an institutional sense. The further addition in C of a complaint *about* complaints – "For pore men dar nat pleyne *ne no pleynt shewe*, / Such a maistre is mede among men of gode" (C.3.214–5, my emphasis) – can only make sense (and avoid redundancy) in an institutional setting. It is not just that men cannot complain, but that they are prevented from actually "showing" their complaints in the forms of bills and petitions.[26] The possible sentence is also appropriate for parliament as the King threatens not a tort judgment but summary banishment: "Excuse þe ȝif þou canst, I can no more seiȝe / For consience acusiþ þe to cunge þe for euere" (A.3.160–1; B.3.173–4, C.3.219–20).

Meed's reply to all of this is curious. While she immediately responds *tu quoque* to Conscience since he too has been known to "maynteyne þi manhod" by meed (A.3.172, B.3.185, C.3.231), her extended rebuttal appears to be a non-sequitur:

> Ac thow hast famed me foule byfore þe kyng here
> For kulde y neuere no kyng ne counseilede so to done . . .
> Caytifliche thow, Consience, conseiledest þe kyng leten
> In his enemyes handes his heritage of Fraunce.
> Vnconnynge is þat Consience a kyndom to sulle
> For þat is conquered thorw a comune helpe, a kyndom or ducherie,
> May nat be sold sothlice . . .
> Forthy y consayl no kynge eny conseyl aske
> At Consience þat coueiteth to conquere a reume . . .
>   (C.3.232–55; cf. A.3.173–95, B.186–208)

---

[26] On "shewe" see Chapter Four n. 45, and the discussion below in Chapter Six.

Conscience's accusations (especially in the A-version) are mostly the sort of legal charges one might expect in an equity court. But Meed's response here is almost entirely political: she immediately turns the debate into a discussion about policy counsel and the conduct of the French wars. The discrepancy between Conscience's accusations and Meed's defense is even more pronounced in the earlier versions, with Meed's very topical references to the events surrounding the Normandy campaign of 1359–60 and the treaty of Brétigny (A.3.176–95) following awkwardly from Conscience's list of complaints.[27] Conscience has said nothing about this, but Meed acts as if war policy is a logical extension of the appeal against her. This was not a judicial concern of courts *coram rege* or of the common law courts, or of the prerogative council only. But it was quite regularly – to the point of obsession by the later 1370s – the subject of investigations and indictments in parliament, which debated the French campaigns as a matter of public finance. During those inquiries, accusations of individual malfeasance were bound up with the events of the war, as they were during the inquiry in the Good Parliament over the loss of holdings in Normandy and the financial improprieties of several senior advisors.[28] So Meed's counter-accusation, "Vnconnyngliche þow, Consience, conseiledest hym thenne / To lete so his lordschipe for a litel mone" (C.3.263–4), could also be bound up with accusations of treason, that is, of attempting to do direct harm to the king's "lordschipe" by vitiating the Crown's interests and holdings. Here, as in the accusations against Perrers and others in 1376, war and the mismanagement of royal finances are all jumbled together.

Again, without reducing this to a topical reference, it is easy to see how a parliamentary context makes such a jumble more sensible. In the parliamentary roll for 1376, for example, the brief summary of Perrers' offenses is presented as part of a set of complaints and general anxieties "for the support [ie. cost] of the war, which the king bears and must continue to bear concerning the prosecution of his claim to France."[29] In later decades – especially in 1388, as we have seen – the accusation of intentionally

[27] On this historical allusion see most recently Baker, "Meed and the Economics of Chivalry in *Piers Plowman*," who resuscitates the thesis of Huppé, "The A-Text of *Piers Plowman* and the Norman Wars."

[28] For an example in the Good Parliament, see specifically the accusations about losses in Brittany including Bécherel and St. Sauveur in 1374–5, *RP* 2.325, discussed extensively by Holmes, *The Good Parliament*, 21–62, 126–34; and with reference to this passage by Selzer, "Topical Allegory in *Piers Plowman*," 262–4. Parliamentary inquiries into the war occurred in 1339, 1344, 1346, 1347, 1348, 1353, 1354 (especially), 1360 (Treaty of Brétigny), 1369 (resumption of the war), 1372, 1373, and 1376. See Butt, 282–354.

[29] *RP* 2.321: ". . . pur la maintenance de la Guerre, que le Roi fait & encores covient de faire entour la prosecution de sa Querele de France."

misleading the king or of mismanaging royal interests became a powerful weapon in parliamentary trials. So it appears Meed has understood the accusations against her as such, and her reply becomes a self-defense against treason and malfeasance.[30] Such charges were increasingly put forward in the parliamentary court of Lords at this time, when the definition of treason itself was a contentious political issue. Langland takes for granted that his audience would have made the connection between Meed's offenses and the way she chooses to rephrase them. Simply put, Meed defends herself as if she has been hauled before the court of parliament, which was in fact a court of trial and record. Her defense has the substantive and rhetorical characteristics of those impeachment hearings that were becoming more frequent.

The setting of a specifically parliamentary inquiry also matches the details of Meed's marriage dispute and its development into a debate on public law. The debate with Conscience occurs as a result of the impending marriage of Meed and False, and Meed has travelled to Westminster because of questions surrounding its legitimacy. As with the marriage in Chaucer's *Parliament of Fowls*, this detail has generated some uncertainty about the kind of court where Meed is presumably seeking the legitimation of her marriage claim. She has been enfeoffed with the lands of False and the size of that *maritagium* is very large and potentially problematic for the king.[31] From an institutional point of view, the procession of Meed and her retinue to Westminster, and before the king, would appear to emphasize the specifically secular threat presented by the wedding. The allegorical rationale for bringing her to Westminster becomes clearer from the detail that Meed is a royal kinswoman, as Theology observes: "And mede is a moylore, a mayden of gode; / A myhte kusse the kyng as for his kynnes womman" (C.2.148–9; cf. B.2.132–3; A.2.96–7); and from the detail that Falsenesse and Favel go with the retinue "to wende with hem to westminstre the weddyng to honoure" (C.2.177; cf. B.2.161, A.2.125), suggesting the conflation of the legal and ludic aspects of the whole procession. As we have seen, one of the traditional functions of parliament was the recognition and quasi-legitimation of marriages of the royal family as well as the nobility.[32] So shortly thereafter, when Peace enters the scene and "puts up his bill" against Wrong, we have been prepared for the scope of the specific accusations of tort that it contains as well as for the more general dynamic of semi-public

[30] The first such impeachment was brought against a former steward of the royal household, Sir John de la Lee, in 1368: see *RP* 2.297–8 items 20–2, and Butt, 329.
[31] See especially Tavormina, *Kindly Similitude*, 21–8, for analysis.
[32] See the discussion in Chapter Four.

debate following it, which is appropriate for the mixed political–judicial environment of a parliament where Meed's wedding is now under review.

To get the best sense of Peace's bill, it is worthwhile to quote it in full from the C-text:

> Thenne cam pees into þe parlement and putte vp a bille
> How wrong wilfully hadde his wyf forleyn
> And how he raueschede Rose the ryche wydewe by nyhte
> And margarete of here maydenhod as he mette here late.
> "Bothe my gees and my grys and my gras he taketh.
> Y dar nat for his felawschipe, in fayth," pees sayde,
> "Bere sikerlyche eny seluer to seynt Gyles doune.
> A wayteth ful wel when y seluer take,
> What wey y wende wel ȝerne he aspyeth
> To robbe me or to ruyfle me yf y ryde softe.
> ȝut is he bold for to borw Ac baddelyche he payeth:
> He borwed of me bayard and brouhte hym hom neuere
> Ne no ferthyng therfore, for nouhte y couthe plede.
> A meynteyneth his men to morthere myn hewes,
> Forstalleth my fayres and fyhteth in my chepynge
> And breketh vp my berne dores and bereth awey my whete
> And taketh me but a tayle for ten quarteres otes;
> And ȝut he manescheth me and myne and lyth be my mayde.
> Y am nat hardy for hym vnnethe to loke."
>
> (C.4.45–63)

The bill is a veritable laundry list of tort complaints. It includes most of the major aspects of trespass in fourteenth century law: assault and battery of person, threats, abduction ("ravishment") and rape, seizure of goods and animals, destruction of property and structures, fraud and misrepresentation, breaking the peace, assault of servants and villeins, and (by implication) just about everything else "wrong" imaginable.[33] The bill is so overdone that its allegorical seriousness is somewhat playfully undercut by its hyperbole. While this is obviously a court scene, we should, I think, take the narrator at his word when he says the bill is put forward in a parliament. Peace's procedure here is completely consistent with the way bills and petitions were submitted to be vetted and heard during parliaments. Moreover it is an appropriately parliamentary setting not just because it makes procedural sense, and not just because the scenario's focus is congruent with a parliament, but also because following the submission of the bill, the narrative continues with a general discussion of the scope of justice

---

[33] A sense of the bill's comprehensiveness can be gained by comparing it to examples of trespass cases digested by Arnold, *Select Cases of Trespass from the King's Courts, 1307–1399*, xxxi–lxxxv.

and maintenance. That is, the narrative proceeds with a *parlement* about the legal and adminstrative policy reforms that should be instituted in the face of Wrong's trespasses and Meed's challenge to the equitable operation of the legal system, which is precisely the kind of "political" debate about local justice that was particularly suited to parliamentary treatment.[34]

Thus what follows is not a judicial decision but a parliamentary debate. Here, with the king and with Reason "bytwene hymsulue and his sone" (C.4.43), we get the distinct impression that it is a formal, communal setting in which Peace makes his complaint not just against the adminstration of royal justice, but against every type of trespass in the realm. When he puts forth his own body as proof of the parlous state of the kingdom –

> ʒut pees put forth his heued and his panne blody:
> "Withouten gult, god wot, gat y this scathe;
> Consience knoweth hit wel *and al the Comune trewe*."
> (C.4.74–6, my emphasis)

– it is overtly Conscience and the "true" commons who are aware; it strongly implies that we should envision this as a trial not simply *coram rege* but before a larger community, and probably in the presence of the Commons in the court of parliament. Nor does it seem insignificant that the C-version of this episode introduces the buzz-phrase *trewe commune*, one of the shib-boleths adopted by the rebels of 1381. This change in particular implies an awareness of how the very notion of "the commons" – institutional and popular, "false" and "true" – was a point of strong ideological contention. Reason declares his demands and his stark principle for judgment ("For *nullum malum* þe man mette with *inpunitum* / And bad *Nullum bonum* be *irremuneratum*" [A.4.126–7; B.4.143–4, C.4.140–41]), and after this dec-laration he is held to be the victor of the debate (C.4.153). The narrative thus presents a legal–political indictment and then a more formal sub-mission of a bill or petition by Peace, followed by an apparently "public" debate.

Toward the end of the scene, the clearest indicator of a parliamentary setting comes with the final declaration of judgment against Meed. All of the major and minor actors – the complainant Peace, the defendant Wrong, the council members and advisors such as Reason, Kynde Wit, and

---

[34] Harding notes that parliament was the locus of national discussion about local justice: "If the series of parliamentary petitions, statutes, and judicial commissions are taken together, local justice and not taxation is seen to be the first great subject of political discussion between the king and the people at large . . . The plaints and bills produced by litigation became a great new means of political communication flowing now from localities to government" (Harding, *Medieval Law*, 185; see also his "Revolt Against the Justices.")

Conscience, Meed, "Clerkes," and others – mill about in the deliberative mix, until the decisive moment when Meed is condemned by Love, Leutee and Conscience, and then derided by the common voice. Here in the C-text, Langland avails himself of an almost irresistible pun:

> Loue lette of mede lyhte and leutee ȝut lasse
> And cryede to Consience, the kyng myhte hit here:
> "Hoso wilneth here to wyue for welthe of here goodes
> But he be knowe for a cokewold, kut of my nose."
> Mede mornede tho and made heuy chere
> For þe comune calde here queynte comune hore.
> A sysour and a somnour tho softliche forth ȝede
> With mede þe mayde out of þe moethalle.
>
> (C.4.156–63)

Here in front of the "court," Meed is authoritatively condemned (with another bit of bawdy), but the sentence is declared not by the king but by Conscience. This is a court where the king sits as a judge but does not in fact render judgment, as in cases tried before the parliamentary peers. Meed, downcast, is then led out of the assembly. With "þe comune" cat-calling after her, we witness an instance of the infamous "common clamor" that was a part of the parliamentary process, as the narrator triply puns on "common": the community, as the Commons, condemns Meed as a common whore – and also, one suspects, as the Commons' whore, making the accusation ironically hypocritical.

With its noisy tumult, characters being led in and out, and general rowdiness, the conclusion of Meed's trial presents the sort of uproar stereotypical of parliaments. We can recall Chaucer's similarly tumultuous portrait in the *Parliament of Fowls*. In the Good Parliament, the roll record notes that William Latimer was *empeschez & accusez par clamour des ditz Communes*, which is a more technical use of the term.[35] And in 1377, the Commons and Lords agreed on a small intercommuning committee, "en petite et resonable nombre," so that important matters could be discussed *sanz mumur, crye, et noise*.[36] The scene in Passus 4 is also comparable to an entry in the rolls of parliament for 1377 when Perrers was again appealed and impeached and her goods were re-confiscated to the Crown, where there is an extraneous note about the Commons' clamor against her:

---

[35] *RP* 2.324. On "common clamor" as a form of indictment by public infamy (i.e., being the subject of multiple complaints), see Harding, "Plaints and Bills," 78–9; see also Steiner, "Commonalty and Literary Form."
[36] *RP* 3.36.

And let it be remembered that it was ordained in Parliament, at the clamor and urging of the Commons (*que al clamour & instance des Communes*), that the said Alice should be sent for, in order to respond thereof (i.e., to the charges against her) in Parliament, and that she should receive what would be determined concerning her.[37]

This little note refers to the start of the parliamentary process, but interestingly it comes at the end of the roll (and after the concluding announcement of a subsidy grant), as if to remind the reader of the public outcry and "clamor" which brought Perrers to the bar in the first place. As with all parliamentary judicial proceedings, Perrers was tried before the Lords; but the Commons were integral as plaintiffs and witnesses. Given this overt record of the public outcry against her (also frequently noted in the chronicle accounts), it seems fair to imagine the kind of vocal scene for which parliaments were notorious. The insults that follow the judgment against Meed in Passus 4 – "Quaint common whore!" – indicate that Langland's image of the king's moot-hall is reminiscent of this: a rowdy parliamentary session with the king in earshot, probably at the head of the White Chamber of the Lords, and not the more subdued proceedings of the King's Bench or Privy Council. In both the historical and the fictional accounts, the accusations finally devolve into a verdict of forfeiture and banishment, and we find a populist appeal that the extorted wealth will be returned to the people harmed.

As the scenario draws to a close at the end of Passus 4, the king and his advisors retire to a private meeting. The king complains to Meed and to men of law that "thorw ʒoure lawe . . . y lese meny chetes" (C.4.169), and when he declares his intent to reform the process of justice, Conscience sagely observes that "withoute þe comune helpe / Hit is ful hard, by myn heued, herto bryngen hit / And alle ʒoure lege ledes to lede thus euene" (C.4.176–8). The repeated phrase "comune helpe" (previously used in Meed's speech, C.3.244) combines the social and financial senses of what is at stake. It will be difficult for the king to get anything done without the goodwill of the community – "comune" and "lege ledes" – *and* without a subsidy aid or "help" of cash from the Commons. Although Meed has been judged, meed is still very much an issue. Immediately thereafter the king appoints Reason and Conscience to administrative positions, calling on Reason to "be my cheef Chaunceller in Cheker and in parlement / And Consience in alle my Courtes be as kynges Iustice" (C.4.185–6). In this way

[37] *RP* 3.15: "ET fait a remembrer, que al clamour & instance des Communes estoit ordeignez en Parlement, que la dite Alice serroit envoiez, pur y ent respondre en Parlement, & resceivre ce que ent serroit ordeignez vers elle."

the king formalizes the administrative roles that Reason and Conscience have already performed for him in guiding his verdict. This bureaucratic change also seems to promise that henceforth the king will be governed by them. By this time we can see that the allegory is in fact *institutional* and not just personal to the king, and that the king must work in concert with the institutional representatives of several bureaucratic offices, all of which – like parliament itself – were elements of monarchical government. Notwithstanding the simple and completely consistent fact that parliament remains an extension of the sovereign's authority, the stress here is on the reform of the government as an exercise in institutional reform. That reform, as Reason states, must come through the king's impartiality – "*audiatis alteram partem* amonges aldremen and comeneres" (C.4.188) – and through a strict control of the documentary tools of royal justice. Doing so will lead, through "loue," to more money for the war effort, that is, the Commons will more willingly provide funds "to wage thyn and helpe wynne þat thow wilnest aftur" (C.4.191–2). In sum, the king will have enough money to both "wage" his retainers and "wage" his war.[38]

So the allegory comes full circle and returns to the issues of money and finance by making Meed unnecessary for the successful "waging and winning" of the war, if only the king will follow Reason and Conscience. Remarkably, we are left with the king in the position of a *petitioner*, since he seeks the best way to ensure payment – meed – by inquiring responsibly and deliberatively through "reason" and law, not through prerogative control. Correlatively, Meed's attempts to buy off justice (as exemplified in the case against Wrong) have been strongly rebuffed by the virtuously reconstituted court of the king. As a result, "Reason" emerges more as an institutional quality than a personal one, a necessary part of rationalized government, which entails, but is not limited to, a king governing with *Loy & Reson*.[39] And Reason *only* emerges – only comes to court – here in the setting of a trial that has forced the king to take a long hard look at his own household, which is not very different from the way Edward III and his later parliaments (like those of Richard II) were at loggerheads over precisely these issues.

This is a wealth of textual details for one small episode, but it is no more daunting in its attention to practical specificity than the poem's other forays into institutional discourses. There are thus several general observations to be made about the trial and its political *mise en scène*. Hallmark issues of

---

[38] Cf. *MED*, sv. "wāge" def. 2 (b), "a salary paid to a provider of military service, soldiers' pay; a payment made to a knight bound by indenture, feudal obligation, etc. to service to or defense of an overlord, a king, etc."

[39] *RP* 2.323.

parliamentary concern (war, misadministration, legal justice, maintenance, payments to foreign ecclesiastics) have been discussed. "The commons" has dismissed Meed out of the moot-hall and, by extension, the royal court. Conscience has counselled the king about the need for community aid, and correlatively Reason has declared his own desire to "amend all realms" of the kingdom – in other words, royal justice must be exchanged for taxes. By Reason's account this includes the equitable administration of the law, the restriction of royal writs issued under the privy seal, a renewed financial commitment to the war freeing the King from foreign dependence (especially on the Lombards) and, lastly, the necessity of cleaning house by dismissing all the king's officers (C.4.176–96). This is, almost to a point, a list of parliamentary demands, and as Jusserand noted over a century ago, we can scarcely ignore the congruence.[40] It is also worth noting that while the marriage of Meed is present in most of its contours from the earliest versions of the poem, these demands clearly emerge only in the C version. In all versions, the episode draws to a curiously unresolved close. We never find out if the wedding is allowed to continue (or if she weds Conscience), and we never learn the resolution of Peace's complaint against Wrong. In a way these questions seem to have been answered, but strictly speaking we do not know. This inconclusiveness perhaps suggests that matters of plot were not Langland's main concern, even though he may have refined his intent only after several efforts. Rather, the point was to represent a formal exploration of the issues of justice and equity, and to exploit those bureaucratic elements which would enable the allegory to deliberate in a suitably contestive fashion, as the simple agreement between the King and Reason in A and B becomes a larger set of reforms in C. But whatever the order of the text's versions, as close reading helps to clarify, the allegory depends upon a parliamentary setting of the king's court, which was the setting that best enabled Langland to represent these current issues in an oblique yet recognizable form. It allowed him, in other words, to find a speaking voice through the *poetical* representation of *political* representation, through a deliberative and contestive imagining of a deliberative and contestive political assembly.

3 PARLIAMENTARY FORM IN THE BARN OF UNITY

I have concentrated on reading the narrative development of Meed's trial as evidence for a specifically parliamentary interpretation, but there are a few

---

[40] Jusserand, *Piers Plowman: A Contribution*, 111–15.

external manuscript cues as well, indicating that it would have been read thus by a contemporary audience. At the point of Peace's parliamentary bill (C.4.45), one manuscript has the marginal annotation in a slightly later hand, "Pes complayneth yn the Parliament house."[41] Notably this term, *huse de parlement*, is recorded for the first time in the chronicle records of the Good Parliament.[42] In another manuscript, at points in Passus 4 where Kane-Donaldson's standardized B-text reads "comunes," the scribe has substituted the potentially more specific "comones" and "comonys," which may refer to a more clearly institutionalized notion of the Commons.[43] And as Kerby-Fulton and Justice have noted, enough manuscripts have an identifiable history of ownership by bureaucratic personnel that it appears "parliamentarians and high-ranking civil servants" were a primary audience for the scribal output of vernacular poetical manuscripts like those of *Piers Plowman*.[44] It makes sense that *Piers Plowman* would both reflect and re-present the world of its textual consumers. In this context, the development of the allegory in Passūs 2–4 shares with the dream of Hoo not only an allegorical and narrative approach to the problem of meed. It also shares the dream, so to speak, of *being able to speak*, of being able to *exprimere gratiosius in conspectu principum huius regni*, following Hoo, or to "withouten mercement or manslauht amende alle reumes" (C.4.182), following Reason. That is, both texts express the desire to speak authoritatively and effectively – and without violence – for real reform, and to speak *for* the community, from the community.

Having based so much of this analysis on specific echoes from the Good Parliament of 1376, it may seem curious to deny (or at least to defer the claim) that Langland was being directly topical about Perrers, or that he had this particular parliament in mind when composing Meed's trial. While the similarities between Meed and Perrers are striking, there remains an apparently insurmountable temporal difficulty. Perrers' troubles took place in the parliaments of 1376–7, and the A-version of *Piers Plowman*, containing the Meed episode largely complete, is fairly firmly dateable to the late 1360s, and almost certainly to sometime between 1368–74. For strict historical

---

[41] MS. M, British Library Cotton Vespasian B.XVI (C-text), fol. 21v.; lines 45–51 are also underlined.
[42] *Anonimalle Chronicle 1333 to 1381*, 83: noted by Butt, *A History of Parliament*, 343.
[43] MS. F, Corpus Christi College, Oxford MS. 201 (B-text), variants collated from Kane-Donaldson and the online edition, *Early Manuscripts at Oxford University* (http://image.ox.ac.uk/show?collection=corpus&manuscript=ms201). It reads (my emphases): at 4.80, "Boþe Concyense and *þe comones* knowe wel þe soþe"; at 4.182–3, "'Sire,' quod Conscience to þe kyng,' but *þe comonys assente* / It is ful hard, by myn heed, herto brynge it . . .'"; and also 4.188–9, "'þerto I assente,' quod þe kyng, 'by Seinte Marie my lady, / *To my counseil þat 3ee kome amongys clerkes and Lordes.*'" A few more variants of this lightly "parliamentarizing" manuscript are noted below.
[44] Kerby-Fulton and Justice, "Scribe D and the Marketing of Ricardian Literature," 217.

topicality, it is not really satisfying to assume that in the mid-1370s, "the Good Parliament was in the air."[45] Nor, alternately, does it appear satisfactory to recast our assumptions about the dating of the A-version to some time later, which would violate several other guiding assumptions about its date.[46] Ultimately there appears to be no simple means for identifying a directly topical relationship between these parallel episodes or for suggesting (responsibly) that Langland encoded the specific events of 1376–7.

However, given that the text has discernible references to parliamentary procedure, it is likely that following 1377, when the poet was probably working on the B and later C revisions, an appreciation of parliament had entered his awareness as it had the community at large. The strict order of the poem's revisions is not as important as its fairly straightforward engagement with the cluster of controversies developing at Westminster and beyond, at a time when the text was demonstrably in circulation. We need not posit, as did Cargill, that the "first four Passūs of *Piers Plough-man* were recited in the streets of London while the Good Parliament was sitting," although it is a telling observation that they could have been, and with a striking appositeness for exactly the kinds of proceedings that eventually unfolded there.[47] At a time when parliament had seized the public imagination, the relationship between Langland's great poem and the kingdom's greatest assembly was more one of a richly shared ideological idiom than of simple partisan reflection. The allegory of the Rats and the Mice also reinforces this parliamentary context, one in which storytelling and political maneuvering, secular and ecclesiastical, went hand in hand. It was a shared environment of narrative and allegoresis, as we have also seen with Gower and Chaucer; as such it suggests a more complex set of relations between the poem and the politics. Langland was certainly working in the long tradition of venality satire.[48] But it is possible, and the sequence of events suggests, that he found himself in a "wag the dog" situation when the elements of his poem began to play themselves out, in a case of life imitating art, with Alice Perrers starring as a Lady Meed at the Westminster courts. His use of a familiar topos, the meed-theme and the figure of Lady Munera, would thus have become resonantly topical.[49] And looking beyond the parallels between Meed and Perrers to the wider context of

---

[45] Selzer, "Topical Allegory in *Piers Plowman*," 265 n. 7.
[46] See most recently Hanna III, *William Langland* and "Emendations"; and Bowers, "Dating *Piers Plowman*," which generally reaffirm the conclusions summarized in Kane, "The Text."
[47] Cargill, "The Date of the A-Text," 362.
[48] See definitively Yunck, *The Lineage of Lady Meed*, 284–306.
[49] Here I am essentially elaborating a position first put forward by Skeat (*Piers Plowman* vol. 2, 31 n. 9), that Langland revised his pre-existing portrait of Meed to be more reminiscent of Perrers.

how other narratives of "meed" – money and finance, not just allegory or character – have such a prominent place in the chronicle accounts, we can intuit a strongly Langlandian feel to the kind of stories that summed up the spirit of the day. It is not that Langland was writing an allegory of contemporary politics, but that contemporary politics were performing, in a very broad sense, what Langland had also – or already – scripted.

At the same time, that poetical script demonstrates just how difficult it was to get an idealized, inspired community to maintain its focus and purpose. Famously the reforms of the Good Parliament were short-lived, although not quite so abortive as some chroniclers (such as Walsingham) later made them seem. Perrers again provides a case in point. She was reinstated to the court following the "Bad Parliament" of January–April 1377 in which the Duke of Lancaster undid many of the efforts of the previous assembly; Peter de la Mare was imprisoned for his role in the Good Parliament.[50] Then in the first parliament of Richard's reign later in October–December 1377, with de la Mare again as speaker, many of the undoings were themselves undone. Perrers was re-condemned, this time with better attention paid to the niceties of legal procedure. Her case went back and forth for several years.[51] Other reforms were similarly contested and re-contested, perhaps providing even more extensively conflictual examples of the ways in which the assembly forum and form – again like the Rats and Mice – could represent both great promise and flat inanity.

A final example of that contrast, set in an implicitly parliamentary framework, comes at the end of *Piers Plowman* in the Barn of Unity episode in B Passus 19, C Passus 21. James Simpson has demonstrated how the scene of the distribution of the crafts "records a Pentecostal scene in which liturgical and civic, or at least occupational, elements are inextricably interwoven."[52] After Will's long spiritual journey and after the joyous climax of the Crucifixion and Resurrection, the poem's return to the earthly community is signalled by the summoning of "the comune" (C.21.214) to receive the distribution of the graces, by Grace, as "tresor" (C.21.225). This treasure, like Hoo's coins, represents a conflation of spiritual and communal wealth. These graces are, essentially, a return to the crafts of the Fair Field of Folk: we see in turn preachers, priests, and lawyers; merchants and

---

[50] Butt, 351–4.

[51] See *RP* 2.329 (initial "impeachment"), 2.374 (reinstatement), and 3.12–15 (re-judgment). In 1378 another bill was brought forth by William Windsor, her husband, contesting the legitimacy of the judgment based on eight "errors" (*RP* 3.40–1). But it was not until 1384 (*RP* 3.186) that Richard II voided the judgment.

[52] Simpson, "'After Craftes Conseil clotheth yow and fede': Langland and London City Politics," 109.

retailers; laborers of the land and on water; scholars and the learned; and the armigerous nobility, "somme to ryde & to rekeuere that vnrihtfulliche was wonne" (C.21.229–45). Each class is again represented. Conscience is crowned "king" with Craft as his steward, and Piers Plowman is named – all in one – "procuratour" and "reue" and "Registrer to reseyuen *Redde quod debes*" (C.21.258–9). Grace then gives the "grains" of the four cardinal virtues to sow on behalf of the community, and by the further counsel of Grace, Piers is advised to "ordeyne þat hous" (C.21.320) to hold his harvest:

> And þerwith grace bigan to make a goode foundement
> And wateled hit and walled hit with his paynes and his passion
> And of all holy writ he made a roef aftur
> And calde þat hous vnite, holy chirche an englisch.
>
> (C.21.325–8)

This unique "house" is thus a barn or granary and also a church, *the* Church, that is the new center of the community. Conscience repeatedly appeals to it in the same terms as Reason's sermon from Passus 5, exhorting the community to "hold in Unity": "my consayl is to wende / Hastiliche into vnite and holde we vs there" (C.21.355–6; also C.22.75, 204–5, 246, 297). "Unity" emerges as the focal location for the final psychomachia in Passūs 21–2. In fitting with the symbolic struggle, the barn and church also become a fortified town or a keep, besieged by the forces of Antichrist (C.22.51–385).

Along with these architectural symbolizations of community (barn, church, castle), Unity develops into a distinctly deliberative communal environment. It is "þe comune" (C.21.379, 391) who are called into Unity and who also, almost immediately, initiate a debate about precisely *what* is required by "unity": what material concessions must be made in order to have the advantages and protection of this newly-founded community? Conscience preaches a strict adherence to *redde quod debes* and to the cardinal virtues as a prerequisite to full fellowship: "'How?' quod alle þe comune; 'thow conseylest vs to ȝelde / Al þat we owen eny wyhte or we go to hosele?'" (C.21.391–2) Before they go to their "house," they need to know how to be properly "hoseled" or shriven. Here the community/commons speaks with one voice in their desire to know the way to Unity. But Conscience's demands immediately set off a stiff debate. A brewer refuses to be governed by the *spiritus iusticie* when he can cheat customers by selling "Both dregges and draf and drawe at on hole / Thikke ale & thynne ale" (C.21.398–400). Next, with an obligatory pun on "cardinal virtues," a "lewed vicory" (C.21.409) bewails the rapaciousness of foreign cardinals. He notes that "the comune *clamat cotidie*" against their unvirtuous depredations, even though these same commons care only for their own "wynnynge" – this is what passes for the *spiritus prudencie* (C.21.416, 451–3). Third, a noble lord invokes the *spiritus intellectus* and *spiritus fortitudinis* to justify his forceful extraction of as much money as possible from his manorial dependants (C.21.459–64). And lastly, a crowned king appeals to the cardinal virtues and the *Spiritus iusticie* to justify his own rapacity:

> Y am kyng with croune the comune to reule
> And holy kyrke and clerge fro cursed men to defende.
> And yf me lakketh to lyue by þe lawe wol y take hit
> Ther y may hastilokest hit haue, for y am heed of lawe;
> ȝe ben bote membres and y aboue alle.
> And sethe y am ȝoure alere heued y am ȝoure alere hele
> And holy churche cheef helpe and cheuenteyn of þe comune
> And what y take of ȝow two y take hit at þe techynge
> Of *spiritus iusticie* for y iuge ȝow alle.
> So y may boldely be hoseled for y borwe neuere
> Ne craue of my comune bote as my kynde asketh.
>
> (C.21.466–76)

Here the king appeals to the traditional corporeal metaphor of the body politic, adapted from 1 Corinthians 12, to justify his actions. But the less obvious point is that the king's claims – that he takes his monetary extractions legally from commons and clergy, that he takes only what he needs for aid and at greatest expedience, and that he is head and defender of the community and judge of all – refer implicitly to the sovereign's position in parliament. Once again, as in the trial of Meed, all of these details make historical sense only in a parliamentary context, since it was, as we have seen, only in parliament where these national questions of finance and justice were debated and legislated. In particular the king's final statement, that he does not "craue of my comune bote as my kynde asketh," makes sense only if we read it as referring to both the "community" *and* the institutional Commons who controlled access to such taxation.[53] The King is not, in fact, overstating or overstepping his prerogatives, even if he presents them in a particularly blustery fashion. Conscience's reply, that the king can have what he needs as long as he uses the wealth to defend the community and to "rewle thy rewme in resoun" (C.21.477–9), is equally consonant with standard parliamentary thinking on the matter.

---

[53] Again, the F MS. takes mild note of this, substituting "commones" (comonis, commonys) for "comune" at B.19.466, 472, and 476.

This regal bluster harmonizes with the self-interested forcefulness of each estate preceding the king, and we can see, in the wider context, how a tacitly parliamentary framework enables this scene to develop. The narrative moves from the political periphery to the center, from the burgess commons (the brewer) to the clergy, nobility, and finally to the king, matching the quadripartite estates model frequently repeated in the rolls of parliament: *le Roi, les Prelatz, les Grantz, et les Communes.*[54] Each of these estates argues for their justification (or bewails their victimization) regarding the financial extractions attendant to their place. The social picture as a whole is one of serial exploitation. The brewer exploits his customers, the higher clergy exploit their sees, the nobility exploit their dependants, and the king exploits everyone. Each complaint deals with money, wealth, and payment, and each category of complaint was the subject of specifically parliamentary legislation. The rolls are rife with contemporary petitions and parliamentary statutes regarding commercial sales (such as those governing brewers); payments to foreign ecclesiastics; abuses of leasing, auditing, accounting, and purveying; and the extent and uses of royal taxation.[55]

So there is good reason for a sense of *déjà vu* when reading these lines: fifteen passūs and thousands of lines later, *Piers Plowman* is still vitally concerned with the issues of meed and money, and of reform. These concerns re-emerge in the context of a communal *parlement* where the desire for unity – and the House of Unity – immediately reveals the un-unified nature of the body politic. Like a contemporary parliament, each estate clamorously demands justice through the voices of single speakers representing collective social groupings. The bourgeois crafts of London city politics, combined with the national estates and the supra-national estate of the monarchy, all try to protect their own interests while making inroads into everyone else's.

---

[54] See the discussion in Chapter One.

[55] A few examples can be highlighted, mostly from 1363 and 1376, but such concerns are omnipresent in the rolls. On assizes of bread and ale (as well as bakers and butchers), see *SR* 1.200–4, and various parliamentary bills concerning commodity sales: sale of sweet wines and wine (*RP* 2.323, 279), export of grain (*RP* 2.350), sale of wool-yarn (*RP* 2.353), export of cloth, grain, and beer (*RP* 2.275–6); sale of fish and other victuals (*RP* 2.276); and, perhaps strangest to modern eyes, strict regulations *de Polaile*, that is, regulating the sizes and prices of chickens (*RP* 2.277). Complaints about greedy foreign cardinals were repeated in 1376 (*RP* 2.336–7, 339, 341), with the perhaps overblown claim that the amount of tax sent to Rome was five times greater than the king's domestic income (*desqueux le taxe amonte a plus que cink foitz le tax dez touz les profitz que appartenent au Roi par an de tout son Roialme* [337]). See a similar bill in 1386 (*RP* 3.222). Complaints were made against seigneurial abuses in purveying (*RP* 2.342) and against the seigneurial lease-farming of Hundreds, *qar par cause des grosses fermes ils font grandes extorsions au poeple* (*RP* 2.333). There is also a vaguely worded petition against irregular royal confiscations (*RP* 2.333).

So what starts out as yet another Langlandian image of a potentially ideal and just society, quickly descends into ineffectual squabbling and rancor. This discord sets the stage for invasion and subversion in the last passus. Here again we can note the fungibility of ecclesiastical and secular institutional forms. Unity is a castle, barn, and church, but it is also, functionally, a parliament, an assembly-place and moot-hall of uniquely national character. As in Thomas Hoo's dream, sacred and secular institutional structures – St. Paul's and Westminster – are conflated for the purposes of the allegory, a conflation enabling the narrative to explore what is at stake in the controversies and political problems of the nation at large. At the same time, Langland appears to have some very specific things to say – about cardinals, brewers, kings, and the like – that both invite and frustrate a more policy-minded way of thinking.

4 CONCLUSION: PIERS PLOWMAN'S REFORM
OF THE PUBLIC VOICE

To return to the sixteenth-century pamphlet I cited at the beginning, it is now suggestively clearer why Piers Plowman would have been an attractive reformation figure not just as a general critic of church and society, but as the mouthpiece for some very specific reforms, "such good polytike lawes and statutes" as the poem itself seems to endorse in the secular environs of the Visio. In Langland's day as later, parliament was the forum where such ideas were publicized. At the same time, it is not really accurate to think of *Piers Plowman* as a "parliamentary" poem in this narrow sense, when by its conclusion the estates-structure and deliberative practice of *parlement* offer another example of a failed polity, one that constitutes itself in Unity only to be swiftly fractured. In Passus B.19/C.21, the descent of Grace as the *spiritus paraclitus* (C.21.206) also reinforces the Pentecostal parliamentary associations of communal assembly. Like ideal parliaments, the "comune" in C.21 is brought together as an inspired convocation, creating another parallelism with the opening sequence of the Prologue. In B, "an Aungel of heuene" (B. prol. 128) speaks the Latin verses of warning (*Sum Rex, sum princeps, neutrum fortasse deinceps* . . . [131–8]), words spoken in C instead by the figure of Conscience (C. prol. 152–9). Where Conscience at the end of the poem presides over the Pentecostal arrival of Grace and the combative *parlement* of the estates in Unity, at the beginning, the pentecostal Angel/Conscience had similarly gathered the *communes* for the foundation of the king's rule. The F manuscript's B-version of the king's arrival in the Prologue again provides the most "parliamentarizing" version of this

founding gesture in which all instances of þe comune are changed to variants of "the commons" (F MS., B.prol.115–21). The ensuing cry of the *vox
populi* in F is even more reminiscent of the biblical-pentecostal tradition of
parliamentary and communal acclamation:

> Thanne cryeden all þe comonys with o voys atonys,
> *Precepta Regis sunt nobis uincula legis . . .*
>   (F MS., B. prol. 143, 145 [144 omitted])

This variant of the commons speaking "with one voice" is limited to a single
manuscript, and of course, for none of these variants must we completely
restrict our understanding of "the commons" only to "the Commons."
Nonetheless the institutional framework of the parliamentary Commons is
detectable behind this initial Pentecostal scene of political foundation in the
same way that it is the formal organizing principle for the reintroduction
of Grace and Conscience at the end. As in the deposition of Edward II
and the acclamation of Edward III, it was in parliament where scenes
like this were played out; indeed Langland's version here is reminiscent
of the Latin-language chronicle records of vernacular acclamations.[56] The
long tradition of Pentecostalist parliamentarism thus initiates the poem's
troubled exploration of kingship and polity just as it concludes it.

   This is to say, the F-manuscript's variant of the commons speaking "with
one voice at once" is precisely where we would expect it to be, authorial
or not, given the tradition Langland is working with. But unlike Gower or
Chaucer, Langland's allegory expresses a desire for speaking that we simply
have not seen, one that self-consciously eschews the final hypostasization
of that voice into the authoritative figure of an individual. Although *Piers
Plowman* implicitly continues, after its end, with the frustrated quest for
its titular hero, Piers the Plowman's representativeness is subsumed by the
poem's other voices of conflict and reform, especially during the explorations of church reform and personal examination in the vast body of
the narrative I have not dealt with here. Again, parliaments have provided
a framework, a beginning-and-end scaffolding that, as in the *Mirour de
l'Omme* and the *Canterbury Tales*, allows the poet to investigate the estates
and society as a whole in a recognizable and meaningful fashion. But as
an exercise in public poetry, *Piers Plowman* exemplifies a striking development away from the very transcendentalism of its own origins. It begins and
ends with images of social *parlement* as inspired gatherings, but this sort of

---

[56] See Chapters One and Two. On the different registers and tones of the Latin passages in this scene,
see Somerset, "'Al þe comonys with o voys at onys': Multilingual Latin and Vernacular Voice in *Piers
Plowman*."

idealized reformation is stopped, repeatedly, by the practical intransigence of a community whose members cannot come together and who do not find a figure like Chaucer's Parson to provide a definitive or authoritative voice. Any such authority is deferred beyond the bounds of the poem itself, perhaps hinting at the Langland-inspired tradition in the poems of the following decades, that take up both his verse style and practical public voice in even more bureacratized ways. As it stands in its own textual multiplicity, *Piers Plowman* provides an image of poetry as the form of engaged public discourse with an irreducible and often troubling multi-vocality. It is almost as if in Langland's hands, the *spiritus paraclitus* could not withstand the variability of its own expressive vehicle, the "common voice," which inevitably devolves – or develops? – into common *voices*, the rancorous and problematic but also vigorous and realistic talking of the community itself. Read generously, then, it is a strong testament to Langland's critical perceptiveness of this tradition that he was able to exploit the capacities of parliamentary form both with, and against, its own foundational assumptions of unity, for the creation of a poem that speaks with both one, and innumerably many, voices.

CHAPTER 6

Petitioning for show: complaint and the parliamentary voice, 1401–14

With Gower, Chaucer, and Langland, I have argued for a discernible trajectory in their engagement with parliamentary form. Without reducing their poetry to *prises de position*, we can, I think, apply some familiar categories to their specifically parliamentary elements. Where Gower appeals, thematically and structurally, to an ideal or noble metonymy of unity in both voice and figuration, and where Chaucer exploits the structures and documentary forms of petition and mediation (with all they entail), Langland's parliamentary allegories of the social estates exploit an even more open-ended representation of diversity – of voice, class, intent, and institution – that, in the end, refuses to be closed. Certainly these categories and qualities are nothing new to any of them; my endeavor has been to demonstrate how the specifically parliamentary tropes of their poetry help to create the enabling conditions for these familiar aspects of their practice. Proceeding from Langland in particular, what we could call his allegorical realism appears to have been received with excitement and a strong sense of its critical possibilities. The remarkable cluster of *Piers Plowman*-inspired poems, all emerging after the revolution of 1399, utilizes a parliamentary–poetic idiom in some of its most vigorous and searching expressions, and so together they fittingly provide the subjects of this last chapter.

By more directly and urgently exploiting parliament as a topic, the secular poems of the Piers Plowman tradition – *The Crowned King, Richard the Redeless*, and *Mum and the Sothsegger* – actually signal the waning of parliament and *parlement* as a resource for the formal arrangement of narrative art. This is not to deny the creativity of their parliamentary allegories. But at a time when the king's parliament became more powerful and more central than it had ever been before, it lost its capacity – or at least, it is no longer looked to, by artists – as a structuring *idea* for the arrangement of narrative. As it strengthens as a topic, parliament weakens as a form.

In one sense, this is a counter-intuitive development. From both a political and literary point of view, the Lancastrian coup was a severe trauma, one captured directly in the contemporary documentary and chronicle sources, and obliquely in imaginative literature. Works like Gower's *Cronica Tripertita* and Creton's *Histoire* (and shorter poems like Chaucer's "To His Purse") were direct responses to the revolution but did not, by and large, go beyond accounts or interested justifications of what happened. In contrast, the secular poems of the Piers Plowman tradition respond by addressing the institutional context and by commenting on the direction of the revolution. They critique not only what happened but where things might go, and the conditions in which things might change for better or worse. Essential to this inquiry is the parliamentary setting of events. In both its execution and justification (as we have seen in Gower's *Cronica*), the revolution of 1399 was a *pro forma* parliamentary event like the dethroning of Edward II in 1327. The change of regimes was also a watershed as the threat of revolt lingered for the next fifteen years, wound up with anxieties about Lollardy, baronial sedition, and popular upheaval. While there was a radical break in the continuity of the monarchy and the Crown's ability to wield political control, there was no such rupture in parliamentary activities. Indeed the revolution augmented the political centrality of parliament for a time and, in the intial weakness of the Lancastrian regime, gave it renewed standing as a legitimating authority for centralized government. That authority was also, as we shall see, the grounds for "showing" complaints, in the formal sense of that phrase. In this newly opened space, the poets of the Piers Plowman tradition found some room for artistic representation.

As Arthur Ferguson argued in his elegant and durable study, these Langlandian poems – particularly *Mum and the Sothsegger* – stand as early landmarks in the development of a social consciousness of "articulate citizenship," which included the proposition that the public expression of grievances was necessary for the proper governance of the realm.[1] But what these poems gain in political expressiveness and "emergent realism" (to use Ferguson's phrase), they pay for in the contraction of imaginary and artistic license. As we have seen in Chaucer and Langland, the petition was a particularly powerful form. With the sudden ostensible (and troubled) freeing of public discourse under Henry IV, the renewed ability to bring complaints and "show" petitions, in the technical sense[2], emerges as a principal focus of literary anxiety. The most direct and sustained contact between political–institutional and literary form in these poems centers on how, and by whom, petitions and complaints can be shown. This borrows from *Piers*

---

[1] Ferguson, *Articulate Citizen*, 3–129.   [2] See Chapter 4, n. 45.

Plowman at the same time that it bureaucratizes the abstractly formulated idea of a bill that Langland used. That is, rather than poeticizing complaints and bills themselves (amorous or political), these poems talk *about* them, and their conditions, in particularly searching ways. Once again parliament is the forum for this deliberation, both explicitly and implicitly. But as these poems look to their predecessors for a way to approach the pressing issues of right representation and public voice, in the very act of doing so, they tend to constrict the forms of narrative artistry they were drawing from. The incompleteness of these poems – setting aside questions of authorial talent and textual exigency – seems to reflect this.

In a way, this conclusion reaffirms the observation that the Langlandian idiom of these works is "a discourse by no means independent of institutional discourses; but the poetic text is nevertheless registered as taking its occasion from the inadequacies of those institutions and their authoritative texts."[3] By bringing a parliamentary–poetical motif into closer contact with its bureaucratic and practical dimensions, *Richard the Redeless* and *Mum and the Sothsegger* expose its limitations as a means of aesthetic criticism. At the same time, these poems show a remarkable breadth of conception when considering precisely who ought to be (or are) the guardians of good governance in the realm. Where *Richard* is concerned with voicing the accumulated complaints against Richard II's hapless rule, the impasse it reaches also shows how the notional desire for renewed public discourse had not been fully worked out, even by those with a professional investment in its operation. Given that the community must speak, and critically; how then to make it work? In a way, *Mum* picks up where *Richard* breaks off, attempting to recast the quest narrative of *Piers Plowman* into an investigation of this issue. But the similar inconclusiveness of *Mum* also demonstrates the dead end that this literary form had worked itself into, when trying to think through the practical question of how best to foster the showing of complaint without also fomenting social division and conflict. These poems provide artful critiques of communal representative practice as much as they criticize poor royal governance, but they start things they cannot finish. Lacking the authoritative closure to communal *parlement* provided by a Parson, and absent the reiterably unending quest for the desired figure of a Piers, in *Mum* the drive for a meliorative and healing authority results only in an inconclusive jumble.

From the particular perspective of parliamentary writing, by the end of *Mum* one has the distinct sense of artistic fatigue, as if an imaginative

---

[3] Simpson, "The Constraints of Satire in *Piers Plowman* and *Mum and the Sothsegger*," 23.

moment had run its course. If this was the case, and poetical *parlement* could no longer provide a strong conceptual framework for imaginative literature, nonetheless there is ample indication that a legacy of public discourse in poetry had been firmly established with its help. Two contemporary petitions provide helpful contexts for understanding this process. So, for the last time, I will accompany an analysis of these poems with some parliamentary storytelling that, like the case of Elizabeth de Burgh, unfolds in fascinating petitions. These documents also give a better sense of the development of vernacular petitioning, which is, in many ways, the proper context for these poems, as they approach the language and vigor of contemporary documentary culture more intimately than any works before them.

I THE RE-EMERGENCE OF PARLIAMENTARY POWER, 1401–14

To understand why and how parliament was re-empowered in the two decades following the revolution, we need to look at the last years of Richard II's reign, when parliament became, in effect, an extension of the royal court. Following the Appellant crisis of 1387–8, Richard's power was at low ebb. He appears to have consciously cultivated a plan to reassert himself, quietly but consistently, over the following years.[4] As Gwilym Dodd has demonstrated, part of Richard's reaction was to assert his dominion over parliament.[5] Throughout the 1390s he exercised control in both direct and indirect ways: extracting taxes with few concessions, increasing the number of shire parliamentarians from the royalist party and his widening affinity, and most strikingly, through the drastic reduction of common petitions. [6] Common petitions, which had been frequently submitted in previous years, were reduced to a near trickle, probably as a result of skillful management by the royalist Speaker, Sir John Bussy, who held the office after 1394.[7] As few as four common petitions were introduced in 1395. It seems clear that Richard was significantly less inclined to deal with problems of the realm in response to public bills. Rather than opportunities for the community to bring forth petitions on behalf of the realm, Richard's later parliaments were forums for the advancement of royal business and, after 1395, for the

---

[4] See generally Saul, *Richard II*, 176–204, 235–69; Butt, 401–50.

[5] Dodd, "Richard II and the Transformation of Parliament."

[6] This was not necessarily the result of direct "packing," as research has indicated: see Dodd, "Richard II and the Transformation of Parliament," 77–8; Lewis, "Re-election to Parliament in the Reign of Richard II." There are indications that the 1397 "Revenge" parliament and the following parliament at Shrewsbury were packed, or at least were perceived so by contemporary witnesses: see *PROME*, 1397 September, "Introduction."

[7] Dodd, "Richard II and the Transformation of Parliament," 75–7.

public representation of royal power. Perhaps the most troubling example of this trend was the case of Thomas Haxey in the January 1397 parliament.[8] A bill submitted to the Lords contained one article criticizing the size and expense of the royal household (which had grown considerably since 1395), and recommended its reduction. Having learned of this complaint from informants among the Commons, the king demanded that its author be identified. Thomas Haxey, a proctor for the abbot of Selby, was named as the author and was handed over for punishment, with the Lords and Commons offering an almost grovelling apology for his offense.[9] Whatever the substance of Haxey's supposed crime of *lèse-majesté*, the message at the time seems clear: parliament should not presume to complain about royal governance or the conduct of the royal household. Parliament was to act as the agent of the king's wishes, not vice versa. By the next parliament in September 1397, the "Revenge" Parliament, the assembly was completely overpowered by Richard's forceful impositions, which included a display of military force during the session. The king was granted the wool subsidy for life, the former Appellants of 1388 were tried and condemned, and later, parliament's authority was transferred to a small committee that continued business after the full assembly had been dismissed.[10] By this point, parliament had effectively been made into an appendage of the royal will. There was little opportunity to show complaint or voice opposition without the real threat of violence.

These well-known facts of Richard's later "tyrannical" rule help to contextualize the delicate balance struck by Henry IV in the years immediately after the revolution. Many later complaints about the ineffectiveness of parliament (as we find in *Richard the Redeless*, for example) look back to this troubled period specifically.[11] The articles of deposition brought against Richard included the illegalities of almost all of these impositions upon parliament, even when similar procedures had been exercised in prior assemblies.[12] After 1399, Henry's more conciliatory stance appears to have been a calculated response to set himself apart from his predecessor, even as the new Lancastrian regime was frankly Ricardian in its desire to control

---

[8] On the Haxey case, see Butt, 424–7; Saul, *Richard II*, 369–70; *PROME*, Richard II, 1397, January, "Introduction"; Dodd, "Richard II and the Transformation of Parliament," 78–80.

[9] *RP* 3.339. Haxey was condemned to death for having encroached upon the king's "royal estate and liberty" (*son Roiale Estat et Liberte*). His sentence was later commuted and then dismissed.

[10] Saul, *Richard II*, 366–94; Butt, 427–39; the parliamentary committee was set up after the Shrewsbury session of January 1398.

[11] See McFarlane, "Parliament and 'Bastard Feudalism,'" 3.

[12] As Butt notes (439), the parliamentary committee of 1398 resembled previous extra-parliamentary councils assigned to deal with petitions outside of regular sessions. On the articles of deposition see *RP* 3.416–32; for analysis see also Giancarlo, "Murder, Lies, and Storytelling."

214 Parliament and Literature in Late Medieval England

dissent.[13] After the deposition, however, a new tone enters the record of the crown's dealings with parliament, as both the king and the assembly worked out the boundaries of what could be said to, or demanded of, the other, while not pushing the relationship to the brink of a mutually destructive crisis.

Interestingly, this new approach included Henry's direct and relatively informal interactions with parliament. He occasionally addressed the assembly in person and argued *in propria persona* about points of policy and finance.[14] In 1401 at the start of the first regular parliament after the revolution, the roll records Henry IV declaring his desire for a comprehensive and orderly assembly that would attend to its responsibilities in a timely fashion. Immediately after his election as Speaker, Arnold Savage requests assurance that the Commons would be given sufficient time for "good advice and deliberation, without being requested suddenly to reply to the most burdensome matters at the end of parliament, as had been the case before."[15] It is not clear if Savage was criticizing Richard's practices or the practices of the first parliament under Henry only thirteen months prior, but the former seems more likely. The king is recorded as responding with the nonplussed assurance that he had "no such subtlety" (*nule tiele subtilitie*) in mind. Shortly after this there is a plea that the king should not pay any heed to tale-bearers or rumors of the Commons' deliberations put forward "by anyone . . . before such matters had been put to the king by the advice and assent of all the commons"; this was allowed as well.[16] These assurances augmented the limited protections provided by the Speaker's protestation, and it was probably a new sense of expressive opportunity about speaking *simpliciter* that accounts for the generous record of Savage's activities as Speaker in this parliament.[17] The roll records the submission of multiple requests orally, *par bouche*, which the king defers to answer before having them put into writing; a request for assurance that the business of parliament would be enrolled or "engrossed" (*enactez & engrossez*) in a timely manner; a request that the Commons' petitions be answered *before* the granting of subsidies; and, toward the end, a particularly deferential

---

[13] See especially Strohm, *England's Empty Throne*.

[14] See Dodd, "Conflict or Consensus: Henry IV and Parliament, 1399–1406," and "Henry IV's Council, 1399–1405"; Clark, "Magnates and their Affinities in the Parliaments of 1386–1421."

[15] *RP* 3.455: ". . . avoir bon advys & deliberation, sanz estre mys sodeinement a respons de les pluis chargeantz matires au fyn de Parlement, come il ad este usez devaunt ces heures."

[16] *RP* 3.456: "et q'il ne vorroit oier nulle tiele persone, ne luy doner credence, devaunt qe tieles matires feussent monstrez au Roy, par advis et assent des toutz les Communes, solonc le purport de leur dit prier."

[17] See Roskell, "Sir Arnald Savage of Bobbing."

request for "grace and pardon" if the Commons had spoken or acted in any manner displeasing to the king.[18]

Clearly all of these procedural and rhetorical gestures move away from the strict position of subordination that Richard had cultivated for parliament, at the same time that the tone of exchange adjusts to take advantage of the rhetorical space opened up by the grandiose Ricardian *regimen parliamenti*. The request for "grace and pardon" in the 1401 parliament, reminiscent of the self-abasing apology submitted in the Haxey case of 1397, demonstrates the simultaneously humble and aggressive stance adopted by the Commons with regard to its own capacities as a speaking body. The request itself is recorded in the deferential terms of bodily and rhetorical submission:

Also, on the said Thursday, the last day of parliament [10 March], the said commons, humbly kneeling, prayed of our lord the king that in case they, or any one of them, through ignorance or negligence, had acted wrongly in any way, either in their speech, or contrary to his royal estate, thus in any way incurring the displeasure of his royal person, it might please our same lord the king out of his benign grace to grant them full grace and pardon.[19]

Displays of this sort were not normal prior to the 1390s. Such pretension to overarching regality, combined with the showy abasement of the Commons, was the kind of behavior Richard had been faulted for, particularly by Walsingham.[20] But with Henry, the dynamic had changed. However polite the plea (and notwithstanding Henry's relatively relaxed approach), this and the other recorded instances of petitions for grace are, in fact, more the result of the Commons' – and particularly Savage's – effective *resistance* to the king's demands for money.[21] Indeed, this is the important point of kneeling: having resisted Henry on substantive matters, the Commons can defer to him on symbolic ones. What looks from a distance like toadying is actually a hint of the Commons' ability to control its agenda, and at the same time,

---

[18] For the initial submission of oral petitions see *RP* 3.456; the recording of business, *RP* 3.457–8; the effort to have all petitions answered prior to the subsidy grants (which Henry resisted), *RP* 3.458; the request for general pardon, *RP* 3.466.

[19] *RP* 3.466: "Item, le dit Joefdy, le darrein jour du Parlement, les ditz Communes humblement engenulantz, prierent a nostre Seignur le Roy, q'en cas q'ils, ou ascun de eux, par ignorance ou negligence soi avoient aucunement mespris en parol ou en fait encontre son Roial Estat, qe purroit aucunement tourner a displaisance de sa Roiale persone, q'il pleust a mesme nostre Seignur le Roi de sa benigne grace leur ent faire pleine grace et pardone."

[20] See Saul, "Richard II and the Vocabulary of Kingship," 854–9.

[21] The St. Albans *Chronicle* notes that Savage "set out the case for the commons so clearly, so eloquently and so admirably, especially to the effect that they should not in future be burdened by taxes or tallages, that he won the praise of all that day" (qui tam diserte, tam eloquenter, tam gratiose, declaravit communitatis negotia, praecipue ne de caetero taxis gravarentur, aut talliagiis, quod laudem ab universis promeruit ea die). *Chronicon Angliae*, 335, cited in *PROME*, Henry IV 1401, "Introduction." See also Brown, "The Commons and the Council in the Reign of Henry IV," 11–12.

to act with a petitionary show of deference that secures its own position. Other examples are found later. In 1404 when Savage was again Speaker, the roll records a request that the king not be offended by the Commons' complaints about the governance of the realm because they do not proceed from any *sinistre information* or *malvoise entencion*.[22] In the roll of the Long Parliament of 1406, the Speaker John Tiptoft apologizes for the Commons and denies the *sinistre report* that they had spoken inappropriately of the king's royal person. He re-asserts their love as *loialx lieges* of the king.[23] And in 1411, Henry IV's last parliament, a similar declaration of fidelity is made to counter the *graund murmur* that the king held ill will (*pesantee*) against his subjects in parliament. The declaration is made in a petition requesting a show of his good grace, which the king grants *de sa grace especiale*.[24]

The difference, then, was in the disposition of the political actors in their public petitionary shows, and in how the Commons could manipulate their subordinate stance to extract assent from the king. During these years the Commons also increasingly policed the control of their own voice and documentation. In 1401 they strengthened the procedures for proper enrollments of official parliamentary records. In 1404 they reluctantly granted an irregular tax, but only on the condition that no record of it be left in the rolls and that it set no precedent for future taxation; our knowledge of it comes only from outside sources.[25] In 1407, when Thomas Chaucer was speaker, conflict arose after Henry went first to the Lords to begin negotiating the size of a subsidy and only secondly presented the proposal to the Commons. Although there was no real attempt to force the proposal, they were nonetheless alarmed that the customary sequence – with the Commons initiating specific grant proposals – had not been followed. As a result, a schedule of indemnity was recorded in the roll making their objection a matter of record.[26] Later in 1413, in the first parliament of Henry V's reign, the speaker of the Commons, the lawyer William Stourton, was dismissed from office almost immediately after election because he agreed to a request made by the king without first presenting it to the Commons for approval.[27] Among the many agendas and programs pursued aggressively during these parliaments (not the least being the prosecutions

[22] *RP* 3.523.   [23] *RP* 3.569.   [24] *RP* 3.658.

[25] See Butt, 468; Walsingham, *Ypodigma Neustriae*, 404. Similarly in the 1410 parliament, anti-clerical petitions were submitted along with attempts to soften the anti-Lollard statutes, but these were suppressed from the parliamentary record: Butt, 480.

[26] *RP* 3.611. See Butt, 478.

[27] Butt, 487. The relative insignificance of the matter (the king requested that petitions be submitted in writing) makes clear that the issue was Stourton's procedural mis-step, not the request itself.

of the Lollards and efforts to control royal expenditures) the control over parliament's public self-representation – its showing of *itself* – was a persistent concern.

The apogee of parliament's power came during the Long Parliament of 1406. This assembly sat for three sessions from March to December and was the longest parliament yet held at Westminster. It was also the most active since the Good Parliament of 1376, engaging in a sustained struggle with the king over practically every significant issue of governmental control.[28] Over the course of the sessions, the rolls record the speaker renewing his Protestation no fewer than six times, as well as seeking "pardon" for any offence he may have caused.[29] Conflicts over the issues at stake – taxation and revenues, royal expenditure and resident aliens in the king's court, the Glendower rebellion in Wales and rebellions in the north, the wars in France and Scotland, secure shipping, the composition of a royal council – were heated and at times gave way to open bickering between the king and parliament. The young and forceful speaker, Tiptoft, was appointed with Henry's approval and was probably a royal nominee, and he emerged as a skilled mediator during the Commons' most successful exercise of power in a generation.[30] He guided the parliament's resistance to the king's demands for immediate grants, and a number of independent magnates were appointed to oversee Crown expenses. Tiptoft himself was made treasurer of the household. By the end of the assembly a council was put in place that "ruled the king almost as if he were a minor."[31] True to parliament's increased sense of expressive self-control, the Commons demanded that a committee of MPs be present when the official roll was engrossed.[32] Henry's failing health was certainly a major factor in his relative weakness and the length of the assembly, but overall the records make it clear that the legislative initiative had shifted to the Commons and parliament.[33] Although the Commons maintained their respectful deference (and exploited it), the situation had almost completely reversed Richard's domination of a decade earlier.

---

[28] For good summaries of this long and complex parliament see especially *PROME*, Henry IV, March 1406, "Introduction"; Butt, 470–5; and Brown, "The Commons and Council in the Reign of Henry IV," 12–29.
[29] *RP* 3.568, 569, 572, 574, 577, 579.
[30] See Roskell, "Sir John Tiptoft, Commons' Speaker in 1406," and Pollard, "The Lancastrian Constitutional Experiment Revisted: Henry IV, Sir John Tiptoft, and the Parliament of 1406."
[31] McFarlane cited in *PROME*, "Introduction," fn. 27.
[32] *RP* 3.585. The petition also asks that the petition itself be enrolled, which it was.
[33] Biggs, "The Politics of Health: Henry IV and the Long Parliament of 1406."

2 RIGHTEOUSNESS AND COMPLAINTS:
TWO PETITIONS FROM 1414

In fact the balance of power had swung so abruptly back in favor of parliament, historians have remarked that Henry IV was subjected to unprecedented challenges and restrictions emanating from the Commons.[34] From our perspective, the importance of this shift lies not just in parliament's renewed legislative power, but in the re-emergence of petitions as the means for public representation and voice. Two documents provide unique perspective on this development. Following the contraction of petitioning under Richard, the Lancastrian regime saw a re-effloresence of parliamentary bills and petitions. The roll for 1406, for example, contains thirty-six common petitions, and later parliaments record similar numbers.[35] Henry IV apparently cultivated this resumption of familiar practice in an effort to gain popular standing, and attention was paid to ensuring the sovereign's readiness to regularly hear and answer petitions.[36] Two noteworthy petitions, both from the start of the reign of Henry V, bear witness to the way the Commons and the community approached parliamentary petitioning in this new environment. In a common petition submitted during Henry V's second parliament in April 1414 (Figure 7, Item x.22), the Commons asserts its official prerogative, not just as a body of petitioners but also as assenters, that is, as legislators and co-sharers of law-making power with the king.

This unique English document bears quoting in full:

Oure soverain lord, youre humble and trewe lieges that ben come for the commune of youre lond by sechyn on to youre ri3t ri3twesnesse, that so as hit hath evere be thair liberte et fredom, that thar sholde no statut no lawe be made of lasse than they yaf ther to their assent: consideringe that the commune of youre lond, the whiche that is, et evere hath be, a membre of youre parlement, ben as well assentirs as peticioners, that fro this tyme foreward, by compleynte of the commune of eny myschief axkynge remedie by mouthe of their speker for the commune, other ellys by peticione writen, that ther never be no lawe made theruppon, et engrosed as statut et lawe, nother by addicions, nother by diminucions, by no maner of terme ne termes, the whiche that sholde chaunge the sentence, et the entente axked by the speker mouthe, or the peticions biforesaid yeven up yn writyng by the manere forsaid, withoute assent of the forsaid commune. Consideringe oure soverain lord,

---

[34] Elton, *"The Body of the Whole Realm,"* 37, notes that "through all the long years of Henry VI's minority . . . the regency government was frequently in trouble with its own members but never subjected to the sort of attack from the Commons which had troubled Henry IV in 1404, 1406, and 1411."

[35] The 1407 parliament roll records twenty-eight, thirty-three in 1411, twenty-four in 1413.

[36] *RP* 3.587. See Biggs, 'The Politics of Health." One provision of 1406 called for the king to set aside two days a week (Wednesdays and Fridays) for hearing petitions.

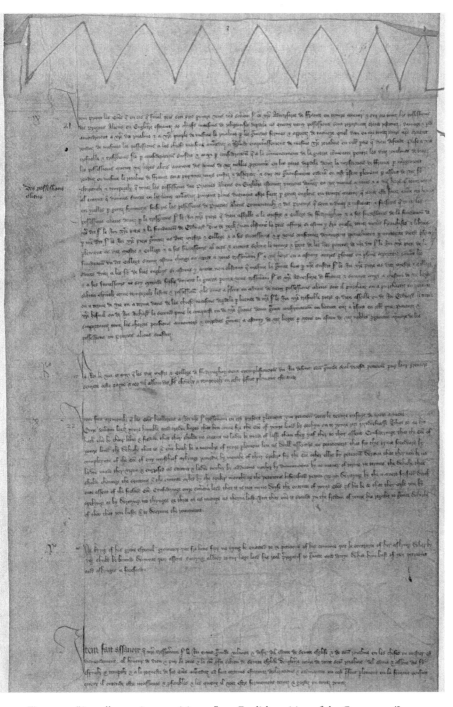

Figure 7. "As well assentirs as peticioners": an English petition of the Commons (Item x.22) from April 1414 parliament at Leicester. National Archives C 65/74/3 (reduced). © 2006 The National Archives

that it is not in no wyse the entente of youre communes, ȝif hit be so that they axke you by spekyng, or by writyng, too thynges or three, or as manye as theym lust: but that evere it stande in the fredom of your hie regalie, to graunte whiche of thoo that you luste, et to werune the remanent.[37]

In terms of its historical significance, this bill is no longer considered the constitutional landmark it was once thought to be. It was probably motivated by Henry's actions following the previous parliament, when he unilaterally amended six out of ten petitions that had been enacted.[38] Nonetheless it is a remarkable statement, all the more notable for its unassuming qualities. It is recorded in the official parliament roll unobtrusively, and it employs the traditional terms of "humble lieges" coming forward to the king's court of justice. The petition's blasé assertions – that the Commons had been always been present in parliament, that they had always "ben as well assentirs as peticioners," and that their assent had ever been necessary for the creation of law – are simply false, historically speaking. There is in fact a neatly circular irony to it (perhaps visible to its drafters) insofar as the text itself is a petition, asserting the "assenting" and not merely "petitioning" power of the Commons, by *petitioning* the king and his "riȝt riȝtwesnesse" to acknowledge it.[39] The real point of the exercise is not to assert constitutional principles or to re-configure the basic relations between Crown and parliament. Rather it is to secure, in an institutional and documentary way (that is, in the practice of the assembly and the "engrossing" of the record), a licit and recognized control of the *voice* of the Commons: control over the additions, diminutions, terms, petitioning, engrossing, and "sentence" that might effect what is recorded as "axked by the speker mouthe" or by "the peticions biforesaid yeven up yn writyng." This is an attempt by parliament to protect its own expressive capacities in the free control of its speech and writing. The petition clarifies (in its last sentence) that all statutes are still also controlled by the *hie Regalie* of the king's assent. But in this scheme neither can anything be asserted as law *without* the Commons' assent. Thus the petition envisions a fundamental check on the *representation* of what is, or is not, the public voice, by means

---

[37] *RP* 4.22; text with corrections taken from *PROME* Henry V 1414 April, x.22.

[38] See especially Chrimes, *English Constitutional Ideas*, 159–64, who refutes Stubbs' broad interpretation of the petition; Butt, 487–9. As Butt notes, it was "more than stretching the truth" to assert the Commons had always been assenters to statutes (488). See also Brown, "Parliament, c. 1377–1422," who notes that while the claim was untrue, "it is the making of the claim that is significant, and the wording of statutes shows that the commons' claim was not utterly wild" (128).

[39] Henry V's recorded response is similarly circumspect, conceding "fro hens forth no thyng be enacted to the peticions of his comune, that be contrarie of hir askyng, wharby they shuld be bounde withoute their assent," but "savyng alwey to our liege lord his real prerogatif, to graunte and denye what him lust of their peticions and askynges a foresaide" (*RP* 4.22).

of the subtle reconfiguration of how the public can have a legitimating voice through the recognized and recorded assent of the Commons.

The petition is also obviously unique because out of the numerous enroll-ments and acts for this parliament, it is the only one in English. It is the first common petition put forward in English and an "Englishing" of procedure, asserted at a time when Lollards and others were similarly pressuring the ecclesial establishment. But as an internal institutional gesture, its justifi-cation is unclear. Like the several English documents enrolled during the 1397 and 1399 parliaments, this small petition may have warranted English so as to be accessible to a wider audience. But in this case – even more so than during the revolution – it is not at all clear who that audience might have been.[40] There is no surviving record of the petition having been published or circulated beyond the roll of the parliamentary record, and the text itself gives little sense of who would have been reading it beyond parliamentarians, clerks, or other professional personnel.

Notwithstanding the possible functionality of its English, we can rather think of it as an exercise in textual self-imagining. Particularly at a time when the vernacular was increasingly put forward as a medium for national expres-sion in literature, devotion, and politics, this petition does indeed stand forth as a small landmark. Where a common petition recorded in Anglo-French or Latin would have been both unremarkable and in a way more sensible, the English of this bill signals the intersection of still-developing vernacular expression with the desire to speak in a warranted and unified voice, one with its "entente" intact and granted a level of independently protected status. This we might consider to be its subtextual but strong motivation. It is an exercise in both linguistic and representational boot-strapping, a small attempt to speak about the issue of speaking – the ability to petition and assent – in a language that can address its own environ-ment. The petition signals, in short, a desire to speak that is simultaneously in a necessary relationship with, but independent of, the sovereign royal structure of power that warrants it. It stands both within, and outside, the documentary form of official record that is also its subject. In a way its "audience," then, in addition to the men who wrote and read it, is the very roll itself, the context ("engrosed as statut et lawe") it directly addresses and that records it. It is speaking *in* a common voice *about* speaking with a common voice, for the first time, in the documentary record *of* parliament's common voice.

---

[40] On the use of English in parliamentary records, especially following the 1362 Statute of Pleading, see Ormrod, "The Use of English: Language, Law, and Political Culture in Fourteenth-Century England," 781–7; for the English documents of 1397 and 1399 see Giancarlo, "Murder, Lies, and Storytelling."

I will return to this inside-outside relationship a bit later in considering what is, I think, the same institutional dynamic evident in the contemporary poetry of *Mum and the Sothsegger*. The second petition I want to consider is also addressed in English, but from a different standpoint and towards a different end. The records for the second parliament of 1414, held in November, include a bill and lengthy *schedula* from one Thomas Paunfield, a resident of the vill and manor of Chesterton in Cambridgeshire, a small farming community. A small Anglo-French petition addressed to parliament, in which Paunfield calls himself *un des frankes tenauntz nostre tres redoute Seigneur le Roy*, is accompanied by a much longer version written in English.[41] Where the French petition succinctly summarizes Paunfield's complaint in standard form, language, and length, the accompanying English document is massive, extending over two large folios and eight columns in the printed *Rotuli Parliamentorum* edition.[42] It expands the petition into a fully-fledged and detailed narrative.

As we have seen in previous documents, English petitions from suitors to the courts were not unheard of in the fourteenth century, and probably many more were written than survived. All the same, the Paunfield petition is simply unprecedented in its size and scope (Figure 8). There is nothing quite like it elsewhere in the extant medieval English parliamentary records.

The English petition begins by describing to the Lords and Commons how Paunfield has been kept from submitting his bill because of an unjust judgment of outlawry:

To the Worshipeful and Wyse Syres, and Wyse Communes, that to this present Parlement ben assembled; Besecheth mekely ȝoure pore Bedeman Thomas Paunfeld, oon of the fre tenantz of oure liege Lord the Kyng, of his Maner and Tounshipe of Chestreton, in the Shyre of Cambrigg, that ȝe wole considere how that I persuede diverse billes byfore oure liege Lord Kyng Henry the Fourthe, fader to oure liege Lord the Kyng that now is, and hise worchepful Lordes and Communes, in his Parlement holden at Westminster, the x day of Fevrier, the xiiii ȝer of his Regne [i.e. the assembly of 10 February 1413].

To the whiche billes myne adversaries repleiden by mouthe, and enformeden the Kyng and the worchepeful Lordes Spirituelx and Temperelx in that Parlement, how that I was outlawed by heye record of trespace, wherthurgh that I ne oughte not to ben herd nor answered of no maner compleynt in my billes writen, but ȝif it se were that I hadde brought my Chartre in myn hond, whereby that I myghte have answered in lawe to all maner of persones, that ony Replicacions wolden have maked aȝeyns ony Article of my billes.

[41] *RP* 4.56; National Archives SC 8/23/1141, 1143a–b.
[42] *RP* 4.57–61. The English version is not included in the recent *PROME* edition. See "Henry V, November 1414, Appendix," item 6, for summary My overall analysis here of Paunfield's petition has greatly benefited from the forthcoming work of Gwilym Dodd, "Thomas Paunfield, the 'heye Court of rightwisnesse,' and the Language of Petitioning in the Fifteenth Century."

Figure 8. The Paunfield Petition in English, folio 1 of 2. National Archives SC 8/23/1143a
(reduced and excerpted, approx. 16.5 × 32 inches). © 2006 The National Archives

And worchepeful and discrete Sires, that myghte I not done that tyme, for I wiste not how I was endited and outelawed of what maner trespace . . .[43]

The initial complaint is about Paunfield's complaint and the restrictions he has met in trying to get his case heard. As a result of his outlawry and the harrassment by his opponents, "I myghte not have been remedied, ne myne neyghebores nother, so sone at that tyme lyk as we oughten to have ben of right, and as me thoughte we shulde ben here, and that was for cause of meyntenance that was aȝeyns us, and ȝit is."[44] Having acquired a stay in the king's court against the outlawry and with the purpose "for to declaren the entente of my billes for the kynges avantage," Paunfield has submitted his petition to parliament, "in this heye Court of rightwisnesse, where as most truste and hope to have rightwisnesse and lawe, rather than I schulde in ony other Court," to make his plea for royal judgment.[45]

As becomes clear after the long account of his procedural wranglings, the case involves both Paunfield personally and the entire community of Chesterton. Paunfield, submitting this bill on behalf of Chesterton (as he apparently has done throughout the course of the affair), maintains the town's status as an independent royal desmesne, "the whiche [is] holden of the tenure of anxien demeyn."[46] This is against the prior and canons of Barnwell abbey in Cambridgeshire, who claim Chesterton as the abbey's freehold with customary duties due to the abbey; they assert the tenants of Chesterton "as for her [their] bonde bore men and her [their] bonde lond holderes."[47] Simply put – and this is what makes the whole bill so compelling – Paunfield's petition asserts that he and the residents of Chesterton are not the serfs and slaves of the abbey of Barnwell; they are freeholders of the king. Paunfield is petitioning in parliament for his freedom and for the freedom of his home town. They have resisted the abbey's attempts to force them "into thraldom and into bondage" by pursuing their rights in the king's courts.[48] The abbot and canons have prosecuted him in particular (Paunfield asserts) with repeated extortions, assaults, and even unlawful imprisonment for up to seven years; the petition itself indicates that he was still imprisoned at the time it was submitted to parliament on his behalf in 1414.[49] His appeal to the Crown and the Crown's documentation

---

[43] *RP* 4.57. Text is taken from the *RP*, compared to National Archives SC 8/23/1143a–b.
[44] *RP* 4.57.   [45] *RP* 4.57.   [46] *RP* 4.57.   [47] *RP* 4.58.   [48] *RP* 4.59.
[49] As the petition outlines, the prior and canons pursued a commission of *oyer et terminer* against Chesterton "after [i.e., based on] the fourme of a Statut mad upon bonde bore men and bonde landholderes"; but this statutory restriction, which was made "the ferste ȝer of Kyng Richard the Seconde, in his tendre age," should not apply to the free tenants of the Crown, which Paunfield asserts they are: "and that we wele preve, and declare by oure evydence, wreten in the Kynges Eschekker at

is explicitly made through the intercessory authority of the Commons in parliament:

> Wherfore, we beseche ȝow mekely, discrete and wyse Communes of this present Parlement, that ȝe preye for us to oure liege Lord the Kyng, and to hise worchepeful Lordes of this present Parlement, in savynge of the right of the Coroune of Yngelond, and of the fredam, and the fraunchise that was endowed therto, in the tyme our worthy Kynges progenitour Seint Edward, that he wole have compassion and pite of these grete mischiefs and falsetes, so done to hise fre tenantz of his Coroune byforeseyd; and to ordeyne, at ȝoure preyere, resonable and intierie remedie in this partie, for Goddes love, and for Seynt Charite, after the fourme that sueth, if it be lykyng to ȝow.[50]

The case is summarized appealingly at this point in the text, but this semi-conclusion comes only half-way through. The bill continues for another folio and hundreds of words more, like a speech by an orator determined to get his point across. In fact this was probably the intent: the French cover bill contains a request *qe lez articles en une Rolle ent fait comprises puissent estre lisez en plein Parlement*, which probably refers to the attached English schedule. It may have been read out loud in an effort to have the petition avowed and endorsed by the Commons on behalf of Paunfield, as the case summarized formally and abstractly in the Anglo-French plea comes out in verbose, emotional, and plaintive terms in English. As a result the bill is baggy and disorganized, but it contains the same formal elements that would be found in any bill in Latin or French: an appeal of wrong, a gesture towards the protection of the Crown's putative interests (repeated several times in the long complaint), entreaties to compassion and pity and to "Goddes love" for a just and reasonable judgment on behalf of the plaintiff. Parliament is the "high court of righteousness" in which the free tenants of Chesterton will finally have their day of royal justice, with the

---

Westminster" (*RP* 4.58). In the petition he asks for the king's grace "to walken at large to pursue these materes that ben folwynge in my bille" because his opponents "hav persued me nowe, and holden me in prison, sithen Seynt Katerynes day twelve Monthes last passed into this tyme," notwithstanding a "graunt and ordinaundce" of liberty already issued by the king (*RP* 4.57). The "Statut" of Richard II in question may conflate two distinct pieces of legislation, the ordinance of servants and laborers (*RP* 3.45, 2 Ric. 2 Stat 1, c. 8), and the restrictions on seeking exemplifications from Domesday in order to assert privileges of "ancient desmesne," instituted in Richard's second year (*RP* 3.21–2). The witholding or contesting of customary services had previously been motivated by disputed appeals to Domesday: see Faith, "The 'Great Rumour' of 1377 and Peasant Ideology." Paunfield's reference to the Exchequer records may refer to the Exchequer copy of Domesday or to some other enrollment concerning the status of Chesterton. Regarding the appeal of ancient desmesne against villeinage, the Paunfield case is very similar to the case of Richard and William Spink, brought against Thomas Lisle, the bishop of Ely, in 1346–8 and later: see Musson and Ormrod, *Evolution of English Justice*, 132–3.

[50] *RP* 4.58.

Commons as their mediator. The appeal stresses the proper performance of the documentary process (the submission of bills, recognizance of charters, performance of enrollments) in order to secure the right to sue in the king's courts without hinderance, so it also reveals a mature understanding of the documentary requirements of the petitionary procedure.

For modern readers it is easy to be attracted to Paunfield's petition as a statement of ideals that it does not contain. Nowhere is "thraldom" or "bondage" condemned, only the attempt to make "bonde cherles" out of *them*. Serfdom itself is not questioned. Nor would the residents of Chesterton be exempted from all dues and services as "fre tenantz annexed to his [the king's] worthy Coroune"; rather those dues (which, the petition notes, would be more than those paid by the priory) would be payable to the king.[51] Freedom and franchise are here, as ever in medieval England, discrete and frankly saleable commodities. The strongest appeal is to the king's unilateral rights as the property-holder, franchise-granter, and profit-taker of the town. As such, the case again exhibits parliament's centrality to legal issues of property and the "savynge of the Kynges ryght."[52] At the same time, the bill overtly tries to hold the king to a prior commitment: it pointedly requests that Henry honor a grant of petitionary liberty (the right to sue in parliament) putatively made to Paunfield on Good Friday at Langley, shortly after his accession.[53] The language and the form of the petition, and its sheer size and forcefulness, make it a unique witness to the appeal of parliamentary petitioning in the Lancastrian years. Indeed a bill like this under Richard hardly seems possible; and as Paunfield names himself several times as the "suytor of this Bille," it is clearly a personal statement from a man who suffered repeated frustrations in the legal system.

Without too much interpretive violence we can also note the English bill's creative gestures in its light employment of legal metonymy and allegory. Like the dream vision of Thomas Hoo but in a very different form too, this story sounds almost Langlandian, as if Paunfield were an imaginative figure of Simple-Justice-Denied. At the same time he speaks repeatedly *on behalf of* Chesterton as the community's representative, although he never uses this phrase or anything like it. His personal appeal – which never stops being personal – melds into a communal petition, as frequently his "I" slips into

---

[51] *RP* 4.59.   [52] *RP* 4.60.

[53] *RP* 4.56: the French bill specifically requests the freedom to petition in parliament "en mesme le manere come notre dit Sr. le Roy luy graunta de sa grace especial le bon Vendredy a Langeley, l'an de son graciouse regne primer," that is, the previous year, shortly after the 1413 assembly which gathered on 3 February but was apparently unable to conduct much business before Henry IV's death on 20 March. Henry V acceded to the throne on 21 March 1413.

"we" and back again. At one point Paunfield urges that all the free tenants of the Chesterton township – or twenty-four of them, a traditional jury quorum – be granted a writ to come to parliament and bear witness to his assertions and to the falseness of the obligations imposed by Barnwell. What the villagers would be supporting is not just the legal appeal, but specifically Paunfield's own probity as a representative speaker, "that my wordes ben trewe."[54] He opposes the priory's "sumptuouse wordes of pride" and the "presumptuouse wordes" of their claim to his own words, which stand, as he does, both metaphorically and metonymically for the community as a whole.[55] The lengthy petition is thus rhetorically comparable to other such legal and petitionary declarations in parliament, particularly at its end, where it presents the legal fiction of an assault *per vi et armis* and the humorous, quasi-allegorical naming of one priest – "Sire Johan Outlaw, Prest and Chanon, sometyme Priour of Bernewell" – as Paunfield's supposed assailant.[56] Our copy of the text concludes with an appeal to the assent of the "discrete and wyse Communes that to this present Parlement ben assembled," along with the king and Lords, for amends to the damages suffered by Paunfield personally. To the end, the man and his community are essentially coterminous.[57]

As different as they are, these two bills share not just the English language, although that is certainly important. Paunfield's bill, like the Commons' English bill in the previous parliament, exhibits both a stirring aggressiveness in its aims and a palpable anxiety about the position from which it can petition to the judgment of parliament. Coming forward and showing in the vernacular, Paunfield's voice also stands both within and outside the assembly it addresses. The fundamental question is whether he (and Chesterton) can even *presume* to appeal to this court, or whether (as asserted by the priory) they have no standing before it at all. In a vernacular that was still a documentary anomaly, both petitions stress the importance of showing complaint and of making visible the mechanisms by which their voices could be heard. This need to show – that is, this necessity of making the criticisms and demands *visible*, even if only to the critics and

<hr/>

[54] *RP* 4.59.
[55] *RP* 4.59–60: "Nevertheles, the forseide Priour and Chanons, and her servantz, hav not governed hem aȝeyn us, lyk as we have done to hem, but heyly hav offenden aȝeyns us, & aȝeyns her bonde, and namely, aȝeyns me Thomas Paunfeld." The specific assertion is that the priory did not observe a Chancery recognizance stipulating that the parties are supposed to keep the peace with one another.
[56] *RP* 4.60.
[57] *RP* 4.61. The smaller French petition is endorsed with the standard instructions for the plaintiff to pursue the case at the King's Bench and according to the common law. The English text is illegible at the end of the damaged parchment.

demanders themselves – motivates the documents as they both manipulate and go beyond (in Paunfield's case, way beyond) the basic criteria of public parliamentary petition. And in both cases, a plain vernacular appeal is made to the "righteousness" of the assembly that would ratify, and be empowered by, their anxious appeals to the king's sovereign power.

3 *THE CROWNED KING* AND *RICHARD THE REDELESS*: CRITIQUES OF PARLIAMENTARY SHOWING

In the context of developments leading up to 1414, Paunfield's and the Commons' bills stand out as examples of what has been called, in the wake of the revolution, the Lancastrian practice of "writing visible," of strategic "framing and analyzing . . . largely through the adoption of textual models and rhetorical tactics drawn from the bureaucratic and legal culture."[58] They are immediately accessible examples of bills and petitions that themselves thematize the need for a visible public voice. Of course these *are* legal and bureaucratic documents, so we would hardly expect them to take any other forms; but the language of their expression places a new emphasis on the public accessibility of what is being said and claimed. That is, following the trauma of Richard's reign and the Lancastrian usurpation, a new emphasis on the simple ability to speak at all, in a public forum, was a large part of the anxiety evident in both the assembly record and the poetry. In this regard, the petitions stand in the same milieu as the poems being composed at the time.

Moving from these petitions, we can approach the major alliterative works of the Piers Plowman tradition with a better understanding of the parliamentary context that informs them and from which they draw much of their immediacy. In the shortest poem of the group, *The Crowned King*, the opening scenario of the narrator's valley-vision overtly takes its cue from the Visio of *Piers Plowman*.[59] It implicitly assumes a parliamentary framework of taxation for war subsidy and the opportunities for showing complaints that such demands entailed. As the dreamer–narrator stands "high on an hill," he looks in a dale to see the gathered community:

> Ther y sawe in my sight a selcouthe peple –
> The multitude was so moche it myght not be noumbred.
> Me thought y herd a crowned kyng of his comunes axe

---

[58] Grady, "The Generation of 1399," 204.
[59] All textual citations of *The Crowned King, Richard the Redeless*, and *Mum and the Soothsegger* are from *The Piers Plowman Tradition*, ed. Barr.

A soleyn subsidie to susteyne his werres,
To be rered in the reaume, as reson requyred,
Of suche as were seemly to suffre the charge;
That they rekened were riche by reson and skyle
Shuld pay a parcell for here poure neighbowres;
This ordenaunce he made in ease of his peple.

(33–41)

Obviously this opening scenario is not intended to reflect a formal parliament or setting at Westminster, and neither does the "soleyn subsidie"
reflect any particular event or grant. Nonetheless, the vision of the realm
as "comunes" in a "dale" embodies the quasi-idealized and bureacratized
version of a common assembly called to grant taxes. A speaker of sorts, the
"clerk," kneels to respond to the king. The style of his response is important.
First the clerk requests permission "to shewe you my sentence in singuler
noumbre" (46) – that is, point by point – for which the king grants him
leave. The clerk then launches into a lengthy but polite harangue about
the performance of good rule. Among the various standard advices offered
for virtuous governance, the clerk emphasizes that the king's education
should cultivate his ability to "show" himself properly in parliamentary
deliberation:

Lere lettrewre in thy youthe, as a lord befalleth,
Whan thou to parlement shall passe there lordes shull pere;
For to her of thy wysdom they woll awayte after;
And though her speche be but small, the more be here thoughtes;
For yif thou have no science to shewe of thy-self,
But as a brogour to go borowe pore mennes wittes,
That were most myscheef that myght a lord befalle,
Ther as wyse men haue wrapped her wittes togidre.

(113–20)

The point of *lettrewre*, "literature," is not simply the moral improvement
of the king but the improvement of his ability to "show" himself in public
discussion. Here in *The Crowned King* an updated version of the clerical
(and rather more radical) "lene lunatik" of Langland's Visio is recognizably
aligned with an identifiable speaking position from which the Commons
could make a response to the king's demands. These kinds of moral exhortations became common stuff in the *Fürstenspiegel* genre in the fifteenth
century. But again, the salient point is not just that this reveals an early
practice of articulate citizenship or of king-counselling in state formation.
Rather, from beginning to end – from the "crowned kyng" assembled with
the "comunes" in the dale, the advice on justice, the meeting with "thi

peres," the quietly critical assembly awaiting to hear the king's "wysdom" –
the poem emphasizes the publicly deliberative demands of good rule. The
clerk's showing of his exhortation is an exhortation to better showing, at all
levels: in pleas in the law courts, among the nobility and peers, and even,
as it turns out, for the king himself in parliamentary assembly, where he
too must show his wisdom. At the poem's end the king is exhorted to take
his example from Christ, in the same terms:

> The condicion of a kyng shuld comfort his peple. . . .
> *And taketh a siker ensample that Crist hym-self sheweth,*
> Of alle the seyntes in heven that for hym deth suffred . . .
> . . . for love of that Lord aloft now they dwelle
> With that crowned kyng that on cros dyed;
> Ther Crist in his kyngdom comfort vs euere,
> And of his high grace graunte vnto vs alle
> Prosperite and pees, pursue we thereafter.
>
> (133, 137–44, my emphasis)

The "comfort" of the king should imitate the final comfort of Christ, who
"sheweth" an example in the same way the king himself should show forth
to his subjects. By this point the meaning of the term has become decisively
spiritual, even though the ending prayer for "prosperite and pees" expresses
an earthly desire. The showing of the poem's beginning in the clerk's appeal
to the king has thus led, subtly but fluidly, to the spiritual showing of its end,
as the form of the Clerk's public petition develops into courtly exhortation
and finally into religious petition ("graunte vnto vs . . ."). From a thematic
point of view, nothing could be more natural than these combinations of
hortatory forms. But they require a framework in which regal publicity can
be conjoined with both spiritual and communal well-being, and with the
voice of a speaker that is institutionally and poetically hortatory.

The Crowned King thus speaks from a perspective that is simultaneously
in and out of the formal governmental structures sanctioning its criticism.
Critical speaking and public petition of the right kind, poetical and political, is what the community needs. The miserable failure of precisely this
mechanism is a topic of *Richard the Redeless*, which has the most caustic
contemporary portrait of parliamentary behavior out of all these works.
Textually, *Richard the Redeless* takes its cues from three coordinate forms:
historical chronicle, legal bill of complaint, and Langlandian allegory. Probably written shortly after 1399, the four passūs of the incomplete poem give
a nearly full accounting of the various accusations against Richard's rule.
The vigorous but uneven verse is permeated with allusions to contem-

porary events surrounding the deposition.[60] More than voicing a formal
record or propagandistic restatement of the accusations against the king, the
narrative voice of *Richard* seems almost personally offended by the king's
ignorant mismanagement. The poet is both well-informed and angered,
and his litany of complaints almost directly glosses the *gravamina* of his
deposition.[61] Richard surrounded himself with flatterers and exploiters who
abused both the royal power and the community, which left the people no
one to show their complaints: "For non of youre peple durste pleyne of her
wrongis, / For drede of youre dukys and of here double harmes" (1.139–44).
It is, repeatedly, the inability to lodge formal complaints that motivates
much of the energy behind the verse: "for wo, they ne wuste to whom
for to pleyene" (1.151). Richard is faulted for not trusting "the comoune"
and for having advisors who were "all to yonge of yeris" (1.165, 176). His
retainers are figured as harts running wild throughout the kingdom (2.1–
27), abusing everyone and particularly abusing the king's authority and
voice:

> For they acombrede the contre and many curse seruid,
> And carped to the comounes with the kyngys mouthe,
> Or with the lordis ther they belefte were,
> That no renke shulde rise reson to schewe.
> They plucked the plomayle from the pore skynnes,
> And schewed her signes for men shulde drede
> To axe ony mendis for her mys-dedis.
>
> (2.28–34)

Here, in an example of the lexical punning extensively analyzed by Barr,
the poet combines senses of *schewe* for ironic effect. By means of the display and abuse of Richard's livery, people were prevented from showing
their complaints as "Reason" – right legal procedure – would require.[62]
Richard's justification for distributing his livery was false, and the allegorical symbolism of the practice leads to a harsh critique of the king's
blameworthy officers, Bushy, Scrope, and Green (2.135–67). At this point

[60] See, most fully, the apparatus provided by Barr's edition and the notes in Day and Steele, who edited
the poem as part of *Mum and the Sothsegger*.
[61] Noted by Barr in the notes to her edition of the poem, and by Scattergood, "Remembering Richard
II," 211–17.
[62] And later in the passus, Reason itself reiterates this point, stating the necessity of "showing" for the
sovereign's well-being in uncorrupted judiciary processes: "But yif God haue grauntyd the grace for
to knowe / Ony manere mysscheff that myghtte be amendyd, / Schewe that to thi souereyne to
schelde him from harmes . . ." (2.72–4). "Reason" here, as Barr notes, is the proper operation of the
law that makes equitable judgment "whane the pore pleyned that put wer to wrongis" (2.87): *Signes
and Sothe*, 137–8, 143.

the rather awkward and headlong combination of symbolic elements –
deer, bushes, "schroup," "grene," Henry arriving as "the fawcon" among
lower birds (2.152–4, 160) – leads to an abbreviated bird assembly judging
the captured "bagge," or Henry Bagot,

> This lorell that ladde this loby awey
> Ouere frithe and forde for his fals dedis,
> Lyghte on the lordschepe that to the brid longid,
> And was felliche ylaughte and luggid full ylle,
> And broughte to the brydd and his blames rehersid
> Preuyly at the parlement amonge all the peple.
>
> (2.170–5)

The reference is almost certainly to the 1399 deposition parliament and
the later proceedings against Richard's supporters. This chronicler's style of
writing momentarily forces the poet to drop out of the allegory and into
catachresis, referring to "the peple" instead of birds. In the background
may be the model of Chaucer's parliament of birds, but it is not developed. Rather the emphasis is on the justice wrought by "this egle" (2.176,
190), Henry Bolingbroke, who not only brings the lesser birds to account
but also "kenned clerliche as his kynde axith" (2.191). Passūs One and
Two accordingly form a cohesive unit in which a chronicle-like account
of Richard's offenses and downfall are compacted into a summary of complaint as well as an historical summary, loaded with heraldic and onomastic
allegory.

This amalgam of motifs carries the complaints into Passus Three. In a
way, the poet seems simply unable to let them go. The narrator begins
by declaring "I wolle schewe as I sawe till I se better" (3.5), and not see-
ing anything better, continues to describe the same abuses in even greater
detail. This longest and most opaque section of the poem continues the
beast allegory, which then turns into an account of high politics and the
mistreatment suffered by specific lords, criticisms of taxation, and a complaint about sumptuary abuses (3.11–181). Both the stereotyped complaints
and the particular exhortations for reform (for example, that young and
inexperienced councillors should be removed from the court [3.190–206])
continue the accusations of almost complete malfeasance, as does the brief
allegory of "Witt" and "Wisdom" wandering the kingdom, beleaguered
and excluded from the court (3.211–46). Once again, it is not just complaints, but the abuse of the *procedures* of complaint, that provokes the
poet's greatest anger and most creative versifying. The procedures of the
itinerant royal justice courts are mocked, and Richard's infamous company

of Cheshire archers – the "chyders of Chester" who terrorized the king's opponents in the later 1390s – exemplifies the abuse of maintenance in a parody of court procedures:

> They prien affter presentis or pleyntis ben yclepid,
> And abateth all the billis of tho that noughth bringith . . .
> For chyders of Chester where chose many daies
> To ben of conceill for causis that in the court hangid,
> And pledid pipoudris all manere pleyntis . . .
> Thei had non other signe to schewe the lawe
> But a preuy pallette her pannes to kepe,
> To hille here lewde heed in stede of an houe.
> They constrewed quarellis to quenche the peple,
> And pletid with pollaxis and poyntis of swerdis,
> And at the dome-yeuynge drowe out the bladis,
> And lente men leuere of here longe battis.

(3.306–7, 317–19, 324–30)

The joke here (dense as it is) lies in the lexicon of the law applied to the lawlessness of Richard's thugs. To "plead piepowders in all manner of plaints" – that is, to appeal to the procedures of ad-hoc "piepowder courts" of fairs and markets – was tantamount to simply ignoring proper legal procedure altogether.[63] The king's guards substituted pole-axes and sword points for pleas and plaints, and their visible insignia "to schewe the lawe" were not justice's coifs ("an houe") but military garb. At the same time, the abuse is aligned with the itinerant royal courts that wrongly "abate the bills" of plaintiffs. Force and legal corruption are co-implicated. The utter lack of any licit authority willing to hear men's plaints is made worse by the fact that true men of the law – including perhaps the poet himself – were effectively cut out of the legal procedure of pleading: "for selde were the sergiauntis soughte for to plete, / Or ony prentise of courte preied of his wittis, / The while the degonys domes weren so endauntid" (3.348–50). This abasement of legal showing ends only with the advent of "the sonne that so brighte schewed" (3.367), another reference to Henry IV's usurpation.[64] The "better show" sought at the beginning of the passus thus comes to fruition in the felicitous symbolism of yet another of Bolingbroke's heraldric emblems, the sun, which represents (ironically enough) the return of proper legality and the demise of Richard's "felouns" and "devourours

[63] Explained by Barr, *Piers Plowman Tradition*, 285 n. 319; see also Day and Steele, *Mum and the Sothsegger*, 103 n. 319. As Barr notes elsewhere (*Socioliterary Practice*, 69), through these polysemic juxtapositions "the poet of *Richard the Redeless* demystifies the political artifice in order to foreground the lawless brutality of Richard's policies."
[64] Barr, "Richard the Redeless," *Piers Plowman Tradition*, 286 n. 365–8.

of vetaile" (3.369–70). The way the poet presents it, the storm has cleared
with Henry's ascent. This new sun of Lancaster offers the kind of public
visibility and clear-sightedness that would allow right reason to take its
proper place in the kingdom.

Notwithstanding its obvious Lancastrian bias, we can see that the poem's
consistent concern with proper pleading and showing – and with the legal
procedures of right representation – motivates the otherwise incongruent
shift from king to parliament in the last extant passus. Moving from complaints about Richard's abuses and sheer stupidity, Passus Four critiques
parliament for practicing a related but different kind of abuse. As with the
courts and the royal retinue, parliament is distorted by the king's actions;
the scene is generally held to be a thinly veiled portrait of the Shrewsbury parliament of 1398.[65] In the scant ninety-odd lines of the incomplete
passus, not only does the *Richard*–poet include a remarkable amount of
institutional and satirical detail, he manages as well to raise the fundamental question of just what, and how, parliamentary representation was
meant to show for the nation. The writs for calling the election of the
shire knights, "to schewe for the schire in company with the grete" (4.30),
are rigged. After the opening of the parliament and the declaration of the
summons, the parliamentarians respond to the king's demands with an
evasion:

> But yit for the manere to make men blynde,
> Some argued ayein rith then a good while,
> And said, "We beth seruantis and sallere fongen,
> And ysent fro the shiris to shewe what hem greueth,
> And to parle for her prophete and passe no ferthere,
> And to graunte of her gold to the grett wattis
> By no manere wronge way but if werre were;
> And if we ben fals to tho us here fyndyth,
> Euyll be we worthy to welden oure hire."
>
> (4.44–52)

This passage is noteworthy as the first quotative and non-allegorical discussion, not just of parliament, but of the representational principles central
to its deliberative identity. Although the poet apparently feels that the MPs
are arguing wrongly ("ayein rith" or "against right"), there is in fact nothing

[65] See Barr, *The Piers Plowman Tradition*, 287–91; Day and Steele, *Mum and the Sothsegger*, 104–6.
On the 1398 parliament at Shrewsbury, which lasted just four days starting 28 January, see Butt,
435–9; Saul, *Richard II*, 380–1. It is indexed as part II of the September 1397 parliament in *PROME*.
As Butt notes, Shrewsbury was the assembly in which the Bolingbroke–Hereford dispute was first
made public, presaging the eventual Lancastrian rise to power.

absurd or irresponsible in their objection. Strictly speaking, the argument is correct: the primary job of parliamentarians (at least from a subordinate perspective) was to put forward the concerns of the localities and to show complaints; grants of taxation were traditionally in response to exigencies of war or extraordinary emergency.[66] The broader question is also an important one: how far are representatives allowed to go in showing for their constituents? What is their speaking power and authority? Rather than being an otiose issue, if it accurately represents the kind of deliberation that actually took place in 1398, this response may reflect the savvy tactics employed by the MPs when they were faced with Richard's forceful extractions. Instead of outright refusal, they plead incompetence, in the sense that the representatives are simply not *authorized* to speak beyond certain bounds.[67] This was in fact a common enough assertion, both by the men who went to parliaments in the later fourteenth century and, in the shire courts, by the constituents who elected them and often tried to limit their tax-granting freedom.

However, even if read so generously, this parrying maneuver only heralds the loss of show as well as the individual malfeasance of the parliamentarians themselves. They become allegories of emptiness and ill effect:

> Than satte summe as a siphre doth in awgrym,
> That noteth a place and no thing availith;
> And some had ysoupid with Symond ouere euen,
> And schewed for the shire and here schew lost;
> And somme were tituleris and to the kyng wente,
> And formed him of foos that good frendis weren . . .
> And somme slombrid and slepte and said but a lite;
> And somme mafflid with the mouth and nyst what they ment;
> And somme had hire and helde ther-with euere . . .
>
> (4.53–8, 62–4)

This portrait of the MPs is pointed and satirical, but also varied and humorous. They mumble and sleep, scheme and backbite. Some are so "soleyne and sad" (4.66) that they make no sense of their own conclusions. Some start fierce but go awry, others do nothing. Some go only with the crowd, others refuse to go anywhere. Artistically, the parliament becomes an assembly very much like Gower's parliament of vices and demons in the *Mirour*

---

[66] Noted by Cam, "The Relation of English Members of Parliament to their Constituencies," who calls the parliamentarians' response in *Richard the Redeless* an "orthodox and respectable line to take" (232).

[67] Even if it was the case, eventually the parliament of 1398 was pliant in meeting Richard's demands, granting him the wool and skins custom for life (with the stipulation that it was not a precedent for later kings). See Butt, 437.

de l'Omme, or more closely, like the allegorical figures of Langland's assemblies. But the capacity or direction of the representation is reversed. Where before the allegory was implicitly applied to real-world figures within a larger scheme of narrative, here the actual historical (and chronicle) allusions of the poem provide the explicit textual foreground out of which the allegory develops. That is, instead of presenting symbolic figures that are meant to be read back into the world, *Richard* portrays men, with all their failures, who are then made into symbolic parodies of themselves.

As Grady has remarked, the representation of the parliament in *Richard* is thus "equidistant from literary parliaments on the one hand and real parliament rolls and chronicle accounts on the other," but with this important difference from its predecessors.[68] The rather cryptic observation that the parliamentarians "schewed for the shire and here schew lost" (4.56) indicates that the assembly's debased showing, the loss of true representation and voice, is still the poet's main regret. In showing themselves thus for their localities, "they" – ambiguously either the MPs or their constituencies – lost the very thing they were assembled to achieve. At the abortive end of the passus, singular profit, bribery, and fear bring silence to both the parliament and the poem:

> Some parled as perte as prouyd well after,
> And clappid more for the coyne that the kyng owed hem
> Thanne for comfforte of the comyne that her cost paied,
> And were be-hote hansell if they helpe wolde
> To be seruyd sekirly of the same siluere.
> And some dradde dukis and Do-well for-soke . . .
>
> (4.88–93)

With that, the verse itself is forsaken, uncompleted. Like many parts of *Richard*, this concluding criticism is opaque but decipherable. Some representatives made more effort and noise ("clappid") for the money the king owed them individually than they did for the good of the communities that sent them and paid their wages.[69] They were promised gifts and sureties ("hansell") – essentially bribes – if they helped others to gain what they wanted from the "the same siluere," the king's treasury. Representatives become mere agents for individual gain, all feeding from the same trough. With the mention of Do-Well – the most direct reference to *Piers Plowman* in the poem – the narrative stops short. In the manuscript, the verse stops

---

[68] Grady, "The Generation of 1399," 224.
[69] For some examples of this in the 1406 parliament, see Pollard, "The Lancastrian Constitutional Experiment Revisted," 106–7.

mid-page and there are several missing folios and a blank folio following, perhaps indicating that the remainder of the poem simply was never copied. Whatever its manuscript history, thematically the narrative seems to have backed itself into a corner such that its own ability to show and to speak have been lost. Like the parliament itself, *Richard the Redeless* lapses into mere ineffectiveness, and ultimately silence, where before it had entered into its critical task with a passion.[70] The shift from criticisms of the king and court to the "knyghtis of the comunete" and "citiseyns of shiris" (4.41–2) thus widens the scope of its critical purview, but at the same time it blurs the focus of the satire to the point where the poetical display of the community's cries – the public voice for a public good – is threatened with the very loss it was engaged to avoid.

Clearly this is poetry operating very near to the documentary forms that were also engaged to provide similar ameliorative gestures (or corrective accounts) for proper petitionary showing. But it operates with a much more negative cast, as the voice of *Richard the Redeless* seems both empowered and nullified by the kind of redelessness it attempts to expose. As a therapeutic expression it seems unable, in the end, to negotiate its own urgent questions of just how far that voice can go in fulfilling the demands that brought it into being, and of how a parliamentary institution can avoid becoming merely another means for abuse. Like the assembly, the poem thus seems marked for premature failure. The multitude of figures and responses embodied by the parliamentarians cause it to collapse under a kind of centrifugal pressure. The image of too many figures attempting to answer too many demands, some right and some wrong, offers an anxious example of parliamentary representation in verse that itself has only a tenuous hold on its own representational capacities. As a result, the kind of focused exhortation found in *The Crowned King* has its inverted counterpart in the witlessness of *Richard*'s king and parliament, neither of which can represent the proper showing of a public voice so sorely desired by the poetry.

4 *MUM AND THE SOTHSEGGER*: SHOWING AS HEALING

The last and most complex poem of the group is a fitting end-piece not only for the texts of this chapter but for this study as a whole. Although no longer considered the work of Langland himself, *Mum and the*

---

[70] Similar readings are put forward by Barr, *Signes and Sothe*, 44, and Grady, "The Generation of 1399," 225.

Sothsegger is a remarkably well-composed (if incomplete) Langlandian meditation on the conditions of public speech. Possibly written by the same
author as *Richard the Redeless* at a later date, it picks up many of the same
concerns with speech and access, and it focuses on the anxieties surrounding right representation evident in *Richard*. It is more successful both as
poetry and as a meta-commentary on the conditions of poetry and complaint, which it approaches from a distinctly documentary point of view.
Mum also stands out as a particularly searching meditation on the therapeutic or prophylactic limits of idealized speech, poetical and political. As
Wawn has succinctly described it, "the poem indeed offers a remarkably
self-conscious anatomy of and apology for the poetry of articulate citizenship."[71] Again, my purpose in approaching the work via parliament is
not to discount the poet's criticism of the assembly, although it is notable
that the caustic portrait of parliament in *Richard the Redeless* finds no real
counterpart here. In *Mum*, the need for showing is fundamentally a need
for health; the alignment of public showing with social healing is stronger
than the urge to satirize. But the deliberations on a healthy political economy come to yet another quizzical non-conclusion, less under the stress of
parliamentary malfeasance than an apparent impasse of conceptualization.
The poem simply seems unable to represent how, precisely, the desired
social and political unity could be functionally or artistically represented.
As with *Richard the Redeless* we could ascribe this failure to the poem's res-
idence on the traumatic Ricardian/Lancastrian historical divide, or even,
as Wawn and Ferguson have argued, on the border between medieval and
early modern mentalities. In the light of its preceding tradition, the poem's
parliamentary elements help to explain the functional shortcomings of this
successfully unsuccessful poem.

   At the risk of manifest repetitiveness, we can note (as we would expect
by now) that *Mum* begins with the same set of complaints we have seen
elsewhere concerning the ability to show complaints. Out of the several
officers of the royal court and courts that are presented (treasurer, chancellor, justices, judges, sergeants), it is the office of "Sothsegger" that is
seldom seen; the truth-teller goes begging for service and appointment (1–
53). Where the Sothsegger's hard words cause discomfort ("the pure poynt
pricketh on the sothe / Til the foule flessh vomy for attre" [52–3]), false
flatterers spread pleasing lies that grow like weeds. The results are an ignorant king who does not know the true state of the realm, and an oppressed

---

[71] Wawn, "Truth-Telling and the Tradition of *Mum and the Sothsegger,*" 284, proceeding from Ferguson,
Articulate Citizen, 75–85.

community that cannot show its complaints (129; 133–8). Although he promised improvement when he first became king, Henry has fallen short of his assurances. Despite the common clamor, communities can find no voice to show themselves:

> But whenne oure comely king came furst to londe,
> Tho was eche burne bolde to bable what hym aylid
> And to fable ferther of fautz and of wrongz,
> And romansid of the misse-reule that in the royaulme groved,
> And were behote high helpe, I herde hit myself . . .
> But the king ne his cunseil may hit not knowe
> What is the comune clamour ne the crye nother,
> For there is no man of the meeyne, more nother lasse,
> That wol wisse thaym any worde but yf his witte faille,
> Ne telle thaym the trouthe ne the texte nothir,
> But shony forto shewe what the shire meneth,
> And beguile thaym with glose, so me God helpe,
> And speke of thaire owen spede and spie no ferther,
> But euer kepe thaym cloos for caicching of wordes.
>
> (143–7, 156–64)

The reluctance of representatives to show "what the shire meneth" is another implicit complaint against parliament, as it was in *Richard the Redeless*. The freedom to "romans[e] of the misse-reule" also implies that the renewed openness for complaint was particularly a vernacular or "romance" possibility; there was hope to speak openly – and perhaps even artistically – about what was wrong with the government. This hope ended with oppressions at least as bad as those under Richard: "and yf a burne bolde hym to bable the sothe . . . / He may lose his life and laugh here no more, / Or y-putte into prisone or y-pyned to deeth" (165–8). The result is the suppression of "trouthe," who is beaten and bound "in bourghes and in shires" so that "he shoneth to be seye forto shewe his harmes" (172–5). Common clamor goes unheard, community complaints go unshown.

Unlike the narrator of *Richard the Redeless*, the speaker of *Mum and the Sothsegger* decides to investigate further and, if possible, to do something about the sorry state of affairs. The ensuing journey takes him from community to community in an updated version of Will's internal journey in *Piers Plowman*, with the difference that this journey is entirely external and social. He proceeds from the schools of the seven liberal arts and the bookish masters of the universities, to the friars and their four orders, and through the institutions of the regular clergy. These encounters elicit some pointed digressions on clerical behavior and ignorance. Afterwards the

narrator takes an abbreviated tour through a representative secular community in the courts and a mayor's hall. But it is clearly the Church that elicits
the greatest criticism and dissatisfaction. Each encounter with a new community gives the narrator the chance to ask about the public accountability
practiced there, whether "Mum" rules or "Sothsegger." Invariably it is the
former, as those who wield the greatest spiritual responsibility for speaking
the truth – the clergy – fall far short. Prefacing all of these encounters is
what he calls a "general rule" taken from the books of the doctors,

> But glymsyng on the glose, a general revle
> Of al maniere mischief I merkid and radde:
> That who-so were in wire and wold be y-easid
> Moste shewe the sore there the salue were.
>
> (314–17)

The whole scenario is profoundly Langlandian. Like Will's encounter with
Truth's pardon that both motivates his quest and provides its proleptic
answer, this principle – a wound, to be healed, must first be revealed – is
set forth at the beginning of the narrator's journey and is also its object.
What he knows intellectually he must test experientially, in the world. But
through all the gatherings and assemblies claiming to speak the truth, he
only finds mum: strategic, self-serving, and dishonest silence that "maketh
many cautelles" (689). The relation of sothsegging to mum is metaphorized
as the difference between wellness and illness. At one point even Mum himself analyzes the conflicts among the nobility (the "grucching of grete that
shuld vs gouuerne" [759]) as a kind of unhealthy royal headache: "for there
the heede aketh alle the lymes after / Pynen whenne the principal is put to
vnease" (763–4). The narrator responds by calling this a healing observation that should be made public (770–4); but Mum, quite in character, will
not risk going forward. The narrator glumly wanders through the secular
landscape and sees the downtrodden figure of Sothsegger "sitte in a shoppe
and salwyn his woundes" (847). Discouraged by the omnipresent illness,
while "rolling in remembrance" (858) of the places he has been, the narrator falls asleep and launches into the main body of the poem's narrative
commentary.

The substance of that commentary, and its frame, are a unique alter-
ation of Langlandian settings in alliterative verse. The narrator lapses into a
dream–vision in familiar fashion, but the parameters of the episode reflect
a new set of corollaries informing the allegory. Contemporary documentary practices – not just of petitions but of documents in the aggregate –
provide the literary substrate for the vision and the eventual object of its

progress.[72] The narrator's journey through the dream–landscape also differs significantly in setting from *Piers Plowman*. Langland's Will had many
places to walk through, but none so strongly echoed the topoi of the *hortus
conclusus* and garden of *deduit* as does the beautiful valley the narrator sees,
"yn a cumbe cressing on a creste wise" (878). Filled with green fields and
woods, lovely mansions and meadows, "swete sightz" (890) and a natural
abundance of fauna of every type, it is a garden of plenty. It also represents
a vision of human plenitude in the form of a landed estate:

> Thenne lepte I forth lightly and lokid a-boute,
> And I beheulde a faire hovs with halles and chambres,
> A frankeleyn-is fre-holde al fresshe newe.
> I bente me aboute and bode atte dore
> Of the gladdest gardyn that gome euer had.
>
> (944–8)

Here at the Franklin's garden, we are, proverbially, somewhere east of Eden;
it is a place of surpassing beauty and fructuousness. The Franklin too
is attractive and agreeable, a figure of both wise age and a certain fresh
("vresse") youthful vigor. The description is worth quoting in full:

> But so semely a sage as I sawe there
> I sawe not sothely sith I was bore,
> An olde auncyen man of a hunthrid wintre,
> Y-wedid in white clothe and wisely y-made,
> With hore heres on his heede more thanne half white,
> A faire visaige and a vresse and vertuous to sene.
> His eyen were al ernest, eggid to noon ille,
> With a broode besmet berde ballid a lite,
> As comely a creature as euer kinde wrought.
> He was sad of his semblant, softe of his speche,
> Proporcioned at alle poyntes and pithy in his tyme,
> And by his stature right stronge, and stalworth on his dayes,
> He houed ouer a hyve, the hony forto kepe . . .
>
> (954–66)

With the possible exception of Haukyn the Active Man (or of his own
self-portrait in the C-version of *Piers Plowman*), Langland never composed
any portrait like this. For its structured personal observation, verisimilitude
(notwithstanding the "hundred winters"), control of narratorial assessment,
and judicious choice of detail, we must look instead to the portraits of
Chaucer's "General Prologue" for its analogues and probable inspiration.

---

[72] On this point see extensively Steiner, *Documentary Culture*, 177–90.

Indeed, with his white hair, arresting but pleasant visage, sanguine disposition and ample (if not necessarily fat) proportions, he bears more than a
passing resemblance to Chaucer's own Franklin. The two also bear comparison insofar as they are, as becomes clear, inverse versions of the same
seigneurial ideal. While Chaucer's Franklin is a portrait of rural lordship
in the practice of expenditure and consumptive excess – the Saint Julian
of his county – here in *Mum*, the Franklin beekeeper is a model of sober
pastoral productiveness, and his freehold is an example of the countryside
put to good use. He is a gardener and grounds-keeper, one who obeys
the law by stewarding his property well ("as longeth to this leyghttone the
lawe wol I doo" [978]) and who fulfills a longstanding stereotype of the
vavasour as a kind of "*homme moyen intellectuel* of late fourteenth-century
England."[73] In retrospect the marvellous fecundity of the surrounding valley – its fishes, coneys, chestnuts, cherries, pears, plums, hares, hounds,
sheep, harts, hinds, and everything else – takes on the reflected pleasance
of the Franklin's intelligent lordship. Here, the poem implies strongly, is an
image of all the realm's true riches. They can be be found in the environs
of a well-run shire estate, the truest version of a garden of plenty.

This profoundly ideological vision is certainly "a sort of *locus amoenus
aristocraticus*," as Grady has called it, at the same time that it offers both
a dream-allegory soliciting interpretation and a recognizable social ideal,
unrealistic only in its hyperbole.[74] Immediately following the introduction
of the Franklin, the narrator's questions about his bee-hive solicit a long
explanation of the hive's social structure and governance. The Franklin
describes the bees as an orderly natural society ("the bee of alle bestz beste
is y-gouuerned / Yn lowlynes and labour and in lawe eeke" [997–8]) with a
king and community that are exemplars of productiveness and organization.
This creates an additional layer in the poem's symbolic political homology.
As the country as a whole is metaphorically and metonymically analogous
to the Franklin's estate, so both of them are reflected in the hive. It is a
model kingdom and monitory exemplum. For although it is natural, it is
not perfect: while most of the bees in the hive live lawfully by "reason"
(1036) and good order, the drones are parasitic wastrels who deceive the
worker bees and harm the hive through their unproductive consumption.
The beekeeper himself stands watch outside the hive, killing the drones as
they try to enter (966–9). When the narrator asks why the worker bees do

---

[73] Pearcy, "Chaucer's Franklin and the Literary Vavasour," 33. See also Olson, *The Canterbury Tales and
the Good Society*, 264–5 (and references), who notes that Franklins could be called upon to represent
their villages in the king's courts and parliament.
[74] Grady, "The Generation of 1399," 212.

not simply get rid of the drones themselves, the Franklin responds that the bees are working too hard "aboute comune profit" (1078) to worry about the drones. When the bees realize what has happened, they react "and quellen the dranes quicly and quiten alle thaire wrongz" (1084–6). But this reaction is too little too late, as the presence of the Franklin implies. In any case the narrator – who cagily declines to interpret the exemplum ("hit hath muche menyng who-so muste couthe, / But hit is to mistike for me . . ." [1088–9]) – immediately puts to the Franklin the question of the mastery of Mum versus Sothsegger.

The transition from the opening complaints of the poem to the sequential vision of the valley and freehold, and from there to the inner allegory of the beehive, is abrupt and somewhat awkward, but intentionally so. It resembles the transitions between the waking/reading and sleeping/dreaming episodes of Chaucer's early poems, and like the juxtapositional structure of the *Parliament of Fowls* or the *House of Fame*, it forces the reader to make the correct connections between narrative moieties.[75] In response to the question, the Franklin says he will "go as nygh to the grounde as gospel vs techeth" (1113) about the true dangers of Mum. He immediately offers an analysis with parliament at its center. The principal evil of Mum has been to silence the "showing of sores" in parliamentary assembly. The poet employs an extended medical metaphor:

> For of al the mischief and mysse-reule that in the royaulme groweth
> Mvm hath be maker alle thees many yeres,
> And eek more, a moulde, I may wel aduowe;
> And principally by parlement to proue hit I thenke,
> When knightz for the comune been come for that deede,
> And semblid forto shewe the sores of the royaulme
> And spare no speche though thay spille shuld,
> But berste out alle the boicches and blaynes of the heart
> And lete the rancune renne oute a-russhe al at oones
> Leste the fals felon festre with-ynne;
> For as I herde haue, thay helen wel the rather
> Whenne the anger and the attre is al oute y-renne,
> For better were to breste oute there bote might falle
> Thenne rise agayne regalie and the royaulme trouble.

(1115–28)

Of all the parliamentary texts we have seen, this passage in *Mum and the Sothsegger* makes the strongest connection between the showing of public grievances in parliament and the overall health of the realm. The specific

---

[75] On this aspect of inset Ricardian narratives see Burrow, *Ricardian Poetry*, 62–3.

allusion to rebellion (the "rise agayne regalie") probably refers to the several revolts Henry experienced between 1400 and 1408; but it is the general principal of showing complaint, rather than any particular event, that stands out as the salient point. The medical metaphor also stands out sharply if we keep in mind the contemporary context. Well within living memory England had suffered repeated and severe bouts of the bubonic plague.[76] The "boicches" or boils of the realm needing to be exposed and lanced to let out the swelling poison ("attre") are like buboes. The image strikingly evokes the desperate measures taken to hold back the tide of disease. Now it is the community's complaints that must be heard and relieved in order for healing to begin, as it is the plague of Mum that infects the realm like a black death. But the Lords' and Commons' refusal to show in parliament leaves these sores "salveless":

> The voiding of this vertue doeth venym forto growe
> And sores to be salueless in many sundry places
> Sith souuerayns and the shire-men the sothe haue eschewed
> Yn place that is proprid to parle for the royaulme
> And fable of thoo fautes and founde thaym to amende . . .
> Thay wollen nat parle of thoo poyntz for peril that might falle,
> But hiden alle the heuynes and halten echone
> And maken Mvm thaire messaigier thaire mote to determyne,
> And bringen home a bagge ful of boicches vn-y-curid,
> That nedis most by nature ennoye thaym there-after.
>
> (1129–33, 1136–40)

Instead of curing ills, Lords and shire knights ("souuerayns and the shire-men") simply bring them back home, "boicches" unopened in a bag. The Franklin seems to speak here from personal knowledge, as several of the narrative's motifs (health, showing, and documentary practice) are connected. The necessity of complaint is aligned with the specifically parliamentary procedure through which the national peripheries petition to the political center, and it also appears that the Franklin's concern with parliament, the place that is "proprid to parle," is a semi-professional one. As well as a rural estate-holder, he is, by implication, a parliamentarian, speaking from his own experience. He stands for exactly the kind of seigneurial figure whose political identity had coalesced in the fairly exclusive bourgeois club of the "shire-men." In this aspect he is again comparable to (and perhaps

---

[76] See Gottfried, *The Black Death*, 58–67, 129–35. Following the pestilence of 1347–51, major reoccurrences of plague hit the British Isles in 1361–2, 1369, 1375, 1379, 1381–2, 1390, 1399–1400, 1405–6, and 1411–12.

inspired by) Chaucer's Franklin, that regional figure who was himself "full ofte tyme . . . knyght of the shire."

If we take this as a plausible identification, then *Mum*'s Franklin's perspective on the necessity of public speech aligns directly with the comments in both *Crowned King* and *Richard the Redeless* about showing petitions in assembly. Like those poems, *Mum and the Sothsegger* reacts directly and artfully to the contemporary anxiety about petitionary access and reform through parliament. The fundamental problem at the source of the rest of the realm's ills is Mum, and the Franklin takes it as his duty to demonstrate the evils: "that shal I shewe the by exemples y-nowe" (1150–5, 1156). The urgency of this showing is underscored by his example of the evils brought on by Satan. If the image of the freehold and the figure of the Franklin appear Chaucerian, his further explanation of the evil caused by Mum sounds like something drawn from Gower's *Mirour de l'Omme*. Lucifer "leyeth his lynes" (1161) and snares man in lust and covetousness until he simply will not listen to any truth-teller; man is tempted and seduced by Mum who brings him, and himself, to destruction in falseness (1157–1200). So the Franklin exhorts the narrator "that thou lieue in no lore of suche lewed gomes" (1202) and to stay true to the Sothsegger, whose proper habitation is enfeoffed in the estate of man's heart, "as hooly writte techet" and as Adam was possessor "in paradise terrestre" (1224–8). As in Gower's *Mirour*, parliamentary structure combines with property metaphors in the image of "Man," *l'omme*, as a singular and unified figure of what should be, ideally, a unified body politic. This figure is used to exhort the dreamer. In the end of his dream the narrator is urged by the Franklin to make good on his "boke-makyng" (1281) – the composition of the poem itself – with which he should "feoffe" the king, so that it may afterwards be copied by knights as an example. The dream ends on this missionary note (1277–87).

This central dream-sequence is neither as labored nor as entirely derivative as my summary makes it sound, and the skill of the *Mum* poet is consistently evident in the flow of the vision as well as in the ease with which its various parts are linked together. When the narrator emerges from the dream and proceeds to the final scene, the tone and framework change once again, so it is worthwhile to pause over the challenging significance of the Franklin beekeeper. As a discrete figure he practically demands to be read allegorically, but as an allegory of *what* is unclear. He stands over the hive as a guardian and external figure who is nonetheless intimately concerned with its well-being. While the hive (like the Franklin's estate) presents a very traditional georgic image of contemporary social polity, interpreting the beekeeper's position is more difficult, especially in the context of Richard II's deposition and the incipient Lancastrian rule. While it is tempting to read him as a figure for the usurping Henry Bolingbroke (or, more abstractly, perhaps as a newly intervening royal authority) it would appear to be a category error to align the completely human figure as a substitute for the *bee* king, the natural head of the hive. Nowhere does the dream impeach the bees' sovereign or the hive's monarchy. There is no hint of the deposition in the Franklin's actions either, as he does not kill or threaten the leader of the hive. And the beekeeper's destruction of the drones seems symbolic less of the actions of the king than of the constant parliamentary anxiety (and legislative efforts) that the royal courts be kept clear of wastrel hangers-on and sycophants.[77]

The Franklin beekeeper's significance is therefore, I think, more abstract – and in some ways less satisfying – than a direct allegory of Bolingbroke. The Franklin displays no pretensions to kingship, and what we read of his political philosophy is resolutely but not completely deferential to kingly authority. He is a human worker-bee of sorts, but he is also the ultimate parasite on the hive as a whole, implicitly extracting from it a heavy tax of honeyed wealth. He stands as a singular figure and speaker, but a speaker *for* this community of the hive of which he is, and is not, an integral part. He is in fact something of a leviathan in relation to it. As he provides a voice and power to its disparate members – who are, we recall, too busy to police themselves effectively – he speaks soberly and authoritatively in his collective wisdom. Fundamentally, the Franklin represents his charge by husbanding it responsibly and by answering its needs, just as he does for the freehold as a whole. The Franklin beekeeper is, in short, an oddly appropriate hypostasization of the fantasy of effective and licit parliamentary power, precisely because he is the *single* supra-communal power who can see what is going on throughout the body of the hive. He is a figuration of the idealized ability to speak and act as a corporate whole, and with one voice, as a unified "national" figure that is both within and outside the community that gives him sustenance.

Thinking back to the fantasy of the committee-to-one in the *Modus Tenendi Parliamentum*, we can see how the Franklin beekeeper similarly stands both with, and across from, the sovereign social structure he is charged to speak for and protect. Read in this way, it is perhaps the most

---

[77] Similar anxieties about the unproductive and parasitic clergy may also be implied, echoing contemporary Lollard complaints. See Barr, *Socioliterary Practice in Late Medieval England*, 158–75.

flatteringly grandiose image of parliamentary identity we have yet encountered. In its immediate historical context the beehive allegory becomes another form of "showing," not of complaint, but of a symbolical model for the narrator–dreamer, and thus for readers, to take as a lesson in practical politics. The Franklin's perspective is simultaneously subordinate to existing structures and critical of them from a supposedly outside or impartial point of view. The kingdom – and even the king – needs a husbandman–guardian, one with the secure country values of a bourgeois shire-man. As we have seen in other parliamentary narratives, here in *Mum*, poetry and dream–vision offer the best chance for formulating this functionally *impossible* arrangement, and for expressing it effectively.

The Franklin beekeeper thus resolves the narrator's doubts so that he comes out of his sleep emboldened and ready to take on the role of healer or salver by voicing the complaints of the realm: "thenne softe I the soores to serche thaym withynne, / And seurely to salue thaym and with a newe salue" (1338–9). Immediately following this declaration is the striking and oft-remarked image of the bag of books filled with every kind of document and "pryue poyse" (1344). The "books" are in fact a collection of documentary petitions and complaints, especially against the clergy. The subject matter, context, and timing of the documents (these complaints are gathered in a bag "that was not y-openyd this other half wintre" [1347], that is, bi-annually at wintertime) suggest that the narrator is now adopting the *functional* identity of a parliamentarian presenting petitions in one of the (roughly) twice-yearly sessions of the assembly. The complaints themselves reflect the sorts of petitionary efforts characteristic of the Commons in the early Lancastrian years. The dream's "bag full of boicches" has been supplanted by this bag full of books, but in context they are the same thing: a collection of sore complaints to be brought forth by a representative who carries the voice of the community to the king's court for redress. The various documents ("a quayer of quitances," "a rolle of religion," "a paire of pamphilettz," and more [1347, 1364, 1370]) all contain various accusations, especially against the clergy. One document, "a copie for comunes" (1388), contains the texts of rumors that, in a homely detail, make things worse by inflaming popular anger: "thaire tales been so trouble that tournen men thoughtz; / The more that men musen on thaym, the madder they been after" (1392–3).

If this were the extent of the poem's engagement with public governmental showing, *Mum and the Sothsegger* would stand out as a particularly idealized secular representation of the hope for good reform. The poem shifts in the last four hundred lines to a predominantly policy-making mode of poesy, offering specific suggestions for improvement in the realm's governance. But it does so by way of the curious exemplum of "Changwys," or Genghis Khan (1414), who is introduced through this documentary sequence. Like the Franklin, he needs explication. Specifically after the rumor-mongering of the "copie of comunes," Changwys is invoked as a representative of a strong central leader exemplifying control not just of wild rumor and dissent, but of public deliberation about government in general. Tale-bearers and gossips will "mellen . . . with matieres to moustre thaire wittes" (1411). In contrast, the seven nations under Changwys' rule were initially divided and in danger of total destruction by their enemies until the "principalz" followed a "voice" and made Changwys their king (1424–5). Once king, Changwys immediately consolidated his power by ordering the death of his nobles' sons and heirs, and by demanding ownership and control of their lands. After the nobles submitted, Changwys returned their lands to them and took their counsel, "and wroughte alle with oon wil as wise men shuld" (1452). He then led them to conquer their enemies, regaining all the territory they had previously lost (1453–6).

Even by medieval standards this a particularly grim exemplum. The narrator explicates it by immediately trying to clarify the licit bounds for public complaint:

> Now by Crist that me creed, I can not be-thenke
> A kindely cause why the comun shuld
> Contre the king-is wil ne construe his werkes.
> I carpe not of knightz that cometh for the shires,
> That the king clepith to cunseil with other;
> But hit longeth to no laborier; the lawe is agayne thaym.
>
> (1457–62)

How are we to read this strange juxtaposition? The poet has clearly gotten himself into an uncomfortable (and potentially risky) position where he wants to sanction *some* form of licit public complaint – the "knightz that cometh for the shires" – while making a strong, Changwys-like proscription against any general dissent or criticisms aimed at the fundamental authority of the monarch. If before it appeared that the Franklin sanctioned the practice of criticism wholesale, the correlative figure of an absolutist despot, a Khan violently compelling total loyalty, goes to the opposite extreme. Changwys arises from *within* the community, is raised up by it, and then grimly rules it not by suppressing wastrels but by suppressing the very nobles who raised him in the first place. Proceeding from this counter-example

of Changwys, the commons (as opposed to the Commons) are told quite
frankly to shut up with their complaints:

> Thus clappeth the comun and knocketh thaymself,
> For the tayl of thaire talking teneth thaym ofte . . .
> Thay finde many fautes and faillen most thaymself
> Of deedes of deuete that thay do shuld.
> Thay shulde loue loyally the lordz aboute,
> That thay mighte lerne a lesson of thaire lowe hertz
> To reule thaym by reason and by right lawe.
>
> (1469–70, 1475–9)

Loyalty is the thing: the commons should listen to lords "and obeye to
thayre bidding and bable no ferther, / For suche lewed labbing the lande
doeth a-peire" (1482–3). The commons should know their place from the
example of Changwys "and construe no ferther" (1486), a vaguely threatening conclusion to the passage.

If up to this point we (or anybody else) were tempted to read the *Mum*
poet as a nascent democrat or populist, this figure of total central control sharply reverses our expectations. It appears to be an almost complete
retreat from the opening of the poem where, as we have seen, the narrator complained that "yf a burne bolde hym to bable the sothe" (165)
he was subjected to imprisonment or worse, not to mention the "general
revle" that complaints must be shown to be healed (314–17). At different
levels, this backtracking may have had multiple motivations. The fear of
widespread popular rebellion, incipient local wars waged by recalcitrant
nobles, the threat of sedition and heresy which provoked an especially
harsh clampdown under Archbishop Arundel's Constitutions in 1409, and
the widespread abuse of legal pleading (which the poet goes on to decry
at length): all of these would have provided ample reason to draw back
from a call for unfettered public complaint. And yet the poem appears
to be caught in a bind between precisely these two poles, and it develops into something of a self-consuming artifact. Calling for the expression
of complaints in the public sphere as no poem before it, it also offers
the fantasy of strong-willed, univocal centralized authority that comes
across, perhaps startlingly, as a proleptic portrait of Tudor-era absolute
monarchy.

It is in this dialectic between centripetal and centrifugal forces, mediated
by the model of legal documents, that *Mum and the Sothsegger* staggers
toward its inconclusive conclusion. The narrator rummages around in the
bag full of books and finds, among other things, a "librarie of lordes" (1626,

1626–82) that actually urges the restraint of the nobility and a reformed upbuilding of the monarchy:

> For trusteth right treuly, talke what men liketh,
> And wendith and trendith twys in oon wike,
> And clepith to your cunseil copes and other,
> And pleyne atte parlement, but yf the deede prouue
> That the coroune in his kinde come ynne agaynes,
> Clene in his cumpas with croppes and braunches,
> Lite and a lite, right as the lawe asketh,
> Wel mowe we wilne and wisshe what vs liketh
> And eeke waite after welthe but as my witte demeth,
> Oure wynnyng and worship wol be the lasse
> With knight and with comune til the king haue
> Alle hoole in his hande that he haue oughte.
>   (1671–82)

Both the comment about "wending and trending twice in one week" (that is, the two days a week set aside by parliamentary statute in 1406 for hearing complaints) and about "pleyn[ing] atte parlement" clearly refer to the formal institutional channels of parliament as the means for gaining royal access. But if the royal estate itself is not returned to its proper full growth ("with croppes and braunches"), no one, nobility or commons, will benefit from weak royal power. The poet acknowledges that they are dealing with a weakened monarchy, not a Changwys. It must be remade, "lite and a lite," into the strong central authority the country needs. So this document about lordship is actually more focused on restoring strong kingship; otherwise all of the parliamentary maneuvering and public reform simply will not work. Other documents in the bag include "a copie of couetise" (1683, 1683–96) criticizing the rich who covetously hold on to their wealth until their death; a "title of a testament" (1697, 1697–1722) exposing the way heirs refuse to honor the charity mandated in a testator's will; a "poynt of prophecie" (1723) mocking the currency of Merlin's prophecies and the fruitless attempts to predict the future[78]; and a "cedule" (1734) accusing the knights and clergy of not being "knytte in conscience" (1739) to their duties and good behavior. And with that, before the completion of the documentary sequence, the poem comes to an abrupt halt in the damaged manuscript. Like *Richard the Redeless*, *Mum and the Sothsegger* stands physically incomplete as well as conceptually uncompleted. It is not

---

[78] Parliamentary statutes of 1402 and 1406 in fact attempted to ban such political agitation and prophesying: *RP* 3.508 (on sedition in Wales), and 3.583–4 (against the Lollards) .

possible to reasonably speculate, from the extant trajectory of the poem, where or how it might have concluded.

On the one hand we could readily conclude, as Grady has argued, that "for *Mum*, even more than for *Richard*, parliament is part of the problem, not part of the solution."[79] Like other governmental and bureaucratic structures – indeed, more so – parliament has been infected and distorted by Mum. But at the same time, the thinking and poetical organization of *Mum* is deeply influenced by specifically parliamentary forms of discourse, and the poem itself, in the end, becomes parliamentary as an incomplete exercise in publicly submitting various documentary petitions in the manner sanctioned by the Franklin beekeeper. In this case, documentary form *is* parliamentary form: the collection, submission, and public showing of complaints. If the poem faults this process, it does so only because it has so much riding on it, artistically and politically, and because the process of complaint has been distorted for so long. To mix our metaphors (as the poet does), we could say that the bag of books containing the sores of the realm is left open, and so it provides a structuring framework for the ending part of the narrative, which remains incomplete and was probably uncompleteable in an environment of political expressive risk. Similarly the tension between the opposed figures of the poem, the Franklin and Changwys, is left unreconciled. Looking forward, this is also an accurate reflection of the contemporary ideological impasse between decentralized local forces and the increasing power that would be put at the royal center, especially after Agincourt. But we cannot fail to miss that *Mum* itself is a metatextual compendium *of* complaint, one that criticizes the bureaucratic environs of parliament precisely through its own self-annulling failure to show the things it most desperately wants to.

What the documentary form of *Mum* thus provides is not exactly an estates satire, although it can be compared to one. Again drawing a comparison to the estates of Gower's *Mirour*, or to Chaucer's *Parliament of Fowls* and *Canterbury Tales*, we can see more clearly how the documentary substitutions of the *Mum* poet move his Langlandian formula away from an emphasis on character in favor of a stress on complaint. Instead of gathering people or estates, it collects bills; the assembly-function of poetry is reduced to its basic parchment participants and to the physical documentation so central to the petitionary process, as opposed to an extended fantasy of art or experience of character. Indeed, despite his compelling portrait, ultimately it is not even a figure like the Franklin who steps forward to make the

---

[79] Grady, "Generation of 1399," 227.

poem's petitionary declarations. In the end, the documents almost seem to submit themselves. This decharacterization or depersonalization is perhaps the logical end-point of a mode of poetry that began with an emphasis on the *individual* coming forward, a "man" (*l'omme*) or other figure, to show plaint and seek redress. Between the urgings of a Franklin and the threat of a Changwys, it is, in the end, the complaints themselves as books in a bag that must be made to speak, and to bear speaking legitimacy, for whatever healing they can muster.

5 CONCLUSION: PARLIAMENT, PETITION, AND IMPASSE

As I have suggested here, we can read the opposed figures of the Franklin and Changwys as correlative figurations of early Lancastrian political fantasy. They represent, on one side, the sagely virtuous shire-man from the periphery who speaks the *sothe* of complaint and popular voice as a country/county representative, and who acts as a peripheral guardian of the national interest; and on the other, the strong martial leader raised up from within the political center, who provides focus, discipline, and control, eliminating dissent and consolidating power, and who acts as the object of unifying identity for the polity as a whole. They are opposed but mutually dependent. In the post-revolution context of the early 1400s, these two institutional figures – strong parliamentarian, strong monarch – provided the fodder for this bureaucratic verse in a style that Steiner has usefully termed "obtrusive writing," the artistic imagining of institutional documents in which "the poem is the incisive critic; its documentary practices are its distended subject."[80] In the case of the poems of the Piers Plowman tradition, it is, repeatedly, the act of showing complaint that provides both the impetus for versifying and the object of complaint itself. The poems criticize their own activity to the extent that, in *Mum*, the material tools of complaint – books, cedules, bills of various kinds – become the only representative voices heard by poem's end. As a "parliament" poem, or a poem of *parlement*, *Mum and the Sothsegger* thus extends and effectively completes the focus on petitionary voice and complaint we have seen elsewhere.

But in doing so, it also makes manifest a representational conflict that is not easily ignored. As a representation of representation, *Mum* has the unique distinction of being the one poem to introduce an authoritative figure – and partly, a political philosophy – that would disallow its own writing. As Ruth Mohl has noted, "as a legist rather than a religious allegorist

---

[80] Steiner, *Documentary Culture*, 144; see 143–90.

the author of *Mum* makes clear that the real power of the people lies in their representation in Parliament and not in malicious gossip and disloyalty."[81] But therein lies the rub. While maybe we can draw these boundaries – that is, between right representation and disloyal discourse – certainly *Mum* and the other poems have a harder time of it. There were no guarantees that even the best-intentioned, most loyally-conceived complaint-poems would not be accused of sedition or disunity. This is not a failure of their parliamentary currency, but a product and necessary risk of it. For we can hardly fail to recognize the irony that, as an extra-representative and unofficial public expression of complaint, the poem which *invokes* a Changwys is exactly the sort of popular discourse that would be suppressed *by* him. In a way, this is the point where the representational poetical animal starts to eat its own tail, making itself incomplete by design.

To bring this analysis back around to the petitionary examples with which I began, we can derive further insight by speculating how bills such as the Commons' vernacular petition–assertion of assenting authority, and Thomas Paunfield's petition on behalf of himself and Chesterton, would have been viewed by the *Mum* poet. The question is germane, given their temporal and lingual (and topical) proximity. Would these cedules and bills have been viewed as good things or bad things, as the legitimate representative voices of the community, or as an illegitimate suppression of the king's authority and power (the former) and as an abuse of the law and the king's courts by unruly or uppity commons (the latter)? Of course there is no way to tell, but it would have been an immediately relevant question about the *representational capacity* of these forms of discourse, especially in their documents, as the media and means of public *parlement*. In this sphere, poetry was investigating the same parameters of public and institutional speech, and it ran similar risks. We can recall that when Thomas Haxey was condemned by Richard for his overreaching bill in parliament (like Keighley long before him), it was the bill itself that came first and that was circulated independently, and for which Richard had to demand the public identification of its author so as to mete out punishment. Both the Commons' and Paunfield's bills present themselves as coming forward and speaking on behalf of their communities as acts of public showing, and in differing allegories, as revealing the "boicches" needing cure. Were we to read Thomas Paunfield himself as another or lesser version of the Franklin beekeeper – a rural figure daring to speak on behalf of his small, hive-like community – we could get a sense of the expressive risk, and possibilities,

---

[81] Mohl, "Theories of Monarchy in *Mum and the Sothsegger*," 38.

that were attendant upon complaining at parliament, even if you had your petitions in the bag.

However, by this point even in literary works the assemblies no longer resemble the notional assemblies of Gower or Chaucer, as we find, in all the poems of the Piers Plowman tradition, nothing like parliaments of fowls or allegorical *parlements*. The shift toward a plainer documentary reality was perhaps, as I have suggested, a step away (or backward) from the delights of high art. But in return, toward the end of this parliamentary-poetic tradition, we nonetheless encounter a set of works that make a good show for themselves as aesthetic representatives of the desire for effective speech and common voice, in all of its complexity.

Conclusion:
speaking with one voice

'*And as to the causes of social change, I look at it in this way – ideas are a sort of parliament, but there's a commonwealth outside, and a good deal of the commonwealth is working at change without knowing what the parliament is doing.*'

– George Eliot, *Daniel Deronda*[1]

* * *

By 1415, the particular moment in late medieval England for parliamentary poetry, if not the poetry of *parlement* and discussion, had largely run its course. As much as anything else, the success of the Lancastrian regime's military ventures eased internal tensions for a time.[2] National anxieties could be exercised through their projection upon Lollards as embodiments of the internal enemy, and by the reign of Henry VI, the literary manifestation of a public voice had shifted to different models. Gone were parliaments and public speakers of broad social identification, replaced by the example of a Lydgatean laureate exercising his craft as an approximate sovereign or poet-king but not as a *vox publica* in the mode of a mediatory speaker. The minority of Henry VI in particular, following his accession in 1422, introduced new challenges and problems that simply did not provoke a parliamentary model of artistic response. While parliamentary procedures and authority were largely solidified and continued to develop during the Wars of the Roses, even parliamentarian authors like George Ashby and Thomas Malory pay little attention to the assembly. Or if they did focus on parliament – as in a few of Malory's changes to the Morte d'Arthur narrative – it was in forms that looked back to the older ideals of baronial assembly with little influence of a communal model. By 1422, it is not entirely as if the previous fifty years had never happened. But in this respect, close to

[1] George Eliot, *Daniel Deronda*, ed. Cave, 524–5. Book IV, Chapter 42: Goodwin speaking to his companions at Mordecai's round table, with Deronda present.
[2] See generally Butt, 485–566.

it: public poetry changed its identity, as community concerns found new avenues for expression that left in abeyance the kinds of *parlement* analyzed here.

In large part, this shift comes about because civic culture and the literary styles used for public consumption, representation, and commentary had moved on to new forms: mummings and disguisings, exempla, drama, the triumph, new lyric models and modes, and other genres that would be associated with the high literary practice of the English Renaissance. Literary art began to be categorized, culturally, much more *discretely*, as a realm with its own recognizable shapes and genres. No need then, to borrow from something like a parliament or forms such as documentary petitions. The identifiable "public" also tended to contract to the overlapping spheres of baronial and royal courts, leaving out much of the bourgeois-clerical constituency and ethos so central to Ricardian and Lancastrian literature. There were no Good Parliaments of the fifteenth century nor parallel poetical reflections of them. Chaucer – or at least some of his work – was looked to, and provided, a literary model for this artistic condensation of forms and audience. Lydgatean spectacle and show, drawing from father Chaucer, nonetheless moved the focus of representativeness away from the mediatory forms of *parlement* and middling estates-society so characteristic of Chaucerian style and towards (or back to) the king as figurehead and ideal, a sovereign who stands as representative of, and to, the realm in his body and office.[3] This was, of course, hardly a foreign idea for medieval poetry and politics; the king as "head of all" would have been as comfortable to Langland as it was for Lydgate. But in a time of chronic dynastic uncertainty, the flexibility provided by earlier styles of *parlement* and the representation of rancorous estates could not as readily be afforded. Narrative and poetic art thus adopted more clearly typified genres, developing in new directions.

While this study has stressed the specific formal and bureaucratic models of assembly and petition, it has also made clear that these modes also led to a broadly reconceptualized understanding of what a *public* could be, or ought to be, in literary exercise. The trajectory of the shift from a baronial to a communal model shows how, for the period, many of the assumptions about licit public discourse in fact remained the same or similar over time. The desire for a speaking and representative unity never really loses touch with both a transcendentalized notion of divinely ordained *unanimitas* and a demotic appeal to a common voice, even as the identity of that voice

---

[3] For analysis see Nolan, *John Lydgate and the Forms of Public Culture*; Lerer, *Chaucer and His Readers*.

changed radically. During a period when the realm of social and political discourse was being recast from above – especially by Richard II's attempts to adopt a Valois-influenced style of divine kingship[4] – and from below – in the protests of rebels, Lollards, and other subaltern and peripheral communities – the forms of parliament and *parlement* analyzed here provide unique glimpses of a self-consciously mediatory aesthetic practice. These expressions of the dialectic of *unitas* and *communitas* carry on an attempt, as I have argued, to think about their social world in terms that can negotiate the dual threats of coercion and violence from both above and below. The multiple tropes and figurations of this dynamic – the fantastic committee-to-one and pseudo-Arthurian assemblies; parliaments of fowls and bags of boicches; prudential women, anxious petitioners, and properties of *l'homme*; barns of Unity and houses of Provence; franklin beekeepers and despotic khans; the mum and the mumbling as well as bold-speakers and truth-tellers – all have in common the organizing notional forum of parliamentary assembly, its political space and petitionary venue. Familiarly enough, individual interests and public good repeatedly clash here in the conflicts of diverse voices. They *are* one, and many, at the same time, and in the same public writing.

This is to say – in a necessarily polemic formulation – that the lessons to be drawn from the practice of these poets are relevant to our own artistic, political, and public lives as critical examples of a *juste milieu* aesthetic: not just the literature of middlemen, but the literary exploration of what it means to seek a common ground. They raise the perennial challenge, within our literary and constitutional tradition, of finding a common voice, and of defining the procedural legitimacy that might attain to it. This is *not* to claim that the poetry actually fulfills our demands – or even its own – of "true" representation and representativeness, whatever that might mean in a given historical context. Indeed the practice of each author raises the troubling question of whether *any* representation, artistic or electoral, can ever be adequate to its world. Nonetheless, they do try. And their remarkable achievements of new voices and identities, as represented in all of these works, project the thought-provoking power of exactly the distance or gap between the representation and the represented that is the fundamental condition of both artistic and political possibility. Instead of thinking of the mediatory role sought by these poets as a merely tepid response to other, more pressing changes, we can visualize their practices as significant efforts arising from the juncture between firmer and less yielding

---

[4] See especially Staley, *Languages of Power in the Age of Richard II*.

(one could say entrenched) polemical and social positions, practices of an almost negative capability. In the space amidst tyrant kings, elite courts, oppressed groups and angry mobs, there were parliaments and poets. In this regard (as the saying goes) surely the middle of the road is the best place to get run over; and in the later fifteenth century the definition of the "public" and *communitas regni* continued to be violently contested down to Cade's Rebellion and beyond, often in explicitly parliamentary terms.[5] But the *moyen* and medium of parliamentary poetry in the later fourteenth and early fifteenth centuries also offered artists a fairly wide latitude for investigating the concepts and practices of representation, and of representing representation. For men of talk and *parlement*, this was a natural space to inhabit.

In conclusion, to adapt Eliot's formulation in *Daniel Deronda* as it is spoken at Mordecai's round table – itself a not-too-subtle representation of an intellectual *parlement* – the period was thus also a time for the remarkably productive intersection of "ideas," parliament, and a vibrantly unstable commonwealth, each element not as easily distinguishable from the other as Goodwin's arrangement makes them, and each drawing from the others as engines of change, wittingly or unwittingly. I have stressed the role of mediatory form most strongly in Chaucer, and the poets of the Piers Plowman tradition also display a remarkable capacity for imagining (or bewailing) bureaucratic and petitionary forms as methods of practical intermediation. But it is perhaps best stressed by Gower that the means and modes of *parlement* have an irreducible ethical valence. The task of public speaking, whether communal or individual – or of a *vox communis* as earthy *vox populi* and heavenly *vox Dei* – is also a civic responsibility of the first order, one that should be adopted by poets and politicians only with a strong sense of *both* its radical contingency *and* its profound centrality to the civic culture that gives it a home. In this sense, the best of these late medieval English poets, in their roles as public speakers, conjoin the pleasure, thoughtful challenge, and occasional humor of narrative artistry with the parliamentary forms of their times, to produce arts, and voices, that still resonate intimately with our own.

---

[5] See Watts, "The Pressure of the Public," for an excellent overview and analysis.

Bibliography

DOCUMENTARY AND MANUSCRIPT SOURCES

National Archives SC 8/20/962 (Deumarcz petition, c. November 1381)
National Archives SC 8/20/997 (Mercers' petition, 1388)
National Archives SC 8/23/1141 (Paunfield petition, Anglo-French, November 1414)
National Archives SC 8/23/1143a–b (Paunfield Petition, English schedule, November 1414)
National Archives SC 8/192/9579 (Drayton petition, 1344)
National Archives C 65/74/3 (parliamentary roll, April 1414, membrane 3)
British Library MS. Cotton Vespasian B.XVI (*Piers Plowman* MS. M, C-text)
Corpus Christi College, Oxford, MS. 201 (*Piers Plowman* MS. F, B-text)

PRIMARY SOURCES AND REFERENCE WORKS

A Book of London English, 1384–1425. Eds. R. W. Chambers, R. W. and Marjorie Daunt. Oxford: Clarendon, 1931.
A Latin Dictionary. Eds. Charlton T. Lewis and Charles Short. Oxford: Oxford University Press, 1991 [1879].
Anglo-Norman Dictionary. Eds. Louise Stone and William Rothwell. London: Modern Humanities Research Assoc., 1977, 1992.
Anglo-Norman Political Songs. Ed. Isabel Aspin. Oxford: Basil Blackwell, 1953.
The Anonimalle Chronicle, 1307–1334. Ed. Wendy R. Childs and John Taylor. Yorkshire Archaeological Society, 1991.
The Anonimalle Chronicle 1333 to 1381. Ed. V. H. Galbraith. London: Manchester University Press, 1927.
Aquinas, Thomas. *Summa contra gentiles.* 5 vols. Trans. Vernon J. Bourke. Notre Dame: University of Notre Dame Press, 1956.
Aquinas, Thomas. *Summa theologiae.* Trans. Fathers of the English Dominican Province. Rev. Daniel J. Sullivan. Chicago, London: Encyclopædia Britannica, 1952.
The Assembly of Ladies. In *The Floure and the Leafe, The Assembly of Ladies, The Isle of Ladies.* Ed. Derek Pearsall. TEAMS. Kalamazoo, MI: Medieval Institute Publications, 1990, pp. 29–62.

Athelston. In *Middle English Verse Romances.* Ed. Donald B. Sands. Exeter: University of Exeter Press, 1986, pp. 130–53.

Biblia Sacra, iuxta Vulgatam Versionem. 3rd ed. amended. Ed. Boniface Fischer et al. Stuttgart: Deutsche Bibelgesellschaft, 1969, 1983.

Brewer's Dictionary of Phrase and Fable, Revised & Enlarged. New York: Harper & Brothers, n.d. [c. 1949].

Bromyard, John. *Summa praedicantium omnibus Dominici gregis pastoribus, divini verbi praeconibus, animarum fidelium ministris, & sacrarum Literarum cultoribus longè utilissima ac pernecessaria.* Antwerp, 1614 [c. 1330–52].

Capgrave, John. *The Life of Saint Katherine.* Ed. Karen A. Winstead. TEAMS. Kalamazoo, MI: Medieval Institute Publications, 1999.

Carlyle, Thomas. *On Heroes, Hero-Worship, and the Heroic in History.* Ed. Carl Niemeyer. Lincoln, Nebraska: University of Nebraska, 1966 [1841].

Chaucer Life-Records. Eds. Martin M. Crow and Clair C. Olson. Oxford: Oxford University Press, 1966.

Chaucer, Geoffrey. *The Riverside Chaucer.* 3rd ed. Ed. Larry D. Benson et al. Boston: Houghton Mifflin, 1987.

Chrétien de Troyes. *Arthurian Romances.* Trans. William W. Kibler, Carleton W. Carroll. New York: Penguin, 1991.

Chrétien de Troyes. *Erec et Enide.* Publié par Mario Roques. Classiques Français du Moyen Age. Paris: Librairie Honoré Champion, 1981.

Chrétien de Troyes. *Le Chevalier au Lion (Yvain).* Publié par Mario Roques. Classiques Français du Moyen Age. Paris: Librairie Honoré Champion, 1982.

The Chronicle of Walter of Guisborough. Ed. Harry Rothwell. Camden Society 3rd series, vol. 89. London: Royal Historical Society, 1957.

Chronicon Angliae, ab anno domini 1328 usque ad annum 1388. Auctore monacho quodam Sancti Albani. Ed. Edward Maunde Thompson. Rolls Series, London, 1874. Kraus reprint, 1965.

Dante Alighieri. *Monarchia.* In *Opere di Dante Alighieri.* A cura di Fredi Chaipelli. Milan: Mursia, 1963, pp. 333–90.

The Dictionary of National Biography (DNB). 22 vols. Eds. Leslie Stephen and Sidney Lee. London: Oxford University Press, 1885–1901.

The Dictionary of National Biography (DNB). On line edition. Oxford University Press, 2004. http://www.oxforddnb.com/

Dictionnaire de l'ancien français. A. J. Greimas. Paris: Larousse Bordas, 1997.

Eliot, George. *Daniel Deronda.* Ed. Terence Cave. New York: Penguin, 2003 [1876].

Favent (Fovent), Thomas. *Historia siue Narracio De Modo et Forma Mirabilis Parliamenti.* Ed. May McKisack. Camden Miscellany 3rd ser., vol. 14. London: Camden Society, 1926.

Flores Historiarum. 3 vols. Ed. Henry Richards Luard. London: Eyre & Spottiswoode, 1890.

Foedera, conventiones, literæ et cujuscunque generis acta publica. Ed. Thomas Rymer. London: A. & J. Churchill, 1703–35.

Geoffrey of Monmouth. *The Historia Regum Britanie of Geoffrey of Monmouth.* 5 vols. Vol. 1 Bern Burgerbibliothek MS. 568. Vol. 2 The First Variant Version: A Critical Edition. Ed. Neil Wright. Cambridge: D. S. Brewer, 1984, 1988.

Glover, Robert. *Nobilitas politica vel civilis: personas scilicet distinguendi, et ab origine inter gentes, ex principium gratia nobilitandi forma* . . . Londini: Typis Gulielmi Jaggard in via Barbicanea, 1608.

Gower, John. *Mirour de l'Omme (The Mirror of Mankind).* Trans. William Burton Wilson, rev. Nancy Wilson Van Baak. East Lansing: Colleagues Press, 1992.

Gower, John. *The Complete Works of John Gower.* 4 vols. Ed. G. C. Macaulay. Oxford: Clarendon Press, 1899–1902.

Gower, John. *The Major Latin Works of John Gower.* Trans. Eric W. Stockton. Seattle: University of Washington Press, 1962.

The Harleian Miscellany: A Collection of Scarce, Curious, and Entertaining Pamphlets and Tracts, as well in Manuscript as in Print, Selected from the Library of Edward Harley, Second Earl of Oxford. 10 vols. Eds. William Oldys and Thomas Park. London: Printed for John White and John Murray, 1808–1813.

Havelok the Dane. Ed. G. V. Smithers. Oxford: Clarendon Press, 1987.

The Holy Bible, Douay Rheims Version, Translated from the Latin Vulgate. Rev. Bishop Richard Challoner. Rockford, Illinois: Tan Books and Publishers, 1971 [1899].

Isidore of Seville. *Isidori hispalensis episcopi etymologiarvm sive originvm.* Ed. W. M. Lindsay. 2 vols. Oxford: Clarendon, 1911.

Knighton, Henry. *Knighton's Chronicle 1337–1396.* Ed. and trans. G. H. Martin. Oxford: Clarendon, 1995.

Langland, William. *Piers Plowman: The A Version. Will's visions of Piers Plowman and do-well.* Ed. George Kane. Berkeley: University of California Press, 1960, 1988.

Langland, William. *Piers Plowman: The B Version. Will's visions of Piers Plowman, do-well, do-better, and do-best.* Ed. George Kane and E. Talbot Donaldson. Berkeley: University of California Press, 1988.

Langland, William. *Piers Plowman: The C Version. Will's visions of Piers Plowman, do-well, do-better, and do-best.* Ed. George Russell and George Kane. Berkeley: University of California Press, 1997.

Langland, William. *The Vision of Piers Plowman.* Ed. A. V. C. Schmidt. New York: E. P. Dutton, 1978.

Langtoft, Pierre (Peter). *The Chronicle of Pierre de Langtoft.* 2 vols. Ed. Thomas Wright. London: Longmans, 1868.

Lydgate, John. *Temple of Glas.* Ed. J. Schick. Early English Text Society. London: Kegan Paul, 1891.

Malory, Thomas. *Works.* 2nd ed. Edn. Eugène Vinaver. Oxford: Oxford University Press, 1971.

Mannyng of Brunne, Robert. *The Chronicle.* Ed. Idelle Sullens. Binghamton, NY: Medieval and Renaissance Texts and Studies, 1996.

Manual of Law French. 2nd edn. Ed. J. H. Baker. Brookfield, Vermont: Scolar Press, 1990.

Middle English Dictionary (MED). Eds. Hans Kurath and Sherman M. Kuhn. Ann Arbor: University of Michgan Press, 1952–2001. http://ets.umdl.umich.edu/m/mec/

Middle English Romances. Ed. Stephen H. A. Shepherd. New York: Norton, 1995.

Modus Tenendi Parliamentum. Eds. and trans. Nicholas Pronay and John Taylor. In Pronay and Taylor, *Parliamentary Texts of the Middle Ages*, pp. 67–99, 103–14.

Mum and the Sothsegger. Eds. Mabel Day and Robert Steele. London: Early English Text Society, 1936.

The N-Town Play Cotton MS Vespasian D.8. Ed. Stephen Spector. 2 vols. Oxford: Early English Text Society, 1991.

Oxford English Dictionary (OED). 3rd edn. updated. Oxford University Press, 2005. http://dictionary.oed.com/

The Parliament Rolls of Medieval England (PROME). CD-ROM edition. Eds. Chris Given-Wilson *et al*. Leicester: Scholarly Digital Editions and The National Archives, 2005.

Parliamentary Texts of the Later Middle Ages. Eds. Nicholas Pronay and John Taylor. Oxford: Clarendon, 1980.

Patrologia Latina Cursus Completus. 221 vols. Ed. J. P. Migne. Paris: 1844–65. Full text database: *Patrologia Latina Full Text Database*, Chadwyck-Healey, 1995.

The Piers Plowman Tradition. Ed. Helen Barr. London: J. M. Dent, 1993.

Pyers plowmans exhortation, vnto the lordes, knightes and burgoysses of the Parlyament-house. London: Imprinted by Anthony Scoloker dwelling in the Sauoy tentes. without Templebarre [c. 1550]. Early English Books (1475–1640) 122:18; STC (2d edn.) 19905.

Le Roman de Brut de Wace. Ed. Ivor Arnold. 2 vols. Paris: Société des Anciens Textes Français, 1938, 1940.

Rotuli Parliamentorum Anglie Hactenus Inediti. Eds. H. G. Richardson and George Sayles. Camden 3rd Series, vol. 51. London: Camden Historical Society, 1935.

Rotuli Parliamentorum ut et petitiones et placita in parliamento [1278–1503]. 6 vols. Ed. J. Strachey *et al*. London: 1767–77.

The Sermons of Thomas Brinton, Bishop of Rochester (1373–1389). 2 vols. Sister Mary Aquinas Devlin (ed.). Camden 3rd Series, vol. 85. London: Royal Historical Society, 1954.

Sir Orfeo. In Stephen Shepherd (ed.). *Middle English Romances*, pp. 174–89.

The Song of Lewes. Ed. C. L. Kingsford. Oxford: Clarendon, 1890.

Statutes of the Realm. Ed. A. Luders. 11 vols. London, 1810–28.

The St. Albans Chronicle. The Chronica maiora of Thomas Walsingham I, 1376–1394. Ed. and trans. John Taylor, Wendy R. Childs, and Leslie Watkiss. Oxford: Clarendon Press, 2003.

Thomas Wright's Political Songs of England from the Reign of John to that of Edward II. New Edition. Ed. Peter Coss. Cambridge: Cambridge University Press, 1996.

The Vision of William Concerning Piers Plowman. 2 vols. Ed. W. W. Skeat. Oxford: Clarendon, 1924.

The Westminster Chronicle, 1381–1394. Ed. and trans. L. C. Hector and Barbara F. Harvey. New York: Oxford University Press, 1982.

Vita Edwardi Secundi. The Life of Edward the Second, by the so-called Monk of Malmesbury. Ed. and trans. N. Denholm-Young. London: Thomas Nelson and Sons, 1957.

Walsingham, Thomas. *Ypodigma Neustriae, a Thoma Walsingham, quondam monacho monasterii S. Albani conscriptum*. Ed. H. T. Riley. London: Longman, 1876.

The Wedding of Sir Gawen and Dame Ragnell for Helpyng of Kyng Arthoure. In Stephen Shepherd (ed.). *Middle English Romances*, pp. 243–67.

Ywain and Gawain. In Stephen Shepherd (ed.). *Middle English Romances*, pp. 75–173.

SECONDARY STUDIES

Aers, David. "Class, Gender, Medieval Criticism, and *Piers Plowman*." In Britton J. Harwood and Gillian R. Overing (eds.). *Class and Gender in Early English Literature: Intersections*. Bloomington: Indiana University Press, 1994, pp. 59–75.

Alford, John A. (ed.) *A Companion to Piers Plowman*. Berkeley: University of California Press, 1988.

Alford, John A. *Piers Plowman: A Legal Glossary*. Cambridge: Cambridge University Press, 1988.

Ankersmit, F. R. *Aesthetic Politics. Political Philosophy Beyond Fact and Value*. Stanford: Stanford University Press, 1996.

Ankersmit, F. R. *Historical Representation*. Stanford: Stanford University Press, 2001.

Ankersmit, F. R. *Political Representation*. Stanford: Stanford University Press, 2002.

Arnold, Morris S. *Select Cases of Trespass from the King's Courts 1307–1399*. London: Selden Society, 1985.

Askins, William. "*The Tale of Melibee* and the Crisis at Westminster, 1387." *Studies in the Age of Chaucer, Proceedings* 2 (1986), 103–12.

Baker, Denise N. "Meed and the Economics of Chivalry in *Piers Plowman*." In Denise Baker (ed.). *Inscribing the Hundred Years' War in French and English Cultures*. Albany, NY: SUNY Press, 2000, pp. 55–72.

Baldwin, Anna. "The Historical Context." In John Alford (ed.). *A Companion to Piers Plowman*, pp. 67–86.

Baldwin, Anna. *The Theme of Government in Piers Plowman*. Cambridge: Cambridge University Press, 1981.

Barr, Helen. *Signes and Sothe: Language in the Piers Plowman Tradition*. Cambridge: D. S. Brewer, 1994.

Barr, Helen. *Socioliterary Practice in Late Medieval England*. Oxford: Oxford University Press, 2001.

Barron, Caroline M. "William Langland: A London Poet." In Barbara Hanawalt (ed.). *Chaucer's England. Literature in Historical Context.* Minneapolis: University of Minnesota Press, 1992, pp. 91–109.

Bennett, J. A. W. "The Date of the A-Text of *Piers Plowman.*" *PMLA* 58 (1943), 566–72.

Bennett, J. A. W. "The Date of the B-Text of *Piers Plowman.*" *Medium Aevum* 12 (1943), 55–64.

Bennett, J. A. W. *The Parlement of Foules: An Interpretation.* Oxford: Clarendon, 1957.

Benson, Larry. "The Occasion of *The Parliament of Fowls.*" In Larry D. Benson and Siegfried Wenzel (eds.). *The Wisdom of Poetry: Essays in Early English Literature in Honor of Morton W. Bloomfield.* Kalamazoo, MI: Western Michigan University, 1982, pp. 123–44.

Biggs, Douglas. "The Politics of Health: Henry IV and the Long Parliament of 1406." In Gwilym Dodd and Douglas Biggs (eds.). *Henry IV: The Establishment of the Regime.* York: University of York Medieval Press, 2003, pp. 185–202.

Black, Antony. "The Conciliar Movement," In J. H. Burns (ed.). *The Cambridge History of Medieval Political Thought*, pp. 573–87.

Black, Antony. *Council and Commune. The Conciliar Movement and the Fifteenth-Century Heritage.* London: Burnes & Oates, 1979.

Black, Antony. *Political Thought in Europe, 1250–1450.* Cambridge: Cambridge University Press, 1992.

Bloch, Howard R.. *Etymologies and Genealogies: A Literary Anthropology of the French Middle Ages.* Chicago: University of Chicago Press, 1983.

Boureau, Alain. "L'adage *vox populi, vox dei* et l'invention de la nation Anglaise (VIIIe-XIIe siècle)." *Annales: economies sociétés, civilisations* 47 (1992), 1071–89.

Bowden, Muriel. *A Commentary on the General Prologue to The Canterbury Tales.* New York: Macmillan, 1959.

Bowers, John M. "Dating *Piers Plowman*: Testing the Testimony of Usk's *Testament.*" *Yearbook of Langland Studies* 13 (1999), 65–100.

Boyle, Leonard E. "The Date of the *Summa Praedicantium* of John Bromyard." *Speculum* 48 (1973), 533–7.

Brown, A. L. "The Commons and the Council in the Reign of Henry IV." *English Historical Review* 79 (1964), 1–30.

Brown, A. L. "Parliament, c. 1377–1422." In R. G. Davies and J. H. Denton (eds.). *The English Parliament in the Middle Ages*, pp. 109–40.

Brown, A. L. *The Governance of Late Medieval England, 1272–1461.* Stanford: Stanford University Press, 1989.

Burns, J. H. (ed.). *The Cambridge History of Medieval Political Thought, c. 350–c. 1450.* Cambridge: Cambridge University Press, 1988.

Burrow, J. A. *Ricardian Poetry. Chaucer, Gower, Langland, and the Gawain Poet.* New Haven: Yale University Press, 1971.

Burrow, J. A. "The Audience of Piers Plowman." In *Essays on Medieval Literature.* Oxford: Oxford University Press, 1984, pp. 102–116.

Burrow, J. A. "The Poet As Petitioner." *Studies in the Age of Chaucer* 3 (1981), 61–75.

Butt, Ronald. *A History of Parliament: The Middle Ages.* London: Constable, 1989.

Cam, Helen M. "From Witness of the Shire to Full Parliament." In *Law-Finders and Law-Makers in Medieval England*, pp. 106–31.

Cam, Helen M. "Mediaeval Representation in Theory and Practice." *Speculum* 29 (1954), 347–55.

Cam, Helen M. "Stubbs Seventy Years After." In *Law-Finders and Law-Makers in Medieval England*, pp. 188–211.

Cam, Helen M. "The Community of the Shire and the Payment of its Representatives in Parliament." In *Liberties & Communities in Medieval England*, pp. 236–50.

Cam, Helen M. "The Relation of English Members of Parliament to their Constituencies in the Fourteenth Century." In *Liberties & Communities in Medieval England*, pp. 223–35.

Cam, Helen M. "The Legislators of Medieval England." In *Law-Finders and Law-Makers in Medieval England*, pp. 132–58.

Cam, Helen M. "The Theory and Practice of Representation in Medieval England," in *Law-Finders and Law-Makers in Medieval England*, pp. 159–75.

Cam, Helen M. *Law-Finders and Law-Makers in Medieval England.* London: Merlin Press, 1962.

Cam, Helen M. *Liberties & Communities in Medieval England.* Cambridge: Cambridge University Press, 1944; Barnes & Noble, 1963.

Cargill, Oscar. "The Date of the A-Text of Piers Ploughman." *PMLA* 47 (1932), 354–62.

Carlson, David R. *Chaucer's Jobs.* New York: Palgrave Macmillan, 2004.

Chrimes, S. B. *English Constitutional Ideas in the Fifteenth Century.* Cambridge: Cambridge University Press, 1936.

Clanchy, M. T. *From Memory to Written Record. England 1066–1307.* 2nd edn. Oxford: Blackwell, 1993.

Clark, Linda. "Magnates and their Affinities in the Parliaments of 1386–1421." In R. H. Britnell and A. J. Pollard (eds.). *The McFarlane Legacy. Studies in Late Medieval Politics and Society.* New York: St. Martin's Press, 1995, pp. 127–53.

Clarke, Maude V. "The Lancastrian Faction and the Wonderful Parliament." In *Fourteenth Century Studies.* Oxford: Clarendon, 1937, pp. 36–52.

Clarke, Maude V. "Forfeitures and Treason in 1388." In *Fourteenth Century Studies.* Oxford: Clarendon, 1937, pp. 115–45.

Clarke, Maude V. "Committees of Estates and the Deposition of Edward II." In *Medieval Representation and Consent.* London: Longmans, Green, 1936; repr. Russell & Russell, 1964, pp. 173–95.

Coffman, George R. "John Gower, Mentor for Royalty: Richard II." *PMLA* 69 (1954), 953–64.

Coleman, Janet. *English Literature in History, 1350–1400. Medieval Readers and Writers.* London: Hutchinson, 1981.

Collette, Carolyn. "Heeding the Counsel of Prudence: A Context for the Melibee." *The Chaucer Review* 29 (1995), 416–33.

Copeland, Rita. *Rhetoric, Hermeneutics, and Translation in the Middle Ages. Academic Traditions and Vernacular Texts*. Cambridge: Cambridge University Press, 1991.

Davies, R. G. and J. H. Denton (eds.). *The English Parliament in the Middle Ages*. Manchester: Manchester University Press, 1981.

Davies, R. R. *The First English Empire: Power and Identities in the British Isles 1093–1343*. Oxford: Oxford University Press, 2000.

Davis, Kathleen. "Hymeneal Alogic: Debating Political Community in The Parliament of Fowls." In Kathy Lavezzo (ed.). *Imagining a Medieval English Nation*, pp. 161–87.

de Lagarde, Georges. "L'idée de représentation dans les oeuvres de Guillaume d'Ockham." *Bulletin of the International Committee of Historical Sciences* 37 (1937), 425–51.

Denholm-Young, N. "The Tournament in the Thirteenth Century." *Studies in Medieval History presented to Frederick Maurice Powicke*. Eds. R. W. Hunt, W. A. Pantin, R. W. Southern. Westport, Connecticut: Greenwood Press, 1948, pp. 240–68.

Denton, J. H. "The Clergy and Parliament in the Thirteenth and Fourteenth Centuries." In R. G. Davies and J. H. Denton (eds.). *The English Parliament in the Middle Ages*, pp. 88–108.

Devlin, Sister Mary Aquinas. "Bishop Thomas Brunton and His Sermons." *Speculum* 14 (1939), 324–44.

Dodd, Gwilym. "Conflict or Consensus: Henry IV and Parliament, 1399–1406." In Tim Thornton (ed.). *Social Attitudes and Political Structures in the Fifteenth Century*. Gloucestershire: Sutton, 2000, pp. 118–49.

Dodd, Gwilym. "Henry IV's Council, 1399–1405." In Gwilym Dodd and Douglas Briggs (eds.). *Henry IV: The Establishment of the Regime*. York: University of York Medieval Press, 2003, pp. 95–115.

Dodd, Gwilym. "Richard II and the Transformation of Parliament." In *The Reign of Richard II*. Stroud, Gloucestershire: Tempus, 2000, pp. 71–84.

Donaldson, E. Talbot. *Piers Plowman: The C-Text and its Poet*. Yale Studies in English 113. New Haven: Yale University Press, 1949.

du Boulay, F. R. H. *The England of Piers Plowman*. Cambridge: Cambridge University Press, 1991.

Echard, Siân (ed.). *A Companion to Gower*. Cambridge: Brewer, 2004.

Edwards, A. S. G. "The Early Reception of Chaucer and Langland." *Florilegium* 15 (1998), 1–22.

Edwards, J. G. "'Justice' in Early English Parliaments." In Fryde and Miller, *Historical Studies of the English Parliament. Volume I: Origins to 1399*, pp. 279–97.

Edwards, J. G. *The Commons in Medieval English Parliaments. The Creighton Lecture in History 1957*. London: Athlone Press, 1958.

Edwards, Sir Goronwy. *The Second Century of the English Parliament*. Oxford: Clarendon, 1979.

Elton, G. R. *'The Body of the Whole Realm': Parliament and Representation in Medieval and Tudor England.* Charlottesville: University Press of Virginia, 1969.

Emden, A. B. *A Biographical Register of the University of Oxford to A.D. 1500.* 3 vols. Oxford: Oxford University Press, 1957–9.

Faith, Rosamond. "The 'Great Rumour' of 1377 and Peasant Ideology." In R. H. Hilton and T. H. Aston (eds.). *The English Rising of 1381*, Cambridge: Cambridge University Press, 1984, pp. 43–70.

Ferguson, Arthur. *The Articulate Citizen and the English Renaissance.* Durham: Duke University Press, 1965.

Ferster, Judith. *Fictions of Advice. The Literature and Politics of Counsel in Late Medieval England.* Philadelphia: University of Pennsylvania Press, 1996.

Fisher, John H. *John Gower, Moral Philosopher and Friend of Chaucer.* London: Methuen & Co., 1965.

Fryde, E. B., and Edward Miller (eds.). *Historical Studies of the English Parliament. Volume 1: Origins to 1399. Volume 2: 1399–1603.* Cambridge: Cambridge University Press, 1970.

Fryde, Natalie. *The Tyranny and Fall of Edward II, 1321–1326.* London: Cambridge, 1979.

Galbraith, V. H. "The Modus Tenendi Parliamentum." *Journal of the Warburg and Courtauld Institutes* 16 (1953), 81–99.

Galloway, Andrew. "Gower in His Most Learned Role and the Peasants' Revolt of 1381." *Mediaevalia* 16 (1993), 329–47.

Galloway, Andrew. "Piers Plowman and the Subject of the Law." *Yearbook of Langland Studies* 15 (2001), 117–28.

Galloway, Andrew. "Private Selves and the Intellectual Marketplace in Late Fourteenth-Century England: The Case of the Two Usks." *New Literary History* 28 (1997), 291–318.

Galloway, Andrew. "The Literature of 1388 and the Politics of Pity in Gower's *Confessio amantis*." In Steiner and Barrington (eds.).*The Letter of the Law*, pp. 67–104.

Galway, Margaret. "Geoffrey Chaucer, J. P. and M. P." *Modern Language Review* 36 (1941), 1–36.

Giancarlo, Matthew. "Murder, Lies, and Storytelling: The Manipulation of Justice(s) in the Parliaments of 1397 and 1399," *Speculum* 77 (2002), 76–112.

Given-Wilson, Chris. *Chronicles. The Writing of History in Medieval England.* London and New York: Hambledon and London, 2004.

Goodman, Anthony. "Sir Thomas Hoo and the Parliament of 1376." *Bulletin of the Institute for Historical Research* 41 (1968), 139–49.

Gottfried, Robert S. *The Black Death. Natural and Human Disaster in Medieval Europe.* New York: Free Press, 1983.

Gradon, Pamela. "Langland and the Ideology of Dissent." *PBA* 66 (1980), 179–205.

Grady, Frank. "The Generation of 1399." In Emily Steiner and Candace Barrington (eds.). *The Letter of the Law: Legal Practice and Literary Production in Medieval England*, pp. 202–29.

Grady, Frank. "The Lancastrian Gower and the Limits of Exemplarity." *Speculum* 70 (1995), 552–75.

Gransden, Antonia. *Historical Writing in England c. 550 to c. 1307*. Ithaca, New York: Cornell University Press, 1974.

Green, Richard Firth. *A Crisis of Truth. Literature and Law in Ricardian England*. Philadelphia: University of Pennsylvania Press, 1999.

Hammond, Mason. "*Concilia deorum* from Homer through Milton." *Studies In Philology* 30 (1933), 1–16.

Hanna III, Ralph. "Emendations to a 1993 'Vita de Ne'erdowel.'" *Yearbook of Langland Studies* 14 (2000), 185–198.

Hanna III, Ralph. *William Langland*. Brookfield, VT: Ashgate, 1993.

Harding, Alan. "Plaints and Bills in the History of English Law, Mainly in the Period 1250–1350." In Dafydd Jenkins (ed.). *Legal History Studies 1972*. Cardiff: University of Wales Press, 1975, pp. 65–86.

Harding, Alan. "The Revolt against the Justices." In R. H. Hilton and T. H. Aston (eds.). *The English Rising of 1381*. Cambridge: Cambridge University Press, 1984, pp. 165–93.

Harding, Alan. *Medieval Law and the Foundations of the State*. Oxford: Oxford University Press, 2002.

Harriss, G. L. "The Formation of Parliament, 1272–1377." In R. G. Davies and J. H. Denton (eds.). *The English Parliament in the Middle Ages*, pp. 29–60.

Harriss, G. L. *King, Parliament, and Public Finance in Medieval England to 1369*. Oxford: Clarendon, 1975.

Hay, Malcolm and Jacqueline Riding. *Art in Parliament. The Permanent Collection of the House of Commons*. Norwich: Jarrold Publishing, 1996.

Hines, John, Nathalie Cohen, and Simon Roffey. "Iohannes Gower, Armiger, Poeta: Records and Memorials of his Life and Death." In Siân Echard (ed.). *A Companion to Gower*. Cambridge: D. S. Brewer, 2004, pp. 23–41.

Holmes, G. A. "A Protest Against the Despensers, 1326." *Speculum* 30 (1955), 207–212.

Holmes, George. *The Good Parliament*. Oxford: Clarendon, 1975.

Holt, J. C. "Politics and Property in Early Medieval England." *Past and Present* 57 (1972), 3–52.

Holt, J. C. "The Prehistory of Parliament." In R. G. Davies and J. H. Denton (eds.). *The English Parliament in the Middle Ages*, pp. 1–28.

Horobin, Simon, and Linne R. Mooney. "A Piers Plowman Manuscript by the Hengwrt/Ellesmere Scribe and Its Implications for London Standard English." *Studies in the Age of Chaucer* 26 (2004), 65–112.

Hudson, Anne. "Epilogue: The Legacy of Piers Plowman" In John Alford (ed.). *A Companion to Piers Plowman*. Berkeley: University of California Press, 1988, pp. 251–66.

Huppé, Bernard. "The A-Text of Piers Plowman and the Norman Wars." *PMLA* 54 (1939), 37–64.

Huppé, Bernard. "The Date of the B-Text of Piers Plowman." *Studies in Philology* 38 (1941), 34–44.

Illingworth, W. "Copy of a Libel against Archbishop Neville." *Archaeologia* 16 (1812), 80–3.

Johnson, Lesley. "Robert Mannyng's History of Arthurian Literature." In Ian Wood and G. A. Loud (eds.). *Church and Chronicle in the Middle Ages. Essays Presented to John Taylor.* London: Hambledon Press, 1991, pp. 129–47.

Jusserand, J. J. "*Piers Plowman* The Work of One or of Five." *Modern Philology* 6 (1909), 271–329.

Jusserand, J. J. "*Piers Plowman* The Work of One or of Five: A Reply." *Modern Philology* 7 (1910), 289–326.

Jusserand, J. J. *Piers Plowman: A Contribution to the History of English Mysticism.* 2nd edn. Trans. M. E. R. New York: G. P. Putnam's Sons, 1894.

Justice, Steven. *Writing and Rebellion. England in 1381.* Berkeley: University of California Press, 1994.

Kaminsky, Howard. "Estate, Nobility, and the Exhibition of Estate in the Later Middle Ages." *Speculum* 68 (1993), 684–709.

Kane, George. "The Text." In John Alford (ed.). *A Companion to Piers Plowman,* pp. 175–200.

Kantorowicz, Ernst. *The King's Two Bodies: A Study in Mediaeval Political Theology.* Princeton: Princeton University Press, 1957, 1997.

Kellogg, Eleanor. "Bishop Brunton and the Fable of the Rats." *PMLA* 50 (1935), 57–68.

Kelly, Henry Ansgar. *Chaucer and the Cult of Saint Valentine.* Netherlands: E. J. Brill, 1986.

Kerby-Fulton, Kathryn and Steven Justice. "Scribe D and the Marketing of Ricardian Literature." In Kathryn Kerby-Fulton and Maidie Haimo (eds.). *The Medieval Professional Reader at Work: Evidence from Manuscripts of Chaucer, Langland, Kempe, and Gower.* University of Victoria: English Literary Studies, 2001, pp. 217–37.

Kerby-Fulton, Kathryn and Steven Justice. "Reformist Intellectual Culture in the English and Irish Civil Service: The *Modus Tenendi Parliamentum* and its Literary Relations." *Traditio* 53 (1998), 149–202.

Kerby-Fulton, Kathryn, and Steven Justice. "Langlandian Reading Circles and the Civil Service in London and Dublin, 1380–1427." *New Medieval Literatures* 1 (1997), 59–83.

Kerby-Fulton, Kathryn. "Langland 'In His Working Clothes'? Scribe D, Authorial Loose Revision Material, and the Nature of Scribal Intervention." In A. J. Minnis (ed.). *Middle English Poetry: Texts and Traditions.* York, England: York Medieval, 2001, pp. 139–67.

Knapp, Ethan. *The Bureaucratic Muse. Thomas Hoccleve and the Literature of Late Medieval England.* University Park, Pennsylvania: Penn State University Press, 2001.

L. B. L. [Lambert B. Larking]. "'Probatio Aetatis' of William de Septvans." *Archae-ologia Cantiana* 1 (1858), 124–36.

Landman, James. "Pleading, Pragmatism, and Permissable Hypocrisy: The 'Colours' of Legal Discourse in Late Medieval England." *New Medieval Literatures* 4 (2001), 139–70.

Lavezzo, Kathy (ed.). *Imagining a Medieval English Nation.* Minneapolis: University of Minnesota Press, 2004.

Lerer, Seth. *Chaucer and His Readers.* Princeton: Princeton University Press, 1993.

Lewis, N. B. "Re-election to Parliament in the Reign of Richard II." *English Historical Review* 48 (1933), 364–94.

Loomis, Roger Sherman. "Edward I, Arthurian Enthusiast." *Speculum* 28 (1953), 114–27.

Lord, Robert Howard. "The Parliaments of the Middle Ages and the Early Modern Period." *Catholic Historical Review* 16 (1930), 125–44.

Lyon, Bryce. *A Constitutional and Legal History of Medieval England.* 2nd edn. New York: Norton, 1980.

Maddicott, J. R. "Parliament and the Constituencies, 1272–1377." In R. G. Davies and J. H. Denton (eds.). *The English Parliament in the Middle Ages*, pp. 61–87.

Maitland, F. W. *The Constitutional History of England.* Cambridge: Cambridge University Press, 1931.

Manly, J. M. "The Authorship of *Piers Plowman*." *Modern Philology* 7 (1909), 83–144.

Manly, J. M. *Some New Light on Chaucer.* New York: Henry Holt, 1926.

Mann, Jill. *Chaucer and Medieval Estates Satire.* Cambridge: Cambridge University Press, 1973.

Marongiu, Antonio. *Medieval Parliaments. A Comparative Study.* Trans. and adapt. S. J. Woolf. London: Eyre & Spottiswoode, 1968.

Marx, C. W. *The Devils' Parlament and the Harrowing of Hell and Destruction of Jerusalem.* Heidelberg: C. Winter, 1993.

Marx, C. W. *The Devil's Rights and the Redemption in the Literature of Medieval England.* Cambridge: Brewer, 1995.

McCall, John P. "The Trojan Scene in Chaucer's *Troilus*." *English Literary History* 29 (1962), 263–75.

McCall, John P. and George Rudisill, Jr. "The Parliament of 1386 and Chaucer's Trojan Parliament." *Journal of English and Germanic Philology* 58 (1959), 276–88.

McFarlane, K. B. "Parliament and 'Bastard Feudalism.'" *Transactions of the Royal Historical Society* 4th ser. 26 (1944), 56–65.

McFarlane, K. B. *The Nobility of Later Medieval England. The Ford Lectures for 1953 and Related Studies.* Clarendon: Oxford, 1973.

McKisack, May. *The Parliamentary Representation of the English Boroughs During the Middle Ages.* Oxford: Oxford University Press, 1932.

McKisack, May. *The Fourteenth Century, 1307–1399.* Oxford: Oxford University Press, 1959.

Michaud-Quantin, Pierre. *Universitas. Expressions du mouvement communautaire dans le moyen-age Latin.* Paris: Librairie philosophique J. Vrin, 1970.

Middleton, Anne. "The Audience and Public of *Piers Plowman.*" In David Lawton (ed.). *Middle English Alliterative Poetry and its Literary Background.* Bury St. Edmunds, Suffolk: D. S. Brewer, 1982, pp. 101–23, 147–54.

Middleton, Anne. "The Idea of Public Poetry in the Reign of Richard II," *Speculum* 53 (1978), 94–114.

Mohl, Ruth. "Theories of Monarchy in *Mum and the Sothsegger.*" *PMLA* 59 (1944), 26–44.

Mooney, Linne. "Chaucer's Scribe." *Speculum* 81 (2006), 97–138.

Moore, Olin H. "The Infernal Council." *Modern Philology* 16 (1918), 169–93.

Musson, Anthony, and W. M. Ormrod. *The Evolution of English Justice: Law, Politics and Society in the Fourteenth Century.* London: Macmillan Press, 1999.

Musson, Anthony. *Medieval Law in Context. The Growth of Legal Consciousness from Magna Carta to the Peasants' Revolt.* Manchester: Manchester University Press, 2001.

Myers, A. R. "Parliament, 1422–1509." In R. G. Davies and J. H. Denton (eds.). *The English Parliament in the Middle Ages*, pp. 141–84.

Nolan, Charles J., Jr. "Structural Sophistication in the 'Complaint Unto Pity.'" *The Chaucer Review* 13 (1978), 363–72.

Nolan, Maura. "Metaphoric History: Narrative and New Science in the Work of F. W. Maitland." *PMLA* 118 (2003), 557–72.

Nolan, Maura. *John Lydgate and the Forms of Public Culture.* Cambridge: Cambridge University Press, 2005.

Oakley, Francis. *The Conciliarist Tradition. Constitutionalism in the Catholic Church 1300–1870.* Oxford: Oxford University Press, 2003.

Oliver, Clementine. "A Political Pamphleteer in Late Medieval England: Thomas Fovent, Geoffrey Chaucer, Thomas Usk, and the Merciless Parliament of 1388." *New Medieval Literatures* 6 (2003), 167–98.

Olson, Paul A. *The Canterbury Tales and the Good Society.* Princeton: Princeton University Press, 1986.

Ormrod, W. M. *Political Life in Medieval England, 1300–1450.* London: St. Martin's Press, 1995.

Ormrod, W. M. *The Evolution of English Justice. Law, Politics, and Society in the Fourteenth Century.* New York: St. Martin's Press, 1999.

Ormrod, W. M. "The Use of English: Language, Law, and Political Culture in Fourteenth-Century England." *Speculum* 78 (2003), 750–87.

Ormrod, W. M. *The Reign of Edward III.* Stroud, Gloucestershire: Tempus, 2000.

Ormrod, W. M. "A Problem of Precedence: Edward III, the Double Monarchy, and the Royal Style." In J. S. Bothwell (ed.). *The Age of Edward III.* York: York Medieval Press, 2001, pp. 133–53.

Ormrod, W. M. "Who Was Alice Perrers?" *Chaucer Review* 40 (2006), 219–29.

Owst, G. R. "The 'Angel' and the 'Goliardeys' of Langland's Prologue." *MLR* 20 (1925), 270–9.

Palmer, J. J. N. "The Parliament of 1385 and the Constitutional Crisis of 1386." *Speculum* 46 (1971), 477–90.

Palmer, J. J. N. *England, France and Christendom, 1377–99.* London: Routledge and Kegan Paul, 1972.

Patterson, Lee. "'What Man Artow?': Authorial Self-Definition in The Tale of Sir Thopas and The Tale of Melibee." *Studies in the Age of Chaucer* 11 (1989), 117–75.

Patterson, Lee. *Chaucer and the Subject of History.* Madison: University of Wisconsin, 1991.

Payling, Simon. "The Politics of Family: Late Medieval Marriage Contracts." In R. H. Britnell and A. J. Pollard (eds.). *The McFarlane Legacy. Studies in Late Medieval Politics and Society.* New York: St. Martins Press, 1995, pp. 21–47.

Pearcy, Roy J. "Chaucer's Franklin and the Literary Vavasour." *Chaucer Review* 8 (1973), 33–59.

Pearsall, Derek. *The Life of Geoffrey Chaucer.* Oxford: Blackwell, 1992.

Peck, Russell A. "The Politics and Psychology of Governance in Gower: Ideas of Kingship and Real Kings." In Siân Echard (ed.). *A Companion to Gower.* Cambridge: D. S. Brewer, 2004, pp. 215–38.

Peck, Russell A. *Kingship and Common Profit in Gower's Confessio Amantis.* Carbondale: Southern Illinois University Press, 1978.

Pieper, Willy. "Das Parlament in der me. Literatur." *Archiv für das studium der neueren sprachen und literaturen* 146, n.s. 46 (1923), 187–212.

Pitkin, Hannah. *The Concept of Representation.* Berkeley: University of California Press, 1967.

Pocock, J. G. A. *The Ancient Constitution and the Feudal Law. A Study of English Historical Thought in the Seventeenth Century. A Reissue with a Retrospect.* Cambridge: Cambridge University Press, 1987.

Pollard, A. F. "The Authorship and Value of the 'Anonimalle' Chronicle." *The English Historical Review* 53 (1938), 577–605.

Pollard, A. F. *The Evolution of Parliament.* London: Longmans, Green, 1920.

Pollard, A. F. "The Lancastrian Constitutional Experiment." *Parliamentary History* 14 (1995), 103–19.

Porter, Elizabeth. "Gower's Ethical Microcosm and Political Macrocosm." In A. J. Minnis (ed.). *Gower's Confessio Amantis: Responses and Assessments.* Cambridge: Brewer, 1983, pp. 135–62.

Powell, J. Enoch, and Keith Wallis. *The House of Lords in the Middle Ages. A History of the English House of Lords to 1540.* London: Weidenfeld and Nicolson, 1968.

Prestwich, Michael (ed.). *Documents Illustrating the Crisis of 1297–98 in England.* London: Royal Historical Society, 1980.

Prestwich, Michael. "Parliament and the Community of the Realm in Fourteenth Century England." In Art Cosgrove and J. I. McGuire (eds). *Parliament & Community.* Belfast: Appletree Press, 1983, pp. 5–24.

Quillet, Jeannine. "Community, Counsel and Representation." In Burns, J. H. (ed.). *The Cambridge History of Medieval Political Thought*, pp. 520–72.

Rayner, Doris. "The Forms and Machinery of the 'Commune Petition' in the Fourteenth Century." *English Historical Review* 56 (1941), 198–233.

Richardson, H. G. "John of Gaunt and the Parliamentary Representation of Lancashire." *Bulletin of the John Rylands Library* 22 (1938), 175–222.

Richardson, H. G. "The Commons and Medieval Politics." *Transactions of the Royal Historical Society* 4th ser., 28 (1946), 21–45.

Richardson, H. G. "The Origins of Parliament." *Transactions of the Royal Historical Society* 4th ser., 11 (1928), 137–83.

Richardson, H. G. and G. O. Sayles. "The King's Ministers in Parliament, 1272–1377." *The English Historical Review* 46 (1931), 529–55.

Richardson, H. G., and G. O. Sayles. "The Parliament of Carlisle, 1307 – Some New Documents." *English Historical Review* 53 (1938), 425–37.

Roskell, J. S. "Sir Arnald Savage of Bobbing." In *Parliamentary Politics in Late Medieval England*. 3 vols. London: Hambledon Press, 1981, vol. 3, pp. 65–80.

Roskell, J. S. "Sir John Tiptoft, Commons' Speaker in 1406." In *Parliamentary Politics in Late Medieval England*. 3 vols. London: Hambledon Press, 1981, vol. 3, pp. 107–50.

Roskell, J. S. "Sir Peter de la Mare, Speaker for the Commons in Parliament in 1376 and 1377." *Nottingham Medieval Studies* 2 (1958), 24–37.

Roskell, J. S. "Thomas Chaucer of Ewelme." In *Parliamentary Politics in Late Medieval England*. 3 vols. London: The Hambledon Press, 1983, vol. 3, pp. 151–91.

Roskell, J. S. *The Commons and their Speakers in English Parliaments 1376–1523*. Manchester: Manchester University Press, 1965.

Rosser, Gervase. "Going to the Fraternity Feast: Commensality and Social Relations in Late Medieval England." *The Journal of British Studies* 33 (1994), 430–46.

Saul, Nigel. "The Despensers and the Downfall of Edward II." *English Historical Review* 99 (1984), 1–33.

Saul, Nigel. "Richard II and the Vocabulary of Kingship." *English Historical Review* 110 (1995), 854–77.

Saul, Nigel. *Richard II*. New Haven: Yale University Press, 1997.

Sayles, George O. *The Functions of the Medieval Parliament of England*. London: Hambledon Press, 1988.

Sayles, George O. *The King's Parliament of England*. New York: W. W. Norton, 1974.

Scammell, Jean. "The Formation of the English Social Structure: Freedom, Knights, and Gentry, 1066–1300." *Speculum* 68 (1993), 591–618.

Scanlon, Larry. "King, Commons, and Kind Wit: Langland's National Vision and the Rising of 1381." In Kathy Lavezzo (ed.). *Imagining a Medieval English Nation*, pp. 191–233.

Scanlon, Larry. *Narrative, Authority, and Power: The Medieval Exemplum and the Chaucerian Tradition*. Cambridge: Cambridge University Press, 1994.

Scattergood, John. "Remembering Richard II: John Gower's *Cronica Tripartita*, *Richard the Redeless*, and *Mum and the Sothsegger*." In *The Lost Tradition*.

Essays on Middle English Alliterative Poetry. Dublin: Four Courts Press, 2000, pp. 200–25.

Scott, Florence R. "Chaucer and the Parliament of 1386." *Speculum* 18 (1943), 80–6.

Selzer, John L. "Topical Allegory in *Piers Plowman*: Lady Meed's B-Text Debate with Conscience." *Philological Quarterly* 59 (1980), 257–67.

Simpson, James. "'After Craftes Conseil clotheth yow and fede': Langland and London City Politics." In Nicholas Rogers (ed.). *England in the Fourteenth Century. Proceedings of the 1991 Harlaxton Symposium.* Stamford, England: P. Watkins, 1993, pp. 109–27.

Simpson, James. "The Constraints of Satire in *Piers Plowman* and *Mum and the Sothsegger.*" In Helen Philips (ed.). *Langland, the Mystics, and the Medieval English Religious Tradition.* London: D. S. Brewer, 1990, pp. 11–30.

Simpson, James. "The Other Book of Troy: Guido delle Colonne's *Historia destructionis Troiae* in Fourteenth and Fifteenth-Century England." *Speculum* 73 (1998), 397–423.

Simpson, James. *Piers Plowman: An Introduction to the B-Text.* New York: Longman, 1990.

Somerset, Fiona. "'Al þe comonys with o voys at onys': Multilingual Latin and Vernacular Voice in *Piers Plowman.*" *Yearbook of Langland Studies*, 19 (2005), 107–36.

Somerset, Fiona. *Clerical Discourse and Lay Audience in Late Medieval England.* Cambridge, 1998.

Staley, Lynn. *Languages of Power in the Age of Richard II.* University Park, Pennsylvania: University of Pennsylvania Press, 2005.

Steiner, Emily and Candace Barrington (eds.). *The Letter of the Law. Legal Practice and Literary Production in Medieval England.* Ithaca, NY: Cornell University Press, 2002.

Steiner, Emily. "Commonalty and Literary Form in the 1370s and 1380s." *New Medieval Literatures* 6 (2003), 199–221.

Steiner, Emily. "Inventing Legality: Documentary Culture and Lollard Preaching." In Steiner and Barrington (eds). *The Letter of the Law. Legal Practice and Literary Production in Medieval England*, pp. 185–201.

Steiner, Emily. "Langland's Documents." *Yearbook of Langland Studies* (2000), 95–107.

Steiner, Emily. *Documentary Culture and the Making of Medieval English Literature.* Cambridge: Cambridge University Press, 2003.

Stillwell, Gardiner. "John Gower and the Last Years of Edward III." *SP* 45 (1948), 454–71.

Stokes, Myra. *Justice and Mercy in Piers Plowman. A Reading of the B Text Visio.* London: Croom Helm, 1984.

Stow, George B. "Richard II in John Gower's *Confessio Amantis*: Some Historical Perspectives." *Mediaevalia* 16 (1993), 3–31.

Strohm, Paul. "Politics and Poetics: Usk and Chaucer in the 1380s." In Lee Patterson (ed.). *Literary Practice and Social Change in Britain, 1380–1530.* Berkeley: University of California Press, 1990, 83–112.

Strohm, Paul. "Saving the Appearances: Chaucer's Purse and the Fabrication of the Lancastrian Claim." In Hanawalt, Barbara (ed.). *Chaucer's England: Literature in Historical Context*. Minneapolis: University of Minnesota Press, 1992, pp. 21–40.

Strohm, Paul. *Social Chaucer*. Cambridge, Massachussetts: Harvard University Press, 1989.

Strohm, Paul. *Hochon's Arrow. The Social Imagination of Fourteenth-Century Texts*. Princeton: Princeton University Press, 1992.

Strohm, Paul. *England's Empty Throne. Usurpation and the Language of Legitimation, 1399–1422*. New Haven: Yale University Press, 1998.

Stubbs, William. *The Constitutional History of England in its Origin and Development*. 4th edn. Oxford: Oxford University Press, 1896.

Tavormina, M. Teresa. *Kindly Similitude. Marriage and Family in Piers Plowman*. Cambridge: D. S. Brewer, 1995.

Taylor, John. *English Historical Literature in the Fourteenth Century*. Oxford: Clarendon, 1987.

Tierney, Brian. "The Idea of Representation in the Medieval Councils of the West." In Peter Huizing and Knut Walf (eds.). *Concilium: Religion in the Eighties. The Ecumenical Council – Its Significance in the Constitution of the Church*. New York: Seabury Press, 1983, pp. 25–30.

Tierney, Brian. *Religion, Law, and the Growth of Constitutional Thought, 1150–1650*. Cambridge: Cambridge University Press, 1982.

Tout, T. F. "The English Parliament and Public Opinion, 1376–1388." In Fryde and Miller, *Historical Studies of the English Parliament. Volume I: Origins to 1399*, pp. 298–315.

Tout, T. F. *Chapters in the Administrative History of Mediaeval England*. 3 vols. Manchester, 1928.

Tower, Sir Reginald. "The Family of Septvans." *Archaeologia Cantiana* 40 (1928), 105–30.

Treharne, R. F. "The Nature of Parliament in the Reign of Henry III." In E. B. Fryde (ed.). *Simon de Montfort and Baronial Reform. 20th Century Essays*. London: Hambledon, 1986, pp. 209–34.

Trigg, Stephanie. "The Traffic in Medieval Women: Alice Perrers, Feminist Criticism and Piers Plowman." *Yearbook of Langland Studies* 12 (1998), 5–29.

Turville-Petre, Thorlac. "Politics and Poetry in the Early Fourteenth Century: The Case of Robert Manning's Chronicle." *Review of English Studies* 39 (1988), 1–28.

Wallace, David. *Chaucerian Polity: Absolutist Lineages and Associational Forms in England and Italy*. Stanford: Stanford University Press, 1997.

Watts, John. "The Pressure of the Public on Later Medieval Politics." In Linda Clark and Christine Carpenter (eds.). *The Fifteenth Century IV. Political Culture in Late Medieval Britain*. London: Boydell Press, 2004, pp. 159–80.

Wawn, Andrew. "Truth-telling and the Tradition of *Mum and the Sothsegger*." *Yearbook of English Studies* 13 (1983), 270–87.

Weber, W. C. "The Purpose of the English *Modus Tenendi Parliamentum.*" *Parliamentary History* 17 (1998), 149–77.

Wetherbee, Winthrop. "John Gower." In David Wallace (ed.). *The Cambridge History of Medieval English Literature*. Cambridge: Cambridge University Press, 1999, pp. 589–609.

White, Hayden. *The Content of the Form: Narrative Discourse and Historical Representation*. Baltimore: Johns Hopkins, 1987.

Wilson, R. M. *The Lost Literature of Medieval England*. London, 1952.

Windeatt, Barry (ed.). *Chaucer's Dream Poetry: Sources and Analogues*. Suffolk: D. S. Brewer, 1982.

Yeager, R. F. "John Gower's French." In Siân Echard (ed.). *A Companion to Gower*. Cambridge: D. S. Brewer, 2004, pp. 137–51.

Yeager, R. F. "Politics and the French Language in England During the Hundred Years' War." In Denise N. Baker (ed.). *Inscribing the Hundred Years' War in French and English Cultures*. Albany: SUNY Press, 2000, pp. 127–57.

Yeager, R. F. *John Gower's Poetic. The Search for a New Arion*. Cambridge: D. S. Brewer, 1990.

Yunck, John A. *The Lineage of Lady Meed: The Development of Mediaeval Venality Satire*. Notre Dame, IN: University of Notre Dame Press, 1963.

Zammito, John. "Ankersmit and Historical Representation." *History and Theory* 44 (2005), 155–81.

Index

bills of complaint (*cont.*)
  in *Richard the Redeless*, 230, 232
  Mercers' Petition (1388), 73, 75–6
  propagandizing/partisan uses, 76
  public interest in, 144
  submission process, 68
bills of complaint. *see also* complaint, right of,
    petitions, parliamentary
bird metaphors/allegory
  in *Parliament of Fowls*, 153–63
  in *Richard the Redelesss*, 237
  in *Summa Praedicantium*, 82
  in *Canterbury Tales*, 175
Blake, John, 168
Blancheflour et Florence, 160
Bowden, Muriel, 174
Brembre, Nicholas, 73–6, 159, 167
Brinton, Thomas, 31, 54, 79, 80
  use of 'rats and mice' fable, 182
Bromyard, John, 80–3
Bromyard, John. *see also Summa Praedicantium*,
    83
Brown, A. L., 8
bureaucratic language/procedures
  Chaucer's familiarity with, 130, 133, 151, 174
  Gower's familiarity with, 105–6
  in *Anonimalle Chronicle*, 69–71
  in *Parliament of Fowls*, 155, 157–64
  in parliamentary petitions, 68
  in *Piers Plowman*, 199, 201
Burghersh, Bartholomew de, 55
Burley, Simon, 167–8
Burrow, J. A., 144
Bussy, John, 212
Butt, Ronald, 8

Cam, Helen Maud, 18
Canterbury Tales (Chaucer)
  as estates satire, 251
  mediatory focus, 148
  parliamentarians in, 139
  parliamentary narrative framework, 183,
    207
  representation as theme in, 131
  speaking with one voice in, 149
  the Franklin in, 241, 245
  the Parson in, 208
Canterbury Tales, (Chaucer). *see also* "General
    Prologue", "Tale of Melibee"
Capgrave, John, 139
Cargill, Oscar, 201
Carlyle, Thomas, 18
Changwys exemplum (*Mum and the Sothsegger*),
    248–9
Charlton, Thomas, 10

Chaucer, Geoffrey
  as literary model, 256
  government service, 9–10, 129–30, 151, 164
  parliamentary participation, 131, 152
  rape quitclaim, 92
  traditionalist view of parliament, 20, 85
Chaucer, Geoffrey. *see also Canterbury Tales*,
    Parliament of Fowls, "Tale of Melibee",
    Troilus and Creseyde
Chaucer, Thomas, 10, 130, 216
Chaumpaign, Cecily, 92
Chesterton (Cambridgeshire), Paunfield's
    petition on behalf of, 222, 224–6
Chrimes, S. B., 33
Chronicle (Knighton), 165–7
Chronicle (Langtoft), 38, 39
  Pentecostal model of assembly in, 51
  translation and rewriting of, 40
Chronicle (Mannyng), 41–3
chronicles, chronicle tradition
  in *Richard the Redeless*, 230, 232
  romance baronialism in, 34, 45–6
  romance historiography, 41
church. *see* clergy, 6
church. *see* Conciliar Movement, 6
civil rights, 9
clamor, public/parliamentary
  in *Parliament of Fowls*, 157, 196
  in *Piers Plowman*, 196, 207
  remedies for, 117
classes, see estates, 114
classes. *see* social classes, 276
clergy
  criticisms of in *Mum and the Sothsegger*, 240
  criticisms of in *Piers Plowman*, 206
  participation in parliament, 3, 33, 35, 52, 187
  pictorial representations of, 25
clergy. *see also* convocations, clerical, 276
clerks
  and the development of parliamentary
    literature, 10, 64
  as audience for petitions, 221
  as audience for *Piers Plowman*, 181
  as speaker in *The Crowned King*, 229
Cliff, William, 135
Cobham, Baron, 130, 154
Cobham, John, 94, 104
Coke, Edward, 22
Coleman, Janet, 33
commercial legislation, 5
committee-to-one (*Modus Tenendi
    Parliamentum*), 88, 119, 246
Common Pleas court, 25
Commons, 197
  as representative of whole parliament, 33

282 *Index*

CAMBRIDGE STUDIES IN MEDIEVAL LITERATURE

Lightning Source UK Ltd.
Milton Keynes UK
UKOW03f1400090514

231388UK00001B/67/P